CYNGOR
CEFN GWLAD
CYMRU

COUNTRYSIDE
COUNCIL
FOR WALES

GWASANAETHAU LLYFRGELL
LIBRARY SERVICES

Prif Swyddfa/Headquarters
Plas Penrhos
Ffordd Penrhos
Bangor
Gwynedd LL57 2LQ

Tel: (01248) 385522
Fax: (01248) 355782

Digital Aerial Survey: Theory and Practice

Ron Graham

Aerial Survey Consultant and Research Associate, Geotechnologies,
Bath Spa University College, Bath, UK

and Alexander Koh

Principal Lecturer in Remote Sensing and GIS and DIrector of Geotechnologies,
Bath Spa University College, Bath, UK

Whittles Publishing

CRC PRESS

Boca Raton London New York Washington, D.C.

Typeset by
Whittles Publishing Services

Published by
Whittles Publishing,
Roseleigh House,
Latheronwheel,
Caithness, KW5 6DW,
Scotland, UK

Distributed in North America by
CRC Press LLC,
2000 Corporate Boulevard N.W.,
Boca Raton,
FL 33431, USA

ISBN 1-870325-98-2
USA ISBN 0-8493-1601-4

Printed by Bookcraft, Midsomer Norton, UK

Contents

We gratefully dedicate this book to Joan Graham, and to Timothy and Mary Koh

Preface

During the past decade digital imaging from airborne platforms has been tested and developed in parallel with progressive advancements in digital camera technology. During this period the authors have been privileged to take an active role in the promotion of airborne digital mapping systems and to have worked alongside the few who have pioneered this technology both in the UK and abroad.

Headed by Alexander Koh, Geotechnologies was started in 1991 by a team of specialists in air survey navigation, aerial digital imaging, digital photogrammetry and geographic information systems (GIS). Geotechnologies is a wholly owned subsidiary of Bath Spa University College that has cooperated with numerous air survey companies and clients throughout the world in the field of exploration, mapping, remote sensing and GIS.

After some years of close cooperation involving flying and digital camera systems, Ron Graham joined Geotechnologies as a Research Associate, from which base this book has evolved with the intention of providing a comprehensive background to the theory and practice of digital aerial surveys. In this respect we make no excuses for providing a didactic approach, since the text and associated images are intended as a teaching resource to supplement various instructional programs. Both authors are pilots (PPL) and have considerable experience in aerial survey, digital systems, soft-copy photogrammetry and teaching.

Geotechnology teams have completed over forty digital survey missions evenly spaced across the UK and abroad, with successful operations extending across Europe, the Far East, Indonesia, Africa and South America. From these experiences the Geotechnologies MF-DMC system has evolved through the synergy of numerous flight trials, technical innovation and application to the production of digital aerial photomaps. With continuous upgrading such systems will remain at the cutting edge of solid state imaging technology particularly since the MF-DMC is arguably the first medium-format digital mapping camera to be sold world-wide as a proven direct digital mapping system suitable for all types of aircraft.

Ron Graham PhD, CPhys, FInstP, AMRAeS
Alexander Koh BSc (Hons), MSc

Acknowledgements

We should like to express our appreciation to those friends and colleagues who have helped us with their advice, discussions and aviation field trials while working in this exciting new field of digital data acquisition and mapping. To colleagues at Bath Spa University College, our thanks go to Dr Rick Curr, Dr Esther Edwards and Dr Fiona Strawbridge for their unstinting help, and also to Dr Jon Mills (University of Newcastle), Prof Dr. Franjo Heimes (Fachhochschule Bochum, Gennany), Roger Read (AIS), Dr. Alexander Hinz (Z/I) and Ernie Wickens (Z/I, UK), for their professional advice and contributions to the text. Our thanks also go to Trevor Miller of Kodak and to our professional pilot colleagues, Adrian Barralet and David Smith for use of their aircraft and survey flying assistance.

Last but not least, our thanks go to Dr Keith Whittles our publisher who, with his friendly advice, experience and enthusiasm has made the production of this book such a great pleasure.

Introduction

Digital aerial photography is a non-contact, non-destructive technique of data capture and information extraction for objects located on the earths surface. Rapid developments in digital camera technology and real-time satellite differential global positioning systems (dGPS) have yielded new opportunities for on-the-fly, in-situ digital mapping when used in conjunction with state of the art digital photogrammetric workstations.

This manual examines the systems available for data capture and photogrammetric processing, and provides an opportunity for readers to apply photo-interpretation to reconnaissance and photomapping techniques, and to many planning, resource harvesting, pollution prevention, disaster mitigation and containment requirements.

Geospatial information is an all embracing term that covers mapping, geographic information systems (GIS), and remote sensing. The gathering of geospatial information is well served by digital aerial surveys which allows the synergy of digital imagery and geospatial information to be applied in a wide variety of applications. The National Imagery and Mapping Agency (NIMA) of the USA defines geospatial information as, 'information about any object – natural or man made – that can be referenced to a specific location on the earth.' (King, 2000).

The manual concentrates on on-the-fly digital data capture and processing techniques because decision making processes are significantly enhanced by the timeliness of data collection and information extraction using these technologies. When data obsolescence is problematic during time-critical investigations (with typical data lives of 24 to 72 hours) a rapid turn-around time is imperative. A focus on rapid data capture and delivery to accepted standards are underlying themes of this vocationally oriented manual.

Objectives of this manual

Appreciation of:

(a) The historical basis of aerial photography.
(b) Analogue systems of aerial photography.
(c) Cost-effective applications and commercial deployment of digital aerial photographic services.
(d) Airborne kinematic GPS techniques.
(e) Recent developments in digital aerial cameras.
(f) The integration of aerial photography in GIS.

Understanding of:

(a) The underlying principles of vertical cartographic aerial photography.
(b) Principles and concepts of colour and colour infrared (CIR) digital aerial photographic sensors.
(c) Aerial survey flight track and mission planning.
(d) Survey costings and tender protocols.
(e) Aerial survey navigation.
(f) Ground control acquisition techniques.
(g) The theories and methods of photo-interpretation.
(h) Principles and methods of digital photogrammetry.
(i) Quality assurance issues in data capture, management, DEM and contoured orthophotomap production.

Know how to:

(a) Produce comprehensive flight and mission plans for digital aerial survey sorties.
(b) Produce competitive costing and delivery schedules.
(c) Capture digital aerial photography to specified standards.
(d) Navigate aerial survey platforms (aircraft) to pre-planned mission parameters.
(e) Manage captured data and produce a comprehensive searchable digital aerial photographic index.
(f) Collect ground control for GIS mapping.
(g) Produce DEMs (digital elevation models) from digital stereo aerial photography.
(h) Produce orthophotography at various resolutions.

1 A brief history of aerial survey

Behind every topographic map is an aerial photograph. First developed in World War One as a means of gaining military intelligence from the air, the technology of aerial photography has progressed dramatically since then. Since it has become common practice to scan air films in order to convert the image from analogue to digital form, it is safe to say that future airborne camera developments will be directed towards the digital domain.

In common with most technologies, photogrammetry and mapping have embraced the computer totally, and their mathematical nature means they benefit greatly from the use of sophisticated software. Gone are the large and expensive stereo-comparators and analytical machines, now replaced by a desk-top computer, and stereo viewing glasses. The process of soft-copy photogrammetry or digital photogrammetry is now available to numerous specialists who, with appropriate training, can produce their own digital terrain models (DTMs) and contoured orthophotomaps.

Analogue data capture

The conventional air survey photograph (either negative or positive) is an analogue image, and in order to be computer compatible must be changed into digital form. This is done by scanning the image with a suitable electronic sensor, such as a charge coupled device (CCD), the resulting data is then processed by an analogue-to-digital converter (ADC) and then back into analogue form by way of the digital-to-analogue converter (DAC) for display on the computer monitor.

For economic reasons, mapping (film) cameras are very large. Their square 23 cm image format is designed to cover as large a tract of land as possible in a single exposure. Survey flight is an expensive business, and for very large areas a large format is essential, in terms of area covered for a given scale, and flight-time efficiency. In a working environment that requires clear skies and optimal solar conditions it is important to be able to complete photographic cover as soon as possible – before conditions change! As a consequence these cameras are very expensive, because of their size and sophistication, the control systems and navigation sights, and the added factor that they require large sized rolls of film and processing in expensive laboratories.

Typically, these air cameras complete with their control systems can cost an operator around US$600,000, and they also require a relatively large aircraft to act as a survey platform.

We can expect large format (film) air cameras to be employed for many years yet, mainly for the following reasons:

1. A large format covers a larger area of terrain for any given scale.
2. Currently there is a world-wide availability of survey (film) cameras, which are suitable for existing mapping services offered by most of the established survey companies.
3. Conventional (film) data is compatible with existing mapping equipment, including modern scanning equipment.
4. Resistance to changing technologies (mainly due to client rather than operator).

Indeed, national mapping agencies and many large air survey companies are fully equipped with recently acquired survey cameras, such as the Leica (Wild) RC-20 or RC-30, or Zeiss RMK-TOP air cameras. These expensive cameras, complete with associated survey flight management systems (SFM), such as the IGI CCNS4, or Leica Ascot, give excellent service and will not be made redundant for many years yet. But the nature of primary data acquisition is steadily changing to digital cameras for very good reasons!

Current methods of analogue-to-digital data capture are less than efficient, save for the singular advantage of extensive terrain cover. The various steps include:

1. Primary data acquisition on 23 cm^2 film.
2. Film processing via roller transport (RT) machines.
3. Film scanning with variable scanning apertures.
4. Computer processing and operation.

When compared to digital data capture the above is found to be very inefficient in terms of economy and time. Steps 2 and 3 represent the main expenditure in time and cost in the data capture phase of the map production processing chain.

Film processing is highly expensive since the RT machine requires a firm base and has to be installed through a split darkroom/laboratory with associated chemical storage tanks. The processing chemicals have a very limited storage life, particularly colour developers, and the machines must be regularly cleaned and serviced. The process requires skilled staff to operate and the laboratory must be fed with a regulated water supply, temperature controlled and filtered. Film processing is also difficult, if not impossible, in certain field locations throughout the world.

Film scanning, using a photogrammetric scanner, is common practice these days since it is widely accepted that a scan resolution of 25μm is sufficient for the transfer of geometric information from analogue to digital form (Gong, *et al.*, 2000). This is expensive however, both in equipment and time and, although essential if the data is to be processed by computer, is an extra step requiring skilled staff and essential servicing.

Digital data capture

Here we have only two steps:

1. Primary data acquisition onto a digital camera.
2. Computer processing and operation.

To date, the development of a suitable aerial digital camera for mapping has had to wait for a suitable sensor. That is, a sensor array that is large enough to provide adequate cover with a resolution that can be the equivalent of film capture. Although digital cameras have been used for aerial photography since the early 1990s (Graham & Mills, 1994; Curr & Koh, 1994), the cameras employed have been off-the-shelf CCD types such as the Kodak DCS-200, DCS-420 CIR , DCS-460 CIR and DCS-660. All of these employ small formats such as 9.29 mm × 13.97 mm (DCS-200 and 420 series), or 18 mm × 28 mm (DCS- 460 and 660). The DCS-200 (1992) and DCS-420 (1994) have the same M5 chip with an image array of 1524 × 1012 pixels (each 9 μm^2) giving a total of 1.5 mega pixels (MPx).

By 1996 matters improved with the Kodak DCS-460 CIR camera. Fitted with the M6 chip the image array was now 2036 × 3060, giving a 6 mega pixel array over a 18.48 mm × 27.65 mm format – a very substantial increase in image area, with the same 9 µm pixel resolution. When fitted with a standard 28 mm lens the DCS-460 and 660 types can provide imagery equal to that of 23 cm contact prints made from film, in either monochrome, colour or colour infrared (CIR), provided they are printed on a high quality dye-sublimation, laser or even ink-jet printer.

However, the area coverage, scale for scale, has always been the limiting factor with these non-specific digital cameras when compared to a typical air survey camera. Although cameras such as the DCS-460 and 660 are used extensively for numerous small area projects, particularly in the fields of remote sensing, engineering, coastal and urban surveys etc., they were not purpose designed for aerial survey. Nevertheless, the rapid advances in digital technology and digital data capture are too great to be ignored for long. As a consequence, the main survey camera manufacturers mentioned above, Leica (Wild) and Zeiss, have both merged with specialist software and hardware companies in recent years. We now have: Zeiss/Intergraph (Z/I), and Leica/Helava (LH), and both have had a digital survey camera on offer since 1999.

The new digital survey cameras offered by Z/I and LH differ from each other in their technology, but have one thing in common – they are even more expensive than the survey film-cameras they still manufacture. No doubt these are early days and there will be improvements in the design and price of these cameras. In the meantime, a more appropriate digital air camera is that designed by Geotechnologies, Bath Spa University College, England. Designed as a medium format digital mapping camera (MF-DMC) this system has a 63.16 mm^2 CCD chip housed in a well known medium format camera with an established reputation in the field of small format aerial photography (Graham *et al.*, 1996). These cameras have a square imaging plane of 57.15 mm compared to the square CCD image array of 63.16 mm. The effective imaging area of this system is therefore 3706 × 3706 px which is bounded by a 197 px border.

Integrated within a Hasselblad 555 ELD (SLR) camera, the MF-DMC series of digital cameras incorporate either the Dicomed 4096 × 4096 px chip, or the Kodak Pro Back 4072 × 4072 Px chip, both providing an image sensor array of 16Mpx. Although both sensors are CCDs the Dicomed chip has silicon pixels 15.4 μm^2, whereas the smaller (36.53 mm^2) Kodak chip employs indium tin oxide (ITO) pixels each 9 μm^2. Both chips accommodate conventional colour or false-colour infrared (CIR) images, but the Dicomed has the advantage of a larger footprint (×1.564) at any given photo-scale because of the differences in CCD size with respect to the imaging plane size. The difference does not stop there however, since the Pro-Back model stores its images on Type II CF+ Microdrive storage cards, making it more portable than the Dicomed model which is connected directly to the computer. Fitted with a 40 mm lens with an inter-lens shutter (62.56 mm when used with the Kodak chip) and Firewire interface, the predicted performance of these 16Mpx cameras is to provide sequenced images that can be downloaded in 8 s.

The time taken to download the CCD captured image is an important feature in aerial survey work, and for the Kodak DCS-460 camera (6 Mpx array) the download period is 8–12 s, depending on the quality of the PCMCIA card in use. By comparison, the MF-DMC (16Mpx array) is a great improvement with its 8 s download interval. The importance of this time-interval (ΔT) is made clear when one considers large-scale photography at scale numbers less than 10,000. This is explained in more detail in Chapter 2. Typically, for a 25 cm nominal ground resolution, a 40 mm lens will provide a photoscale of 1:16234 for the Dicomed chip or 1:27778 for the Kodak chip. The Dicomed chip will provide a ground coverage of 0.93 km × 0.93km and the Kodak chip a ground coverage of 1.02 km × 1.02 km. At photo-scales below 1:10,000 stereoscopic cover (with a 60% forward-lap) requires short photo-interval periods, and for the 40 mm lens the required ΔT must be 2–8 s, depending on the ground speed of the aircraft (see Chapter 7).

Kodak cameras, such as the DCS-560, 660 and 760 models manage to download their images much faster than the DCS-460 due to improved bus architecture that incorporate the Firewire (IEEE-1394) interface (see Chapter 5).

The introduction of the Firewire computer data transfer interface is particularly important for the larger chip sizes such as the 4k × 4k pixel arrays employed in the MF-DMC series and the new Kodak DCS-Pro Back camera with its 16MPx sensor.

CMOS digital cameras

Although only CCD sensors have been considered thus far, the industry has longheld the view that a more simple device is on the horizon – the complementary metal oxide semiconductor (CMOS). The CMOS sensor has already been employed in the cheaper low-end cameras, and for some time the CMOS digital camera has been seen as a cheaper and more efficient system with the potential to match the quality of CCD imagers. Their main advantages are economy of manufacture (and retail prices) and lower power consumption, using only 10 to 20% of the power of a comparable CCD. They also tend to have fewer defects but unfortunately CMOS imagers have greater noise levels than CCDs. Unlike CCDs which must transfer their charges through neighbouring pixels, each CMOS pixel has its own amplifier and output, which means it can be read-out independently and so permit faster image downloads – an important feature for aerial photography (Graham, 1998).

Although the Kodak KAC-1310 SXGA CMOS imager has yet to be installed in a camera we can expect this sensor, or others like it, to be exploited very soon. The KAC-1310 CMOS features integrated timing control, and each pixel on the sensor is individually addressable allowing the user to control 'Window of Interest' (WOI) subsampling, resolution, exposure, gain and other image processing features.

Developments early in 2001by Foveon Inc (USA) indicate that a future generation of professional CMOS digital cameras will offer a serious challenge to CCD systems. The Foveon II for example is a CMOS 16Mpx sensor manufactured with 0.18μm CMOS process technology which enables more pixels to be packed within a given physical area and with greater quality than existing CCD types. Another Foveon CMOS sensor with a 2k × 2k pixel array will soon be marketed as the Hasselblad DFinity digital camera (see Chapter 5).

Advantages of the digital survey system

While respecting the established role of conventional, large format, aerial cameras, there can be no doubt that digital primary data acquisition offers significant advantages over film in certain areas. Although a 23 cm format exposure collects more than 15 times data than that captured by the MF-DMC, the role of the digital camera should not be dismissed in such simplistic terms. More importantly one must respect the fact that CCD and CMOS technology is improving rapidly, and whereas only a few years ago the concept of digital primary data was considered improbable, it is now fully accepted and shows even greater promise for the future.

The following, generally accepted, advantages for digital primary data acquisition are based on research projects as well as commercial operations.

1. The primary data can be accessed immediately the survey aircraft has landed, or even during the flight.
2. Typically, a calibrated Kodak DCS-460 CIR camera can deliver 1:10,000 scale mapping (colour infrared) over a 10km × 5km block with a ground resolution of 50 cm. The resulting data are then processed with soft-copy photogrammetry to produce DTMs and contoured orthophoto mosaics, within eight hours of the survey aircraft landing.
3. The entire digital process is conducted without film processing.
4. The process is free from chemistry and no darkroom or laboratory is required.
5. Primary data is immediately available for computer processing in a digital photogrammetric workstation (DPW) using a large library of software suitable for line mapping, GIS and remote sensing.
6. Expensive and time consuming film scanning is no longer required.
7. Small and medium format digital cameras are less expensive than conventional (film-based) mapping cameras and can be employed in smaller and less expensive aircraft.
8. Image quality and resolution match conventional requirements.
9. Whereas film-based colour infrared data needs to be processed by a skilled laboratory technician, digital CIR data can be accessed and processed by the client. The very significant advantage here is that the specialist can work with the false-colour image to find the required result, rather than having to accept the singular example provided by the photographic technician.
10. Digital image files are more easily stored and accessed (and at less expense) than rolls of 23 cm air film.

Survey navigation with digital air cameras

As with all modern survey flights digital surveys can also be planned and operated with global positioning system (GPS) equipment. In keeping with smaller and less expensive cameras it is prudent to employ less expensive GPS units to fly survey lines within a pre-planned block.

All survey flight planning starts with a request to cover a specified area at a certain scale, and with a suitably scaled map (usually 1:50,000 or even 1: 25,000). The area of interest (AOI, or survey block) is marked with the required survey flight lines and the map coordinates for each line are noted. Using off-the-shelf GPS units, the pre-planned waypoints are then entered (in WGS-84 coordinates) into the GPS unit. The survey is flown, using point-to-point navigation techniques to considerable accuracy by using the moving map window to place the aircraft on the pre-planned flight line to an accuracy of 8 m. The performance of these GPS units can be further enhanced by supplying it with high frequency differential collection data which will allow for each photo-centre to be displayed as a GPS waypoint, allowing the camera operator to manually trigger an exposure at the exact ground point.

Since the restrictive selective availability (SA) was removed by a USA act of Congress on May 1st 2000 and the availability of the wide area differential system (WADS), positioning accuracy can now reach 3 m in planimetry and 5 m in heighting. As a consequence accurate aerial surveys can be planned and flown without having to rely too much on GPS ground stations for differential GPS (dGPS).

Whereas the conventional (and expensive) optical navigation sight was an essential part of airborne survey equipment, it has now been relegated to secondary duties in most commercial survey firms. It is used primarily to determine atmospheric conditions when exposing photographs from high altitudes, employing the old adage *"if you can see the ground clearly through the navigation sight, then it should be OK to take photographs!"*. But for digital cameras, where shorter focal length lenses are employed, flying heights are much lower and the need for an optical sight is totally unnecessary.

The main use of the navigation sight is to determine wind-drift in order to keep the survey aircraft on track, but with GPS this is no longer required since the ground speed and track (trk) of the aircraft are displayed on the GPS screen. Wind-drift is then easily calculated by checking the aircraft's track over the ground, against its heading (hdg) or compass direction. The camera must then be turned towards the wind-corrected angle by means of a drift-mount in order to keep the images square to the flight-line (see Chapters 6 and 8).

2 Principles of digital aerial photography

Bearing in mind the interdisciplinary nature of aerial survey photography it is not surprising to find the subject permeated with a mixture of units, sciences, rules and technologies. For example, the reader will find a mixture of imperial and metric units in calculating the working parameters of a typical aerial survey – mainly due to rules of aviation where altitude and height must be quoted in feet – whereas spot heights on a map will be quoted in meters. Similarly, we might find the air speed indicator (ASI) in a survey aircraft reading in either, mph, km/h or knots, and conversion of all these units to meters/second is a necessary requirement for flight planning. The reader is therefore directed to Appendix A for assistance in these various unit conversions.

The nature of aerial survey

Aerial surveys can be divided into two main groups: vertical and oblique, and although the latter is not a significant part of this industry oblique photography might well be required for certain applications, such as industrial sites or coastal surveys.

In military applications, for reconnaissance, vertical and oblique photography roughly share the work in terms of strategic and tactical cover.

Vertical aerial survey

Vertical photography implies that the optical axis of the camera is as close to vertical as possible, and although it is virtually impossible to ensure that the lens axis is perpendicular to the ground (apart from the fact that the terrain would need to be flat) the problem is one of keeping the aircraft steady or 'straight and level'. Stabilised mounts help in this respect and are an important (if expensive) feature with modern large format air cameras. A general rule is that vertical photographs are acceptable for photogrammetry provided they are exposed with less than 5° of tilt; typically, an aerial survey is flown so that tilt (nose down or up) of any single image is <3°, and the relative tilt between any two consecutive frames less than 5°.

Vertical photography and basic photogrammetric issues

Vertical photography is used for topographic mapping, and the layperson usually assumes that a vertical photograph is the same as its map counterpart, except for contours and symbols. There is some excuse for this assumption of course: first because of the obvious spatial relationships between map and photograph; and second because of the well known practice of fitting and matching consecutive photographs to form a mosaic. Indeed, the uncontrolled mosaic has its uses in both military and civil applications, and has until recent times had the advantage of being produced much faster and more cheaply than the cartographer's map (computerised mapping has changed this however). Nevertheless, a map differs from its primary data source in a number of important ways. Not least of these is the metric or geodetic accuracy of the map compared to the photograph. A photograph is a perspective view, in contrast to the strictly orthogonal view of a map.

The image points on a vertical photograph are displaced from their true plan position for two reasons: camera tip and tilt, and height displacement. To these distortions must be added image distortions: lens aberrations, translated image motion, atmospheric refraction and, for film, dimensional instability of the material.

Basic photogrammetric considerations

Photogrammetry is the applied science of obtaining reliable measurements from photographs. In topographic survey work some of the complex problems that face the photogrammetrist can be reduced considerably if the air survey crew (pilot and navigator/camera operator) do their work correctly. An important feature in all aerial surveys is obtaining suitable coverage with the maximum degree of accuracy, and as economically as possible. In this respect the first major consideration is photo-scale (the image scale of the primary data), where a reduction in the photo-scale has a two-fold effect:

1. A smaller photo-scale reduces the overall accuracy to which ground detail may be coordinated, in both planimetry and height.
2. A smaller photo-scale is more economic since it reduces the number of overlapping photographs necessary for the stereoscopic cover of a given area. This, in turn, reduces the number of costly ground control points, number of photographs and downstream plotting efforts.

The compromise between accuracy and economy has many side issues which require careful mission planning, particularly where block size, terrain and aircraft selection are concerned, and involves not only the solution of technical problems but logistical and economic factors as well (see Chapters 6 and 7).

The geometry of a vertical photograph

In photogrammetric terms there are nine orientation elements of a near-vertical photograph: six 'outer orientation' elements and three 'inner orientation' elements.

Outer orientation

3 translations: X, Y, Z.

3 rotations: tip (ϕ) phi, tilt (ω), swing (κ) kappa.

Note: The aviation counterparts to the above rotational elements are:

Pitch (tip), nose up or down.

Roll (tilt), wing up or down.

Yaw (swing), nose left or right.

Inner Orientation

Principal distance (PD): (calibrated focal length: C_k).

Principal point (PP): (position of PP: 2 shifts, x and y).

The inner orientation elements refer to the survey camera and, as a consequence, are known to a high degree of accuracy. The principles of photogrammetry depend on the accuracy of the camera, and for this reason great store is put on its calibration. As shown above, the three elements of inner orientation include the PD and the exact position of the PP. Whereas the nominal focal length of a camera (f) is good enough for most work it is not sufficiently accurate for metric work. However, for the sake of simplicity in future calculations, we shall always refer to the PD in terms of the symbol f.

The PD (f) is measured from the perspective centre of the lens to the PP; the exact location of the PP being of great importance. During calibration the PP is found and its location recorded with respect to fiducial marks within the focal plane of the camera. Whereas these fiducials are usually marked on the edges of the film plane in 23 cm survey cameras, the corners of the digital chip are usually employed for locating the PP in digital cameras.

Scale (M) and scale number (m)

The scale (M) of a vertical photograph is given (to a first order of accuracy) as:

$$M = f/H \tag{2.1}$$

where f = calibrated focal length, and H = mean height above ground.

(Note: We always refer to height above ground (H) and not altitude, which is the height of the aircraft above sea level. For hilly terrain H is taken as the mean height above ground, a figure taken by averaging spot-heights or contours on the appropriate map).

It will be noted that Eq. 2.1 provides a value for scale which may be shown as 1/12,000 for values of f = 50 mm and H = 2000 ft. However, this is traditionally shown as the ratio: 1:12,000.

In our calculations for survey flight planning we use the reciprocal of scale, i.e, the scale number (m) as this can be directly employed in subsequent calculations.

$$m = H/f \tag{2.2}$$

Equation 2.2 serves well for the rare conditions where the terrain is flat, but does not take into account either topographic relief or camera tip and tilt. Flying height can usually be controlled to within 1%, but there will always be small variations in scale from one image to another along a given flight-line, particularly in conditions of extreme turbulence. Topographic relief and camera tip/tilt will also cause variations in scale from point to point within each photograph.

Figure 2.1 illustrates the view of a near-vertical photograph taken with a camera tilted by t degrees and a perspective centre at o. The PD is given by the line op, and it can be seen that the tilt angle is given by pon, where n is the nadir point (also called the plumb point, vertically below the aircraft). The principal line lies in the plane of the image and passes through the points n and p, and is oriented in the direction of the steepest inclination of the photograph. The bisector of the tilt angle intersects the

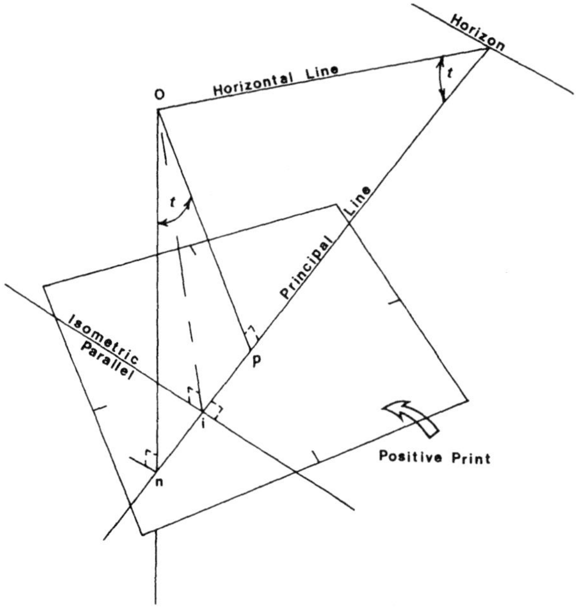

Figure 2.1 *The positive view of a near-vertical photograph. The tilt angle t is given by pOn, where p is the principal point found at the intersection of the four fiducial marks, O the perspective centre and n, the nadir point. In the presence of tilt, photo-scale will vary along the principal line but will remain constant along the isometric parallels.*

image at the isocentre i on the principal line.

It is convenient to consider tilt t as the single resultant of the component tip (ϕ) and tilt (ω). The photo-scale will thus change along the direction of the principal line, but will remain constant along any line that is perpendicular to the direction of tilt. In the presence of camera tilt and terrain elevation, the scale-number of any image point can be calculated from Eq. 2.3.

$$m = (H - h) / (f - q.\sin t) \quad (2.3)$$

where q is the distance of the image point from the isocentre measured in the direction of the tilt, and h is the ground elevation of the associated object relative to the same datum as that used for H (as shown by the elevation AB in Fig.2.2).

The effects of tilt are important to the photogrammetrist, as shapes of ground areas are distorted in a tilted photograph. For truly vertical images (where the PP and nadir point, n, coincide), and for perfectly flat terrain, the nadir point is used as the radial centre for plotting detail. With the nadir point as centre, it may be assumed that all image displacements on a photograph are radial from this point; thus angles subtended by images to the radial centre are assumed in radial plotting to be equal to the corresponding angles on the ground. For the tilted photograph however, displacements are radial from the isocentre.

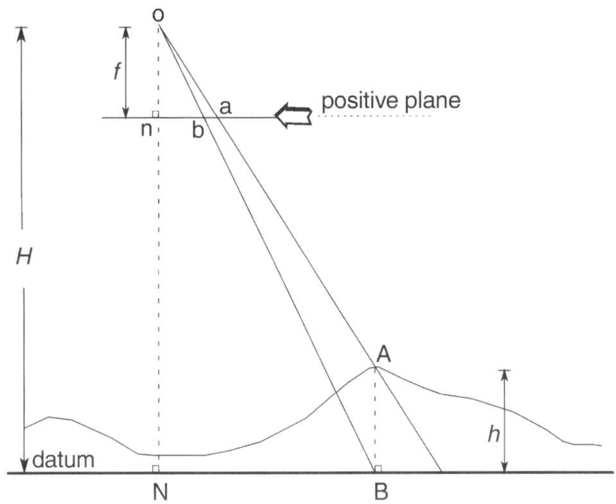

Figure 2.2 *Height distortion for a truly vertical photograph. The height displacement ab is calculated from: ab = na × h/H, where na is the radial distance from the nadir point.*

In Fig. 2.2, height distortion is shown for a truly vertical photograph, where the height displacement ab is calculated from Eq. 2.4.

$$\text{ab} = (na.h)\ / H \tag{2.4}$$

where *na* is the radial distance from the nadir point. Equation 2.4 is valid for conditions where the camera is tilted, and height distortion is always radial from the nadir point.

Summing up: for tilted images of terrain where relief is present, tilt displacements are radial from the isocentre while relief displacements are radial from the nadir point. Strictly speaking therefore, there is no single point on the photograph where the sets of directions on the image and ground are equal. In practice however, the nadir and principal points approximately coincide. Provided that tilt does not exceed 2°, and height variations are not greater than about $0.1H$, then no significant error is introduced into the survey by accepting the PP as a radial centre. This is known as the radial line assumption. Whereas these assumptions are usually made for the 15 cm lens on a 23 cm format, they should equally apply to digitial systems such as the MF-DMC.

For any given photo-scale, planimetric accuracy tends to get better for greater focal lengths (smaller angular fields), but height accuracy decreases rapidly because the height error is approximately inversely proportional to the base/height ratio (Jerie and Visser, 1969). The base of a pair of forward-overlapping vertical photographs (also known as the air base) is the movement of the camera between two air stations along a given flight-line, as shown in Fig. 2.3. Heightings are taken from a stereoscopic pair of images and the amount of relief displacement (Eq. 2.4), for example, is greater for smaller focal lengths.

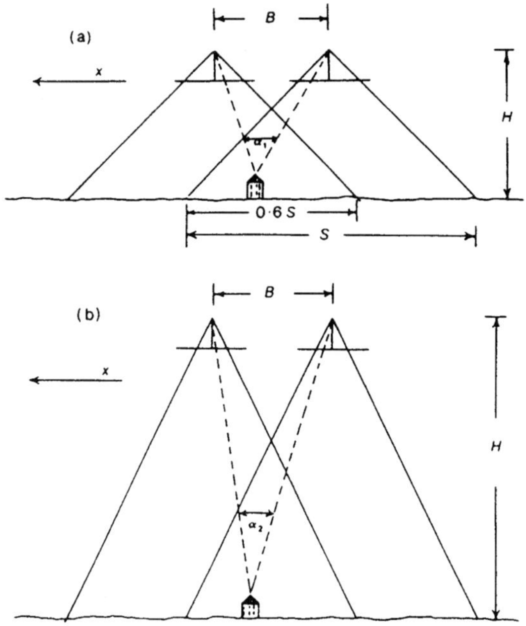

Figure 2.3 *The air-base B of an overlapping pair of photographs is provided by two camera stations along the flight-line. The 60% overlap (0.6S) provides for stereoscopic observations with parallactic angles α proportional to the B/H ratio. (a) Heighting accuracy is favoured by greater B/H ratios, providing greater parallactic angles. (b) With increased flying height H,* $\alpha_2 < \alpha_1$, *and the measurement of heights is less accurate.*

From a quantitative point of view, large B/H ratios favour higher plotting accuracy and are provided for by employing a wide angle lens, so that greater parallactic angles (α) are gained with the increased B/H ratio. For mosaic work, tilt and height displacements may be minimised by increasing the flying height; scale variations will also be minimised.

The normal degree of forward-overlap required to produce sufficient stereo-parallax is 60% of the ground covered by a single photograph, as shown (in the *x* direction) by Fig. 2.3. In order to cover an extensive area of ground (the survey block) a number of flight-lines are flown, each line overlapping its adjacent flight-line by a given amount of side-lap. This requirement sets high standards of survey navigation accuracy which, nowadays, is made easier by GPS tracking. The amount of side-lap (*y* direction) may vary according to economics or specific requirements. For mountainous terrain, or urban areas, a wide-angle lens may be used with excessive amounts (40% to 60%) of side-lap in order to avoid dead areas (due to relief). But on average, side-lap is usually in the region of 25% to 30%, unless mosaic production is anticipated, where it may be increased in order to reduce the size of the central image area of each photograph, thus reducing the effects of tilt and terrain distortion.

Line overlaps in vertical photography

Apart from the occasional single pin-point photograph, most verticals are taken as a series of overlapping flight strips. The generally accepted degree of forward overlap is 60% ± 5%, which provides for a number of conditions:

1. Good stereoscopic cover between successive frames.
2. Full coverage in the event of damage to any frame.
3. Adequate provision against scattered cloud obscuring the mission area (usually sufficient to allow for up to one or two *octa* of light cumulus).
4. Reasonable safety against undue terrain variations, or camera tilt due to turbulence, drift etc.

The basic principles of stereoscopic cover can best be illustrated by considering a stereo-pair of diapositives (Fig. 2.4), and assuming exactly vertical photographs with a horizontal air-base (*B*). Thus, for a given forward overlap between two images caused by a change in camera station, the parallax of a point A is the difference measured in the position between its image points. As shown in Fig.2.4, the right hand photograph is placed over the left hand photograph such that the two PPs are superimposed, and the lines representing the flight direction (x-axis) on the two images are made collinear. Under these conditions the x-parallax of the point a is given by the distance aa″, this distance p_a may be given as:

$$p_a = x - x' \qquad (2.5)$$

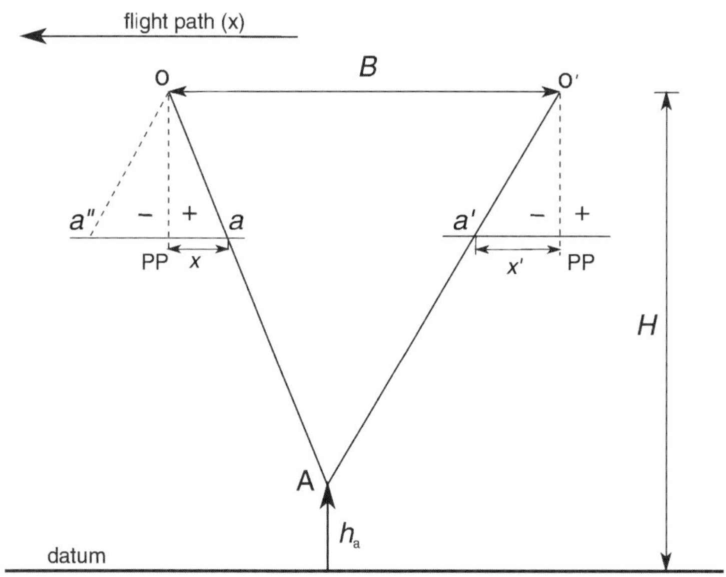

Figure 2.4 *The basic principles of stereoscopic cover. If two diapositives are positioned such that their principal points coincide and their flight directions are made collinear, the x-parallax of point a is given by the distance aa″, i.e* $P_a = x - x'$ *(observe the sign notation).*

This is called the parallax equation.

From Fig. 2.4, and the similar triangles aoa″ and oAo′, we have:

$$P_a = (f.B) / (H - h_a) \tag{2.6}$$

where B is the air-base, f is the PD of the camera lens, H is the flying height above mean-ground (datum), and h_a is the height of point A above the datum. From carefully measured values of x and x' it is then possible to extract a value for terrain height h_a from:

$$h_a = H - (f.B) / P_a \tag{2.7}$$

From Eq. 2.6 we may put:

$$P_a (H - h_a) = f.B \tag{2.8}$$

For a given pair of photographs both f and B have a fixed value; the product $f.B$ is thus a constant. However, p will differ from point to point within the stereo-pair according to the height of the point such that pH = constant; in other words the magnitude of p varies inversely with H. Thus we have:

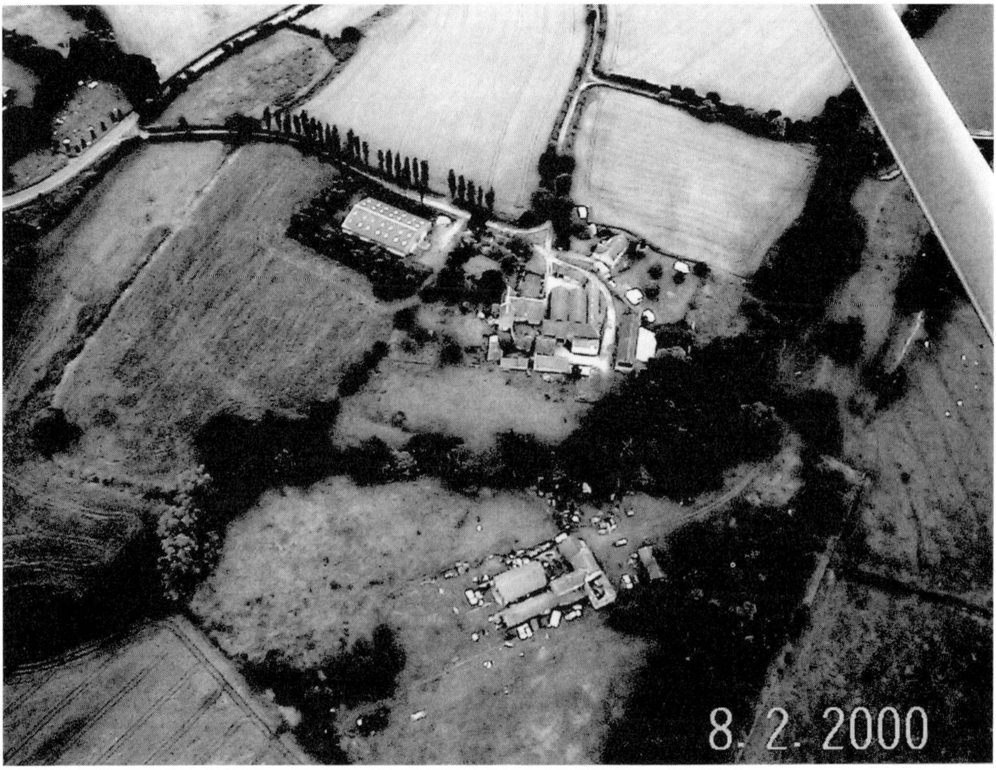

Figure 2.5 *Low oblique (no horizon) taken with the Kodak DC-210 Plus digital camera. Photo: Ron Graham.*

$$pH = \text{constant} \tag{2.9}$$

and by differentiating Eq. 2.9 with respect to H we may determine the rate of change of p with respect to H since:

$$0 = H\,(\mathrm{d}p/\mathrm{d}H) + p \tag{2.10}$$

or

$$\mathrm{d}p/p = -\mathrm{d}H/H \tag{2.11}$$

Equation 2.11 is obtained by differentiation, and is consequently only valid for small increments of H or p. However, provided that only small deviations from true vertical or horizontal are involved, this equation is useful for determining heights of trees or buildings.

The above calculations simply provide a background to the nature of photogrammetry, but it must be emphasised that within recent times, high performance computers and high speed image processing have removed most of these tedious mathematical processes. In addition, lower memory costs, inexpensive mass storage, image compression/decompression techniques and high resolution monitors have made the digital photogrammetric workstation (DPW) a highly efficient and economic part of modern mapping technology. Yet another advantage of the DPW is its ability to accommodate multiple viewers, allowing training time to be greatly reduced because several people can see the same demonstration simultaneously. This also encourages teams of engineers to collaborate on a single project; a practice that was nearly impossible with previous generations of photogrammetric systems (Intergraph Corp, ITC. 1993).

Oblique aerial photography

Obliques are generally categorised as either high obliques or low obliques. A high-oblique includes the horizon whereas a low-oblique does not.

Obliques are easily made and are a popular choice where aerial photography is of immediate importance, e.g, for police work, military reconnaissance, disaster areas or industrial-site surveillance. All that is required is a light aircraft and a cockpit provided with a clear-vision panel. Low-to-medium priced digital cameras are ideally suited for this work, since they allow for swift access to their images, either by an immediate liquid crystal display at the rear of the camera or through a computer. For obvious reasons, obliques are more acceptable to the layman because they are easily interpreted and offer immediate information concerning relative heights of objects and terrain features.

A typical low oblique is shown in Fig. 2.5. Taken with an inexpensive Kodak DC-210-Plus digital camera, this was photographed from a small light aircraft over a farm site in conditions of rain. In Fig. 2.6, we have a high-oblique taken only a few minutes later. Both photographs were taken from an open cockpit at a height of about 1000 ft. The DC-210-Plus camera has a limited CCD array of only 1 million pixels but, as can be seen, the results have adequate resolution and quality.

A particular problem always associated with high-oblique images is the possibility that an important feature may be located near the horizon. Under these circumstances subject matter will always suffer, either from atmospheric effects or from camera-flare.

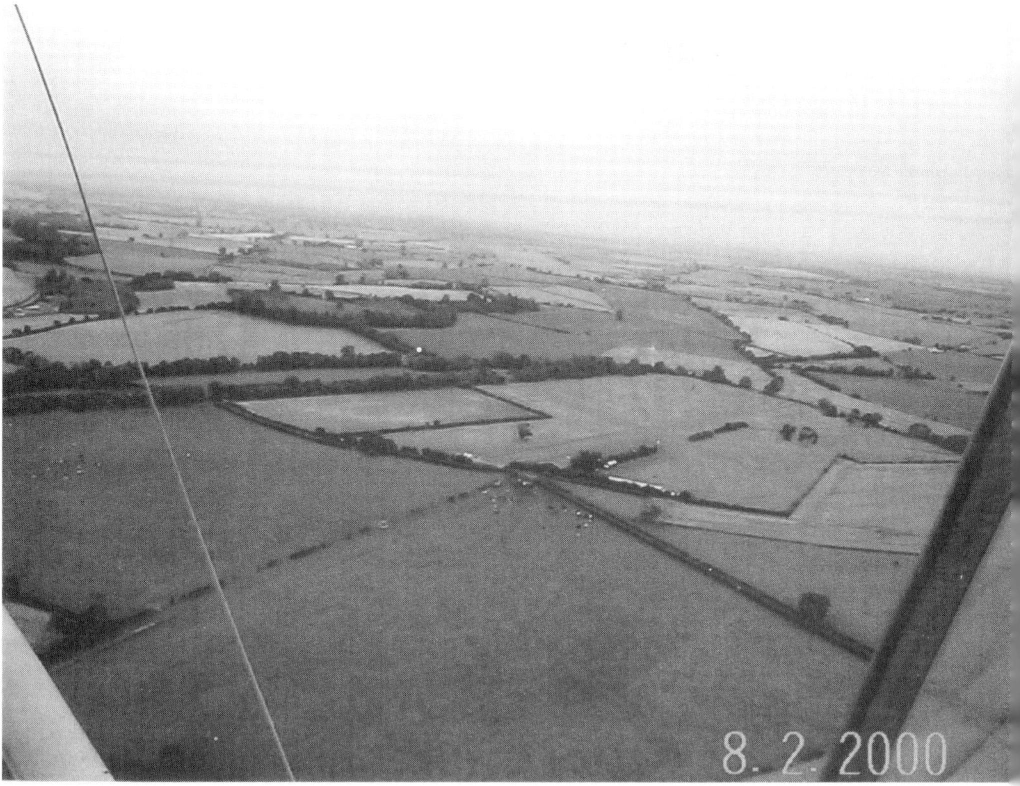

Figure 2.6 *High oblique (includes horizon) taken with the Kodak DC-210 Plus digital camera. Photo: Ron Graham.*

In Fig.2.6 the horizon is slightly obscured by an approaching rain front, but had it been clear there would still be the adverse effects of camera lens flare.

All air cameras (film or digital), will suffer from excessive over exposure along the horizon when recording high obliques. This is due to camera lens-flare, where over-exposed sky light spreads into adjacent image areas of terrain. It is rare for this to be a problem however, since the camera is usually depressed to the principal target leaving the horizon well alone.

Oblique scale(s)

Obviously all oblique images have a continuum of scales depending upon the slant range between the camera and a given point on the ground. The important oblique parameters are illustrated in Fig. 2.7.

Slant range *H'* depends on the aircraft's height H and the angle β made by a direct line between lens and target and the vertical.

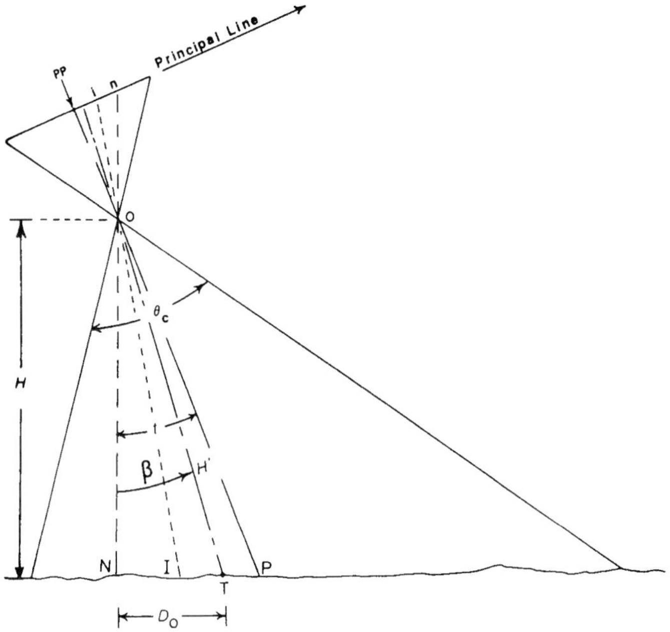

Figure 2.7 *Parameters important to oblique photography (see text).*

$$H' = H.\sec\beta \tag{2. 12}$$

and the oblique scale number (m_o) is:

$$m_o = H'/f = (H.\sec\beta)/f \tag{2. 13}$$

In Fig. 2.7 we see that the slant range to target is the distance OT, and the ground distance from nadir N to the target T is the offset flight-line D_o. The angle of camera tilt (t) is between the vertical ON and the principal axis OP. The distance from the aircraft to the offset flight-line D_o is given by:

$$D_o = H\tan\beta \tag{2. 14}$$

Whereas Eq. 2.13 covers every eventuality for calculating scale number, it is often convenient to refer to a fixed oblique angle t, for the scale-number at ground points N, I and P as follows:

Scale-number at the principal point (pp)

$$m_{o(p.p)} = H/(f.\cos t) = (H.\sec t)/f \tag{2. 15}$$

Scale-number at the isocentre (i)

$$m_{o(i)} = H/f \tag{2. 16}$$

(It should be noted that the scale-number at the isocentre is the same as that for a vertical photograph).

Scale-number at the nadir point (n)

$$m_{o(n)} = H/(f.\sec t) = (H.\cos t)/f \tag{2. 17}$$

The scale at each of these three points will, of course, be continued along the parallels normal to the principal line. The above equations are necessary for the flight planning of oblique missions, and particularly for fixed oblique installations, where the aircraft flies straight and level with a camera depressed at given angle of tilt.

Digital terrain models (DTMs) and digital elevation models (DEMs)

As originally defined by Miller and La Flamme in 1958, 'the digital terrain model (DTM) is simply a statistical representation of the continuous surface of the ground by a large number of selected points with known X,Y,Z coordinates in an arbitrary coordinate field'. Objects such as buildings and other man-made constructions are the main areas of interest for truly 3D DTMs.

After the DTM other terms have been coined which, although presumed to be synonymous, usually refer to quite distinct products. In particular we have the digital elevation model (DEM), where the term elevation refers to the measurement of height above datum and the absolute elevation of the points contained in the model.

The DEM has many applications within the field of surveying and mapping, typical examples being digital orthophotos and programs to derive contour lines, digital slope models and, for visualisation purposes, perspective views.

3 Sensors for aerial photography

Digital imaging sensors are just as capable of providing the same kind of image as film materials, either in monochrome (black and white), full colour or colour infrared (CIR). Like film, they provide an analogue recording of a scene but, unlike film, the image is one of stored electronic charge rather than a latent image stored in a photo-sensitive silver-halide.

The basic imaging sensor is a metal oxide semiconductor (MOS) which can be in the form of either a complementary metal oxide semiconductor (CMOS) or a charge coupled device (CCD). The CMOS sensor shows lots of promise and currently offers a more economic system, whereas at the high-end of the market the Foveon CMOS sensors (see Chapter 5) show promise over the CCD. Neverthless we can expect CMOS to dominate the digital scene within a few years. For the time being however, we must concentrate on the CCD camera which is the system currently in use. This is the sensor type featured throughout the rest of the book, knowing that the principles of digital imagery will remain essentially the same.

The most significant aspect of CCD imaging is its system compatibility with computers. After exposure each cell in the CCD array is 'clocked out' by the systems electronic circuitry so that each CCD (millions of cells) is given a digital code according to its signal strength (image intensity at that point) and x, y position within the array. At this stage of the imaging process the system becomes 'digital', and as such can be stored in the camera – to be subsequently downloaded into a computer.

In common with all popular electronic products, digital cameras will be improved and become less expensive. Currently, only a handful of these cameras are really suitable for precise metric aerial photography. Nevertheless, we may be confident that digital aerial surveys will become the norm in future years.

Semiconductors

The resistance of conductors (as well as insulators and semiconductors) is partly determined by the number of electrons in the outermost energy level – the valence band – of the substance's constituent atoms. Under suitable conditions, such as the application of energy from an external source, electrons can be forced from the valence band into the even higher energy level of the conduction band. This transport of electrons constitutes an electric current. The maximum possible number of electrons in a valence band is eight, and an atom with eight valence electrons is normally an excellent insulator. But elements with only six or seven valence electrons are also found to be good insulators, mainly because the gap between the valence and conduction bands is too great.

Atoms having only one, two or three valence electrons readily accept electrons from, or contribute electrons to, neighbouring atoms and are therefore good electrical conductors. Those elements with four valence electrons in their atoms, and compounds made up of one element with three valence electrons and another with five valence electrons, may be semiconductors.

Semiconductors are used to make solid-state electronic components, and some of these are light-sensitive devices that employ the photoelectric effect. One such photocell is the cadmium sulphide (CdS) photoresistor, which has a resistance that can vary from millions of ohms in total darkness to a few tens of ohms when illuminated. Another device is the metal oxide semiconductor (MOS).

Semiconductors are often 'doped' with controlled amounts of impurities so that the dopant lowers the resistance of the semiconductor to allow more current to flow through the device. If we introduce a pentavalent element (five valence electrons), such as phosphorus, arsenic or antimony, into a pure silicon crystal (the host material, with four valence electrons) then each substitute atom has one more electron than necessary to make a covalent bond. These pentavalent atoms are called 'donors' since they donate an extra electron. And since they are not in a valence band, these excess electrons are free to carry a negative charge and leave behind a fixed positive charge (positive hole) in the substitute atoms. In this way the charge-neutrality condition is preserved.

Silicon doped with phosphorus is a negative type (n-type) semiconductor because the concentration of free electrons (n) is much larger than that of holes (p). But if a trivalent element such as boron, or aluminium is used as the substitutional impurity, a single electron is now missing from the bonding arrangement of elements, and a positive hole is produced with a fixed negative charge remaining in the impurity atom. Materials with an excees of holes are called p-type semiconductors. It is the movement of electron-hole pairs that carry the charge in solid-state junction devices.

The junction diode formed by an interface of p-type and n-type semiconductor materials has the ability to block the flow of electrons in one direction (reverse bias) while permitting electron flow in the opposite direction (forward bias). If electrons are directed into the p-type side of the diode they will not cross the interface of the pn junction, because the electrons already present in the n-type region repel them. But if electrons with sufficient energy are directed into the n-type side they can easily cross over the junction to combine with the positive holes and create an electrical current.

While the diode described mentions electrons as carriers of electrical charge, it is also possible to consider the holes on the p-type side of the junction as being charge carriers because holes continually migrate towards the pn junction to combine with arriving electrons.

The transistor is an important semiconductor employing multiple pn junctions, and although there are numerous types of transistor they all allow a relatively large electric current flowing through the device to be controlled by a very small current or voltage at a third electrode, or gate.

The metal oxide semiconductor (MOS)

Since the mid 1980s MOS technology has superseded the bipolar junction transistor both in sales and in applications, due mainly to its simple structure and low fabrication costs. It is important to discuss MOS structure since the MOS capacitor is basic to the charge coupled device (CCD).

Although a silicon-silicon dioxide MOS capacitor is mentioned here, MOS technology is constantly improving, and insulating materials other than pure SiO_2 are currently under consideration. (Yang, 1988). The basics of a MOS capacitor are shown in Fig. 3.1, where it can be seen that the structure comprises an aluminium gate (Al) over a dielectric material (SiO_2) deposited on a p-type silicon substrate. The band gap of the silicon dioxide insulator is 8eV, and that of the p-type silicon semiconductor 1.1eV, and as there is only a negligible voltage drop in the metal gate, the applied voltage V_G is shared by the voltage across the oxide (V_o) and the surface potential (ψ_s), shown as:

$$V_G = V_o + \psi_s \tag{3.1}$$

The surface potential is the voltage across the semiconductor, and by using the bulk Si as reference, ψ_s can be considered as the potential at the Si- SiO_2 interface. For this reason it is known as the surface potential.

It should be noted that the SiO_2 layer is a good insulator and does not allow the conduction of current between the metal and semiconductor – even under bias, that is, as a dielectric the oxide will, under an applied electric field, cause a displacement of charge, but not a flow of charge.

Depending on the polarity and magnitude of the applied voltage, three different surface conditions are possible: (i) carrier accumulation, (ii) carrier inversion, and (iii) carrier depletion. Although all three conditions are important to the theory of the MOS capacitor, it is the third condition we shall consider here, since this allows us to explain the function of MOS elements in the CCD.

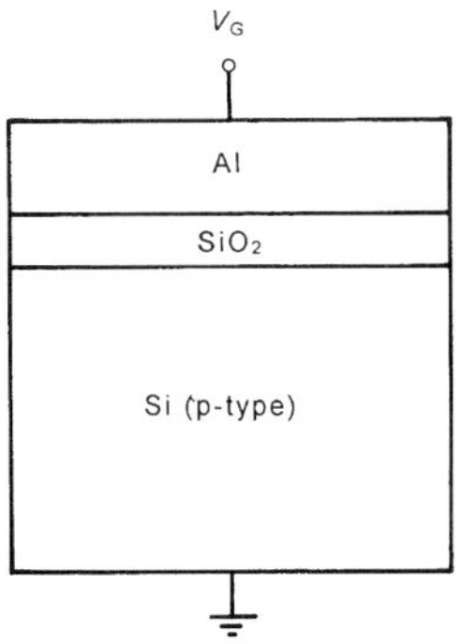

Figure 3.1 *The basic MOS capacitor structure.*

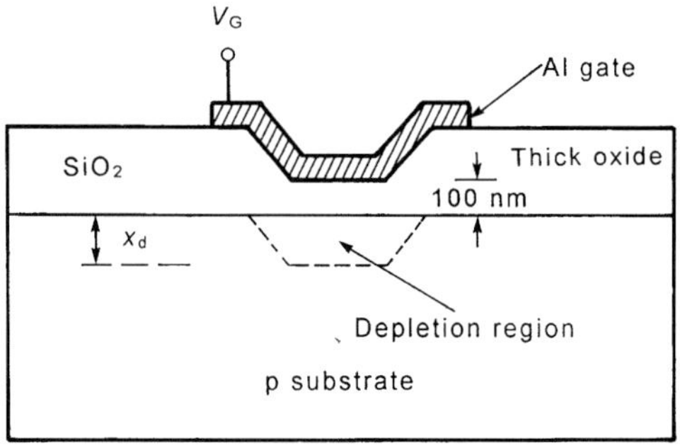

Figure 3.2 *Details of MOS capacitor with aluminium gate.*

In Fig. 3.2 a typical cross section of a MOS capacitor is shown. In this diagram the gate is an aluminium type, but could equally be a semi-transparent polycrystalline (polysilicon) gate as suited to a CCD imaging sensor. Typically the SiO_2 layer will vary from a thin deposit of about 100 nm to a thick one in the region of 1 μm.

When a positive step voltage (up to about 10 volts) is applied to the gate of a MOS, the majority of carrier holes are repelled – resulting in a depletion region of negatively charged acceptor states under the gate, near to the surface of the silicon. In time, electron-hole pairs are generated in the depletion region, and electrons accumulate at the Si-SiO_2 interface to create an inversion layer, while the holes are driven to the substrate.

The surface potential (ψ_s) of a MOS capacitor, as a function of the applied voltage at the gate electrode (V_G), is given by:

$$\psi_s = V_G + Q_s / C_o \qquad (3.2)$$

where: Q_s is the total charge per unit area in the semiconductor surface region (C/cm^2; Note: C is the coulomb, or quantity of electricity transported at one amp/sec); C_o is the SiO_2 capacitance (F/cm^2 where F is in farads).

The oxide capacitance (C_o) is given by:

$$C_o = K_o . \varepsilon_o / x_o \qquad (3.3)$$

where: K_o is the oxide dielectric constant (3.9 for silicon dioxide); ε_o is the free space permittivity (F/m) and x_o is the oxide thickness.

Surface potential is also controlled by the substrate doping concentration, as well as the silicon oxide thickness.

The charge coupled device (CCD)

Essentially a charge coupled device is a silicon integrated circuit of the MOS type with a basic structure as shown in Fig.3.3. A CCD comprises an oxide (SiO_2) covered silicon substrate upon which is formed an array of closely spaced electrodes. Signal information is carried in the form of an electric charge, usually electrons (although opposite polarity CCDs are also possible).

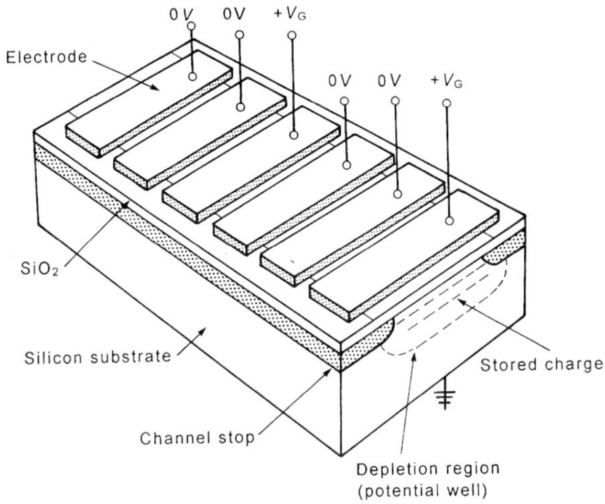

Figure 3.3 *Typical CCD structure.*

The charge is localised under the electrodes with the highest applied potentials, because the positive potential of an electrode (V_G) causes the underlying silicon to be in depletion (Fig.3.2) and so assume a positive potential, which attracts the signal (image photons) electrons. We can then say that the electrons are being stored in a potential-well. The active part of of the CCD (where the charges are stored) is known as the channel, and this region is bounded by electrically inactive p-type channel stops (Fig.3.3).

The term 'charge coupling' refers to the method by which signal charges (which can be photoelectrons created from an image falling on the CCD array) can be transferred from under one electrode to its neighbour next in line.. This is accomplished by taking the voltage on the second electrode also to a high level, and reducing the voltage on the first electrode, as shown in Fig.3.4. By sequentially pulsing electrode voltages between high and low levels, charge signals can be transported down an array of very many electrodes with hardly any loss and with very little noise. This CCD transport system is often compared to the action of a 'bucket brigade' used to convey buckets of water to fight a fire. This simile is made good by the fact that each 'bucket' is a potential well of electrons carried along a 'shift register' to a final output.

The three-phase CCD

The MOS structures within a typical CCD line have their electrodes connected into two or three groups called phases. By changing the voltage of the CCD phases photocharge packets can be moved laterally down the line. A very common system is the symmetrical three-phase CCD, where charges can flow to either right or left as shown in Fig. 3. 5. By connecting up three closely spaced MOS capacitors into storage elements and applying a set of three-phase drive pulses ϕ_1, ϕ_2 and ϕ_3 (typically from +5 to +15 volts), charge signals can be stored under every third electrode in each line of the array.

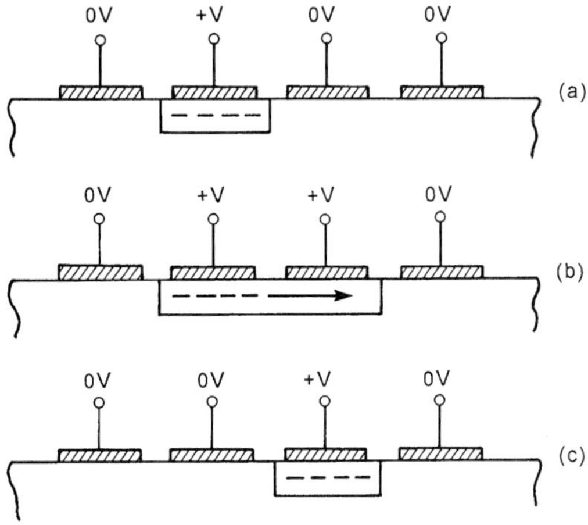

Figure 3.4 *Signal transfer by charge coupling.*

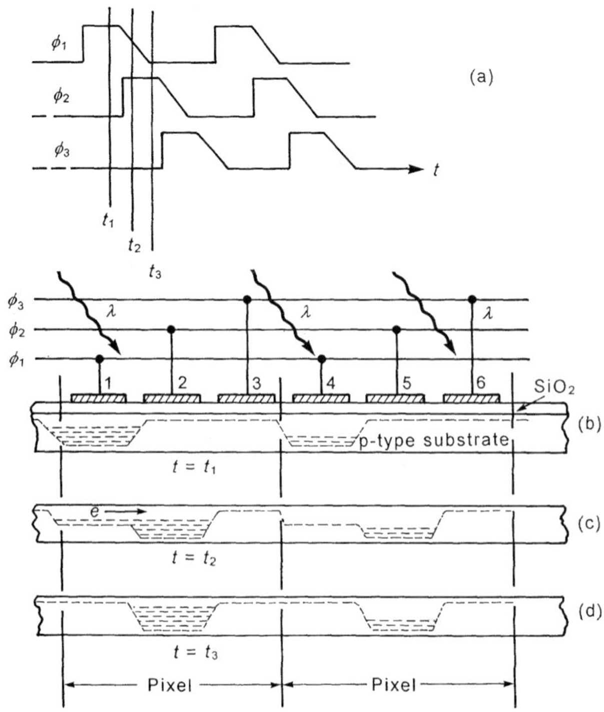

Figure 3.5 *Three-phase CCD, showing storage elements (pixels) and drive pulses.*

It is important to note that, as shown in Fig.3.5, the three drive pulses occupy one electrode width or one pixel. We shall find the pixel to be the most important parameter when discussing CCD chips and their practical characteristics.

Under the three-phase system each storage element (pixel, if the input signal is optically generated) has every third electrode connected to the same clock voltage and consequently three separate clock generators are required (Fig. 3.5a). If the positive voltage applied to ϕ_1 is higher than that applied to ϕ_2 and ϕ_3, surface potential wells are formed under the ϕ_1 electrodes, as explained for Fig.3.4. Charge packets, introduced either optically (image wise, in the form of photons) or electrically, are accumulated in these depletion wells at $t = t_1$. These charge packets may be of different signal strengths. For example, those illustrated in Fig. 3.5b show the charge under gate 4 to be less than that under gate 1. It should be noted that the MOS capacitors must be close enough to allow their depletion layers to overlap; this is necessary so that the surface potential has a smooth transition at the boundaries of the neighbouring electrodes.

In order to move the charges to the right, a positive step-voltage is applied to ϕ_2 to ensure that the potential wells under the ϕ_1 and ϕ_2 electrodes are the same in depth. In this way the charge packets are allowed to spread out to the right, as seen at $t = t_2$ (Fig. 3.5c). Immediately after the pulse to ϕ_2, the voltage at ϕ_1 decays so that the potential wells under the ϕ_1 electrodes slowly rise. The charge packets now spill over to the potential wells under gates 2 and 5 at $t = t_3$ (Fig.3.5d). By repeating the same procedure the signals can then then be moved from ϕ_2 to ϕ_3 and then from ϕ_3 to ϕ_1, and so on. At each full cycle of clock voltages the charge packets advance one storage element (pixel) to the right.

The two-phase CCD

Whereas in a three-phase CCD the potential wells are symmetrical, and charges can flow to either right or left, we have a much simplified system with two-phase clocking (using only two MOS capacitor elements per phase) since the flow can only go in a single direction. Various manufacturers apply either three or two-phase clocking depending on the type of CCD system required for a given purpose. Usually we find that both two-phase and three-phase CCDs employ optically transparent polysilicon-aluminium gates with an overlapping structure of the kind shown in Fig.3.6.

Buried channel CCDs

The CCD charge transfer efficiency (CTE) for silicon surface channel CCDs is as high as 99.99%, but for buried channel CCD types the CTE is even higher at an observed 99.99995%. The difference between these two types of CCD is that in surface channel types (SCCD), the photocharge movements take place at the surface of the semiconductor (at the interface of semiconductor and insulator), whereas with the *buried channel* CCD's (BCCD), signal charges are carried in the bulk of the silicon. The disadvantage of the SCCD is that surface states can adversely influence CTE and noise levels – particularly if the signal strength is low.

A suitable arrangement for overcoming the worst of these SCCD problems is to fabricate the BCCD system, where a diffused n-type layer is placed on a p-type sub-

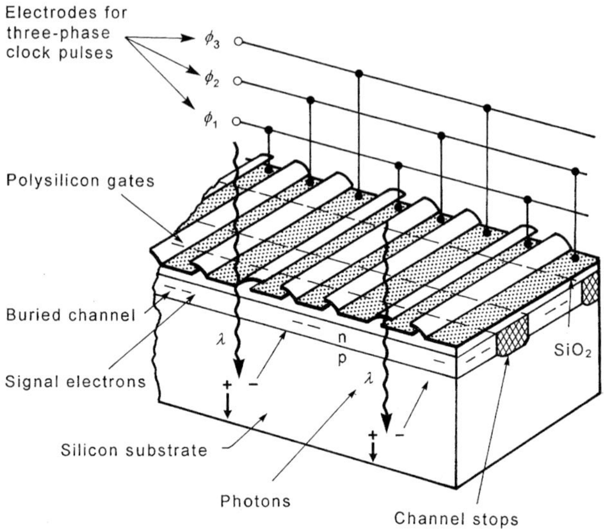

Figure 3.6 *Three-phase buried channel CCD (BCCD).*

strate (Fig.3.6). If a large positive voltage is applied to the channel (via the input and output diodes) a depletion layer is formed under the MOS capacitors. The potential well formed in the n-type buried channel will then store the signal electrons, which can be transferred by the same clock pulses as used with SCCDs. BCCDs have a higher CTE and better noise levels, and in addition higher clocking frequencies can be achieved – up to 100MHz.

Types of CCD image sensors

Although it is possible to define six different types of imaging sensor (Graham, 1998), we shall only consider three here and, for aerial photography, restrict our main interest to one – the single exposure, single area array architecture.

So far we have concentrated on the basic mechanism of CCDs, but now we must turn to CCD imaging sensors in terms of their architecture and pixels. Common to all CCD imaging sensors is the photo-gate (the optical window of the photosite) which is qualified by its fill factor or the percentage of the pixel that can be filled with light. Manufacturers now quote fill factors of 100% for some of their products.

At exposure to image light, each pixel will receive electrons in proportion to the incoming radiation and, as we have seen, each charge packet of electrons is then passed down the line of pixels by the process of charge coupling. Once a charge packet reaches the end of its line it is transferred to the output register and measured.

It is important to remember that the signal received at the output register is still in analogue form, and remains so until put to the analogue-to-digital (A/D) converter. After A/D conversion each individual pixel receives a digital number (DN) according to its strength and corresponding to its sensor location within the array. (Note: The

CCD elements are only equivalent to pixels if the sampling rate at the A/D conversion is the same). Naturally we can expect some of the charge to be lost at each potential well as the signal is passed down the line, but this is only a very small amount with modern CCDs since they generally exhibit CTEs as high as 99.99%, or one electron in 10^5, a negligible amount when one considers that it takes over 10^5 electrons to fill each potential well (Mills, 1996).

CCD linear imaging arrays

The linear (single dimension) array represents the simplest form of CCD imager and has been employed since the early 1970s in applications varying from space-borne military intelligence gathering to flatbed photo-scanners. As shown in Fig.3.7, a single line of CCD pixels is clocked out into the parallel output register. In order to produce a two-dimensional image, a line array sensor has to be used as a scanning device either by moving the linear array over the object, or vice versa. In aerospace imaging the former method is employed by a process known as push-broom, where the space vehicle or aircraft moves over the terrain and, akin to sweeping a floor with a broom, the linear array sweeps forward to scan the terrain in a regular pattern that is read out strip-by-strip via the output register into storage or direct transmission.

The push-broom technique has been instrumental in producing one of the earliest and most important forms of CCD digital imagery, not only for military reconnaissance but also for SPOT (Systeme Probatoire d'Observation de la Terre), the French earth resources satellite cover, and airborne multispectral line-scan imagers such as the Canadian MEIS II. SPOT, for example, employs linear arrays of 6000 elements in its panchromatic mode and 3000 in its multispectral mode. Similar methods are employed for flatbed scanners, using either moving or static arrays.

Most recently a multiple linear array system (in full colour) has been produced for aerial survey applications. This is the L/H Systems ADS40 Airborne Digital Sensor launched at the 19th ISPRS Congress, 2000. In this system three groups of linear CCD lines are arranged in the camera's focal plane to capture information forward, nadir and backward from the aircraft. Each line incorporates 12,000 pixels and provides a full image array through push-broom scanning. The ADS40 is multispectral and highly sophisticated, but since the raw image data has to be rectified using position and attitude data, it is also very expensive. A more detailed account of this camera can be found in Chapter 4.

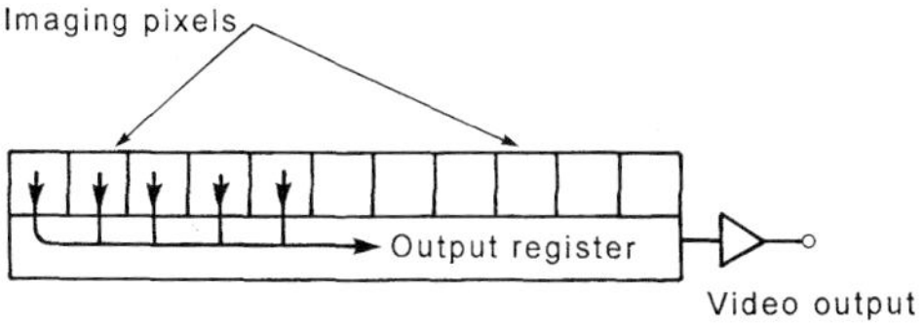

Figure 3.7 *A single-line CCD linear array.*

CCD area imaging arrays

Unlike the linear arrays, area imaging arrays are two-dimensional and allow for a single exposure to capture the image in a single frame – much like that with film. There are three main architectures, but for aerial applications we need only consider two:

1. Full frame transfer arrays (FFTA).
2. Interline transfer arrays (ITA).

Full frame transfer arrays (FFTA)

Current developments in CCD technology certainly favour the FFTA as the state-of-the-art architecture for modern digital cameras, and authors consider this type of digital camera to be the best for aerial survey, both in terms of economy and practical operational efficiency (see Chapter 4).

A typical FFTA architecture is shown in Fig.3.8, where the entire frame is occupied by image-receiving pixels. As a three-phase system, there are three MOS capacitors to each (vertical) storage element, and so a square-shaped pixel is formed by appropriately spaced channel stops. In Fig.3. 8 there are 24 horizontal electrodes and at the bottom of the array is the 'line read-out' of the horizontal shift register, which

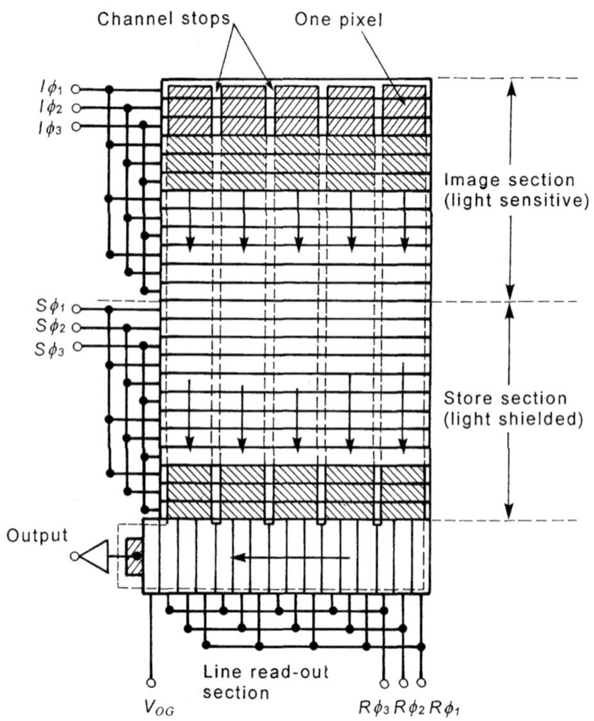

Figure 3.8 *CCD full-frame transfer array (containing only incident light receptors).*

transfers the charges in each pixel-line to the video output amplifier. This amplifier is electrically shielded from the line read-out section by an output gate (OG) which is held at a fixed direct current bias voltage (V_{OG}). The clock pulses applied to the image and shift register sections are designated: $I\phi$ and $R\phi$ respectively.

This device must be considered as an array of horizontal pixels above a number of vertical charge-transfer channels (or columns) defined by channel stop regions. When the image array is illuminated, photons pass through the semi-transparent polysilicon electrodes to generate electron-hole pairs withing the silicon substrate. The electrons then diffuse to the nearest biased electrode where they are collected as a signal packet (Fig.3.5) and the holes diffuse down to the substrate where they are effectively lost (Fig.3.6). A single pixel is therefore a square area (usually between 9–15μm across) bounded by the channel stops and the three (or two, in a two-phase system) electrodes centred on the biased electrode. Although square pixels are mentioned here, recent developments have seen digital cameras fitted with chips bearing octagonal pixels arrayed in a honeycomb pattern. These Fuji Super-CCD octagonal pixels have their electrode stucture integrated with the transmission path, and are rotated at a 45° angle in order to pack the pixels closer together. Fuji claims that their octagonal array improves image quality and allows for faster framing rates (Electronic Imaging, 1999).

In the example shown in Fig.3.8, there is a matrix of five pixels in each of eight rows, and the quantity of charge collected by each pixel is proportional to the local radiation intensity and exposure time allowed for collection. At the end of the exposure time, the entire array of charges is transferred directly to the shift register by applying drive pulses to the electrodes. In this example this would amount to eight pulses in each phase. By applying appropriate pulses to the electrodes of image and shift register sections, all the image-generated charges are moved as a block, one element at a time to the shift register.

Normally the integrated charge detection amplifier is configured to provide a voltage output, where the output corresponding to each pixel (V_p) is proportional to the charge collected (Q_p). This can be achieved through a change of potential on the capacitance (C) of the charge detection node, that is:

$$V_p = Q_p / C \tag{3.4}$$

When fitted to a conventional camera, the FFTA chip receives image exposure via a mechanical shutter in order to prevent image smear. Smear is a problem common to all types of frame transfer systems, and can be defined as the ratio between the change in image illuminance above or below a bright area covering 10% of the sensor extent in the column direction (Shortis and Beyer, 1996). Image smear is proportional to the ratio between illumination and transfer periods, typically in the region of 40:1. So, for a 10% extent on the sensor, the smear will be about 0.25% for a saturated image and would not be noticed normally. But if the image is over-saturated at any point, then the smear becomes apparent as 'image trails'.

All CCD frame transfer imagers can be illuminated either from the top (through the semi-transparent polysilicon gates) or through the back of the substrate provided it is suitably thin. Unfortunately, thin wafer substrates are very fragile, so their use is generally reserved for CCD cameras that are attached to instruments, such as astronomical telescopes or microscopes.

Interline transfer arrays (ITA)

For a given size of imaging chip, the interline transfer architecture requires twice as many pixels as an FFTA, because columns of image sensors (pixels) are interspaced by columns of opaque transfer elements, as shown in Fig.3. 9. Charge packets are accumulated in the sensor elements during exposure, then shifted into the transfer columns and finally transferred, row by row, into the horizontal output (shift) register.

The image is detected as two vertically interlaced modes and can be operated in either (relatively) high resolution or standard TV interlace mode. ITA systems are very common since they are generally used in video cameras, where they are favoured for their improved vertical resolution and integral electronic shutter. It is reported that ITA chips are also employed in the cheaper types of (stills) digital camera, simply because they are available from the video production lines (Hynes, 2000).

CCD charge transfer efficiency (CTE)

The fraction of charge transferred at each gate is called the charge transfer efficiency (CTE) and is given the symbol ε. The fraction left behind, or loss per transfer, is designated with the symbol α. So the sum of these two components is given by:

$$\varepsilon + \alpha = 1.0 \tag{3.5}$$

Since ε determines how many transfers can be made before the signal output is seriously distorted and delayed, it is a highly important figure of merit for a CCD imager. If a single charge-pulse of amplitude P_o is transferred down a CCD register with n transfers, the output will be:

$$P_n = P_o.\varepsilon^n = P_o(1 - n\alpha) \tag{3.6}$$

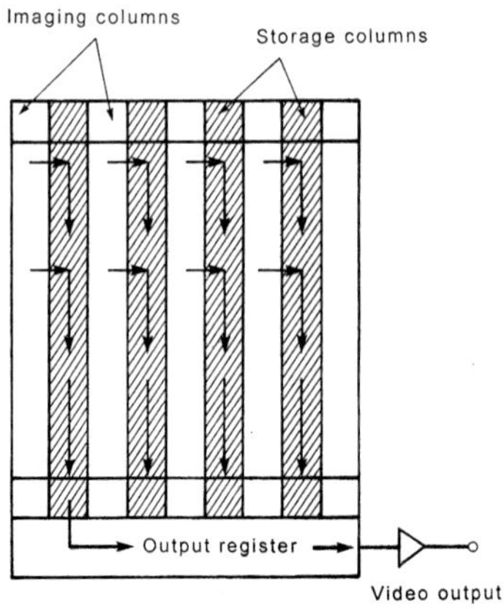

Figure 3.9 *CCD interline transfer.*

When the product $n\alpha = 1.0$, then the original pulse is completely lost and distributed among several trailing pulses (Carnes and Kosonocky, 1981). Obviously α must be very small where a large number of transfers are required, as the following example makes clear. If we consider a 1000 stage shift register and allow an overall loss greater than 10%, then the product $n\alpha \leq 10^{-4}$, and a CTE of 0.9999 is required.

For imaging applications the entire field of CCD stages are biased into deep depletion (Fig.3.2), and then exposed to a focused image for a short period of time as the generation of carriers under a CCD gate is enhanced according to the image illuminance at that point. However, there is a lower limit for the speed of operation of a CCD, where the signal has to be transferred into and out of a stage at a rate that is fast compared with the dark current generation rate at a depleted silicon surface. No stage in a CCD array can be held for a long time in conditions of deep depletion, and noise (such as that caused by dark current) will be continuously added because of thermal generation. Most CCD signal charges usually range from about 10–10^7 electrons. By comparison, a thermally generated dark current density of 1nA cm^{-2} corresponds to about 60 electrons per second under a 1μm^2 gate (Muller and Kamins, 1986).

CCD dark current

Dark current (I_D) arises from the thermal generation of electrons that accumulate in CCD elements and add to the photo-generated signals. A typical value is in the region of 1% of the peak signal level (I_P). At a device temperature of 25°C, typical values are in the region: $I_P \approx 250$nA, and $I_D \approx 3$nA.

Ideally I_D would be uniform – adding equally to the output of all pixels – but there will be some spatial variations due to inhomogeneities in device manufacture, giving a pattern noise that sets a minimum signal level below which imaging is not practical. It is also important to note that the dark signal and its non-uniformity are very temperature dependent and will generally follow the well known diode law:

$$I_D = Ae^{-(V_{bg}/(2kT/q))} \tag{3.7}$$

where: V_{bg} is the band gap for silicon ($\approx$ 1.1 eV); A is a constant; k is the Boltzmann constant (1.38054×10^{-23} J K^{-1}); T is the black-body operating temperature of the device (degrees kelvin) and q is the charge on the electron (1.6021×10^{-19} C).

At normal room temperatures (20–25°C) we can expect values of I_D to follow Eq. 3. 7 quite well over the range –60 to 60°C. Using Eq. 3. 7 with a known dark current value of 3.5nA for a device operating at 25°C (298 K), the constant (A) is found to be 6.88, and when this value is inserted back into the equation, values of dark current can be found for any other temperatures. Values of dark current relative to that found for 25° C (3.5nA) are plotted in Fig. 3.10, from which it can be seen that the dark-current doubling rate parameter is a ± temperature shift of 9–10°C.

Most of the current range of Kodak CCD image sensors suitable for aerial survey have dark current density values smaller than 10pA cm^{-2} (Table 3.1) where the KAF-1600 (DCS-420 camera) and the KAF-6301 (DCS-460 camera) parameters are displayed. But, as can be seen, the dark-current doubling rate is now more sensitive at 5–6°C.

Table 3.1 *Sensor specifications.*

Kodak Sensor: KAF-1600 (M-5 Chip): monochrome, colour and CIR

Image size: 13.97mm (H) × 9.29mm (V)
Chip size: 15.5mm (H) × 10mm (V)
Pixels: 1536 (H) × 1024 (V)
Pixel size: 9μm × 9μm
Optical fill-factor: 100% or 70% (colour)
Saturation signal = 85,000 electrons, or 40,000 electrons (colour)
Output sensitivity = 10μV per electron
Read-out noise (1 MHz): 15 electrons RMS
Dark current < 10pA / cm²
Dark current doubling rate = 5–6°C
Dynamic range (signal/noise) = 72 dB
Maximum data rate = 20MHz
Quantum efficiency = 10% (λ = 450nm), 38% (λ = 550nm), 32% (λ = 650nm)

Kodak Sensor: KAF-6301 (M-6 Chip): monochrome, colour and CIR

Image size: 27.65mm (H) × 18.48mm (V)
Chip size: 29mm (H) × 19.1mm (V).
Pixels: 3088 (H) × 2056 (V)
Pixel size: 9μm × 9μm
Optical fill-factor: 100%.
Saturation signal = 85,000 electrons
Output sensitivity = 10μV per electron
Read-out noise (10MHz): 15 electrons RMS
Dark current < 10pA / cm²
Dark current doubling rate = 5– 6°C.
Dynamic range (signal/noise) = 72 dB
Maximum data rate = 10 MHz.
Quantum efficiency = 10% (λ = 450nm), 30% (λ = 550nm), 40% (λ = 650nm)

(Kodak product specifications by courtesy of Kodak, Rochester, USA)

Sources of noise in CCD systems

There are three main sources of noise in CCD systems, in order of importance: photon shot noise (N_s), dark current noise (N_d) and circuit noise (N_c).

Photon shot noise (N_s)

Owing to the random arrival and absorption of image photons, charge generation is a

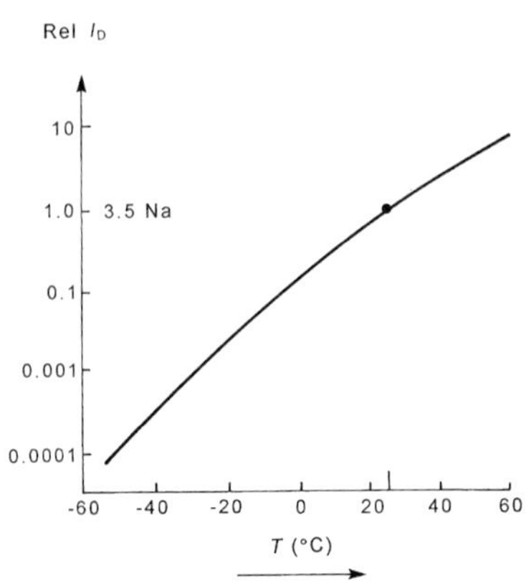

Figure 3.10 *Typical example of CCD dark current (relative to that found for 25°C, 3.5 nA).*

statistical process, and the signal-to-noise ratio (SNR) for the sensed image is at a maximum when the pixels are close to their full capacity (around 10^6 electrons). Photon shot noise is given as the square-root of the signal level (S), given in electrons:

$$N_s = \sqrt{S} \tag{3.8}$$

Dark current noise (N_d)

As shown by Eq. 3. 7, dark current is produced continuously at a rate proportional to the absolute temperature (K) of the sensor material, and is generated at both exposure and read-out phases. Similarly, we find that if we measure the dark current (I_D) in electrons we have:

$$N_d = \sqrt{I_D} \tag{3.9}$$

Circuit noise (N_c)

For a CCD sensor the largest source of cicuit noise is the on-chip amplifier, which is responsible for amplifying each individual pixel charge to a useful level. After each pixel is read-out, the amplifier must be reset to zero, and the uncertainty of the recovered zero level is known as reset noise. Reset noise can be kept low, but this depends on keeping the read-out speed very low. According to one source (Janesick *et al.*, 1990), a specially constructed CCD imager (with 4096 × 4096 pixels) achieved sub-electron circuit noise levels, but requires 64 samples of each pixel and takes 11 minutes to read our an entire image! The sum of all the noise contributions is N, where:

$$N = (N_s + N_d + N_c) \tag{3.10}$$

Signal-to-noise ratio (SNR)

The SNR for an imaging sensor is defined as the ratio between the signal and its noise, or S/N, where N is the sum of the noise contributions listed above. Usually expressed in decibels (dB), the SNR can be equated as:

$$\text{SNR} = 10 \log(S/N) \text{ dB} \tag{3.11}$$

Obviously noise becomes a problem mainly at low image-intensity levels, where the signal (S) is close to the overall noise level (N) called the noise floor. But as the charge capacity of the pixels increases so does the SNR and the dynamic range of the image.

All CCD image sensors have a maximum output signal (or saturation level) and a root-mean-square noise threshold, with voltages V_{sat} and $V_{N(rms)}$ respectively. The characteristic linear response region of the imager lies between these two levels, and when CCD analogue signals are quantised into a binary scale, the dynamic range of the image is typically defined as the ratio between the two levels. Expressed in decibels the dynamic range (DR) is given as:

$$\text{DR} = 20 \log(V_{sat} / V_{N(rms)}) \text{ dB} \tag{3.12}$$

Note: Most modern CCD imagers incorporate a laterel overflow drain to prevent blooming (a once common problem), where excess charge is drained off from bright pixels that are over illuminated. Blooming is the major cause of poor highlight resolution.

CCD sensor linearity

Unlike photographic materials, the CCD sensor provides a linear response between subject and facsimile because the CCD is capable of generating electronic charges in direct proportion to the incident illumination. This is an ideal imaging system, unmatched by any conventional photographic process, and particularly useful for measuring radiometric information from aerial imagery. Provided the CCD signal does not suffer from non-linear features in the amplifier circuit, the output signal (S) from a pixel can be given by:

$$S = \mathrm{k}q^{\gamma} + I_{\mathrm{D}} \tag{3.13}$$

where: k is a constant of proportionality; q is the generated charge (the sensor output is linear when γ is equal to unity) and I_{D} is the dark current signal.

CCD spectral response

The natural spectral sensitivity of silicon CCDs extends from 400–1000 nm and Fig. 3.11 shows the quantum efficiency of these chips vs. wavelength for the Kodak M-5 (KAF-1600) and M-6 (KAF-6301) sensors.

In accordance with international standards, human day-vision is said to extend from 380–760nm, and is known as photopic vision. Further up the spectrum, from 760–1000nm (1µm), is the near-infrared, which is of extreme interest to those involved in aerial photography (see Fig. 3.12).

From Fig. 3.11 we see that a typical CCD sensor is fully capable of recording in the panchromatic (blue, green and red) mode, either in monochrome (black/white), or in full colour (Fig. 3.13). Provided that near-infrared (NIR) sensitivity is not blocked by filters, the CCD can record in this region also, either as pure near-infrared recordings in monochrome (very useful for multispectral photography) or, with the addition of red and green regions of the response curve, as false-colour infrared (CIR).

Most of today's (silicon chip) digital cameras have their natural near-infrared (NIR) sensitivity filtered-out at manufacture. This includes the new indium-tin-oxide (ITO) chips which have incorporated a NIR cut filter, and have also improved blue sensitivity by a factor up to 2.5 (see Fig.3.14). This has to be considered in terms of the general

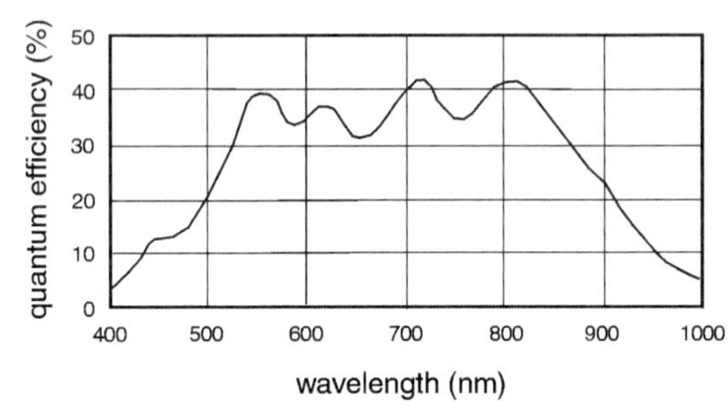

Figure 3.11 *Spectral response of silicon CCD sensor (Kodak M-5 and M-6 chip). Courtesy Eastman Kodak Company.*

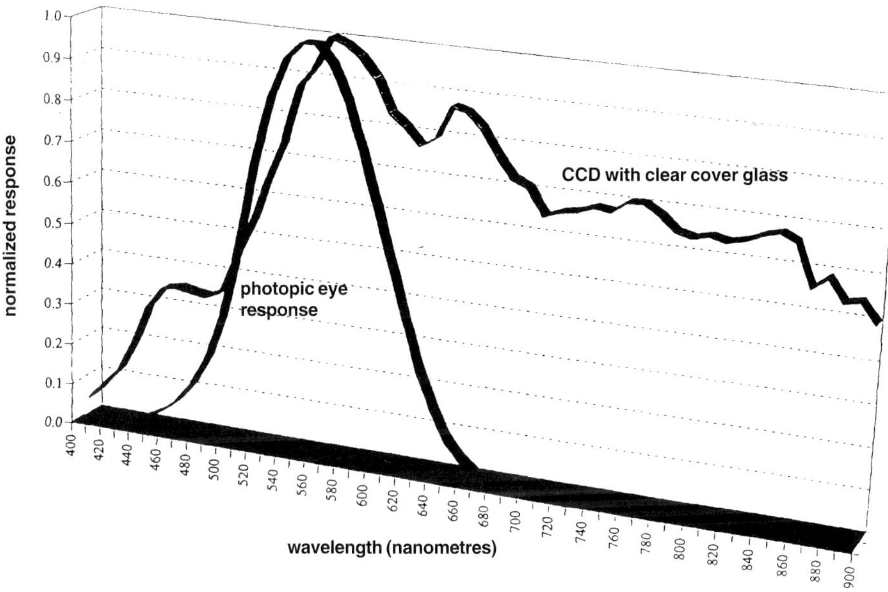

Figure 3.12 *Comparing spectral near-IR response of KAF-1600 with eye. Courtesy Eastman Kodak Company.*

photographic market, where normally there is no use for NIR sensitivity and worse, its presence is undesirable since it spoils natural colour rendition. So nearly all digital cameras have a NIR cut-filter incorporated over the chip. Nevertheless, in the past few years Kodak have allowed three of their high-end CCD cameras to retain their full spectral range, including the near infrared.

The Kodak DCS-200 CIR (colour infrared) model was soon replaced with the DCS-420 CIR camera, both using the M-5 chip. Then came the M-6 chip and the highly successful DCS-460 CIR camera. By using selective front-of-lens filters, these cameras could then be configured for either natural colour, or false-colour infrared (CIR), as described in Chapter 4. It should be noted however, that the Kodak Pro-Back 16MPx camera is normally issued with an ITO chip without NIR sensitivity. But for those who wish to have its NIR sensitivity restored, it is possible to purchase an infrared kit for this purpose, an option highly recommended for aerial remote sensing applications.

Although the DCS-420 was available as a monochromatic camera (in both panchromatic and near infrared models) with a useful role in airborne multispectral photography (MSP), subsequent Kodak digital cameras have all been in conventional colour. Nevertheless, it should be remembered that a colour CCD image can always be converted into a monochromatic record, simply by use of image processing software.

Apart from the Kodak Pro-Back 16MPx digital camera (and its NIR kit option), there are only a limited number of NIR sensitive digital cameras now available since the Kodak range of CIR digital cameras was discontinued in 1999. However, since the

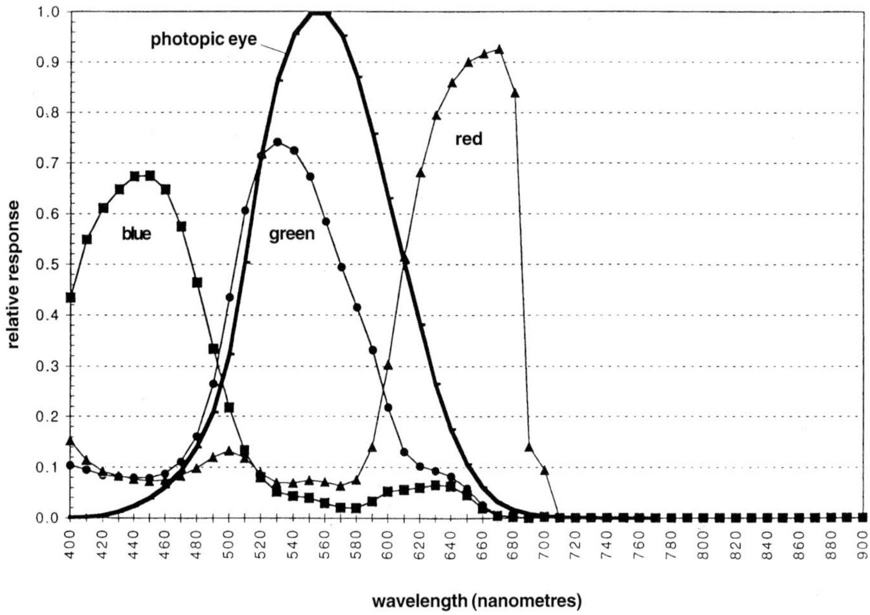

Figure 3.13 *KAF-1600 natural colour response. Courtesy Eastman Kodak Company.*

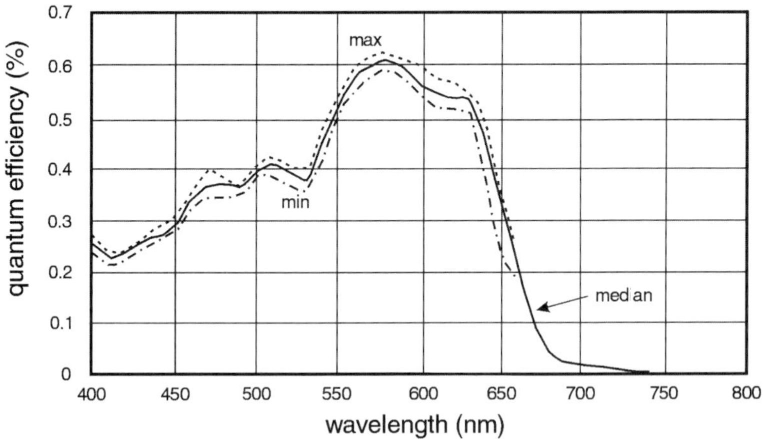

Figure 3.14 *Detective quantum efficiency of ITO sensor KAF-0400E. Courtesy Eastman Kodak Company.*

use of a NIR sensitive digital camera is mainly in the field of airborne remote sensing, it is natural to expect that a camera designed for such work would incorporate both conventional colour and CIR technology, as we find with the Geotechnologies 16MPx MF-DMC camera explained in Chapter 5.

4 Digital camera systems

In common with all cameras, analogue or digital, it is important to consider the basic essentials of an imaging system, and in this respect understand the various terms involved in the disciplines of photometry, radiometry and imaging parameters.

Camera image photometry

Photometry is the science of measuring light, that is, measuring the electromagnetic radiation (EMR) within the visual limits of 380–760nm. But whereas radiometry is pure physics, photometry is also concerned with psychophysics – where the eye mediates between EMR and the brain.

The unit of luminous intensity (I) is the candela (Cd) which, by definition is 1/60th of a square centimetre of the surface of a black-body radiator at the absolute temperature of 2045 K. From this specification and a knowledge of the sensitivity of the human eye it is possible to quantify the physical radiant unit into photometric terms. The human eye sensitivity for daylight (photopic sensitivity) is shown against wavelength (V_λ) in Figs.3.12 and 3.13. The photometric radiation equivalent (PRE) for monochromatic radiation is given by:

$$K_\lambda = 673 \text{ lumen /watt} \tag{4.1}$$

Luminous flux (Φ_v)

The amount of light flowing from a source is known as the luminous flux and is defined as:

$$\Phi_V = K_\lambda \int_{380\text{nm}}^{760\text{nm}} \Phi_{e\lambda} V_\lambda . \mathrm{d}\lambda \ \text{ lumens} \tag{4.2}$$

In a given period of time (t) the luminous energy (camera exposure) is given by:

$$\Phi_v t = 673t \int_{380\text{nm}}^{760\text{nm}} \Phi_{e\lambda} V_\lambda . d\lambda \ \text{ lumen.seconds} \tag{4.3}$$

Illuminance

When a flux (Φ_v) is incident upon a surface of area S it is said to be illuminated, and the illuminance (E) at any point on that surface is given by:

$$E = \Phi_v / S \qquad (4.4)$$

If S is quoted in square meters (m^2) then E is given in lumen/m^2, or lux.

$$E = 673\int_{380\text{nm}}^{760\text{nm}} \Phi_{e\lambda} V_\lambda . d\lambda \ \text{ lumen / m}^2 \text{(or lux)} \qquad (4.5)$$

Reflectance (ρ) and luminance (*L*)

It is well known that all objects reflect light which, in turn, can send the reflected light to a camera. This reflected light is called luminance (L) and, in turn, is subject to the amount of incident light (illumination, E) falling on the object(s). The luminance of a scene can be evaluated from:

$$L = E.\rho / \pi \ (\text{Cd m}^{-2}) \qquad (4.6)$$

where luminance is given in terms of candela per square cm.

For an object (O) with an even and diffusely reflecting surface (ρ), the luminance from that surface will follow Eq. 4. 6 which, in terms of incident flux, is given by:

$$L = (673 / S)\int_{380\text{nm}}^{760\text{nm}} \Phi_{e\lambda} V_\lambda \rho_\lambda . d\lambda \ \ (\text{Cd m}^{-2}) \qquad (4.7)$$

Camera image photometry

An illustration of the total camera image photometry is given by Fig. 4. 1, where a camera lens of relative-aperture N (where N = *f*/*d*), is exposed via a spectral filter (F) of bandwidth F_λ . Under these circumstances the spectrally defined luminance of an object is now given by:

$$L_{o\lambda} = (673 / m^2)\int_{380\text{nm}}^{760\text{nm}} \Phi_{e\lambda} F_\lambda V_\lambda \rho_\lambda . d\lambda \ \ (\text{Cd m}^{-2}) \qquad (4.8)$$

Note: The camera's relative aperture (N) controls exposure to the sensor in conjunction with the shutter speed (t). The term exposure is therefore a function of $N.t$, and (for example) is usually expressed as, say, 1/250 at *f*/4. The actual exposure is usually found from the camera's integral PEM (photoelectric exposure meter).

Image illuminance (E_i)

In simple terms, image illuminance (E_i) is only a function of object luminance and camera aperture, as shown by:

$$E_i = k.L_o / N^2 \ (\text{lux}) \qquad (4.9)$$

where the coefficient k takes care of various lens characteristics. (Note: The unit lux, is

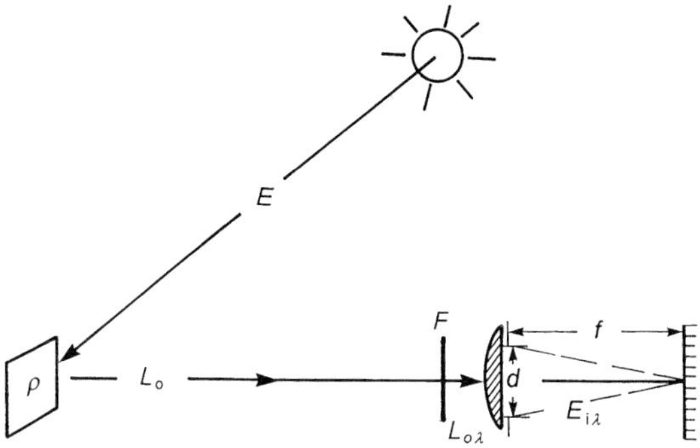

Figure 4.1 *From an illuminance (E), an object with reflectance (ρ) presents a luminance (L_o) incident on the filter (F). The camera lens receives a spectral luminance ($L_{o\lambda}$) through the relative aprture (N=f/d), to provide an image illuminance $E_{i\lambda}$.*

often referred to as the meter candle second, mcs).

If a filter (*F*) is employed then the spectrally-limited (monochrome) image illuminance is given as:

$$E_{i\lambda} = k.L_{o\lambda} / N^2 \text{ (lux)} \tag{4.10}$$

Common to all cameras, image illuminance is complicated by three additional factors, all of which can be integrated under the coefficient *k*:

1. Lens transmission.
2. Non-image light (lens-flare).
3. Off-axis image illumination.

For most modern lenses we can usually ignore the first two factors, as these are of only slight significance. But the third factor can be very significant where wide-angle lenses are employed.

Custom modified SLR digital cameras

Most of the high-end digital cameras, manufactured by Kodak, Fuji, Sony, Canon and Nikon, are based on modified 35mm SLR cameras. The 35mm instrument has established itself not only as a popular camera for amateur photographers, but also as a reliable professional tool. Using 35mm wide film, the image format is 24.0mm × 35.8mm, and the normal focal length lens is 50mm. The 3:2 rectangular format has always been accepted as satisfying both human visual perception and aesthetic considerations, but for aerial photography a square format is more appropriate since it makes survey calculations more simple and easier to alter when survey-flight conditions (mainly weather) change at short notice.

Medium format cameras are generally 5.47cm × 5.47cm square and therefore more appropriate for aerial work. A number of these are available for digital aerial photography, such as the Geotechnologies MF-DMC, the Kodak DCS-Pro Back and the Foveon II CMOS, all with 4k × 4k sensors (16MPx).

In general the normal camera focal length (*f*) is ≥ the diagonal of the image-format and, in turn, provides a normal angle of view. A lens that has a focal length significantly greater than normal is called a long-focus lens and one with a focal length significantly less than normal is designated as a wide-angle lens. Under these terms a typical range of lenses would provide angles of view shown in Tables 4.1 and 4.2.

When fitted with a digital sensor, the 35mm SLR usually employs a chip significantly smaller than the standard film format. The M-5 chip has an image size of 9.29mm × 13.97mm, while the larger M-6 chip has an image size of 18.48mm × 27.65mm. The diagonal for the M-5 format is 16.77mm, while that for the M-6 is 33.26mm. The 'normal' focal length for almost all small format (35mm) SLR digital cameras appears to be a compromise, since they usually are sold with a 28mm lens.

In Table 4.2 the angle-of-view is listed as across the diagonal, because the 60mm square format has more diagonal significance than the 35mm format.

Off-axis image illuminance

Obviously image illumination is best at the frame centre (on the optical axis) and, for reasons of optical geometry, becomes progressively less as it spreads radially towards the edge. This optical phenomenon is quite normal, but a problem where wide angle lenses are employed and particularly so in air survey photography.

Typically, a medium format digital air camera can be fitted with either a normal lens of focal length 80mm, or a wide-angle lens of 38mm. For the mainly economic reasons of ground coverage, many operators will employ a 38mm wide-angle, and accept the fall-off in image illumination attendant with this lens. For most purposes

Table 4.1. *Typical lenses for small format (24mm × 36mm) SLR cameras.*

Designation	Focal length and full field angle (2θ)
1. Super wide-angle	15mm (100°), 18mm (90°), 20mm (84°)
2. Wide-angle	24mm (74°), 28mm(66°), 35mm (54°)
3. Wide-angle (Normal Digital)	28mm (64°)
4. Normal-angle	50mm (40°)
5. Long focus	80mm (25°), 100mm (20°) – 500mm (4°)

Table. 4.2. *Typical lenses for medium format (60mm × 60mm) digital cameras.*

Designation	Focal length and full field angle (2θ)
1. Wide-angle:	38mm (91° diagonal)
2. Wide-angle:	40mm (88° diagonal)
3. Normal-angle:	80mm (52° diagonal)
4. Long focus:	100mm (42° diagonal)

this is not a great problem, but if mosaics are to be made then the computer operator must compensate uneven image illumination by skillful use of software.

The angle θ made between the optical axis and extreme off-axis image points gives rise to less image illuminance ($E_{i\theta}$) at those points, as shown by Eq. 4. 11.

$$E_{i\theta} = E_i . \cos^4\theta \quad (4.11)$$

For wide-angle lenses (such as the 38mm lens on a 6cm format) Eq. 4.11 indicates that edge-of-field illumination is only 20% of that in the centre and would normally require at least two to three times exposure compensation. However, for the MF-DMC series of cameras there is a laboratory procedure and software program that corrects the downloaded images for even illumination without the need for camera over-exposure. Off-axis image illumination is less important for small format SLR digital cameras however, since the chip format is only a fraction of that used for 35mm film, and any significant $\cos^4\theta$ illumination fall-off can be compensated by suitable image processing in Adobe Photoshop® or other software.

Information capacity, file size and spatial resolution

Three of the important characteristics of a digital camera with a regular array of pixels, each with a multilevel capacity (M) of grey-tones or colour, are usually described in terms of: information capacity, file size and spatial resolution.

Information capacity (I_c)

All subjects radiate information in terms of their grey-tone level, or colour. And since we are dealing with digital systems the range of these levels (M) is usually given in binary digits (bits), where the bit is the smallest piece of information that can be stored on a computer and has a binary value of either one or zero. (Note: The byte is a unit used to measure the size of computer files, memory and storage capacity. One byte is made up from eight contiguous bits and stores the equavalent of one character – see Appendix B.)

Information capacity is defined as the maximum amount of information a system is capable of storing under optimum conditions of encoding (Shannon, 1948), and for a multilevel system comprising n pixels with M levels each, the capacity (in bits) is given by:

$$I_c = n \log_2 . M \quad (4.12)$$

If we take the Kodak DCS-420 and 460 cameras as examples, we find their image capture quoted as 12 bits. That is to say 12 bits per red, green and blue, making a total of 36 bits of colour in all. Although these sensors are capable of capturing this amount of information, it is widely accepted that only the best 8 bits (one byte) of data are stored, making the total information capture 24 bits (3 bytes).

It is useful to compare the information captured by a typical 35mm film camera with the same camera fitted with a digital sensor. For example, a 35mm negative on Kodak Plus-X film (ISO 125) might have 2.10^5 cells/cm^2 (Graham, 1998) which means a total of something like 1.7 million pixels within the whole 24mm × 36mm format. If we accept that Plus-X has three density levels (based on a 10σ separation of adjacent density levels) then, in accordance with Eq. 4.12, the information capacity of this frame will be $I_c = (1.7.\ 10^6).\log_2 3 = (1.7.\ 10^6).\ 1.585 = 2.7$ million bits.

By comparison, the Kodak DCS-420i (monochrome version) has 1524 × 1012 pixels (1,542,288 in total) framed in a 9.2mm × 14mm M-5 chip. And with M = 8 bits (2^8 = 256 levels) we have a digital information capacity of $I_c = (1{,}542{,}288).\log_2 256 = (1{,}542{,}288).\ 8 \approx 12.34$ million bits.

Obviously the digital camera is far superior in terms of information capacity. So much so, that the high data capture of these systems can be a problem sometimes. However, this can be solved by compressing the data to a much lower capacity before downloading to the computer.

File size

We have referred to file size in applications of Eq. 4.12, where n is the number of imaging pixels within the sensor and, as we have seen, for colour this is expanded three times to account for the red, green and blue spatial multiplexing required to make a colour image. As a consequence the 1.54 Mb monochrome image of the DCS-420i is interpolated (through spatial multiplexing) to a file size of 4.5Mb in the DCS-420c colour version.

Image file formats

A file format is a structure which defines how information is stored in the file, and how that information is displayed on the monitor or printer. Typical of the many well known file formats that can be used on either Macintosh® or PC platforms are: TIFF (Tagged Image File Format), BMP (Windows® compatible bit-mapped graphic image), DIP (Device Independent Bit-map), PICT (Mac supported), EPS (Encapsulated PostScript) Photoshop and JPEG.

BOX 4. 1

A *bit-mapped* image is composed of a series of dots (pixels) rather than a set of lines (or vectors), and consists of a grid of discrete pixels, each with its own grey value or colour. The bit-mapped image is located within a frame buffer where each pixel (stored as a binary number) has an x, y address that maps to a pixel located in the monitor display. Bit-mapped images consume large amounts of computer memory and can be taken from: (a) digital cameras, (b) scanned photographs or (c) digitised (frame-grabbed) video.

Possibly the most well known format is TIFF which, in its many versions, is a standard file format for bit-mapped graphics images. The TIFF standard also defines data compression techniques and provides for monochrome and colour images.

The BMP format was designed to be used under DOS (disk operated system), Windows, Windows NT and OS/2, and can save both monochrome and colour images up to 24 bit. The DIB format was introduced as a refinement to BMP and today all Windows and OS/2 BMP files are assumed to be in DIB.

PICT is a general purpose format supported by Macintosh and used for storing either bit-mapped or object-oriented-graphics images. PICT bitmaps can provide for grey scale, monochrome or colour with up to 32 bits per pixel (at 32 bits per pixel JPEG compression options are available). PICT format can be saved, opened or imported by most Macintosh programs and some Windows applications, including Photoshop®.

BOX 4. 2

With *object-oriented (vector) graphics* an image is defined by a mathematical process, rather than by a set of dots, and are much more economic with storage space than a bit-mapped image. In addition, object-oriented graphics (unlike bit-mapped images) can reproduce circles or squares without *aliasing* (stair-case stepping of lines) or distortion, and require much less computer manipulation. For this reason object-oriented graphics are mainly used for drawing and CAD (computer aided design) programs.

EPS is the file format of the PostScript page description language, and is device independent, which means that images can readily be transferred from one application to another. However, an EPS file can only be printed on a PostScript-compatible laser printer. EPS can store either bit-mapped or object-oriented images. Using this format images can be placed into programs such as Adobe Pagemaker®, CorelDRAW® and Adobe Illustrator®, which is why EPS is a popular format for exporting grey scale and colour images to page layout and illustration programs.

Photoshop file format is native to Adobe Photoshop software in its various versions, and can generally be opened and saved faster than any other format. It is also preferred for moving Photoshop files between Macintosh and Windows platforms and supports JPEG compression in several ways. With Photoshop 6.0 it is also possible to create editable vector files that can be exported to other programs.

JPEG

JPEG (Joint Photographic Expert Group) format is based on the discrete cosine transform (DCT) algorithm which analyses 8 × 8, or 16 × 16 pixel arrays (cells) within an image (independent of resolution) and performs an averaging of each cell, dramatically decreasing image size. JPEG employs lossy compression techniques that result in some loss of original data and is considered as a baseline standard for this type of image compression.

JPEG 2000

The new JPEG 2000 standard was only completed early in 2001 and is the successor to the original JPEG format developed in the late 1980s. The new JPEG is based on state-of-the-art wavelet techniques that provide better compression and advanced system-level functionality. It has been adopted as an international standard by the ISO and ITU and its power can be harnessed for numerous imaging applications, such as digital photography, remote sensing, image databases, internet, printing and scanning.

JPEG 2000 has a number of advantages over the original JPEG format, including: 40–60% smaller files (without sacrificing image quality), lossy and lossless compression, support for multispectral imagery, CMYK format, and progressive image reconstruction allowing the initial viewing of a low resolution image while transmission is in progress. JPEG 2000 stores a compressed image as a series of increasingly smaller, sub-sampled images at 1/2 size, 1/4 size, 1/8 size, etc. These sub-sampled images can be extracted in compressed form without any processing on the server, allowing the server to transmit an image matched to the screen dimension of the target device.

Image compression and interpolation

Compression of images in order to reduce excessive amounts of image data has been mentioned and, in the opposite sense, we have image interpolation techniques which are essential for creating colour images, as well as other functions. Both of these applications employ mathematical algorithms and are continuously used to modify the raw image data.

Image compression

Digital images usually contain a significant amount of redundant information, and where large image files are concerned these data can be suitably reduced by employing image compression techniques.

Image compression is a method of minimising the number of bytes required to represent an image, particularly where large quantities of digital image data (such as aerial photographs) have to be archived. Image compression algorithms can be classified either as lossless or lossy methods. With lossless compression there is a reduction in the number of bits required to represent the original image, without any loss of information. But with lossy compression, the reconstructed image suffers a certain degree of degradation in exchange for the reduced bits of information, the degree of degradation depending upon the compression ratio. Whereas these compression schemes are vital to the economic storage of mapping films, they have comparatively less importance for digital images acquired by a solid-state camera. To take an example, when a typical monochrome mapping film (23cm × 23cm) is scanned with, say, a 20mm scanning aperture, we have an image file of the order of 100Mb, and three times this amount if the image is in colour.

Image compression is required to compress the number of image-bits to a point where the image is still acceptable, and obviously there are degrees of acceptance. Aerial photographs are a particular example of images which generally have large areas of common tone or colour, and compression ratios of 20:1 or 30:1 are not unacceptable since much of the information is redundant. But for, say, a large scale urban scene, where fine detail has to be preserved, then the compression limit might well be only 2:1.

Compression techniques look at the following redundancies as a means of reducing the size of an image file:

1. Repetition of data.
2. Redundancy in the way the data is encoded.
3. Redundancy between between adjacent pixel values.
4. Pyscho-visually redundant information.

Whereas the first three of the above techniques are lossless methods that leave the original image unchanged (in terms of visual quality) and have very small compression ratios, the fourth method is a lossy compression that can have a ratio as high as 30:1.

Lossless compression

A number of software products can compress images using lossless compression techniques. A typical selection of lossless software for use with Macintosh computers includes: DiskDoubler, StuffIt Delux and Compact Pro. The standard for PC platforms is PKZIP, which is a Shareware DOS application published by PKWare, and for those who prefer to use Windows rather than DOS there is WinZip which features PKZIP to compress files and PKUNZIP to decompress archives.

Lossy compression

Well known lossy compression techniques include JPEG, and Kodak's RADC (Run Adaptive Differential Compression). JPEG was specifically defined to discard information that is not easily perceived by the eye (psycho-visually redundant) and makes use of known facts concerning human vision. The sensitivity of the human eye decreases as the spatial frequency of image detail increases (Van Ness, 1967; Graham, 1975). Also we can detect small changes in luminance (brightness) more easily than small changes in colour (Mullen, 1985). Thirdly, it has been shown that (in photographic prints at least) monochromatic detail is best discriminated in the lower midtones, and that for a continuous tone image containing 6 bits of luminance, about 3 bits contain 80% of the total intelligence (Graham, 1975; Bartleson and Witzel, 1967).

In Kodak's DCS range of digital cameras, RADC compression is used instead of JPEG or other standard compression algorithms, because RADC allows the camera to store more high quality images. Compression with JPEG starts with a full resolution colour image, but it is more efficient to start with pixel values coming directly from the CCD chip, as with RADC, because they contain only one third of the final colour-image file. Thus, for the DCS-420 the 4.5Mb RGB file is compressed in the DSP (Digital Signal Processor) and then stored in compressed form at around 1.5Mb on a standard PCMCIA (PC Memory Card International Association) card.

With the aid of a discrete cosine transformation (DCT) the JPEG algorithm removes visually redundant information by quantising image data in the frequency domain. It then converts it back again (decompression) with its inverse function (IDCT). For colour images this process is carried out separately for the three RGB channels.

The popular Photoshop image-processing software automatically decompresses a JPEG file as soon as it is opened, and when Save is selected from the File menu, JPEG is one of the format choices. A dialogue box then allows one to choose an Image Quality level: Low, Medium, High or Maximum. If Maximum is selected a larger file of higher quality will be produced, and if Low is the choice, then a smaller file of lower quality will be provided.

Interpolation processes

The two most important image interpolation processes are: (a) colour interpolation algorithms for area-array colour filter mosaics, and (b) resolution interpolation for increasing the apparent resolution of an image.

(a) Colour interpolation

Obviously the ideal digital camera has to provide images equal to those obtained with film. This implies a capability for recording full colour images using sophisticated SLR cameras with a wide range of lenses. The type of digital camera that satisfies these criteria is known as the Single Exposure, Single Area-Array Camera and in order to provide colour, it employs a spatial multiplex type of CCD sensor.

It should be noted that colour in a typical digital camera is interpolated from a series of monochrome sensors, since each CCD can only see luminance not chrominance, i.e, they only see in black and white. This type of sensor provides an individual red, green or blue filter over each pixel to create a mosaic chip pattern (Fig. 4.2). Known as a colour filter array (CFA), there are many different filter arrangements possible, but the most popular type used in the colour interpolated mode is known as the Bayer mosaic filter shown in Fig. 4.2 and Fig. 4.3 (colour section). (Note: The Bayer pattern was invented over 25 years ago by Dr. Bryce Bayer of Kodak, who suggested that the three-colour checker-board pattern could be either RGB or CMY, and that the latter would have a much better quantum efficiency and spectral response. Until recently all Bayer filters have been RGB, but Kodak are now offering the superior CMY Bayer filters on their image sensors).

The way in which a single exposure can record all three primary colours is quite complex and can best be explained by looking at the Bayer mosaic in more detail.

At the heart of the spatial multiplex system is an RGB mosaic that sits over the CCD chip and, as shown by Fig. 4.2, the Bayer pattern is a 2 × 2 matrix of two green cells for every red and blue cell. The reason for the 2:1 ratio of green cells is to provide

G	R	G	R	G	R	G	R	
B	G	B	G	B	G	B	G	
G	R	G	R	G	R	G	R	(Single CCD sensor)
B	G	B	G	B	G	B	G	
G	R	G	R	G	R	G	R	

Figure 4.2 *Bayer pattern CFA.*

for improved green sensitivity – in parallel with human eye sensitivity (cf. Fig. 3.13). Known as the Adjacent Pixel Colour Interpolation technique, area-array systems ensure that each pixel-filter is always adjacent to the other two. Because each pixel has to be able to record all three RGB colours, camera software looks at the strength of the missing colours recorded by adjacent pixels, and makes a qualified evaluation of the two missing colours on a pixel-by-pixel basis. As the camera software knows the filter factor for each of the three colours so it can evaluate the correct weighting to apply and then provide the correct colour response. If, for example, the camera was to record a uniform red object, it would not be just the red filtered pixels that created a charge signal, but all of the pixels, red, green and blue! Were this not so there would be open gaps in the resolution.

(b) Resolution interpolation

When the size of a digital image has to be increased it is often necessary to increase its resolution by artificial means. Although this doesn't improve image quality it does at least help to preserve the original resolution. A useful method for increasing the apparent resolution of an image is for the image software to take the mean intensity level of adjacent pixels and put a pixel of that intensity between the two.

In Photoshop software for example it is possible to select three different methods of interpolation: Nearest Neighbour, Bilinear and Bicubic, the poorest quality is with nearest neighbour and top quality with the bicubic option. Interpolation is used under Photoshop's image menu in order to execute such operations as: re-sizing and rotation of an image.

Yet another interpolation function is to increase the resolution (artificially) within the camera. This is mainly a marketing ploy, generally used for the lower priced cameras, and is not recommended for aerial photography where only the highest possible quality is required. Cameras such as the Fuji FinePix (with octagonal pixels arranged in a honeycomb pattern) offer an excellent 3.4MPx on chip, and an interpolated resolution of 6.1MPx, but whereas 3.4MPx is ideal for aerial photography the 6.1MPx quality would be very questionable, particularly since most in-camera interpolation programs use a much simpler algorithm than that provided by computer software such as Photoshop.

Spatial resolution

In previous chapters resolution was referred to in terms of file sizes, and the sensors packing density (pixels-on-chip), and provided we print to one given image size we can say that the more pixels we have on the camera-chip, the higher the resolution. But true spatial resolution is independent of print size and is simply down to the size of an individual pixel. A good example taken from two well known Kodak chips, M-5 and M-6, makes this clear.

Both the M-5 and the M-6 have an identical pixel resolution, where each pixel is 9μm square. But whereas the M-5 has only 1.54MPx in a 9.2mm × 14mm array, the M-6 sports over 6MPx in an 18mm × 28mm array. If we employ the DCS-420 and the DCS-460 to record identical images of a finely detailed scene, then print each image (on the same high quality printer) to, say, 25cm × 20cm, we shall certainly find that the M-6 sensor provides a better resolution than the M-5, since the latter has been pushed too far. But if we now print to only half this size, we will probably not notice any difference in resolution! This is entirely the same for film of course; when large enlargements are required the professional photographer will always employ a larger format!

Although the DCS-420 sensor provides adequate resolution for most purposes and has a proven record for excellent results in aerial photography, it could still be argued that its spatial resolution and image quality is less than that of a medium speed colour film. But with cameras such as the DCS-460 and 660, this argument no longer holds good, as proved by the many professional photographers who use high-end digital cameras for today's commercial work.

Image resolution theory

Resolution theory must always start and end with the human visual system, and it pays to remember that the eye is directly connected to the brain! As a consequence pure physics can never fully account for what we see. Nevertheless, for practical purposes it is possible to split image-resolution into two major parts: optics and sensors.

Lens resolution

A theoretically perfect image point, such as the image of a star seen through a perfect (diffraction limited) lens, will produce a central intensity of that point surrounded by an ever decreasing series of annular rings – known as an Airy disc. If two such points were separated (Fig. 4.4), then these two point would be at the limit of optical resolution, where the central maxima of one coincides with the first minima of the other and the intensity dip between the two points is 18%.

The distance (r) in Fig. 4.4 is known as the Rayleigh limit and is given by: $r = 1.22\lambda N$, but for all practical purposes can be applied as given in Eq. 4.13.

$$r \approx \lambda . N \tag{4.13}$$

where: r = resolution between two image points; λ = dominant wavelength of incident light (i.e, usually as 0.5μm for green light) and N = relative aperture of the lens (i.e, focal length /diameter of lens).

In employing Eq. 4.13 we must remember that λ represents a dominant wavelength, and if we employ a filter with a bandwidth tranmitting between 500 and 700nm, its dominant wavelength may be 600nm (0.6μm). If there is no filter in front of the camera lens we could take the peak daylight sensitivity of the human eye as our value and settle for $\lambda \approx 0.5$μm. Thus, for a lens operating in daylight, with its aperture set at *f*/4, the image resolution (for a perfect lens), is around 2μm.

It should be mentioned that so far we have only considered the theoretically perfect lens, but no such lens has ever been manufactured, and even if it was approached it would only give something like 2μm in a very small patch at the optical centre of the image. However, it is possible for some lenses to provide something like 4μm on the optical axis, but these are rare.

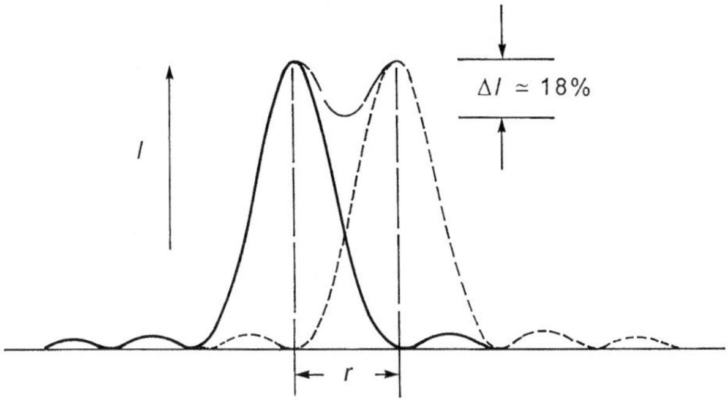

Figure 4.4 *Image resolution (r) for a perfect (diffraction limited) lens. In practical terms r = λN, where N is the f/no. of the lens.*

For the practical testing of spatial resolution we rely on a simple square-wave type of test target with equidistant black and white lines, as shown in Fig.4.5, where the distance between the centre of one black line to the next is the same as r in Eq. 4.13.

We term such charts square-wave since their intensity profile is square, but although sine-wave targets (Graham, 1998) are better (for analysis) their production is far from simple.

Image spatial frequency (k)

For photographic work it is usual to discuss spatial resolution in terms of spatial frequency (k), where k is given in terms of line-pairs per mm, the line-pair being one white line plus one black line. The reciprocal relationship between resolution (r) and image spatial frequency (k) is given by:

$$k = 1/r \quad \text{(line-pairs/mm)} \tag{4.14}$$

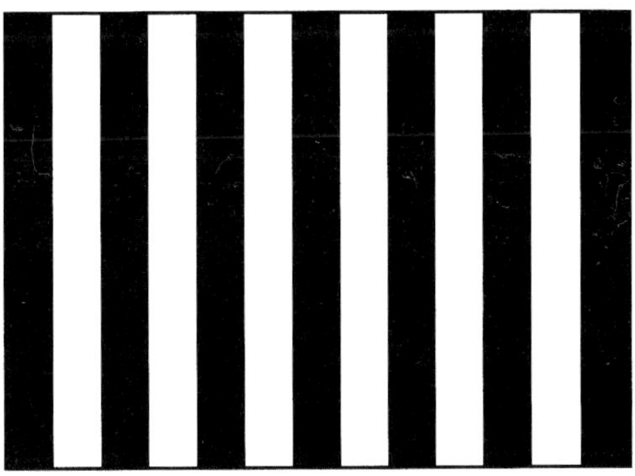

Figure 4.5 *A square-wave test target. Black and white bars are of equal width.*

To a first approximation we can combine the spatial frequencies of lens and sensor and put:

$$(1/k) = \{(1/k_l)^2 + (1/k_s)^2\}^{0.5} \qquad (4.15)$$

A typical example might be a lens capable of an average spatial frequency of, say, 200 line-pairs/mm (at a certain aperture), and when combined with a film providing, say, 100 LP/mm, we have:

$$(1/k) = ((0.005)^2 + (0.01)^2)^{0.5} = \sqrt{((25.10^{-6}) + (100.10^{-6}))} = 0.0112$$

$$\therefore \text{k} = 89 \text{ LP/mm.}$$

As we can see, the overall spatial frequency will always be less than that provided by the lowest element in the camera system.

Contrast and modulation

Image quality is not only dependent upon resolution however. Image contrast is also important, and this, in turn, will mainly depend on the contrast(s) in the original scene. Image contrast (C) is simply expressed as:

$$C = L_h / L_l \qquad (4.16)$$

where L_h = high luminance intensity and L_l = low luminance intensity and can have any value, either for scenes or images. The contrast in the test-target shown in Fig. 4. 5 is very high, in the region of 100:1 or greater. In aerial photography scene contrasts are generally low (ranging from 2:1 to 20:1 approximately) and their associated image contrasts become even lower as flying height increases.

Modulation is a more useful parameter since it quantifies contrast with a scale that corresponds closely with that of visual perception. For example, there is little visual difference between a contrast of 100:1 and 1000:1, and this is well illustrated by the small differences in modulation for these two contrasts. Modulation M is given by:

$$M = (I_{max} - I_{min}) / (I_{max} + I_{min}) < 1.0 \qquad (4.17)$$

For contrasts of 100:1 and 1000:1, their respective modulations are 0.98 and 0.998, whereas for an average sunlit scene (such as experienced in aerial photography) M could range from 0.33 to 0.90 (where the latter value of M would be considered as a very contrasty scene, such as pine trees on a sunlit snow background).

The square-wave target shown in Fig.4.5 is often used to test airborne camera systems, where a ground target of given modulation (M_o) is imaged by an air camera at increasing heights – so that image modulation (M_i) can be evaluated as the photo-scale gets smaller (increasing image spatial frequencies).

Figure 4.6 shows a square wave target imaged at various spatial frequences (5, 10, 20 and 40 LP/mm) and we find that in the region of 5 LP/mm, the square-wave has already lost its sharp edges. By 10LP/mm the image not only becomes sinusoidal in character, but also has less modulation, and so on – until the image is lost within the noise of the system.

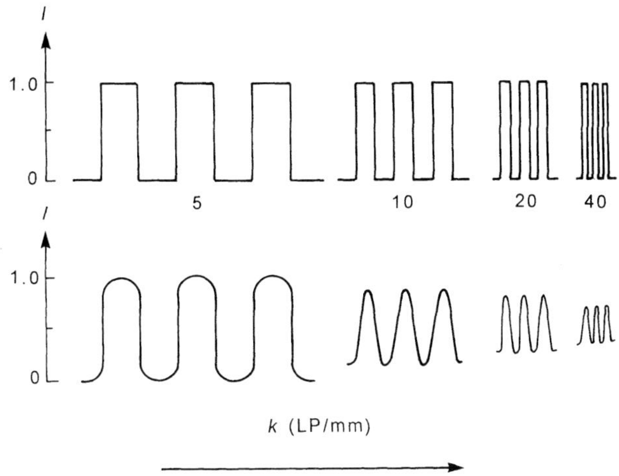

Figure 4.6 *Top: an ideal square-wave target at spatial frequencies (k): 5, 10, 20 and 40 line-pairs/mm. Bottom: their expected reproduction.*

Fourier analysis of a square-wave

The phenomenon shown in Fig. 4.6 is fundamental to image theory and is at the core of most problems experienced in aerial photography, where image degradation from causes such as image motion (blur), atmospheric effects, vibration, scale and poor resolution manifest themselves in loss of edge sharpness and loss of modulation.

The square-wave form shown by Fig.4.5 can be represented mathematically by a Fourier series composed of a fundamental sinewave (with the same spatial frequency k as the square-wave target), plus a series of odd harmonics with spatial frequencies, $3k$, $5k$, $7k$, ...nk. Indeed, a very close approximation to a square-wave would result if the Fourier series were to be summed to about the ninth harmonic. The square-wave function f_x is given by Eq. 4.18:

$$f_x = 2(\sin x + 1/3 \sin 3x + 1/5 \sin 5x + 1/7 \sin 7x + \ldots 1/n \sin nx) \qquad (4.18)$$

From inspection of Fig. 4.6 and Eq. 4.18 we can conclude that image degradation is a combination of harmonic stripping at low frequencies to a loss of modulation at high frequencies.

The modulation transfer function (MTF)

It is obvious from Fig. 4.6 that object modulation (M_o) in a scene suffers on transfer to the image (M_i) and for a given spatial frequency (k) the modulation transfer function (MTF) is given by the transfer factor (T_k) where,

$$T_k = M_{i(k)} / M_{o(k)} \qquad (4.19)$$

CCD arrays: resolution and MTF

Since we traditionally express optical resolution in terms of LP/mm (Eq. 4.14), so we need to equate the pixel frequency of CCDs in the same manner, where the distance between pixel centres (Δp) in µm, provides us with the sampling frequency k_s

$$k_s = 1000 / \Delta p \text{ (pixels /mm)} \tag{4.20}$$

Monochromatic CCD image resolution

A straightforward relationship would suggest that two pixels are equal to a resolution of one line-pair, but in practice two pixels can often fail to resolve one black line and one white line. For this reason it has been suggested (Konecny *et al.*, 1982) that a more reasonable solution is 2.8 pixels = one line-pair, and by others (Makarovic and Tempfli, 1979) that 3.3 pixels would be needed to equal one line-pair. From these figures a suitable compromise for the monochromatic resolution (r_{mono}) of a CCD image (known as the Kell factor) would be:

$$r_{mono} = 3 \text{ Px (mm)} \tag{4.21}$$

and in terms of spatial frequency (R_{mono}) we have:

$$R_{mono} = 1000/ 3 \text{ Px (line-pairs/mm)} \tag{4.22}$$

Colour CCD image resolution

The method of colour interpolation degrades spatial resolution by a factor of √3 and, as outlined above, if three pixels are required for one line-pair, we can put the spatial resolution of a CCD colour image (r_{colour}) as:

$$r_{colour} = 3 \text{ Px.}\sqrt{3} \text{ (mm)} \tag{4.23}$$

and

$$R_{colour} = 1000 / (3 \text{ Px.}\sqrt{3}) \text{ (line-pairs/mm)} \tag{4.24}$$

Thus, for the M-5 chip, with square 9µm pixels, the monochromatic spatial frequency is 37 LP/mm, whereas for the colour image it is only 22 LP/mm. Although it seems reasonable to equate monochromatic pixel resolution with traditional methods, it must be appreciated that solid-state colour resolution is far more complex than that shown by Eq. 4.23, where the CFA algorithm has a large part to play in the overall image quality.

Ground sampled distance (GSD)

A very convenient measure of resolved ground detail is the ground sampled distance (GSD), sometimes called the ground resolved distance (GRD), which has been employed for satellite imagery for a number of years. Although lacking the scientific rigour of optical resolution methods, GSD serves well for CCD imagery where the product of scale number (m_b) and pixel size (Px) provide for a reasonable degree of accuracy, as shown in Eq. 4.25.

$$\text{GSD} = m_{b.}\text{Px} \tag{4.25}$$

Thus, for a digital survey with pixels 9µm square, flown at a scale of 1:20,000, according to Eq. 4.25 we can expect a GSD of the order of 18cm. We can expect GSD values to be a reliable indication of the smallest size of ground object visible in the digital image, and the authors have checked GSD from a number of digital images and found Eq. 4.25 to be highly satisfactory provided there is sufficient contrast (Graham, 1998). Naturally we are not talking about image resolution here (as defined by Figs. 4.4 and 4.5) where two points are being separated in the image, but a more practical expectation of what we can see in terms of ground detail.

The Nyquist sampling theorem

With sensors that have regular cell arrangements (such as CCD imagers with a sampling frequency k_s), unambiguous resolution of image detail with a spatial frequency $k_i > 0.5\ k_s$ is not possible since this would contravene the Nyquist sampling theorem (Pearson, 1975). The theorem states that the sampling of any signal that has a spatial frequency (k_i) close to the sampling frequency (or multiples thereof) gives rise to intensity modulations in the displayed image in the form of 'beats' between the two frequencies (i.e, $k_i \pm nk_s$), commonly called an alias or moiré pattern.

These are most obvious about and above the Nyquist limit and arise because the intensity maxima and minima in the image do not always fully coincide with a sensor element. This is a fundamental limitation of all solid-state image sensors that have discrete sensor elements (such as CCDs) but as the spatial frequency of the sampling systems improves to higher values (such as the M-6 chip), so the problem becomes less important.

The Nyquist limit is given by:

$$k_i \leq 0.5\ k_s \qquad (4.26)$$

The active part of each CCD element is called the channel and this region is bounded by electrically inactive p-type channel stops. The horizontal element spacing (Δp) is defined by the channel stop regions (Fig. 3.6) and the vertical pitch by the centre-to-centre spacing of the CCD elements. These limits provide the optical aperture of the elements (ω), usually expressed in micrometers (µm).

CCD sensor MTF

If we employ a sinusoidal intensity target then the theoretical MTF of a CCD sensor is given by:

$$\mathrm{MTF}_{(CCD)} = \sin(\pi s(\omega/\Delta p) \,/\, (\pi s(\omega/\Delta p))) \qquad (4.27)$$

where s is the normalised spatial frequency ($s = k_i / k_s$).

A typical CCD colour imaging route

Within the digital camera all CCD colour systems start off in monochromatic form, but now there are three channels of data to accommodate. As shown in Fig. 4.7, each RGB data stream will go to an analogue-to-digital converter (ADC), and then, via an 8 or 12 bit frame buffer, to the digital signal processor (DSP) where image contrast and detail are adjusted prior to storage (with or without compression) in the camera's hard disk (PCMCIA or flash-card).

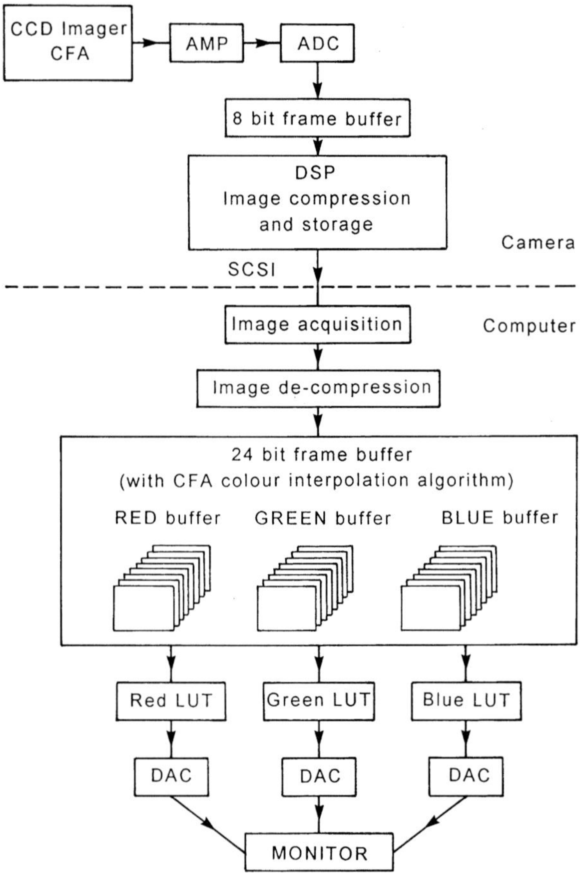

Figure 4.7 *Colour imaging route from CCD imager to the digital signal processor (DSP), image compression and computer (via SCSI interface). After the image has been decompressed, colour signals are sent to respective buffers and look-up-tables (LUTs) before digital-to-analogue conversion (DAC) and presentation at the monitor.*

Image compression is common to most of today's digital cameras, and with the Kodak DCS series takes place within the DSP where it uses the run adaptive differential compression (RADC) algorithm.

An important specification for a digital camera is its pixel depth. Pixel depth is set by the number of bit-planes in the frame buffer, and in order to gain good red, green and blue colour separation it is essential that at least 24 bits of colour are available, i.e, 2^{24} which is 16,777,216 different colours!

After going through the DSP and storage the images are then downloaded through a SCSI (small computer system interface) port to the host computer, where proprietary image acquisition software stores the RGB data in a 24 bit frame buffer for CFA (colour filter array) interpolation. After being processed and stored in the three 8-bit frame buffers, the three digital signals are sent to three LUTs on line between the buffers and the monitor DACs, where real time colour enhancement takes place. Each LUT is effectively a table of numbers that creates an index with pixel values stored in its associated buffer. For 8-bit planes there are 256 entries in the LUT and it is these that are sent to the display. By using LUT entries it is possible to preserve the original digital values in each frame buffer, while the computer operator is free to manipulate LUT data for real time image processing with software – such as Photoshop. The advantage of the LUT system is that it allows for iterative experiments to be made with the image. For example, if the blue pixels are too strong (say a DN value of 150) they can be reduced to a DN value of say 80, without destroying the original (buffer) values.

The colour monitor

Although the bit-mapped image may have a 24-bit capacity, this is not much use if the monitor, or the video graphics card within the computer is not of similar standard.

Monitor resolution is quoted in terms of the number of pixels the screen can display, and also by the VGA (video graphics array) card that supports it. Typically a VGA card will support a monitor that has a resolution of 640 × 480 pixels, with a maximum of 256 colours displayed simultaneously from a pallette of 262,144 (2^{18}) colours.

A higher quality display is provided by the SVGA (super VGA) card, which can support at least an 800 × 600 pixel array with up to 16.7 million colours displayed simultaneously. For photogrammetric applications, an XGA (extended graphics array) card is necessary which can support at least a 1024 × 768 pixel array.

The actual colour displayed on the monitor screen is due to the process of additive colour mixing. The eight major colours are: black, white, red, green, blue, cyan, magenta and yellow. All, with their variations due to hue, saturation and brightness are created from the three RGB primaries. The tiny RGB phosphor dots on the interior screen of the monitor then confuse in the human eye to appear as a resolved point of a given colour.

The colour printer

In a book such as this it is sufficient to say that printing technology has developed as fast as CCD camera technology, and where at one time we required either laser or dye-sublimation printers to produce a good colour image, we can now be satisfied with the ink-jet printers available. Indeed, inexpensive printers such as the Epson Stylus 870, employing an array of 6 inks are able to provide a quality equal to that of film/paper processes. Printers which employ inks work on the subtractive principle of colour synthesis, where RGB data is changed to CMYK (cyan, magenta, yellow and black) before being sent to the printer for hard copies.

Radiometric resolution

CCD linearity was mentioned in Chapter 3 (Eq. 3.13), and unlike photographic film, which has a sigmoid curve relating densities (see Box 4.3) to log exposure, CCD imagers are ideal for measuring radiometric information.

BOX 4. 3

If (I) is the light incident upon a surface of reflectance (ρ), then the opacity of the surface (O) is given by: $O = I/\rho$. Since (I) can be considered as unity, we have $O = 1/\rho$. For example, for $\rho = 0.5$ the opacity = 2. Similarly, for a semi-transparent medium we can put $O = 1/T$ (a photographic negative or dia-positive has numerous transparencies (T) within its image). Density (D) is given as: $D = \log_{10}(1/T)$ or, for prints: $D = \log_{10}(1/\rho)$. The density range of a negative or print is given as: ΔD.

Just as the dynamic range (DR) of a photographic negative or print is given in terms of density range (ΔD) to determine its number of grey levels (or colours), so the DR of a CCD image can be measured (in decibels) by using Eq. 3.12, or, by convention, measure the range of grey levels in terms of bit capacity (binary numbers).

Dynamic range (DR) and image exposure

As stated in Chapter 3, and Eq. 3.12, the DR of a CCD pixel is given in terms of its signal/noise ratio, where:

$$\mathrm{DR} = 20 \log(V_{\mathrm{sat}} / \mathbf{V}_{\mathrm{N(rms)}})\ \mathrm{dB}$$

and if we take the Kodak M-5 and M-6 chips as examples we have the following parameters:

V_{sat} = signal saturation = 85,000 electrons.
$V_{\mathrm{N(rms)}}$ = read-out noise = 15 electrons.
resulting in a DR of 75 decibels.

If over-exposure occurs in film photography the image suffers from two associated problems that are manifest in the highlight regions:

1. poor spatial resolution due to image-spread (irradiation) and,
2. severe loss of grey level discrimination (normal loss of contrast at the shoulder of the $D \log H$ curve).

With CCD images over-exposure can create similar effects (known as blooming) but these effects are now almost unknown due to the incorporation of a lateral over-flow drain where excess charge is drained off from over-exposed pixels.

Pixel depth (bit capacity)

Pixel depth is an important specification for a digital camera, where its ability to separate out various greys-levels and colours is a function of its bit capacity (see Appendix B). Pixel depth (or bit capacity) is set by the number of bit-planes in the frame buffer, and for monochrome images 8 bits ($2^8 = 256$ bit planes) is perfectly adequate. For colour images however it is essential that at least 24 bit colour is available (8 bits per red, green and blue) in order to avoid contouring (where bands of constant intensity between pixels start to appear).

Print luminance (brightness) levels

So far, we have discussed both dynamic range (DR) and pixel depth, and although both of these objective terms are useful for specifying the character of a CCD system, they lack a sense of those subjective explanations common to all analogue systems.

Luminance was discussed in Chapter 4, and its objective value provided by Eq. 4.6. But it is the subjective correlate of luminance that we see and this is called brightness. The two terms are often confused however, and brightness is often employed where it should be discussed as luminance. Brightness is not an easy subject however, mainly because everyone sees it slightly differently, and its correct evaluation (psychophysics) requires specific knowledge of the ambient viewing conditions (Graham, 1975).

Since today's digital images can be printed with a quality equal to that of an analogue print (glossy bromide paper), it is possible to discuss the digital (ink-jet or dye-sublimation) print in the same terms. If we ask the question: "how many grey-levels (or colour levels) can we expect in a print", then we can at least calculate the number of "just noticeable differences" (JNDs) in terms of their small density differences.

If we consider two slightly different brightnesses (JNDs) and determine their respective print densities as (D_{p1}), and a slightly larger one (D_{p2}), then their average density $D_{av} = ((D_{p1} + D_{p2})/2)$, and their differential detection density (dD_p) is given by:

$$dD_p = ((D_{p2} - D_{p1})/D_{av}) \tag{4.28}$$

A typical example would be $D_{p1} = 0.2882$, and $D_{p2} = 0.3010$, which provides a detection density of 0.043. It has been suggested (Bartelson and Witzel, 1967) that a reasonable value for dD_p is of the order of 0.03, or 3%, a figure generally confirmed by other workers in this field (Graham, 1975).

If we now take the maximum density range of a glossy bromide print, $\Delta D = 1.8$, and the generally accepted dD_p value of 0.03, then the so called "continuous tone" image will have (Z) discrete luminance levels in accordance with:

$$Z = \Delta D_p / dD_p \tag{4.29}$$

For a print density range of 1.8 and a differential detection density of 0.03 the value for $Z = 1.8/0.03$ or 60 JNDs, which correlates well with the range of brightnesses suggested by Katz (1935). From these considerations, which include aspects of subjective research, we might accept that a normal glossy print (bromide or ink-jet) can offer a maximum of 60 grey-levels (6 bits).

5 Digital cameras for aerial photography

Common digital cameras suitable for aerial photography

Starting with the Kodak DCS camera, the US Navy Combat Camera Teams employed digital imagers in 1992, and these activities soon expanded with the introduction of the DCS-200 in 1993 (Kodak, 1998). Naturally, these images were of a military nature, but by 1994 a calibrated DCS-200 was being employed for limited airborne mapping (Graham, 1995).

Kodak DCS-200 digital camera

Now out of manufacture, but fitted with the same M-5 chip incorporated in its successor (DCS-420) the DCS-200ci ('c' indicating colour and 'i' internal hard-disk) was housed in a standard single-lens-reflex (SLR) camera – the Nikon 801s. The M-5 chip provides a pixel resolution of 9 μm square, within an overall format resolution of 1524 (H) × 1012 (V) in a 14mm × 9.2mm image format.

One of the earliest digital-camera mapping trials was carried out in 1994 by Ron Graham and Jon Mills (Department of Geomatics, Newcastle University) using a calibrated DCS-200 camera. Flying at 3600 feet in a Cessna 337 cruising at 100 knots ground speed, the 28mm lens provided a photo-scale of 1:40,000. An important lesson gained was the need to put the long edge of the camera format (14mm) in line with the aircraft's axis in order to extend the camera base necessary to gain 60% forward overlap. Although DCS-200 specifications suggested an image download period (to the camera's hard disk) of 3 seconds, in practice we found it closer to 5 seconds and, as a consequence, images could not always be overlapped sufficiently for stereoscopic cover unless surveys were conducted at a small scale. Nevertheless, it was possible to gain good cover of the city of St. Neots as shown in Fig. 5.1 (printed on a laser printer) which was subsequently plotted by Jon Mills on a Leica DVP to provide the map shown in Fig. 5.2.

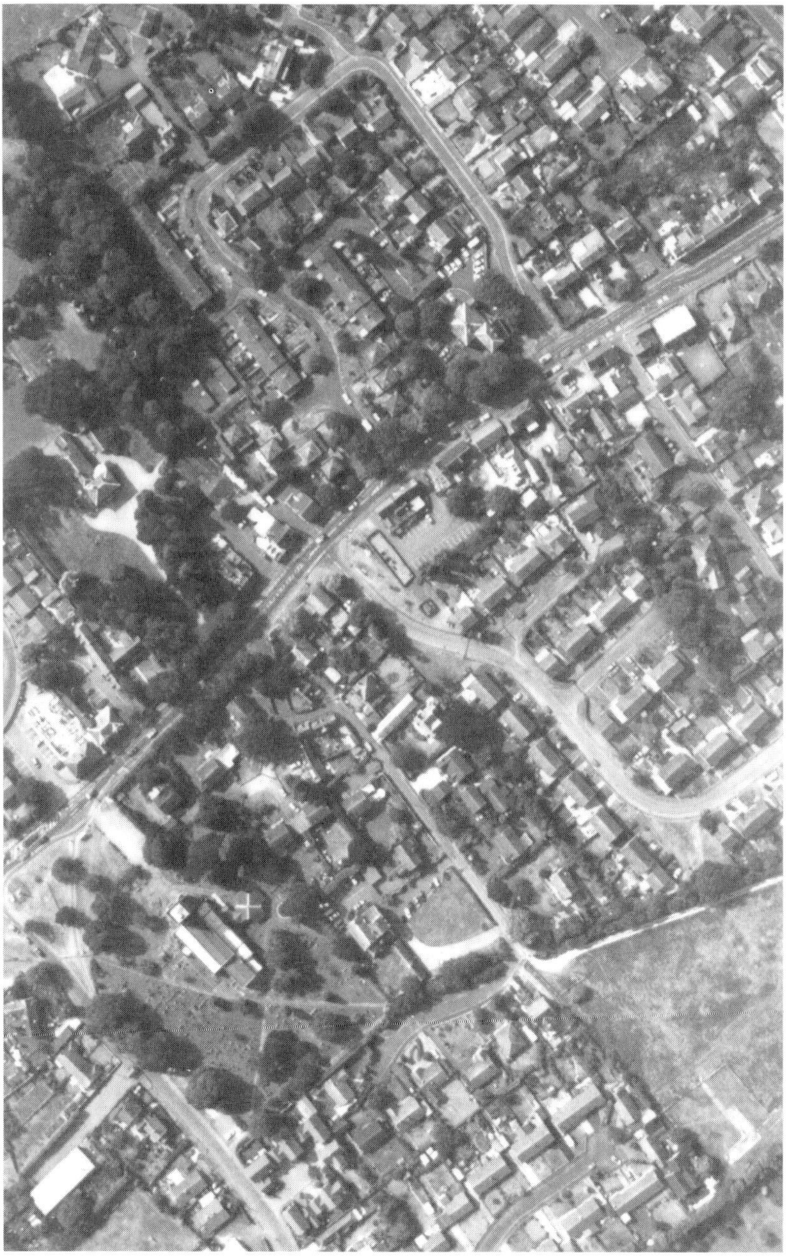

Figure 5.1 *St. Neots, a 1:40,000 photoscale image taken at 3600 feet with a Kodak DCS-200 digital camera (1994). Photo: Ron Graham & Jon Mills.*

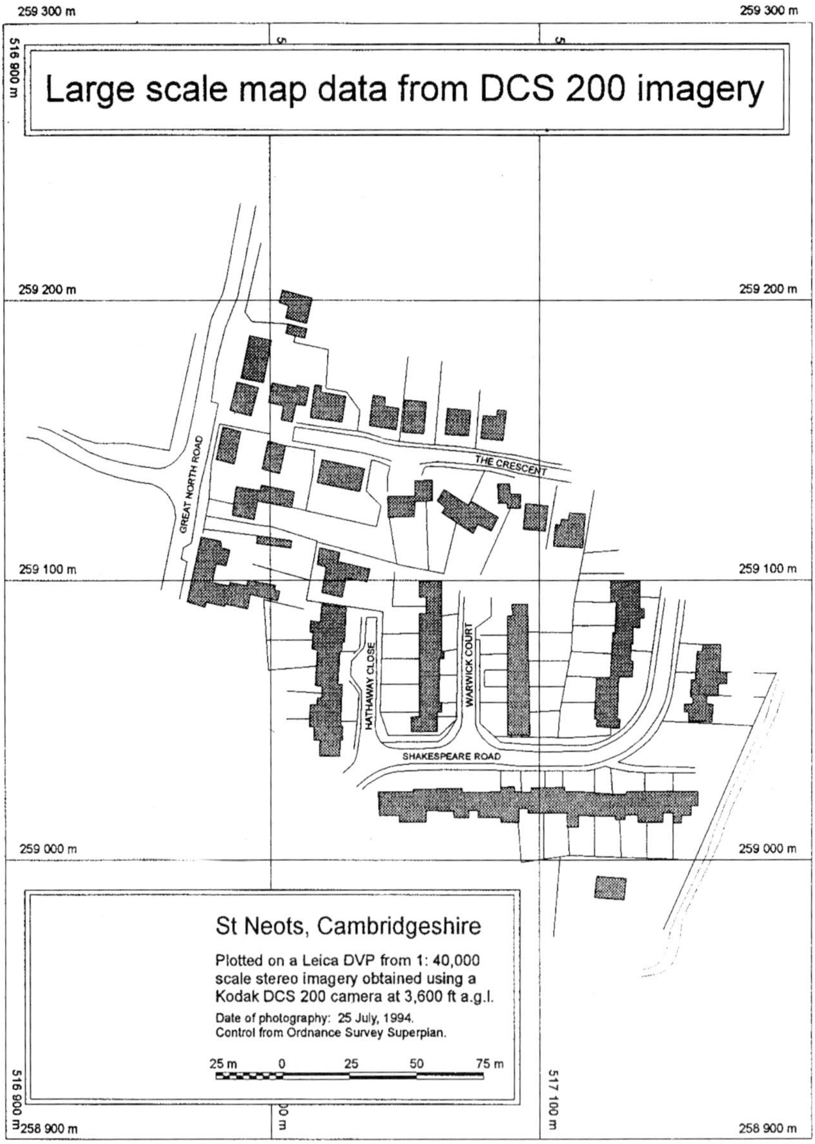

Figure 5.2 *Large scale map detail plotted from the stereo overlap of images 12 and 13 (St Neots) with a Leica DVP.*

The DCS-200ci employs an 80Mb hard disk giving a storage capacity of 50 uncompressed raw images which go to A/D conversion directly on frame capture. Images can be downloaded to the PC through a SCSI port operated by a future domain controller and may be saved in any file format supported by the software running the Kodak TWAIN driver. Information such as time, date of exposure, aperture and shutter settings are automatically tagged to each image.

The DCS-200 was normally operated at a speed rating of 50 ISO since, in common with all CCD cameras, higher speed ratings (100, 200, 400 or 800 ISO) bring about increasing amounts of noise. Downloading each image to disk took a nominal four seconds, initially one second to download 1.54 Mb to the DRAM (dynamic random access memory) and then a further 3 seconds to the hard disk. From known ground truth it was possible to evaluate a GRD of 10 cm for this camera, with an image photo-scale of 1:15,000 printed to 1:1000 on dye-sublimation glossy paper.

DCS-200 camera calibration

In common with all cameras employed for photogrammetric work, the camera lens must be calibrated. The procedure is no different from that used for analogue cameras and can be undertaken with a relatively simple test-field, and computer software.

The infinity focus calibration parameters for the DCS-200 used in producing the map shown in Fig.5.2 are shown in Table 5.1 (Mills *et al.*, 1996). Calibration was carried out at the City University, London, using a free network, self-calibrating bundle adjustment, where a total of six images was taken from four camera stations exposing 41 circular retro-reflective targets. A full description of the self calibration principle can be found in Fryer (1992), whilst a comprehensive account of the calibration of a monochromatic version of the DCS-200 is reported by Van den Heuvel (1993).

A more comprehensive description of the procedure for converting the DCS-200 image to an undistorted metric state is given by Mills *et al.* (1996) where, in the first stage, fiducial marks are created by using a template with marked pixels to represent them. The positions of the fiducials are deduced by extrapolation from the known

Table. 5.1 *Calibration parameters for a Kodak DCS-200 camera (28mm lens)*

Calibration parameter	f (mm)	p_x (mm)	p_y (mm)	k_1 (μm)	t_1 (μm)	t_2 (μm)
Calibrated value:	29.3045	0.0335	0.1933	−169.540	0.025	−0.043
Standard error:	0.0433	0.0706	0.0576	6.952	0.029	0.023

The infinity focus parameters are:
f = principal distance
p_x and p_y = principal point offset from the image centre
k_1 = radial distortions (Note: k_2 and k_3 are not significant here)
t_1 and t_2 = tangential distortions.

coordinates of the calibrated principal point. The template is then overlaid as a transparent layer onto the image being rectified in Adobe Photoshop software. The second stage is to remove any radial and tangential distortions from the image with the use of two displacement maps, one for x and the other for y displacements. Camera calibration data are then entered into a C++ program such that each pixel in the CCD array is interrogated, its centre being determined relative to the calibrated PP position and its displacement (Δx and Δy) being calculated from:

$$\Delta x = x\,(k_1.r^2) + \{t(r^2 + 2x^2) + 2t_2xy\} \qquad (5.1)$$

$$\Delta y = y\,(k_1.r^2) + \{2\,t_1xy + t_2(r^2 + 2y^2)\} \qquad (5.2)$$

where x and y are the image coordinates and r is the radial distance from the calibrated principal point to the pixel centre. Best resampling results are achieved using the cubic convolution interpolation procedure. Resampling to eliminate lens distortion in this way often makes the image appear out of focus, especially at the edges where most distortion takes place. Applying a sharpening filter after resampling will reduce this effect however.

Kodak DCS-420 camera

This camera has been manufactured in five models, all using the M-5 chip (with 36 bit image capture) and installed within a Nikon N-90 SLR camera body, as shown in Fig. 5.3. Image storage is on a removable Type III PCMCIA drive card, and the camera can record approximately1000 images per battery charge, with a one hour recharge.

The ISO equivalent speed settings are 200 to 800 (monochrome, and monochrome IR) and 100 to 400 (colour version). Such ISO speeds are more than sufficient to allow for good exposures of, say, 1/250 or 1/500 second at apertures of *f*/2.8 or *f* /4. In common with all modern cameras, the actual exposure is calculated by the camera's integral PEM (photoelectric exposure meter).

All versions of the DCS-420 have a pixel matrix of 1524 (H) × 1012 (V), each pixel being 9μm square, providing an overall array of 1.54 MPx in a 14mm × 9.3mm image area. The 420 has a dynamic random access memory (DRAM) of 8Mb which, although relatively slow compared with some of the latest digital cameras (the Olympus C-3030 has a buffer RAM of 32Mb), it is sufficient to support a five image burst in just over two seconds. However, although this may prove useful for some applications, in aerial survey the time taken to download each image is 4 to 5 seconds when operating with an intervalometer.

The various DCS-420 models that have been manufactured are:

1. DCS- 420m (panchromatic).
2. DCS-420 IR (monochromatic near-infrared).
3. DCS- 420c (conventional colour).
4. DCS-420 CIR (false-colour near-infrared).
5. DCS-420 GPS (interfaced with a choice of GPS units).

Although it is true to say that the DCS-420c has been the most popular version, particularly for map revision, a number of panchromatic and CIR versions have been found particularly useful for remote sensing applications – such as in forestry (Knapp. *et al.*, 1997; King *et al.*, 1997) and for land-use and natural resources (Bobbe, 1997).

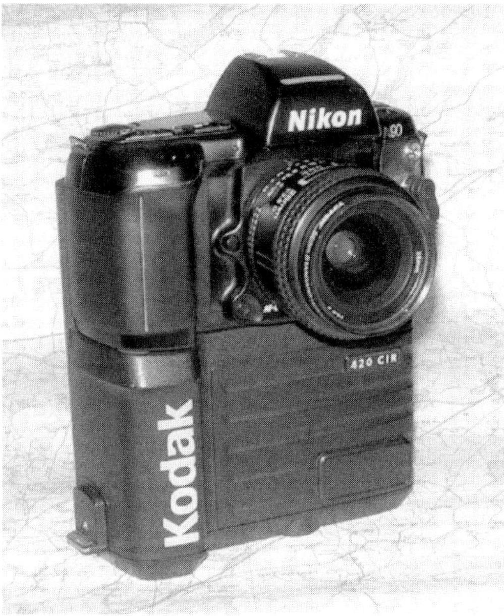

Figure 5.3 *Kodak DCS-420 CIR digital camera.*

DCS-420m and DCS-420 IR false-colour composites (FCC)

Prior to the introduction of the DCS-420 CIR model, early false-colour infrared digital images were made using the DCS-420m in conjunction with the DCS-420 IR camera. The former fitted with a narrow-band red filter ($\Delta\lambda$ = 640nm ± 10.4nm) and the latter with a narrow-band infrared filter ($\Delta\lambda$ = 840nm ± 11.4nm), to provide data for a FCC image (Koh,1996). These two narrow-band spectral channels are known to provide the best data for multispectral photography (MSP) of agricultural scenes. For analogue systems a pan film (red filter) and an infrared film (infrared filter) are necessary and the compared imagery can often show where crop diseases occur, provided that the MSP is taken at the correct time within the crop cycle (Graham, 1980).

The FCC shown in Fig. 5.4 (see colour section) was taken by Alexander Koh using two DCS-420 IR cameras to provide one infrared and one red band image. The subject is a farm in Kenya and was taken at a height of 1000 ft using 18mm lenses, providing a GRD of 15cm. The farm is located in the alluvial plain to the west of Lake Baringo. The area has become progressively more arid and has been heavily overgrazed, resulting in a sparse vegetation cover of Acacia trees and poor grasses.

Although the FCC image is well resolved and well differentiated, the technique is both laborious and time consuming. Processed in Adobe Photoshop the technique involves histogram matching of the different images, image registration, image warping and putting the red image into the blue and green displays of the VDU and the infrared image into the red display. Nevertheless, the FCC does allow for choice of narrow-cut filters according to remote sensing requirements.

Fortunately, since the M-5 chip employs silicon CCDs, the DCS-420 has a natural sensitivity to the near infrared and Kodak soon brought out the DCS-420 CIR model, which made false-colour infrared images directly.

Kodak DCS-420c

The colour filter array (CFA) was mentioned in Chapter 4, as was the popular Bayer mosaic filter (Figs. 4.2 and 4.3). As shown, the Bayer CFA pattern provides two green pixels to each blue and red pixel, this being necessary in order to match the overall CCD response with that of the human eye. Since all of the pixels are sensitive to the near-infrared their IR sensitivity is removed by filtration.

Kodak DCS-420 CIR

Unfortunately the very successful 420 CIR, and its successor the DCS-460 CIR camera were discontinued in the late 1990s. However, it must be remembered that a manufacturer makes a camera for general use and, since aerial survey and remote sensing is not a very large market, the manufacture of a $30,000 camera is not going to be very profitable in the long run! Indeed, most manufacturers take steps to remove the inherent near infrared sensitivity of their digital cameras since most buyers only require a visual response. The Kodak DCS-660 camera is a typical example, where its 6MPx chip is made up of indium-tin-oxide pixels (rather than silicon) a material that has almost no infrared response. Nevertheless, a good number of 420 CIR and 460 CIR cameras still provide excellent service and continue to be extremely useful in the field of remote sensing.

A main source of popularity with the DCS-420 and 460 CIR camera is their capability to capture standard colour or colour infrared photography; this is achieved by

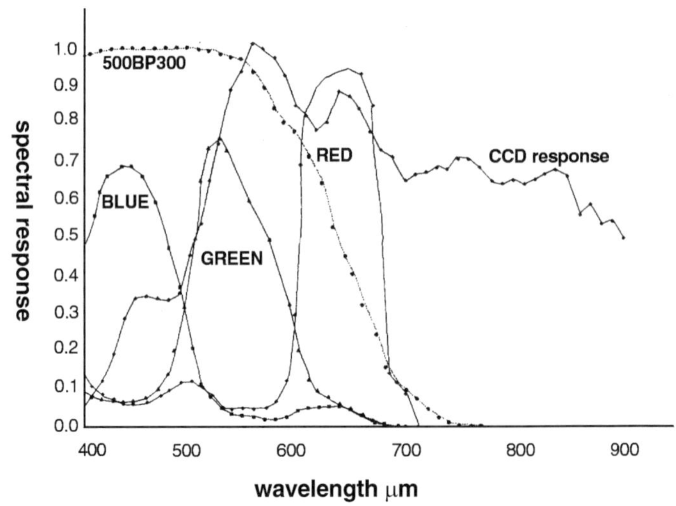

Figure 5.5 *Spectral response of the vis filter. Courtesy Eastman Kodak Company.*

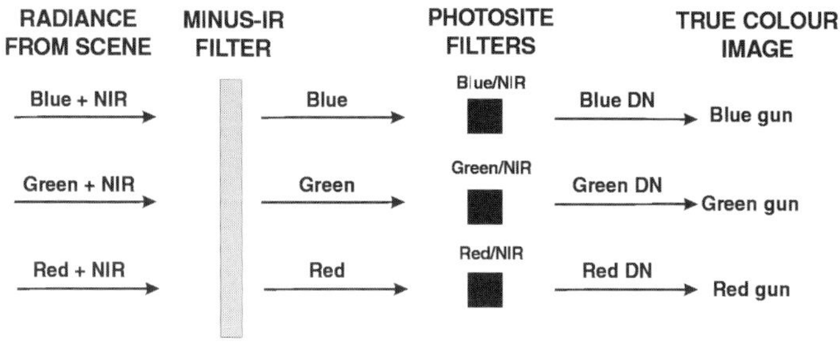

Figure 5.6 *True colour image production using CFA and infrared cut filter. Courtesy Dr E. Edwards.*

changing the filter mounted at the front of the lens and setting the exposure compensation to minus 1.6 or more when configured for CIR.

The spectral response of each red, green and blue pixel is shown in Fig.5.5, where it can be seen that the green response is similar to that of the red and blue pixels. As a consequence the number of green pixels has to be doubled to emulate the dominant green response of the human eye. In order to provide a visual (true-colour) response from the CCD chip it is necessary to fit a 500BP300 filter (vis filter) over the camera lens, as shown in Fig.5.5. Sometimes referred to as a minus IR filter, the 500BP300 filter provides a true colour image as indicated in Fig. 5.6.

For a false-colour image we need to refer to Fig. 5.7 where the 650BP300 yellow filter has been placed in front of the camera lens (the dominant wavelength passed by

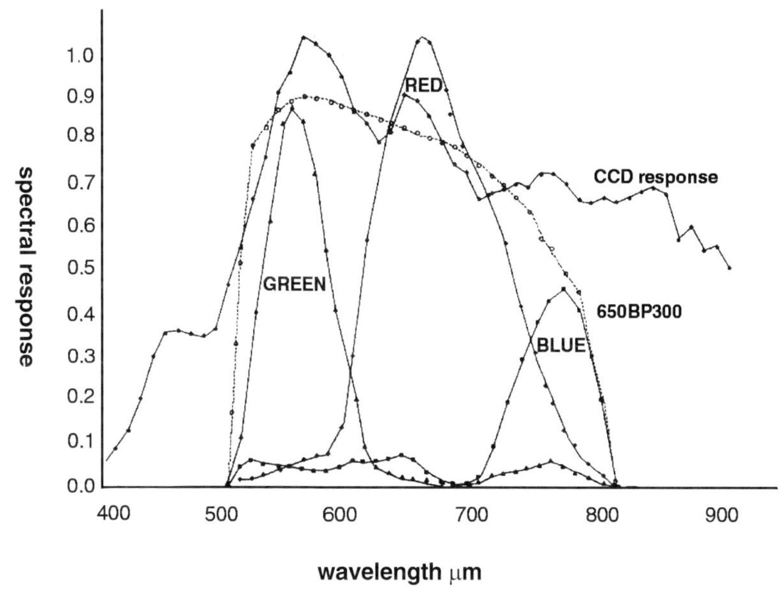

Figure 5.7 *Spectral response of the 650BP300 filter. Courtesy Eastman Kodak Company.*

Table. 5.2 *Storage capacity of type III PCMCIA cards.*

	Number of images per PCMCIA card				
Camera	171 Mb	260 Mb	340 Mb	512 Mb	1 Gb
420 CIR	106	162	212	320	625
460 CIR	27	41	54	82	160

this filter is 650nm, with a side band of 150nm). From Fig. 5.8 we see that the blue pixels now provide a near infrared image directed to the red gun on the VDU, whereas the green and red pixels have their infrared sensitivity subtracted to create blue and green images on the VDU.

It is convenient to mention here that the DCS-460 CIR camera uses the same system as the DCS-420 CIR for its dual image options. But whereas the latter has an interpolated file size of 6.5Mb, the DCS-460 CIR (with four times the image area of the 420) has a file size equal to 18.5Mb. The number of CIR images that can be stored by these cameras depends on the capacity of the PCMCIA cards, and has important implications when calculating a survey mission. The number of compressed image files that can be stored on each of these cameras is shown in Table. 5.2.

DCS-420 GPS

The 420 GPS camera captures imagery and global positioning data simultaneously, so that on each exposure latitude and longitude of the camera location is recorded. The data is stored within the image data block making it available for future identification of the image position. Available camera configurations allow for interfacing with a number of commercially available GPS receivers such as Trimble Ensign XL, Ashtech XII, Motorola VP Oncore and Rockwell PLGR.

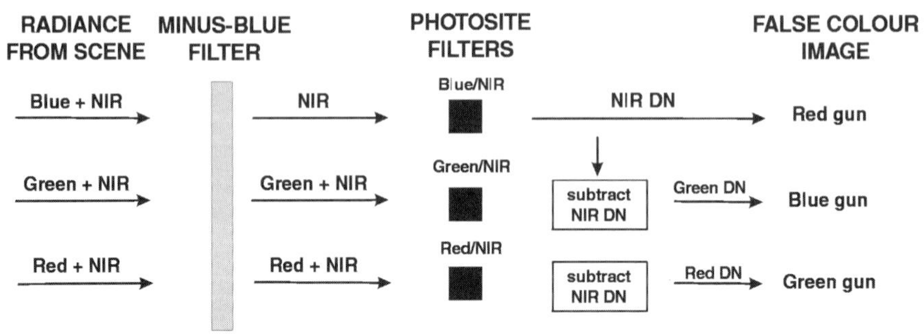

Figure 5.8 *False colour infrared image production using CFA and minus blue filter. Courtesy Dr E. Edwards.*

Although the 420 GPS camera was a customer specific requirement, it was also possible to have the GPS interface retrofitted. A number of DCS-420c and 420 CIR examples are explained in Chapter 15, where their use is discussed in greater detail.

Kodak DCS-460

The DCS-460 came hot on the heels of the 420 series and profited from the extensive research, field experience and marketing of the latter cameras. The most significant difference is the increased size of the CCD chip in the DCS-460. Whereas all of the 420s (and the DCS-200) sport the M-5 chip, with a 9.2mm × 14mm format, fielding 1.54MPx, the DCS-460 models have the M-6 chip with an 18mm × 28mm format containing over 6MPx.

There can be no doubt that the 4× increase in image size improves both quality and resolution when same-size prints from the two cameras are compared. Indeed, any questions regarding the relative merits of analogue over digital imagery were swiftly dispelled as soon as the DCS-460 was employed by the photographic community.

The DCS-460 comes in two versions: the 460 colour, and the 460 CIR, and both employ the same technology as that explained for the DCS-420c and 420 CIR (see Figs 5.5 to 5.8).

DCS-460c

In Fig. 5.9 (colour section) we have an excellent example of the high resolution aerial photography that can be achieved with the DCS-460c. The subject is the campus site of the Fachhochschule, Bochum, Germany, and was flown by Prof. Franjo Heimes, using a 28mm lens supported on his stabilised mount (Heimes *et al.*, 1997).

DCS-460 CIR

When operated in its true colour mode the DCS-460 CIR can also produce high quality imagery (seeFig. 5.10 in colour section). This image is from a series of 60% forward overlap photographs taken with a 28mm lens (1/1000 at *f*/4) at 2600 ft. Taken by Dr. Jon Mills of Newcastle University, these photographs were flown at a photoscale of 1:25,000 to provide an orthophoto map of the Village of Husthwaite, North Yorkshire. A critical examination of Figs.5.9 and 5.10 suggests that the 460c image is of a higher resolution than that taken with the 460 CIR in true colour mode, but this is to be expected, partly because the 460c operates with a simpler algorithm, and also because the camera was operated from a stabilised mount.

A typical DCS-460 CIR record is shown in Fig. 5.11 (colour section) . Taken with a 28mm lens, this false-colour infrared image of an African village was taken by Alexander Koh over Kumasi, Ghana, using Geotechnologies ADPS (Aerial Digital Photographic System) at a height of 1200 ft. Dye sublimation prints at 1:1200 were taken from a series of 1:18,000 photoscale images .

The DCS-460 CIR camera is an ideal tool for both mapping and remote sensing, and although its nominal image download period is far too high at 12 s, it is possible to reduce this to 8 s by using the highest quality PCMCIA card. Nevertheless, the larger format tends to offset this problem somewhat, and with careful mission planning and choice of aircraft, good stereoscopic cover can always be obtained. Quality and resolution are always important features in an aerial photograph and to date, the DCS-460 CIR remains the best off-the-shelf digital camera suitable for mapping, RS and GIS applications. Similar to the 420 series, the DCS-460 camera can be supplied with a GPS interface or the interface retrofitted for use with a large choice of GPS receivers.

Kodak DCS-760 camera

In April 2001 Kodak introduced the 6MPx (ITO) DCS-760 model, with an ISO range of 80 to 400, a CCD array of 3032 × 2008 Px and a much lower price tag of $9000. Housed in the rugged Nikon F5 SLR body the 760 should be good for aerial work since it incorporates a vastly improved IEEE 1394 (Firewire) interface to speed up image transmission. The DCS-760 uses IBM CF+ microdrives and these are available with data storage capacities of up to 1 Gb.

Fujifilm FinePix S1 Pro

Yet another high-end SLR colour digital camera, the Fuji S1 employs a 3.4MPx chip (2304 × 1536 Px) with 'Super CCD technology'. The highly innovative Super CCD chip moves away from the conventional Bayer pattern (see Fig. 4.2) to introduce a honeycomb CFA made up of larger octagonal pixels turned through 45° for maximum density packing. In this radical approach we get greater sensitivity (larger pixels), greater dynamic range and less noise from the 23.3mm × 5.5mm image. A further advantage of the Super CCD is that the horizontal and vertical image resolutions are higher, matching the characteristics of human vision (Larish. J. 2000).

The S1 is built around the Nikon F60 camera and is very reasonably priced at $4000 (body only – lenses extra). There are two LCD screen on the camera back – one for viewing the image and a smaller one for function selection. Four quality levels are available, each selected by function buttons. The top quality mode uses TIFF files, either the traditional RGB (18Mb) or the less memory-intensive YC-TIFF (12Mb). The three lower quality files are JPEG, compressed to: 2.4Mb, 1.2Mb or 0.7Mb when using the highest 6.1MPx (interpolated) resolution. Resolution is selected separately. The raw resolution is 3.4MPx (10.6Mb), but there are options for 2.1MPx (4.1Mb), or 6.1MPx (18.3Mb) images. Sensitivity ranges from 320 to 1600 ISO, and shutter speeds up to 1/2000 are available.

No doubt the S1 will satisfy many photographers looking for a good quality digital camera at a reasonable price, and we can be sure that Super CCD technology will appear in other models at a later date. But although the S1 offers increased sensitivity, selecting the highest resolution has doubtful advantages since this may not offer much more quality over that provided by its raw (3.4Mb) resolution. Also, by invoking the interpolation process, file size is increased before the image is stored to disk which, with the additional processing, slows down writing the image to storage (compact-flash, smart-drive or IBM microdrive) to about 15 s.

Digital cameras designed for aerial photography

Up to now we have only considered small-format off-the-shelf digital cameras that have proven or potential characteristics suitable for aerial survey and remote sensing. For the most part we prefer those with a near infrared sensitivity, so that they can be used for remote sensing as well as metric surveys. However, in recent years both major manufacturers of 23cm mapping cameras (LH Systems and Z/I Imaging) have developed a highly sophisticated digital sensor suitable for photogrammetry and remote sensing. Obviously it was only a question of time before the manufacturers of mapping cameras, such as the RC-30 and RMK-TOP, addressed the question of direct digital imagery, rather than scanning the analogue products of these well known air cameras. But to be fair, we must go back nearly 20 years to find the original digital mapping/remote sensing camera – which is still employed today.

MEIS II: A fully digital airborne mapping platform

The Canadian **m**ultispectral **e**lectro-optical **i**maging **s**canner (MEIS) was developed by the Canada Centre for Remote Sensing (CCRS) 20 years ago to meet the requirements of the mapping and natural resource management sectors for a fully digital map and inventory data base (McColl, *et al.*, 1983). The MEIS system is an airborne multispectral pushbroom scanner that provides a spectral range from 390nm to 1100nm, with ground spatial resolutions ranging from 0.4m to 5m Px GSD, depending on the aircraft's height and speed.

Basically, the MEIS II consists of a multi-element linear array detector of 1728 pixels (Fairchild buried channel silicon CCDs) each 13 μm^2, which is scanned through a total swath width of 39.66° with the real-time image data sampler. The MEIS II system has 8 separate bore-sighted optical channels (lenses) which provide for six very narrow spectral bands (via front-of-lens filters) at nadir, where each channel records 1728 Px resampled to 1024 Px for each scan line.

The design also incorporates a stereo viewing system by adding mirrors to two of the lenses, one directed forward and the other to the rear, resulting in a single-pass stereo data acquisition. The stereo imagery data is important since it is used to develop a DTM for use in the geometric correction of the pushbroom imagery. In addition, an inertial navigation system (INS) and global positioning system (GPS) are also employed to provide rigorous imagery corrections and positioning. Post-processing of the geo-coded pixel data is employed to achieve geometric and radiometric corrections and the production of high quality ortho-images with DTMs.

Since inception the MEIS system has been constantly up-dated and improved in terms of geometric accuracy and data processing. The algorithm for adjusting the imagery and navigation system data is based on rigorous photogrammetric principles and incorporates the standard collinearity and coplanarity conditions, the former for utililising ground control points and the latter for tying multiple flight lines together using features of unknown location common to overlapping flight lines. In this respect the approach is the same as that adopted for conventional photo-mapping projects, except that the algorithm has to be modified for MEIS imagery which, unlike a conventional aerial photograph, does not have a central perspective point. A further modification was also required to accommodate the time-sampled position and attitude measurement data from the INS (Gibson, 1994).

In August 2000, Environment Canada awarded a contract to Aquarius Flight Inc, to acquire digital imagery from Cornwall, Ontario to Trois-Pistoles, Quebec, to cover both the north and south shores (upland) of the St. Lawrence River (Graham and Mills, 2000). The project goals were in support of efforts in the protection and restoration of habitats through a wetland monitoring program. Corrected imagery with full stereo capability is used for precise mapping applications and a full colour ortho-image is generated with sub-meter accuracies and a self-generated DTM. To obtain the required spectral ranges for the monitoring program the St. Lawrence Centre asked Aquarius to configure MEIS in accordance with the channels shown in Table. 5.3.

The final study was accomplished by flying an Aerocommander 680 FL aircraft at 16,000 ft altitude, providing a GSD of 3.5 m. The MEIS II equipment was installed within an IGI GCM-1 gyro-stabilised mount and integrated CCNS4 (GPS) navigation system. The St. Lawrence River project was flown in 18 calendar days, involving 27 flying hours over 3400 linear kilometers and 34 flight-lines.

LH Systems' ADS40 airborne digital sensor

Formally introduced at the International Society for Photogrammetry & Remote Sensing (ISPRS) congress 2000, the ADS40 is claimed to be the first commercial airborne digital camera, and its broad ground coverage and multispectral image collection are set to combine photogrammetric accuracy and remote sensing insight for the first time. Yet, like the earlier MEIS system, the ADS40 employs a pushbroom scanning system that requires post-processing to gain metric accuracy – hardly a 'first time' achievement, even though the LH system exhibits many advanced technological improvements over the MEIS II.

Developed in cooperation with the German Aerospace Centre (DLR), the ADS40 started life around 1998 and, from the start, was strongly influenced by the DLR's high resolution stereo camera (HRSC). The HRSC-A is a narrow angle digital

Table. 5.3 *MIES II St. Lawrence Project: spectral channels.*

Channel	*Wavelength band. (nm)*	*Spectral response*
1 (Stereo)	516.48 – 580.12	Green
2	603.35 – 677.45	Red
3	498.09 – 542.11	Blue-Green
4	717.91 – 782.49	Infrared
5 (Stereo)	516.48 – 580.12	Green
6	417.93 – 479.67	Blue
7	539.50 – 567.10	Green
8	635.57 – 714.63	Red - Infrared

multispectral stereo scanner designed for photogrammetric and remote sensing applications. Employing the 'pushbroom' principle, the HRSC-A incorporates 8 CCD line sensors behind a single optical system and uses forward, nadir and backward-looking linear arrays to provide stereo-panchromatic imagery, as well as multispectral imagery at the nadir position.

Like the HRSC-A, the ADS40 is based on the three-line scanner principle, capturing panchromatic and multispectral information forward, nadir and backward from the aircraft as shown in Figs. 5.13 and 5.14. As the aircraft progresses down a given flight-line, its ADS40 imagery is acquired from a special telecentric (62.5mm focal length) lens, and by high frequency sampling of the CCD lines. The lens field of view (FoV) across track is 46° and read-out frequency of each CCD line (depending on flying height) is in the range 200–800 Hz (Sandau. R, *et al.* 2000).

The ADS40 panchromatic lines

The ADS40 focal plane is populated by 8 CCD lines. The three panchromatic CCD lines are responsible for the forward, nadir and backward-looking views that look after the geometry and stereoscopic cover of the system. All of the linear arrays have pixels 6.5 μm^2 with a dynamic range of 12 bits. Whereas the five multispectral lines have 12,000 Px each, the panchromatic lines are doubled and employ twin-lines each of 12,000 Px with a staggered arrangement that provides a total of 24,000 Px for

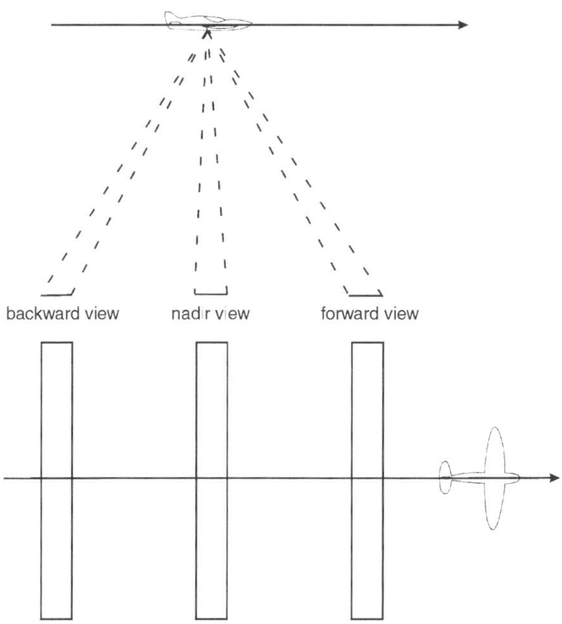

Figure 5.13 *LH Systems' ADS40 airborne digital sensor, based on the three-line scanner principle.*

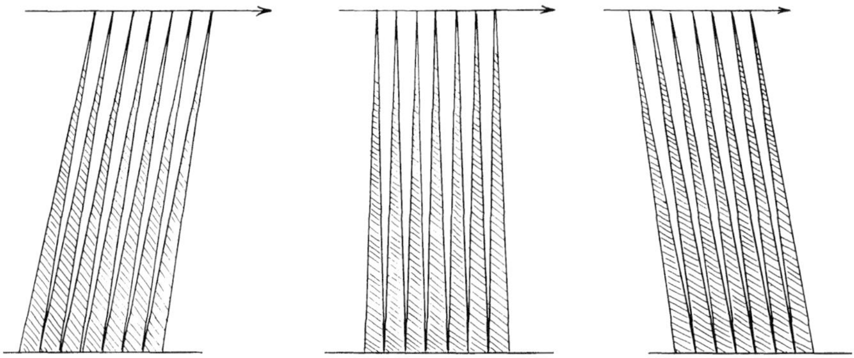

Figure 5.14 *LH Systems' ADS40. Backward, nadir and forward view lines of the ADS40 system.*

improved resolution. The three panchromatic lines offer a choice of three possible stereoscopic pairings, i.e, nadir-to-forward (26°), nadir-to-backward (16°) and forward-to-backward (42°).

Multispectral arrays

In support of the three panchromatic line sensors there are five additional linear arrays, each with 12,000 Px, adjacent to the nadir panchromatic line (Fig. 5.15). These five spectral lines include the usual red, green and blue for true-colour, plus a near infrared (NIR1) and an optional near infrared (NIR2). Table 5.4 provides the spectral bandwidth of all the ADS40 CCD lines.

The three RGB lines are optically superimposed during flight, using a special arrangement where an ingenious trichroid device divides incident light into the red, green and blue, using cascaded dichroitic beam splitters so that no significant energy is lost. The near infrared lines are slightly offset with respect to the panchromatic nadir CCD lines.

Table. 5.4 ADS40 spectral bands.

Spectral band	*Bandwidth* (λ, nm)
Panchromatic	465 – 680
Red	608 – 662
Green	533 – 587
Blue	428 – 492
NIR.1	703 – 757
NIR.2	833 – 887

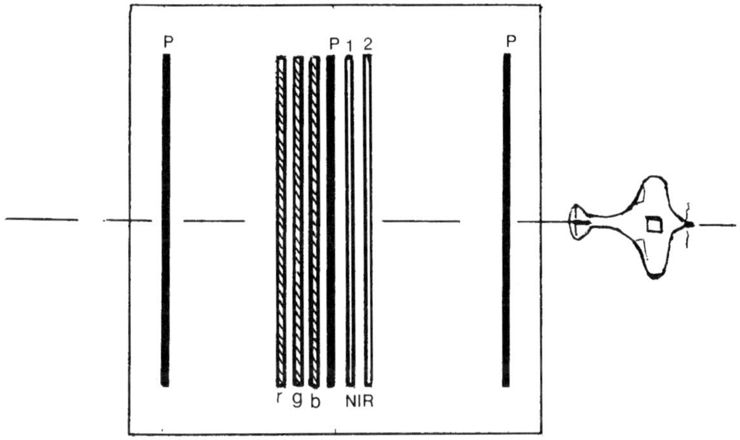

Figure 5.15 *LH Systems' ADS40. Schematic layout of the R,G,B, line., NIR, and panchromatic lines.*

ADS40 spatial and radiometric resolution

The ADS40 sensors are CCD pixels of 6.5 μm^2, and its three panchromatic views provide information for full photogrammetric restitution, with each line bearing two linear CCD arrays, each of 12,000 Px. In this specially developed ADS 40 arrangement, each of the two 12,000 cell linear arrays are staggered by half a pixel to provide a population of 2 × 12,000 Px, thus halving the achievable GSD for any given flying height. Thus, for example, with a lens of 62.5mm and a flying height of 3000m (10,000 ft), the scale number is:

$$m_b = H/f = 3000/0.0625 = 48{,}000$$

and the ground sampled distance (GSD) can be calculated as:

$$\text{GSD} = m_b.\text{Px} = 48{,}000 \times (6.5 \div 2)\ \mu\text{m} \approx 16\ \text{cm}.$$

The limiting spatial resolution factors for this type of sensor are: (a) the maximum read-out frequency of the linear arrays (800Hz), (b) the aircraft's ground speed and (c) the height of the platform above ground.

Measurements of the ADS40 point spread function (PSF) are given in a paper by Schuster and Braunecker (2000), where they detail the procedure for gaining the system modulation transfer function (MTF) by using a fast fourier transform (FFT). The MTF curves characterise the optical performance of the camera system, which is mainly determined by the optics and pixel size, and it is interesting to note that resolution is always better in the direction of flight rather in the cross-track swath direction.

The dynamic range of the ADS40 pixels is 12 bits, with a radiometric resolution of 8 bits (including the effects of the Poisson distribution of the incoming light). It is the Poisson distribution of incoming radiation that determines the signal-to-noise ratio

(SNR) of a CCD (see Chapter 3) and, for a given waveband, the noise of the signal electrons is thus subject to the Poisson statistics of photon noise, as shown by Eq. 3.8.

The ADS40 is claimed to have a SNR of 8–9 bits in a 12 bit dynamic range (Eckardt *et al.*, 2000).

Design philosophy and post-processing requirements

The design philosophy for the ADS 40 is to provide a system that can provide (a) a large field of view, (b) high geometric and radiometric resolution, (c) multispectral imagery and (d) stereoscopic cover. But it appears that (a) is the dominant condition since this directed the choice towards linear arrays and pushbroom scanning in order to gain a large field of view. This choice is justified to some extent by comparing the ADS 40's 12k linear array of pixels against the 7k × 4k area array used in the DMC, or the 4k × 4k area array employed by Geotechnologies MF-DMC. But all airborne scanning systems have a price to pay – and that concerns the extra effort and cost required to correct pushbroom imagery. There can be no doubt that the ADS40 has been well designed, even to the point where the focal plane has a temperature controlled unit that supplies a constant temperature for all the CCD lines. In addition, there is an air filter and drying mechanism to manage pressure differences between different altitudes and possible condensation on the CCD chips.

Like all pushbroom systems the ADS40 images require line-by-line rectification against aircraft flight dynamics (tilt, roll and yaw) during image acquisition, and in order to correct the raw imagery, supplementary data from an on-board inertial measurement unit (IMU) and GPS unit are essential aids in this respect. Fortunately, excellent IMUs are available, which allow precise measurement of the aircraft dynamics.

Expensive software processes are necessary in order to produce traditional photogrammetric products, particularly since GPS and IMU data have been collected during image acquisition and written to the mass memory system (MMS). These two data streams must be post-processed along with optional GPS base station data in order to produce a precise position and attitude stream for every line of imagery. At the end of this processing step there is a single data file for each CCD line, containing the position and attitude for each line of the image. GPS data is recorded in the WGS84 reference system, while the IMU records instantaneous changes in position and attitude of the camera. The ADS40 stores its compressed image data in an on-board MMS with a storage capacity of over half a terabyte, and can provide for survey missions with up to four hours of recording time, at a sustained data rate of 40–50Mb/second.

From the imagery exhibited at the ISPRS 2000 conference it is obvious that the ADS40 is a magnificant achievement, but it remains to be seen what a particular unit will cost since it is a modular system and will depend upon the client's choice. Nevertheless an average price might well be over a million dollars (US) and this could be an economic restriction for a few years yet, particularly for those mapping firms that have only recently invested in expensive film cameras such as the Leica RC-30 or Zeiss RMK-TOP. The basic design outlines of the LH ADS40 and the Z/I DMC are shown in Fig. 5.16.

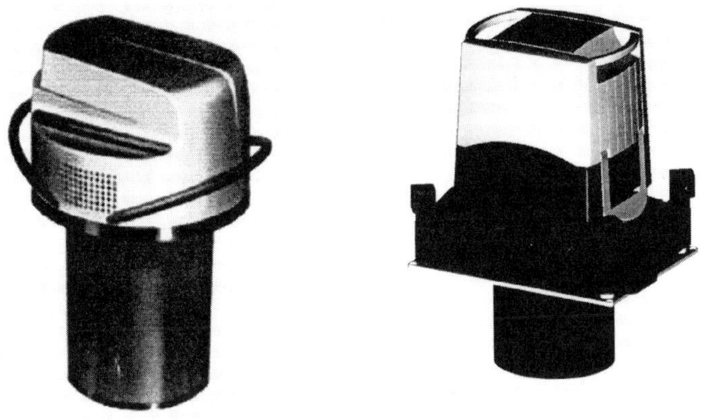

Figure 5.16 *Basic design outline of LH Systems' ADS40 camera (left) and Z/I DMC camera (right).*

Z/I Imaging DMC-2001 system

The Zeiss/Intergraph digital modular camera (DMC) is somewhat simpler in design to that of the Leica Helava ADS40 camera. This is brought about by its area array system which does not require the sophisticated post-processing necessary to rectify the raw image data. One of the basic design features of the Z/I - DMC is to adopt the principle of a central perspective image which, like the film cameras common to both the Zeiss and Leica series of mapping cameras, follows a system established in photogrammetry for almost 100 years. As a consequence, all existing exploitation systems can handle these data, and in many respects the DMC provides an image not much different to that scanned from a 23 cm film image. This close relationship to the Zeiss RMK-TOP system is further qualified by designing the DMC to fit into the T-AS stabilized mount and to be able to accommodate future developments without an significant changes to the camera frame (see Fig. 5.17).

The first production models of the DMC will be known as the DMC-2001, and are expected to be available around June 2002 with prices somewhere in the region of $920,000 (US) for a top-of-the-range model.

The DMC modular approach allows for the combination of several compact camera heads within one installation, offering cross track coverage in the same range as standard wide-angle analogue cameras. In this way customers can select their own appropriate module according to resolution and multispectral requirements. The DMC images have the usual central perspective geometry, thus maintaining interfacing and compatibility to existing softcopy solutions. In their belief that today's digital camera systems cannot replace existing film based systems, Z/I have designed a camera that fits easily into the current film-based workflow to combine the best of both technologies in the most economical way.

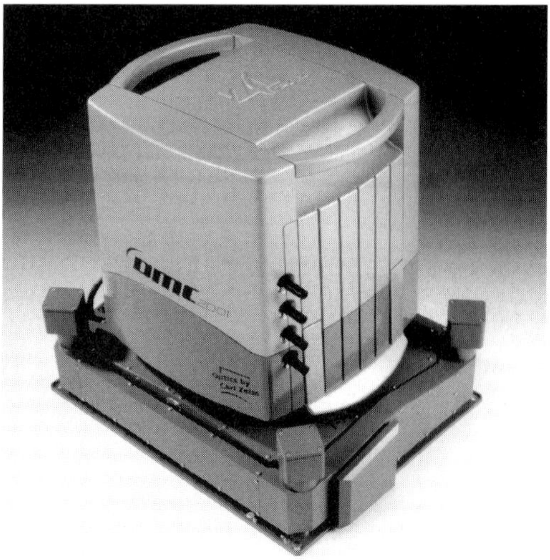

Figure 5.17 *Z/I DMC-2001 digital air camera system fitted into the T-AS stabilised mount. Courtesy Dr Alex Hinz, Zeiss/Intergraph, Germany.*

The DMC modular system

Since it is not (as yet) economically possible to install a single, large area, digital array chip that could approach the format of a 23 cm^2 mapping camera, the Z/I solution is to incorporate several compact camera heads, each with its own lens and CCD chip. The modules are then directed to the scene at slightly displaced field angles (Fig. 5.18) where the four pan modules are surrounded by four multispectral heads. Figure 5.19 illustrates the ground coverage taken by four such camera heads. The principle of parallel image recording has been well established by Zeiss with its reconnaissance cameras, such as the KS-153 and KRb 8/24. The high resolution version of the DMC employs four 7k × 4k large area CCD chips, each with an *f*/4 120mm focal length lens operating in the panchromatic (visual response) mode.

DMC 14k high resolution + multispectral system

Preliminary specifications for all the DMC modules are subject to change, but at the time of writing, the basic optical layout for the 14k high resolution + multispectral system is to have four panchromatic cameras in the centre of the frame, with four multispectral cameras surrounding them at the periphery of the frame. The overall panchromatic resolution (over the ground) is 13,500 Px across track, and approximately 8000 Px along track. The cross track FoV is 74°, formed from two 7k Px dimensions, and the along track FoV is 44°, formed from two 4k Px dimensions. All four of the panchromatic lenses are 120mm *f*/4.

The multispectral array is made up of four 25mm focal length lenses (*f*/4) exposing four channels: R,G,B and NIR. The multispectral chips are of less area resolution, each having a size of 3k × 2k Px. The CCD sensors are Philips types with 12 μm

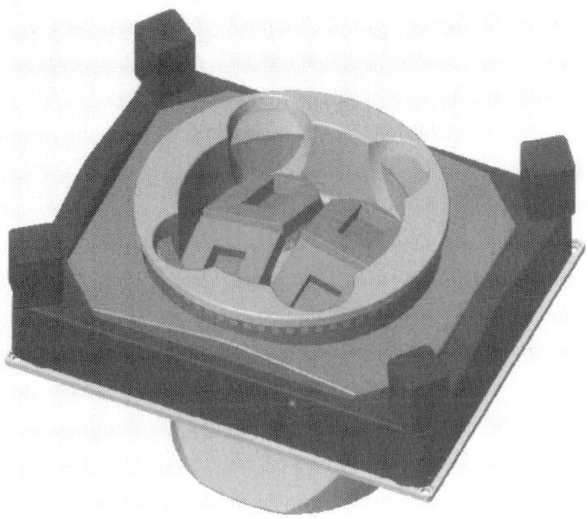

Figure 5.18 *DMC in stabilized platform. Top view onto panchromatic channels. Courtesy Dr Alex Hinz, Zeiss/Intergraph, Germany.*

square pixels (>12-bit capacity), and have a special architecture with four readout registers placed at the corners of the chip. This provides for high readout rates, such that an image repetition frequency of one image every two seconds can be achieved, an important feature for stereoscopic imagery of course.

An electromechanical inter-lens shutter system is employed on each camera, with precise synchronisation of all camera exposures. In addition, a fully electronic forward motion compensation (FMC) of the digital image is available by using the time-delayed integration (TDI) mode during exposure. In this way, compensation for image blur at low altitude and high resolution applications is assured (standard for analogue air cameras since 1982). FMC is implemented on the DMC on a completely electronic basis. In the normal way of reading out CCD pixels in an area-array imaging system, the charge contents of each CCD pixel is transported line-by-line to the readout regis-

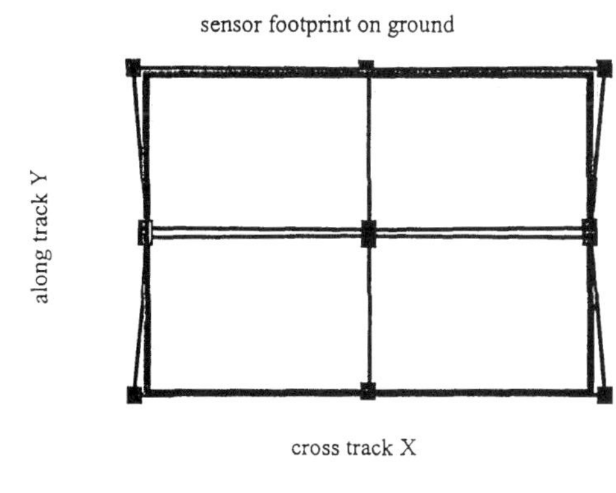

Figure 5.19 *Ground coverage of 4-camera head system.*

ters (Fig.3.8 refers). If this shifting process is performed synchronously to the pixel motion on the ground during exposure, then it is possible to compensate for image motion by means of an electronic procedure where the pixel clock rate is adapted to the image rate (Holst, 1996). In very basic terms this can be explained as follows. During survey-flight operations the format of an area-array digital sensor is such that the CCD pixel charges are read out to their respective readout registers at right angles to the flight path. With this kind of digital system the flight direction is technically called the TDI (time delay & integration) direction (see Fig.5.20) and during the exposure period image blur is compensated electronically during the readout procedure. If we refer to Fig. 5.20 we can see the obvious loss in MTF for the non-TDI image.

Spatial resolution tests

A series of low altitude test flights with a single camera DMC module have been made (Jan.2000), using a twin engined aircraft flying at a ground speed of 140 knots.

As an extreme test, one flight was made at a height of 300 m above ground where a large (6m diameter) Siemens Star test target was positioned. With a 50 mm lens the scale number is 6000, and with 12 μm square CCD pixels, the GSD is calculated (Eq. 4.25) as 7.2cm. An even better result is found from the symmetrically resolved Siemens Star target shown in Fig. 5.21, which indicates 5cm GSD with forward motion blur compensated by 7 Px of TDI (Hinz *et al.*, 2000).

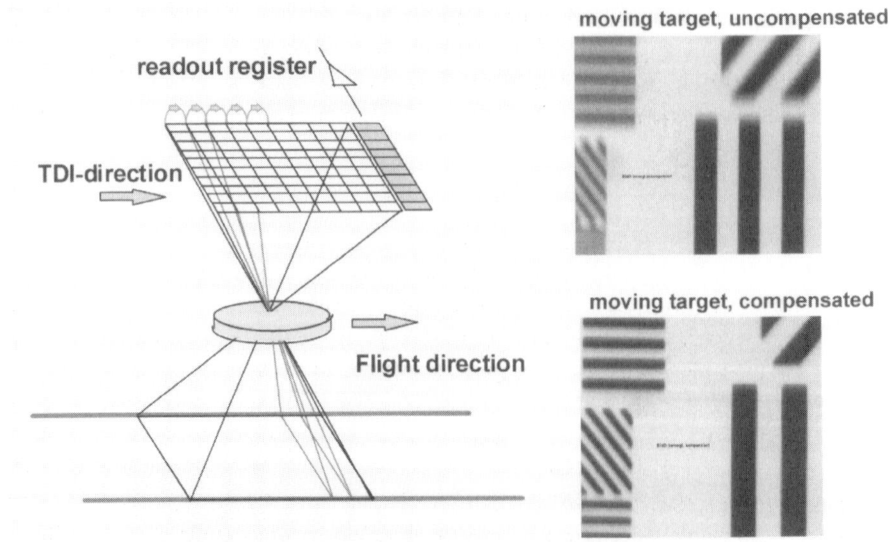

Figure 5.20 *Z/I DMC-2001 System forward motion compensation by TDI (time delay & integration). Courtesy Dr. Alex Hinz, Z/I Germany.*

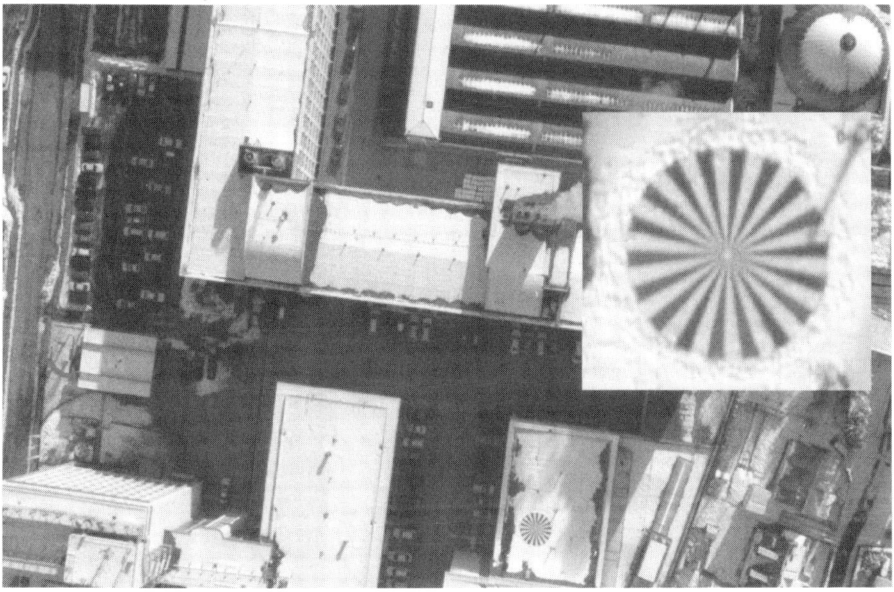

Figure 5.21 *Z/I DMC-2001 System flown over a large Siemens Star target. Courtesy Dr. Alex Hinz, Z/I Germany.*

Forward image motion (FIM)

Forward image motion is an important factor controlling image resolution in both analogue and area-array digital images where, in poor light levels or low flying height, the image exposure time may be too long to avoid significant image blur (Graham *et al.*, 1996) . FIM is a function of a number of parameters where, in accordance with Eq. 5.3, we have:

$$\mathrm{FIM} = f.V.t\,/H \tag{5.3}$$

where f = focal length of lens, V = ground speed of aicraft (m/s), t = exposure time (i.e, shutter speed) and H = height of aircraft above mean ground level.

In terms of air films, the usual accepted limit of FIM is that it should not > 25 μm, but this is usually less in cameras where FMC is operated. It should be noted that FMC is not possible with pushbroom systems. For DMC test quoted above, a shutter speed of 1/140 s would amount to an image blur of 84 μm, or 7 Px.

High resolution DMC tests

Further tests with the High Resolution DMC (four 7k × 4k chips), and 120mm *f*/4 lens have been made, supported by an IGI CCNS4 navigation system. At a flying height of 1100 meters above mean ground level (amgl) a TDI of 10 pixels was employed to gain the image shown in Fig.5.22. The photo-scale number is found as: m_b =

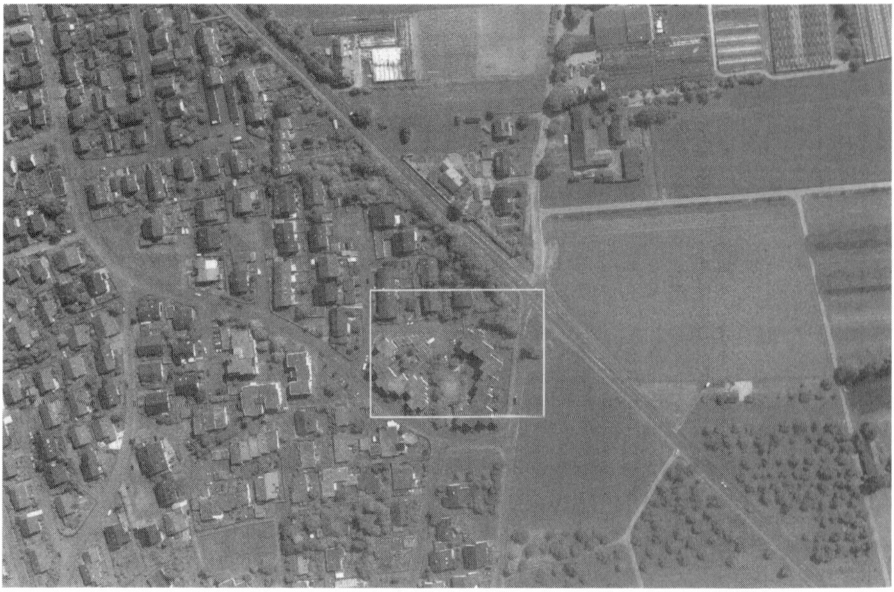

Figure 5.22 *Z/I DMC-2001 spatial resolution test with a TDI of 10 Px. Courtesy Dr. Alex Hinz, Z/I Germany.*

H/f = 1100 / 0.12 = 9166, and the GSD is calculated as 11cm. The original print scale for Fig.5.22 is approximately 1:2500.

When the image of Fig.5.22 is enlarged ×6.8, we find excellent resolution is still preserved as shown by Fig.5.23a, and only when enlarged ×30 (Fig. 5.23b), do we find significant pixelation of the original image.

DMC radiometeric resolution

All of the Z/I DMC modules have a total CCD capacity of 12 bits and, as mentioned in Chapter 4, a pixel depth of 8 bits is sufficient for both monochrome and colour digital imagery. In Fig.5.24a we see a panchromatic image taken by the demonstrator DMC from 6000 feet with a GSD of 40cm. In this 10 bit image (1024 grey values), initial software processing has not provided any detail inside the cooling towers or in the dark shadows they cast. But in Fig. 5.24b, software processing has masked-out these dark areas to reveal the wealth of detail existing in the primary image.

DMC airborne system configuration

A typical DMC installation is shown in Fig.5.25, which is almost identical to existing film camera installations. The DMC camera head has similar dimensions to the Zeiss RMK-TOP camera and is designed to fit into the existing gyro-stabilised mount T-AS. The flight management system, with optional pilot's display and an optional IMU like AEROcontrol can be integrated into the system, opening up the possibility to work without ground control, or with a reduced set of ground control points (GCPs).

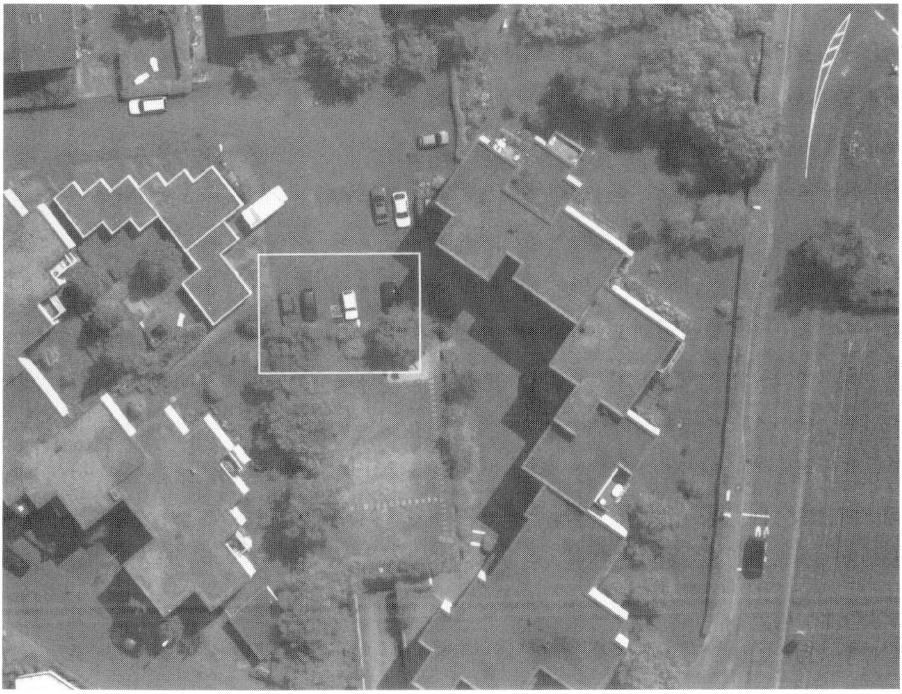

Figure 5.23a *The resolution test image shown in Fig.5.22 enlarged 6.8×. Courtesy Dr. Alex Hinz, Z/I Germany.*

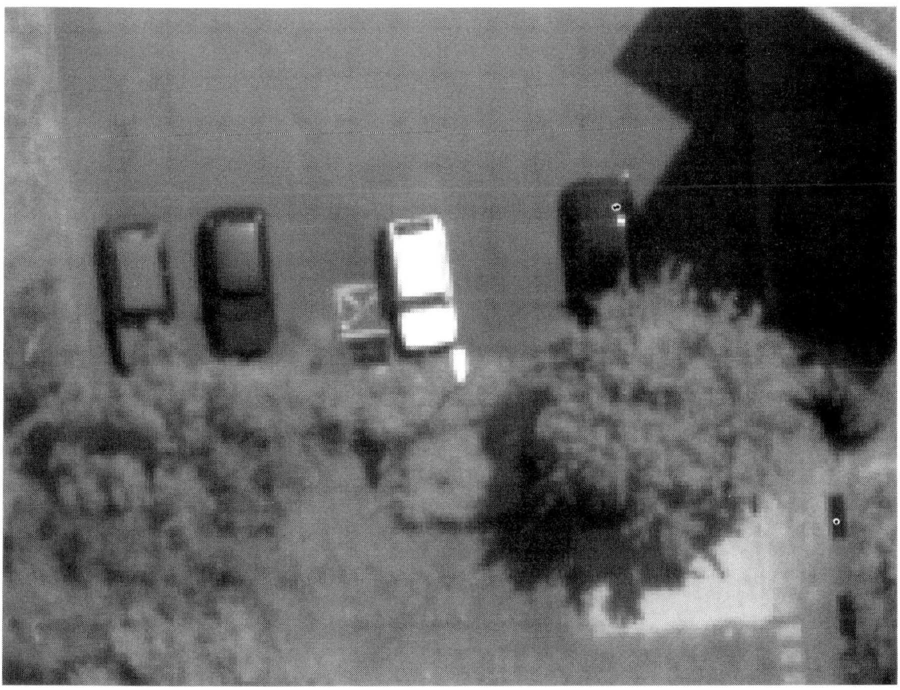

Figure 5.23b *The resolution test image shown in Fig. 5.22 enlarged 30x. Courtesy Dr. Alex Hinz, Z/I Germany.*

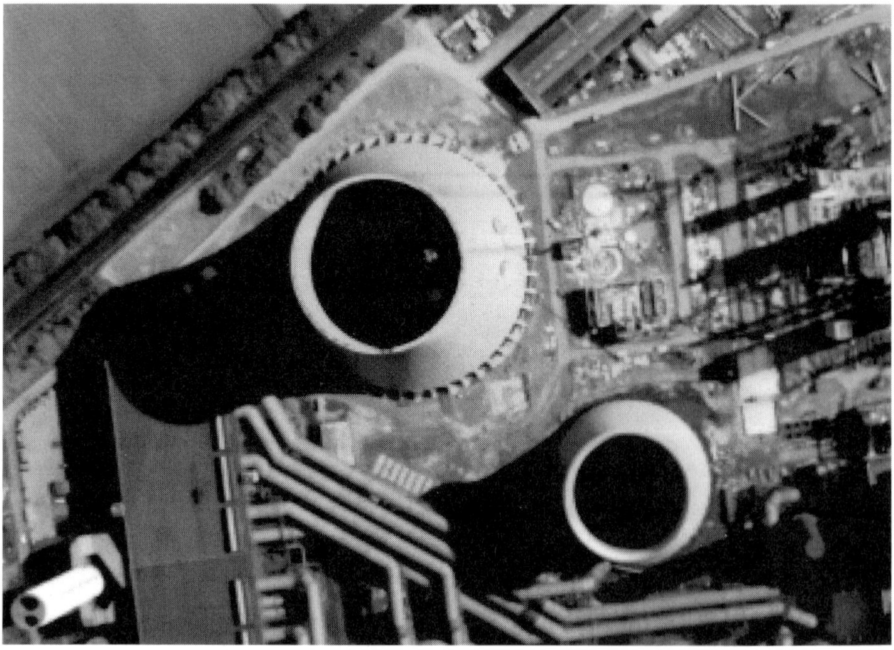

Figure 5.24a *Z/I DMC-2001 image without further processing for shadow detail. Courtesy Dr. Alex Hinz, Z/I Germany.*

The IGI standard CCNS4 and AEROcontrol system has been chosen by Z/I Imaging for guidance positioning, attitude determination and survey-flight management. This integrated system allows for easy mission planning, execution of airborne operations and is the most proven and accurate system available today. The AEROcontrol-IId with IGI's fibre-optic IMU, together with the standard CCNS4 guidance and management unit, build an easy to operate combination for both film and digital cameras. Depending on the GPS constellation and base length, a positioning accuracy better than 0.1m RMS, and attitude accuracy of 0.005° RMS is available in post-processing.

Image data storage

Image data are stored on a RAID (Redundant Array of Independent Disks) hard disk system with removable storage units. The RAID system is placed in a separate housing and connected to the electronics magazine via a high speed FDDI interface. The various storage capacities related to specified DMC models are given in Table.5.5.

The medium format digital mapping camera

Whereas the MEIS II, LH-ADS40 and Z/I- DMC-2001 are all highly sophisticated, purpose-designed, large format digital mapping cameras, they are unfortunately very

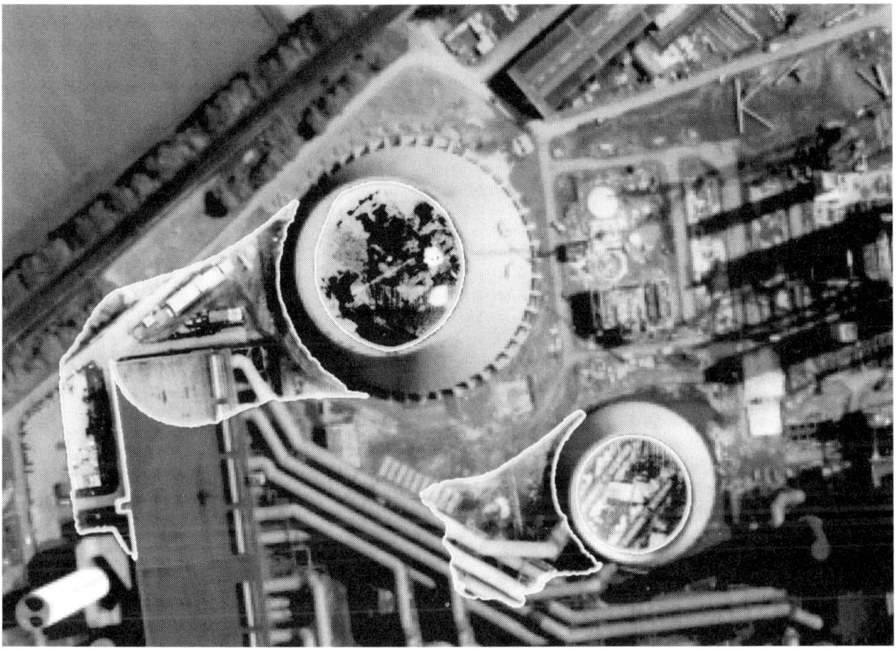

Facing: **Figure 5.24b** *Z/I DMC-2001 image with further processing to reveal shadow detail. Courtesy Dr. Alex Hinz, Z/I Germany.*

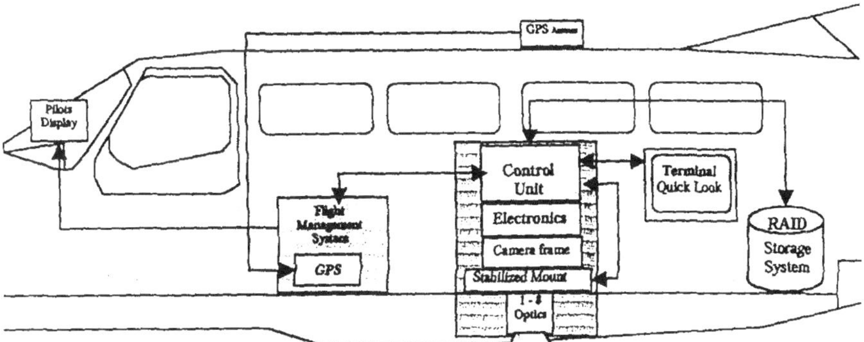

Figure 5.25 *Z/I DMC-2001 camera and survey controls airborne configuration. Courtesy: Dr. Alex Hinz, Z/I Germany.*

Table. 5.5 Preliminary DMC technical specifications.

	DMC model			
	14k Pan plus Multispectral	*7k Single Pan*	*7k Pan & Colour*	*3k Multispectral*
FoV	74° x 44°	39° x 22°	39° x 42°	72° x 50°
Storage Capacity	840 Gb 3000 images	280 Gb 5000 images	560 Gb 3700 images	280 Gb 5800 images
GSD (1:10,000)	12cm	12cm	12cm	12cm
Framing rate	2sec/image	2sec/image	2sec/image	2sec/image
Radiometric resolution	12 bits	12 bits	12 bits	12 bits
Weight without MSS	< 80 kg	< 50 kg	< 65 kg	< 50 kg
Pixel array	13k × 8k (Pan) 3k × 2k (Colour) (RGB & NIR)	7k × 4k (Pan)	7k × 7.5k (Pan) 3k × 2k (Colour) (RGB only)	36 × 2k RGB & NIR
Lens system	Pan: 4 lenses (120mm *f*/4) Colour:4 lens (25mm *f*/4)	Pan: 1 lens (120mm *f*/4)	Pan: 2 lenses (120mm *f*/4) Colour:3 Lens (25mm *f*/4)	Colour: 4 lenses. (25mm *f*/4)

expensive! They are expensive to purchase and to operate in terms of the required aerial platform and installation, plus the specialist expertise essential for the post- processing of their imagery. At the time of writing the latter two cameras are barely out of their prototype stage, and one might reasonably expect numerous development changes in future years as clients become more aware and convinced of their advantages.

As mentioned previously, up to now (with the exception of MEIS II) small format digital cameras have been the main source of airborne digital imagery, and despite their small area coverage, have encouraged the use of airborne digital cameras during the last decade. In the meantime, CCD technology has been constantly improved and in parallel with these developments a number of people in the mapping and remote sensing community have exploited these small-format digital cameras to create a keen interest and acceptance of their use.

Obviously the next step was the development of a larger CCD format than that provided by, say, the DCS-460 and 760 cameras. And although the 18 × 28mm format of these cameras is adequate for many applications (see Chapter 13), a 60mm square format would be more suitable, particularly since this format is well established for military reconnaissance and remote sensing.

Geotechnologies medium format digital mapping camera (MF-DMC)

The MF-DMC was born out of prior experience with the Kodak DCS series of digital cameras (Graham and Mills, 1994; Koh, 1996; Mills *et al.*, 1996). From a number of research and commercial projects, including airborne digital missions in the UK and abroad, the staff at Geotechnologies (Bath Spa University College) looked at the possibility of making their own medium format digital camera designed specifically for aerial survey and remote sensing.

The basic concept was to provide a digital camera to include the following:

1. The host camera will be medium format with 60mm square image dimensions.
2. The host camera must be a quality instrument with a suitable range of lenses, some of which being designated as metric lenses, all of which will be calibrated.
3. Two CCD options should be available:
   (a) Dicomed (silicon) 16MPx chip providing conventional colour and colour infrared (CIR) giving an imaging area 57 mm square with 15 μm pixels.
   (b) Kodak Pro-Back (ITO) chip (with or without NIR kit) giving an imaging area 37 mm square with 9 μm pixels.
4. The host camera must be capable of electrical/electronic remote operation.
5. The camera shutter must be of the inter-lens type, suitable for metric work.
6. All MF-DMCs will employ the IEEE-1394 (Firewire) interface for speedy downloading of each digital image (c. 6–8 s).

Taking all of the above parameters into consideration, the final choice for a host camera was from the well known 70mm format Hasselblad series. Not only do these cameras have a good reputation in the field of photogrammetry, but they also host a highly suitable range of lenses, can be electrically driven and some can be fitted with a large (16MPx) digital sensor at the focal plane. A good number of Hasselblad versions are available and one in particular, the Hasselblad 555ELD has been selected as suitable for digital aerial photography.

4k x 4k (16MPx) CCD sensors

Obviously we can only consider those CCD sensors that are available at the time of writing, but it is obvious that a 4k × 4k (16MPx) square format CCD chip is going to be more useful for aerial photography than a 3k × 2k (M-6) chip, as fitted to the DCS-460 and 760 cameras. Two 4k × 4k chips are currently available and both of them are suitable for the medium format digital mapping cameras.

MF-DMC(1)

Hasselblad 555ELD (SLR) camera fitted with the Dicomed 4096 × 4096 Pixel (16MPx) area-array silicon CCD chip. The chip size is 63.16mm square with 15.4 μm pixels and an associated ISO rating of 100. This is a colour and CIR image sensor with a SCSI II interface. The system is tethered to a Macintosh computer for data storage and processing. A Firewire module to further enhance the data transfer is planned.

MF-DMC(2)

Hasselblad 555ELD (SLR) camera fitted with the Kodak *DCS* Pro-Back 4072 × 4072 Pixel (16MPx) area-array indium-tin oxide (ITO) CCD chip. The chip size is 36.65 mm square with 9 μm pixels and an associated ISO rating of 100. This is a colour image sensor with a NIR kit option for CIR imagery and has a Firewire interface tethered to either a Macintosh G3 or G4 computer. In its portable (in-flight) mode, the MF-DMC(2) can be operated with or without a tethered G4 computer. In its most convenient configuration the camera is simply connected to the Quantum (QB2) battery via its MDC3 cable and images are stored in two 1 Gb compact flash (CF+) cards held in the ProBack body. Alternatively, the computer can be added to the same configuration with images downloaded by Firewire.

Geotechnologies MF-DMC(1) colour and CIR DMC

The MF-DMC(1) is hosted by the Hasselblad 555ELD camera fitted with the Dicomed 16MPx chip. The Dicomed 4096 × 4096 pixel array, with 15.4 μm square pixels, was selected for the MF-DMC(1) since it provides an image area of 57.15 mm square and has the advantage of being a silicon CCD with unrestricted near infrared (NIR) sensitivity.

The 16MPx array doped with an RGB Bayer pattern (see Fig. 4.2) enables the the MF-DMC(1) to be used for normal colour with a 500BP300 (VIS) filter placed in front of the lens. This filter has a dominant pass wavelength of 500nm, with side-bands of 150nm on each side (see Figs. 5.5 and 5.6). Alternatively, when employed in its near infrared (CIR) mode the VIS filter is replaced with a 650BP300 (minus blue) filter to provide a CIR image (Figs 5.7 and 5.8).

It is interesting to note the Dicomed sensor has 15.4 μm square pixels, whereas the usual Kodak chips (silicon or ITO) have pixel sizes of 9 μm. Similarly, the Fuji FinePix S1 Pro and other Fuji models employing 'Super CCD' technology (such as the 2.4MPx, FinePix 4700) have larger (octagonal) pixel diameters in the region of 15 μm! In the classical sense a smaller pixel size favours spatial resolution of course, but unlike film-based imagers, digital systems employ such things as interpolation, CFA and, in Fuji's case, a honeycomb arrangement designed to improve resolution.

Obviously larger pixels must offer certain advantages, as listed below:

1. Quantum efficiency (photon-to-electron conversion) is higher since signal response is directly proportional to pixel area.
2. Signal-to-noise (S/N) ratio is higher as pixel area increases.
3. Less illumination is required to achieve a desired S/N level, allowing the image to appear less grainy.
4. Increased dynamic range. The larger the pixel area, the larger the charge capacity, and the higher the signal level. A pixel is saturated when further increases in illumination do not create a corresponding increase in signal voltage. Consequently, larger pixels improve dynamic range because they hold more charge, so brighter objects do not saturate (and overflow) the pixel.
5. The larger (15.4 μm square) pixel increases the overall image sensor area when compared to the smaller (9 μm square) pixel. As a consequence, for the same

16MPx array, the Dicomed has a sensor size of 57.15 mm compared to 36.65 mm for the Pro-Back.

The decision which MF-DMC model to buy may centre on cost, since the Dicomed version (MF-DMC(1)) is roughly 50% more expensive than the Pro-Back (MF-DMC(2)) model. But on technical grounds the MF-DMC(1) offers certain advantages, the main one being its increased ground footprint, due to the 57.15 mm image size, which in turn allows for much better base/height ratios for a given photo-scale. Other advantages include the larger dynamic range available from the 15.15 μm pixels . A larger than normal dynamic range may be essential when imaging alpine terrain for example, where dark pine forests under mountainous shadow are contiguous with sunlit snow fields.

On the other hand, the MF-DMC(2) offers greater portability through its Quantum QB2 power pack, as well as the use of CF+ Type II microdrives for data storage. These features could be a deciding factor where aircraft cabin space is limited, and the need to carry a dc/ac inverter to power the system (as with the Dicomed) can be avoided. Other advantages with the Pro-Back are the possibility of slightly better spatial resolution due to the 9 μm pixels (but this may be at the cost of a lower S/N ratio although there is no evidence of this in practice) and an image-display LCD, incorporating a menu for histogram image control as well as an intervalometer menu.

The 555ELD is an SLR camera fitted with an electric motor-drive (for cocking the shutter) and can be supplied with a useful range of Zeiss lenses according to client specifications. The 555ELD is designed for use with a digital-back (the D designation standing for Databus) and connections on the camera's magazine mount interface directly with corresponding connections on the digital-back. A special release port on the camera front can be used to activate the digital-back. Using the optional infrared-release unit and infrared-remote-control, the camera can be operated without cables from distances up to 10 meters.

The most useful range of lenses for aerial photography are: (i) the Zeiss Planar *f*3.5/100mm with a field-of-view (FoV) of 42°/30° (diagonal / horizontal); (ii) the standard Planar *f*2.8/80mm with a 52°/38° FoV, (iii) the wide-angle Distagon *f*4 / 40mm lens with a FoV of 88°/67° and (iv) the *f*3.5/30mm wide-angle Distagon (FoV: 108°/83°) which is fitted with interchangeable inter-lens filters (spectral and anti-$\cos^4\theta$) to reduce image illumination 'fall-off'. All of these lenses are fitted with an inter-lens Compur shutter (maximum speed 1/500 second), and all lenses are calibrated for photogrammetry by Geotechnologies.

Depending on various mission parameters, the 80mm Planar lens may be the best choice for mapping purposes since it is noted for its flatness of field, and although the 40mm and 30mm lenses are entirely suitable regards mapping accuracy, they are retrofocus types, where the rear nodal plane (from which the focal length is measured) is behind the rear lens element, in order to provide room for the SLR mirror. Neverthless, distortion is particularly well controlled in both of the Distagon wide-angle lenses and (as with all lenses) they work best when the aperture is set one stop down from maximum, i.e, *f*5.6 for both of these W/A lenses.

Image capture with the Dicomed 4k × 4k chip is 17Mb, which is interpolated (Bayer pattern) to 48Mb in RGB colour. Compared to the DCS-460 the MF-DMC(1) has over seven times the image area of the Kodak camera and, with its square format, represent a more efficient system for aerial photography – particularly when it comes to survey flight planning and practice. Figure 5.26 compares two of the Kodak small-format cameras with the MF-DMC, where we have: (a) Kodak DCS-420 CIR (9 × 14mm), (b) Kodak DCS-460 CIR (18 × 28mm) and (c) the MF-DMC(1) with its 60mm square format.

Figure 5.27 shows the CCD sensors for the DCS-420 CIR and MF-DMC and the relative sizes of the two chips, and the magazine-like clip-on back of the MF-DMC (1).

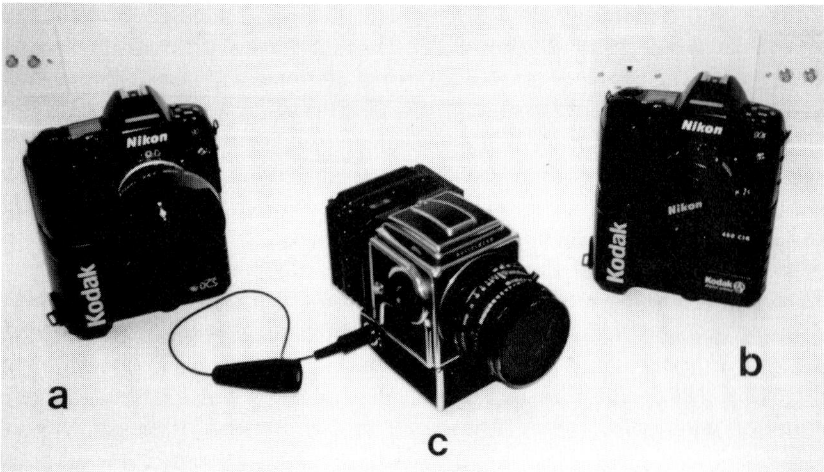

Figure 5.26 *Small and medium format digital cameras. (a) Kodak DCS-420 CIR. (b) Kodak DCS-460 CIR. (c) Geotechnologies MF-DMC (Hasselblad conversion).*

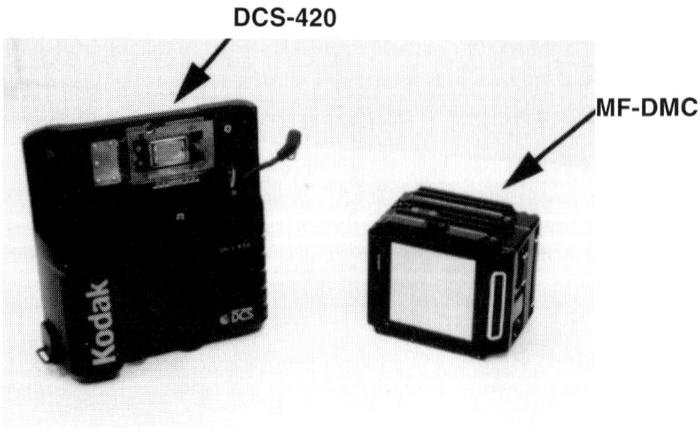

Figure 5.27 *Comparison of CCD digital camera sensors.*

In operational terms, flying at 2000 ft amgl (610m), the 80 mm (standard) lens will cover its 57mm square format at a photoscale of 1:7625 and cover a ground area (S^2) of 434m × 434m, or 188,356 m^2 (18.835 hectares) while, at the same height, the 30mm Distagon will provide a photoscale of 1:20,300 and cover a ground area of 1159m × 1159m (134 Ha). Nevertheless this lens is not recommended for accurate photogrammetry. The main advantage of the wide-angle lens is to enable surveys to be flown under low cloud cover, not only in northern europe where, in the UK for example, much of the summer cloud is just above 3000 ft, but in many tropical zones where mountainous areas and constant cloud cover often lower operational ceilings to 2000 ft or less.

An additional advantage with the 30mm lens is the increased base/height ratio (see Chapter 7) where, for 60% forward overlap and at the same flying height, the 30mm lens gives a *b/h* ratio of 0.76, which is nearly three times that provided by the 80mm lens. This may be of major importance where tight contours are to be plotted, but on the other hand, the 80 mm lens will always offer better image resolution and a more even field of image illuminance – a quality consideration that could take priority where fine detail and mosaics are required.

The MF-DMC(1) is shown in Fig.5.28 in company with the complete airborne survey kit. From left-to-right we have the Apple-Mac Power Book G4 laptop, then the modified Haselblad 555ELD complete with Dicomed back and 40 mm lens (MF-DMC1) and on the right, for precise navigation (accuracy in the order of 0.75 m) a

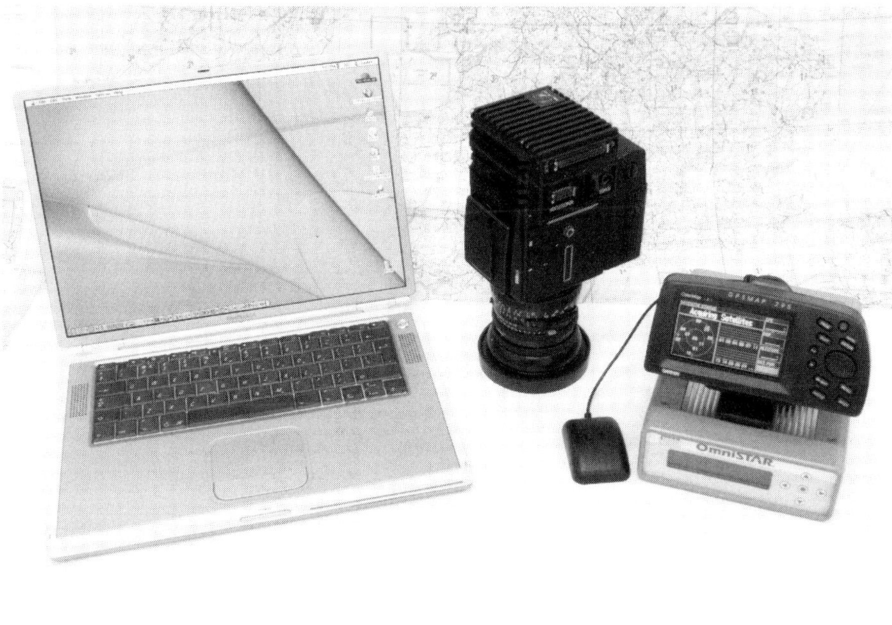

Figure 5.28 *MF-DMC(1) digital air camera complete with 40mm lens and Dicomed 16MPx sensor, on the left is the Apple-Mac Power Book G4 laptop and (right) a Garmin GPS Map 295 receiver on top of the OmniSTAR 3000LR 12 channel dGPS unit.*

Garmin GPS Map 295 sat on top of an OmniSTAR 3000LR 12 channel, real time dGPS system (the aircraft and ground antenna are not shown here). OmniSTAR data is logged onto the on-board laptap in terms of latitude and longitude for each photo-centre.

The MF-DMC(2) with the Pro-Back sensor is similar in appearance to the MF-DMC(1), and operates with similar equipment to that shown in Fig. 5.28. Hasselblad 555ELD camera lenses are connected to the Pro-back via a shutter sync cord so that the Pro-Back knows when the lens shutter opens and closes. Images captured using the DCS Pro-Back are saved in a proprietary format with a .DCR extension. With the 30mm lens at 2000 ft, the DMC(2) will cover a ground area of 752m square (56.5 Ha) and provide a *b*/*h* ratio of 0.49.

Aircraft power supply for the MF-DMC systems

Light and medium sized aircraft normally have a dc power supply of 28 volts (although there are still aircraft flying with 12–14 volt supply), and the primary source is via an alternator powered by a running engine. The alternator produces alternating current (ac) which is converted into direct current by diodes incorporated in the alternator to act as rectifiers. Output from the alternator is controlled by a voltage regulator and an overvoltage sensor protects the system from possible damage.

For conventional survey cameras, electrical power requirements are matched to the normal 28V dc aircraft supply, although this often has to be supplemented with special electrical systems where power requirements exceed the norm. However, for many small and medium format cameras, they can be operated perfectly well by their own battery supply, as can GPS navigation units and intervalometers.

Both of the airborne MF-DMC cameras can be tethered to a Macintosh computer via a Firewire interface. Also, both systems are ideally operated from their own battery power source (sufficient for the average survey duration). Alternatively a 240

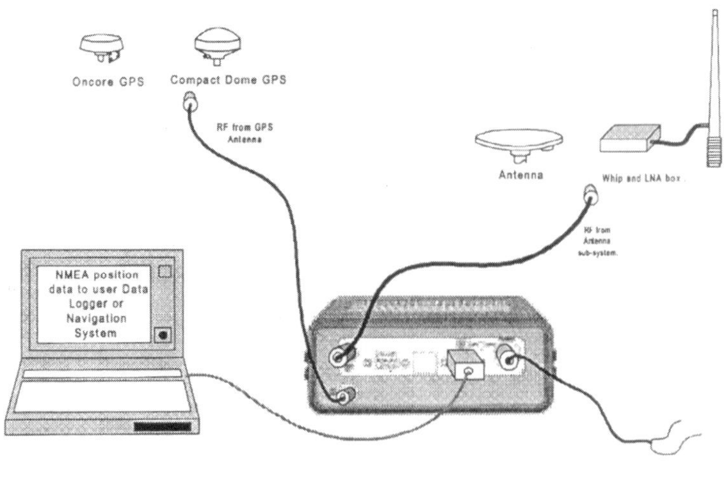

Figure 5.29 *OmniStar 3000 LR system.*

volts ac power supply can be provided by a suitable 28V (dc) to 240V (ac) invertor.

Figure 5.29 shows the OmniStar 3000 LR12VBS system operating in VBS mode, where the GPS engine is configured to output NMEA format position and data telegrams. The GPS position and quality information can be viewed on the VBS menu display, where the differential mode can be ascertained by the state of the Q value.

With its 16MPx sensor, the MF-DMC image is superb and equally matched by the Apple-Mac LCD screen quality. Figure 5.30 (see colour section) shows two MF-DMC(1) images exposed at 1/500 at *f*/4 with an 80 mm Planar lens. The top image is in natural colour and the lower image in RGB infrared colour. In addition the screen can accommodate various menus and data.

Geotechnologies MF-DMC(2) Colour and (optional) CIR DMC

Hosted by the same camera as the MF-DMC(1), and with the same range of lenses, the MF-DMC(2) differs mainly in its choice of sensor: the Kodak Pro-Back with ITO (indium-tin-oxide) chip. This 36.65 mm square sensor is the Kodak KAF-16801CE with a 4072 × 4072 pixel array (16MPx) and 9 μm square pixels. Somewhat less expensive than the MF-DMC(1) the MF-DMC(2) normally operates in conventional colour only. However, an infrared option is available with the purchase of an infrared conversion kit (a local modification can also be applied, see Chapter 12) The 16MPx sensor has a file size of 48Mb (R, G, B) and operates with an exposure rating of ISO 100.

As mentioned, the MF-DMC(2) can be flown either in a computer-tethered QB2 battery configuration, where the stored images are directly downloaded to Kodak's Camera Manager software via the 400Mbps IEEE 1394 (Firewire) or, for improved mobility, simply linked to the QB2 battery with images stored in CF cards (CF+ microdrives) which can be downloaded after the aircraft has landed. From airborne trials, we find that a 1 Gb card can store up to 60 typical air survey images at a rate of about one frame per 8 seconds. With a suitable PC card adapter, the CF cards can then be downloaded into the computer via a PCMCIA Type II slot. Various CF+ microdrives with good shock resistance are available, ranging from 340Mb through 512Mb to 1Gb units. The Pro-Back is also fitted with a removable infrared blocking filter (to improve colour quality), but this can easily be removed, and with a Wratten 12 or 15 yellow filter placed over the lens, the blue channel can be sampled in the software to provide a good (monochrome) near-infrared record (see Chapter 12).

The KAG-16801CE is a high quality CCD sensor with 2-phase register clocking. Each pixel on the 4072 square pixel chip contains anti-blooming protection by means of a lateral overflow drain, thereby preventing image corruption due to high levels of illuminance. This ITO sensor has a high output sensitivity of 12 μV/e and a low dark current of 10pA/cm^2 at 25°C, its charge transfer efficiency (CTE) is as high as 99.999% and the sensor has a typical dynamic range (Eq. 3.12) of 71dB.

MF-DMC modification of off-the-shelf cameras

Since early 2001 a number of manufacturers have combined their interests to provide 4MPx and 16MPx digital cameras designed for the commercial, studio and industrial photographer. Most professional photographers are familiar with medium format cameras and now that these larger digital chips are available they are an attractive option to film, particularly since most photographers now scan their films.

Two new digital cameras by the Foveon company are of great interest since these incorporate three CMOS chips on a colour separation prism, one is a 2k × 2k CMOS camera called the DFinity, and the other is the Foveon II with 4k × 4k CMOS chips. As mentioned in Chapter 3, CMOS sensors show a lot of promise for the future of digital cameras, and we can expect the Foveon products described here to be exciting examples of future CMOS developments.

Foveon II CMOS digital camera

Foveon Inc, a Silicon Valley based producer of image sensors, has announced its next generation of professional digital cameras and the Foveon II is expected to retail at $23,900. The complementary metal oxide semicon ductor (CMOS) has long been forecast as the the economic future for digital cameras, and the Foveon II must be considered as the cutting edge of today's digital camera technology since it also employs a colour separation prism onto which three CMOS 4k × 4k sensors are faced. In this fashion the tri-colour sensors create three full planes (RGB) of colour information integrated into a single exposure, instead of the usual CFA interpolation process employed in most CCD digital cameras where the final colour image is made up of one third real and two-thirds interpolated pixels (as with a typical Bayer filter mosaic). With the Foveon system we not only get a finer colour image, but without the need for an interpolation algorithm (to fill-in missing colour values).

The Foveon sensor is based on a proprietary 0.18 μm analog CMOS fabrication process developed in collaboration with the National Semiconductor Corporation and incorporates a square array of 4096 pixels in a 22 mm × 22 mm chip (5.4 μm pixels) with an estimated ISO speed of 100. And when connected to a Firewire interface exposures can be repeated at 2 second intervals.

Foveon II electronic shutter

An important feature of the Foveon II is its fully electronic shutter providing exposure times up to 1/8000 second, and although shutter speeds higher than 1/1000 second are unlikely to be used for aerial survey work (particularly since the sensor is limited to ISO 100) there is still the advantageous absence of moving parts prone to low temperature failure. With mechanical shutters set at anything from 1/200 to 1/500 second, the charge carrying electrons are allowed to drain away from the pixels until the last fraction of the exposure period, they are then integrated for that preset time and read out. A fully electronic shutter is a welcome improvement over mechanical types since the exposure of 16.8 million pixels is terminated at precisely the same moment without lag between rows, columns or subset regions of the imager.

Hasselblad/Foveon DFinity CMOS digital camera

The Hasselblad/Foveon *DFinity* is a 2k × 2k (4MPx) digital camera employing the same type of colour separation prism as the Foveon II, where by placing CMOS sensors on each of the three prism exit faces, the colour of each point in the scene is sampled by three different colour chips, one red, one green and one blue. The three-chip system results in a cleaner system which, without the need for interpolation, provides an image that can be enlarged much more (and without aliasing) than that from a single chip camera. Again, there are no reasons why this 4MPx camera should not be used for aerial work, but at only one quarter the image size of the Foveon II, it is hardly likely to compete with other off-the-shelf digital cameras.

Interior orientation of digital cameras

For the photogrammetrist an important consideration is the interior orientation of a metric camera. That is to say, the lens focal length must be more than just nominal, it must be known with great accuracy and its value shown in the calibration report (a typical example is shown in CD Table 12.6). In addition, the image centre (IC) must be accurately defined, and for film cameras this is accomplished by putting at least four fiducial marks at the centre of each edge of the image format. These fiducials are then recorded on each image frame within the film and the IC can be found simply by intersecting the paths from opposite fiducial marks.

Once the IC is known then the calibrated focal length can be referred to the photogrammetric principal point (PP) which, for a perfect camera-lens system would be the image centre, but in practice the PP is always offset a few niicrons from the IC.

The lack of fiducial marks in digital cameras seems to have suggested to some that these cameras are unsuitable for photogrammetry. Yet nothing could be further from the truth! Indeed, fiducials are totally unnecessary with digital sensors since the number of pixels in each array is known to perfection, and by intersecting the corners of the CCD array the CI can be found. Camera calibration is then found by recording a projected target with the digital camera (from a group of known locations) and once the target images have been entered into suitable computer software an accurate calibration can be found (see CD Table 12.6).

Modern solid-state technology employs MEMS (micro electro mechanical systems) to fabricate CCD and CMOS sensors by etching away plastic in layers after exposure to synchrotron radiation through a mask. Because the device masks are so small, synchrotron radiation (of X-ray wavelength) has to be used since wavelengths of light are too large for accurate fabrication of these microscopic devices. The masks form a negative image of the parts of the device to be formed, and once exposed the plastic is etched away from those areas exposed by the synchrotron radiation leaving the MEMS device formed from the plastic. The plastic is then coated with metal to create the final solid state device, or is used as a master to create further MEMS of the same type. In such a way CCD and CMOS sensors are built with great accuracy and precision.

With film however, fiducials are necessary due to non-uniform distortions within the emulsion, and while the magnitude and direction of these distortions can never be known with any certainty, the fiducials at least provide a measure of acceptable accuracy, Such distortions are known to be in the region of 3 μm (average) and can be as high as 8 μm with normal processing (*Manual of Photogrammetry* 4th Edition) and must be expected for a medium such as gelatin, which swells and contracts through processing.

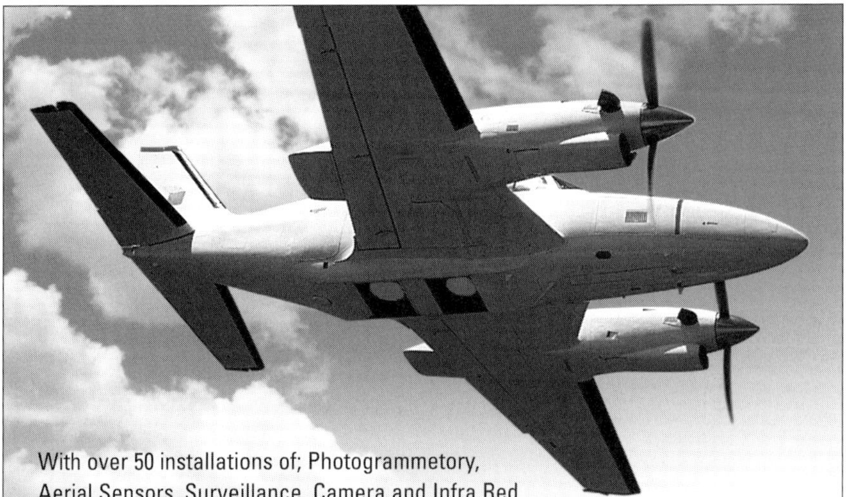

6 Survey aircraft, camera mounts and intervalometers

Survey aircraft

Provided there is suitable provision for the type of air camera employed, almost any type of aircraft can and has been used for the purpose of aerial survey. In this respect we can always say that a twin-engined, pressurised aircraft with a legally modified camera hole in its belly is ideal. If a 23cm mapping (film) camera is being used, or the LH-ADS40, or Z/I -DMC, then such an aircraft would be the first choice in platform since the camera, mounting and control units are large and heavy and the aircraft might be required to fly at, say, 35,000 ft. But not all survey missions require such expensive platforms, and for medium altitude operations (8000–12,000 ft) a single-engined aircraft could be perfectly adequate, just as a light aircraft or helicopter would prove useful for small format aerial photography (SFAP). By SFAP we include all types of camera up to 70mm format (Graham *et al.*, 1996) and this expression also covers digital cameras up to that size.

Survey requirements

Selecting the most suitable aircraft for all types of mapping and remote sensing is like asking " how long is a piece of string?" In general, the large air survey firms mainly use light-to-medium twin-engined aircraft. These may be piston, turbo-prop or even jet, but they will usually be selected for economic and logistic reasons satisfying all or most of the considerations shown in Table 6.1.

Each topic listed Table 6.1 is best considered when we investigate the type of aircraft involved, all mission requirements and the type of camera employed.

Table 6.1 *Survey aircraft: considerations and choices*

Range and duration
Aircraft ground speed
Maximum altitude
Stability
Certified camera installation (STC modifications)
Economic factors

Range and duration

The aircraft's range and duration can be important for different reasons. Firstly, when operating in some countries it may only be possible to reach certain areas from distant airfields. Desert areas, remote islands, tundra and forest regions particularly apply. Secondly, even when operating within a reasonable distance of base, the task may require a lengthy duration over the mapping area. Tidal mapping, remote sensing and 'double surveys' (where different films, or lenses are employed over the same area) are typical cases that require extra airborne duration.

Aircraft ground speed

An aircraft may be ideal in every respect, but when compared to other types, may be rather slow. This may not be important while engaged in photography, but it becomes a problem when transit time to the mapping area is excessive. Air survey missions must be executed during good weather. Unduly slow transit flights can often miss a good 'weather window' at the target area, and possibly the opportunity to fly to another area where weather conditions are better. There are not many clear (survey) days in the year, and flight crews can easily be waiting weeks for a clear spell over a certain area, so mobility is an economic factor in the survey game.

However high speed is not always desirable in a survey aircraft, indeed there are certain conditions where the reverse is true! We have mentioned previously the problem of lengthy download periods with digital cameras such as the DCS-460, where periods of 8 seconds or more inhibit stereo-cover at a large photo-scale when successive photographs (at 60% forward overlap) require photo-cycles shorter than the download period (see Chapter 7). Under these circumstances it may be necessary to employ aircraft that can safely fly at around 50–60 knots ground speed. Fortunately there are several light aircraft that can do this, as can helicopters.

Maximum altitude

As more fully explained in Chapter 7, the higher an aircraft flies over the ground the smaller the scale and greater the ground coverage. So, if an operator has a camera with a 15cm (6 inch) lens (the 'standard lens' for an analogue camera) and a client wants cover at, say, 1:32,000, then survey flight would be at 15,000 ft amgl. But if the client wanted a scale of 1:64,000, the operator would now need a pressurised aircraft with a service ceiling of at least 34,000 ft. The alternative would be to use a wider angle lens, but this would not be an ideal option in terms of image quality, and would most likely be turned down by the client. As a consequence, most of the big survey firms have aircraft capable of flying at over 30,000 ft, particularly for large area mapping worldwide.

Stability

In general, the larger the aircraft the greater the stability for survey flight, particularly where rough and turbulent weather is common. For areas where flying conditions are both difficult and very turbulent a heavy twin-engined machine is often selected. A typical example is survey flying in Sarawak (Malaysia), where cloud cover forces survey flight down to a few thousand feet and extreme turbulence is common. As a consequence a heavy twin feederliner/freighter, the Short 360 Skyvan, is used because its stability and endurance make it an excellent platform in such conditions.

Survey flight is usually undertaken in calm, cloud-free conditions, and a small single-engined aircraft can usually be flown "straight and level" without difficulty. But if flight-lines are long, or the terrain difficult to follow, then keeping the aircraft straight and level becomes tiring for the pilot if he/she has to constantly feed control inputs throughout the mission. For small format digital-camera surveys, a single-engined light aircraft is usually adequate and, unless the aircraft has poor stability in terms of flying a straight line, the pilot should be able to keep a constant altitude with wings level for lengthy flight-lines.

Certified camera installation

In most countries survey modifications to an aircraft must be undertaken by qualified engineers to comply with air safety regulations. Even for small modifications, such as putting a hole in the bottom of a single-skinned aircraft, it can be costly. For aircraft needing a survey modification a supplemental type certificate (STC) is required. This certificate, issued by the appropriate aviation authority, contains the necessary technical specifications for modifying the aircraft type. Once raised, and paid for, it then becomes necessary for all other owners of the type to purchase the STC from the original owner before modifications can be made. Both the FAA and CAA (Civil Aviation Authority of the UK) provide stringent rules regarding aircraft modifications and survey operators must be aware of them.

Economic factors

Naturally there is no point in operating an expensive aircraft if a more economic type can do the same task. Although there are many types to choose from, there are only a few complete with survey modifications. Bearing in mind the essential considerations of Table.6.1, we must also remember that a digital air camera, navigation system and avionics are also expensive and a cheaper choice of platform could be a false economy. There are many options, and it may be prudent to purchase a second-hand aircraft already fitted with a camera-hole but needing a pair of new engines, than to purchase a new machine that has to be modified.

Aircraft servicing, crew requirements, fuel, hangerage and landing fees, all have to be considered in making the final choice. Fuel is a particularly important feature since aviation gasoline (Avgas) is more expensive and often difficult (or impossible) to get in some parts of the world. As a consequence the turboprop survey aircraft has a definite advantage since Avtur is available world wide (airliners use it) and is also cheaper.

A selection of survey aircraft

Twin-engined aircraft

A well known and reliable aircraft for survey is the Piper Navajo Chieftain (PA-31) (Fig. 6.1). The Chieftain, powered by two turbo-charged piston engines is a Commut-

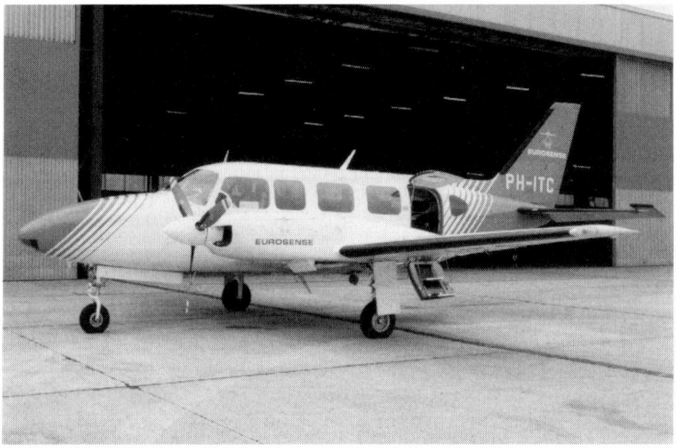

Figure 6.1 *The PA-31 Piper Navajo Chieftain, popular survey adapted aircraft.*

er Aircraft with a good speed (210 kts), range (950 nm) and duration. For turbocharging, the engine exhaust gases are used to drive a turbine which, in turn, forces high pressure air into the air-intakes. Tubocharged engines (Avgas) thus provide for improved climb performance, better performance from high altitude airstrips and hot climates, and most of all give a higher service ceiling. The PA-31 is easily fitted with two large format air cameras, and although it has a useful service ceiling of 24,000 ft, an aircraft such as the Beechcraft (Raytheon) King Air may be required for missions flown at 30,000 ft plus.

What might be considered as top of the range for a survey aircraft is the Beech King Air 350 (Fig. 6.2). This Commuter-liner is certainly expensive (c. $4.5M), but has

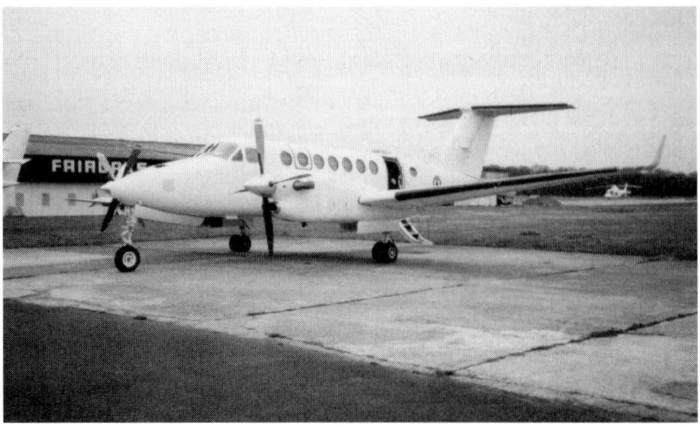

Figure 6.2 *Beech (Raytheon) KingAir 350, long range air survey aircraft modified with two camera holes. Survey ceiling 35,000 ft (pressurised).*

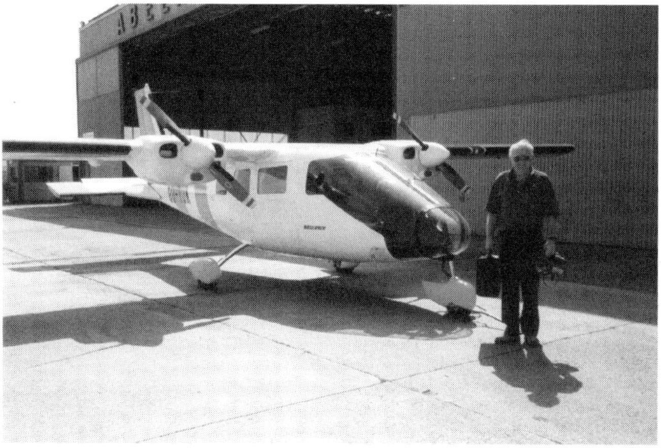

Figure 6.3 *Partenavia Observer – a sleek survey aircraft. The Partenavia P68B is similar but without the glazed nose.*

the advantage of satisfying all of the considerations shown in Table.6.1. With a maximum speed of 314 kts, and normal cruise of 303 kts, the King Air 350 has a maximum range of 1850 nm (with 45 minutes reserve fuel) and a service ceiling of 35,000 ft. With a two-camera configuration, turboprop engines (Avtur) and excellent stability the King Air is highly suitable for lengthy survey flight operations, world wide. Other Beech turboprops include the King Air models 90, and B200, both with excellent records in aerial survey.

The Partenavia Observer most clearly resembles a survey aircraft. It has a fully glazed nose, high wing and sleek fuselage and is an ideal aircraft for medium type surveys (Fig. 6.3). The Partenavia is available in a number of versions, including the P68B (sans glazed nose), which the authors often use. The power plants are piston engines and the aircraft has a maximum cruise of 165 kts.

The Cessna 337G (Super Skymaster) is a very useful survey aircraft and is operated in this capacity by at least two survey firms in the UK. Employing two piston engines in centre-line thrust (push-pull) the Skymaster has a max-cruise of 205 kts and can easily accommodate most survey cameras.

One of the popular platforms for aerial survey is the Britten-Norman Islander. With a max-cruise of only 130 kts, a range of 750 nm and a service ceiling of 16,000 ft the Islander is limited for some survey applications, but it continues to serve well for island work and small surveys, particularly where rough field operations are necessary.

Still going strong in the survey scene is the twin-engined Piper Aztec. With a max-cruise of 180 kts, this light business aircraft can be fitted with turbocharged engines and has a proven record in aerial survey world wide.

Single-engined aircraft

Among the single-engined aircraft adopted for aerial survey, the Cessna 206 in all its

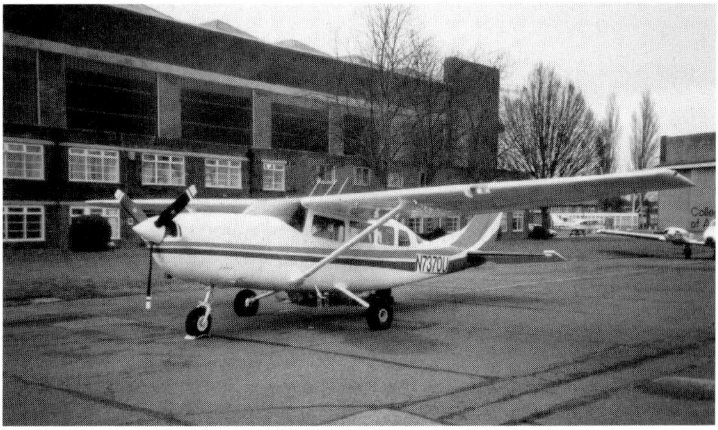

Figure 6.4 *Cessna 206 A single-engined aircraft with an excellent record as an air survey platform.*

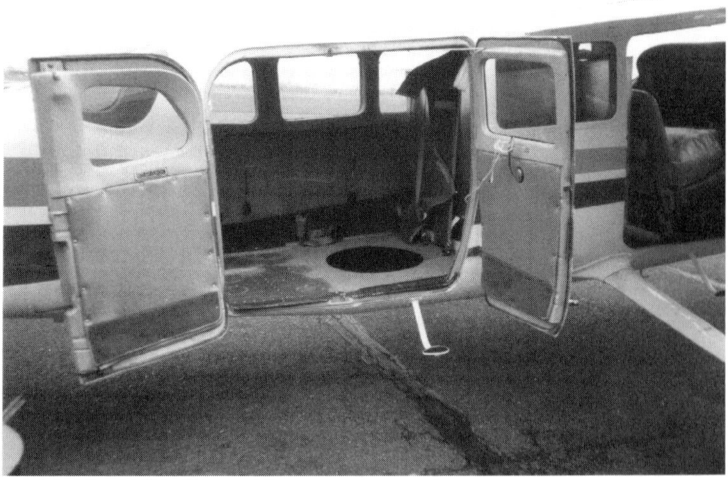

Figure 6.5 *Cabin interior of Cessna 206.*

variants has an excellent record. As a six or seven-seat light aircraft (Fig.6.4) it has sufficient room to fit the largest air camera, complete with mounting and control console (Fig.6.5), and can offer a cruise speed of 148 kts.

Similar to the Cessna 206 but smaller, are the Cessna 180 and 182. With a capacity for four passengers these machines have the same cruise speed as the 206 and are capable of carrying a conventional mapping camera for medium range surveys.

Although an excellent four-seater, the Cessna 172 is too small for carrying a large mapping camera, nevertheless it is extremely useful for SFAP and can be equipped with a modified r/h door (see Fig. 6.6) to carry a medium format camera. The 172 is the best selling light aircraft ever built since 1950. It has many variations but they are all easy to fly and, on average, at 75% power have a cruise of 120 kts, and a range of 440nm at 8000 ft (with 43 minutes reserve). The quoted service ceiling is 13,000 ft. The Cessna 172 also has a good slow-speed performance, where it is possible to fly (with flaps down) at about 52 knots indicated air speed (IAS).

Whereas the Geotechnologies MF-DMC system may be the first of its kind, it is safe to predict that it will not be the last! Indeed, there is sufficient experience with small format digital cameras to support the MF concept, and we can expect this type of airborne digital camera to be a mapping standard in future years. That said, it opens up an entirely new range of suitable platforms for aerial survey, including small light aeroplanes (SLAs) and kit built light aircraft.

Kit-built light aircraft

There are numerous kit-built aircraft that can be used for aerial survey work and their popularity is ever increasing, mainly due to the use of composite materials and economy of manufacture. We shall consider one such aircraft here, mainly because it has excellent characteristics for aerial survey and because the authors have personal flying experience with Aero Designs' Pulsar.

The Pulsar is a two seater and typical of modern light aircraft design. Mostly comprised of pre-moulded sandwich composite materials, the Pulsar combines strength with lightness and employs aluminium plates for hard-points. With side-by-side seating it is comfortable to fly and is a little wider at the shoulders than a Cessna 152 (Fig.6.7). Powered by a 66 HP Rotax 582, the Pulsar has a 75% power cruise of 113 kts, and a safe slow speed cruise in the region of 50 kts (IAS). The Pulsar XP is an 80 HP version powered by a Rotax 912 (4-stroke liquid cooled) engine, and has similar characteristics but with slightly higher speeds. For both models, the service ceiling is 15,000 ft and the range is 434nm.

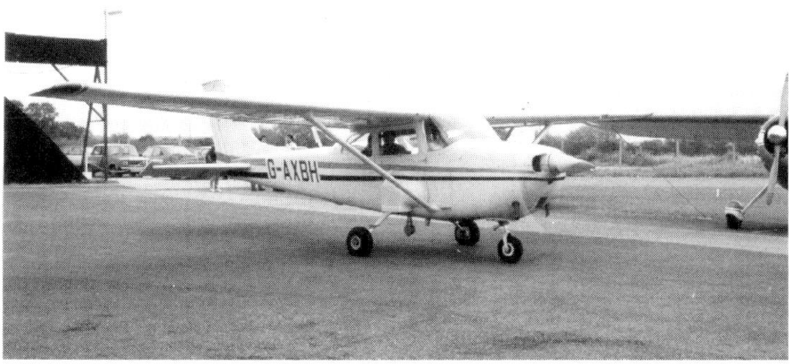

Figure 6.6 *Cessna 172, an ideal aircraft for small and medium-format digital air cameras.*

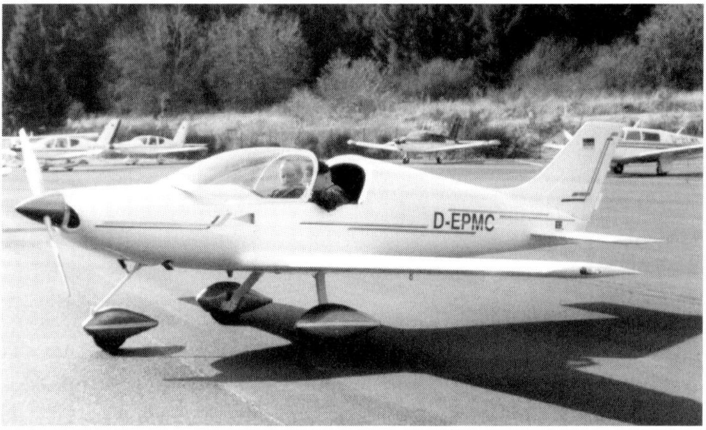

Figure 6.7 *The Pulsar XP kit-built aircraft, a highly suitable platform for small and medium-format digital cameras. It can also be fitted with the Bochum stabilised mount.*

One of the main advantages of the Pulsar is its stability where, due to its generous wing and tail area plus its centre of gravity, it can be trimmed to fly hands-off indefinitely – an extremely useful characteristic for survey flight! One particular Pulsar has been built around a highly sophisticated stabilised mount designed for small and medium format aerial photography, and will be ready for trial flights early in 2002. The prime mover for this project is Prof. Dr. Franjo Heimes, a photogrammetrist at the Fachhochschule, Bochum, Germany who, along with the authors, is a keen advocate of small and medium format digital surveys.

Very light aeroplanes (VLA)

Certified by the European Joint Aviation Agency (JAA) is a new category of aircraft which, under the Joint Airworthiness Regulations (JARs), covers mainly kit-built aircraft up to 750kg. This category, known as a very light aeroplane (VLA), is the result of modern technology and its integration with composite materials including carbon fibre, aluminium, GRP, light-alloy, PVC foam-filler, Kelvar, plywood and moulded fibreglass.

Although full international standards regarding VLAs are not yet agreed, we can expect to see many more of these aircraft in the near future, mainly because their performance as trainers easily outstrips that of many traditional two seater light aircraft such as the Cessna 150/152. Highly regarded VLAs now available include the French Ban-Bi VLA, and the Italian Partenavia P92 Echo, both of which are certified to fly in the VLA category.

Ban-Bi MCR01 VLA

The Ban-Bi MCR01 is of carbon-fibre composite construction and can be supplied either in kit form or ready built. As a side-by-side two seater with ample luggage space behind the pilot, this VLA could easily be fitted with a digital camera and drift mount, with possible in-flight access to the camera. The MCR01 VLA is a low-wing tricycle undercarriage machine that can cruise at c. 140 kts (75% power), stall at 34 kts, and has a range of 540 nm (with no reserves). A large range of power units are available for this aircraft, including the JPX 90HP 4TX90M and 80HP Rotax 912.

The Ban-Bi family also includes the same design in two other weight categories. Allowing for various types of operating licence and aircraft performance, we have the MC100 (aluminium light aircraft) and the Ban-Bi MCR01 ULM (small light aircraft), both machines having a very similar performace to the VLA.

Partenavia P92-S. Echo VLA

The P92-S Echo VLA is a high wing two-seater aircraft with excellent pilot visibility. Its tricycle undecarriage is fitted with wheel spats, and the machine can be powered by either a 100HP Rotax 912-S, or the 81HP Rotax 912. This very popular (all metal) VLA is fitted with Fowler flaps and also has electric trim. Designed as a short take-off and landing (STOL) aircraft, the Echo VLA can unstick at 100 m, clear a 15 m obstacle in a 200 m take-off, and land within 100 m. The Echo VLA has a designed maximum take-off weight (MTOW) of 550kg, and an operational MTOW of 500kg. Its maximum speed is125 kts, and its 75% cruise is quoted as 105 kts. The stall (with flap) is 33 kts, and the aircraft has a service ceiling of 14,800 ft.

Small light aeroplanes (SLA)

Originally termed microlights (or ultralights), the SLA is the CAA definition for a microlight that flies under the new weight limit of 450 kg all-up-weight (auw), and has a stall speed limit of 35 kts. Many of these SLAs are ideal for small and medium format digital survey cameras, but in the UK they can only be employed for research as microlights (SLAs) cannot be used for commercial work.

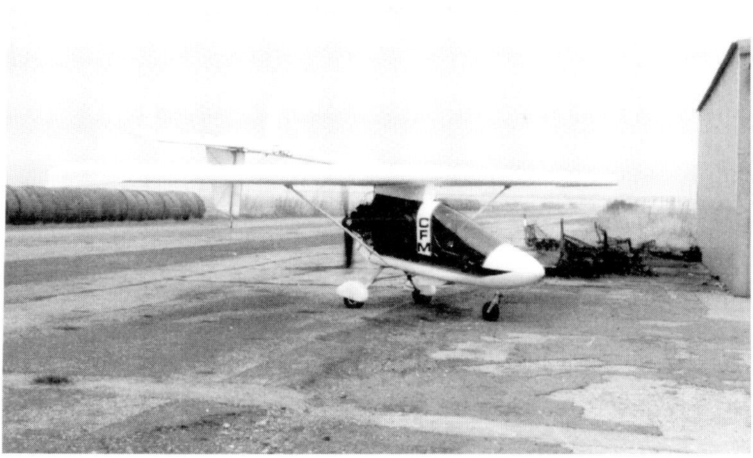

Figure 6.8 *The CFM Shadow small light aircraft (SLA), a highly useful SF and MF air camera platform.*

The CFM Shadow

An SLA with an exceptionally good record is the CFM Shadow. This aircraft has twice been flown (solo) from the UK to Australia, not as an SLA, but in its previous microlight weight of 390 kg. Originally conceived as an aerial work platform it has also been employed by the military, customs, and police forces world-wide, carrying cameras and thermal imagers for various surveillance duties. Best described as a pod and boom pusher (see Fig.6.8) the Shadow is available in a number of variations and can be purchased as a kit or fully assembled. A two-seater (tandem) aircraft, one of the major design features of the Shadow is its inherent stability throughout the entire flight envelope where, for example, it is virtually impossible to stall the aircraft in any situation (Graham, 1988a).

With a slow speed capability of 35–39 kts (IAS) the Shadow is ideal for digital air surveys, but since camera installations are in the rear cabin, camera mountings must be carefully isolated from engine vibrations. As an SLA the latest version is the Shadow Star-Streak powered by a Rotax 618 (74 HP) giving a minimum level-speed of 39 kts (IAS) and a maximim level speed of 113 kts (IAS). The Star-Streak can operate at a ceiling of 25,000 ft and has a useful range of 260nm.

The Thruster

Much of the authors' research with the DCS range of digital cameras has been with the Thruster microlight (Fig. 6.9) which has allowed us to experiment with the Kodak DCS-200, 420 CIR, 460 CIR and the DCS-660 cameras (Graham and Mills, 1997, 2000; Koh, 2000). The Thruster is a side-by-side two seater with excellent rough field performance and can fly (MTOW) as slow as 36 kts (IAS), very often experiencing a ground speed of only 30 kts depending on prevailing winds.

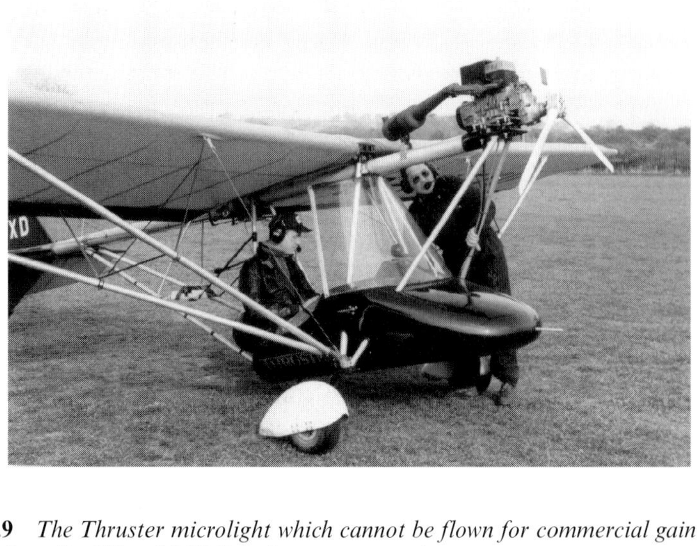

Figure 6.9 *The Thruster microlight which cannot be flown for commercial gain but is an ideal platform for SF and MF digital survey research.*

We usually fly the T300 version (Rotax 503 engine) which provides an endurance of 3 hours 20 minutes at 50% power (economic cruise of 50 kts) and is perfect for the short photo-runs necessary to test cameras and mountings.

The latest version is the Thruster T600 which can be supplied with either nose or tail wheel and has a fully enclosed cockpit. The T600 is powered by a Rotax 582 water-cooled engine and can provide a maximum level speed of 75 kts, an economic cruise of 61 kts and an IAS stall of 30 kts. It has a range of about 165nm at economic cruise and a service ceiling of 12,000 ft.

Jet aircraft

Few pure jets are used for aerial survey since their flying and maintenance costs are much higher than piston aircraft. Nevertheless, a number of operators employ business jets such as the BAe Jetstream 41, or the Learjet 35/36. Both of these aircraft can be certified (STC) with either a camera hole in the belly or, for the Learjet, be fitted with a special camera-pack modification under the fuselage. These jets have a fast transit capability and are useful for extensive surveys. The Jetstream 41 is a 29 passenger feeder-liner with a useful twin role, and sports a cruise speed of 290 kts, a range of 774 nm and a service ceiling of 26,000 ft. But the Learjet, with a cruise of 418 kts, a range of 2710nm and a service ceiling of 45,000 ft has a much greater potential for serious long range high altitude mapping and is an economic platform in this respect.

Helicopters

Helicopters have traditionally found little favour for mapping, mainly due to the difficulty of installing a large 23cm air camera in the cabin, vibration problems and high operating costs. However, digital cameras can now be mounted outside the cabin and, being small, are easily isolated from vibrations. But above all, the helicopter can fly slow enough to allow for the long download periods common to some digital cameras.

The Robinson R22 (two-seat) light helicopter can be a useful platform for small digital camera surveys. The R22 is mainly used for pilot training, but often employed for surveillance work, crop spraying and photography and in the latter role is both economic and practical where platform positioning is difficult, particularly over urban or industrial areas. Although the R22 (Fig. 6.10) has mostly been used with video cameras, it is still possible to employ a digital camera provided it is well protected from airflow and vibrations common to external mountings. Nevertheless, it is not an ideal choice for serious mapping since its maximum speed (97 kts) and range (320nm) are hardly adequate. But its service ceiling of 14,000 and hover ceiling of 6,900 feet, make it a useful platform for spot photography and surveillance.

One of the best utility helicopters for aerial work is the Bell 206 JetRanger, one of the world's most popular helicopters. The 206 combines simplicity with relatively low operating costs and is used for a large variety of work. Seating up to five people, the 206B-3 model has a max-cruise of 116 kts, a range of 395nm (with full fuel) and a service ceiling of 13,500 ft. The usual camera mounting is either in a pod below the glazed nose, or between the skids.

As mentioned before, almost any aircraft (fixed wing or rotary) can be used as a

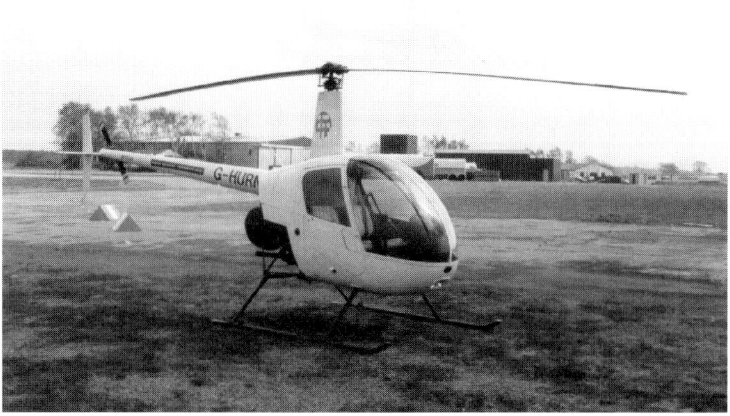

Figure 6.10 *The Robinson R-22 two-seat helicopter.*

camera platform, as the authors found when flying a series of digital mapping tasks in New Guinea (see Chapter 13). Using a Bell 412, this Indonesian version (NBell- 412) was specially modified to fly at 20,000 ft and fitted with a heavy lifting hoist for copper mining operations at 13,000 ft. The four-bladed machine has a cruise of 124 kts at sea level and a range of 375nm, which we found very useful for mapping both at sea level and at 18,000 ft, using an externally mounted DCS-460 CIR camera. Aircraft and crew are shown in Fig.6.11, with Ron suitably harnessed for operating the camera from an open cabin door. Although the outside air temperature (OAT) was – 6°C, the

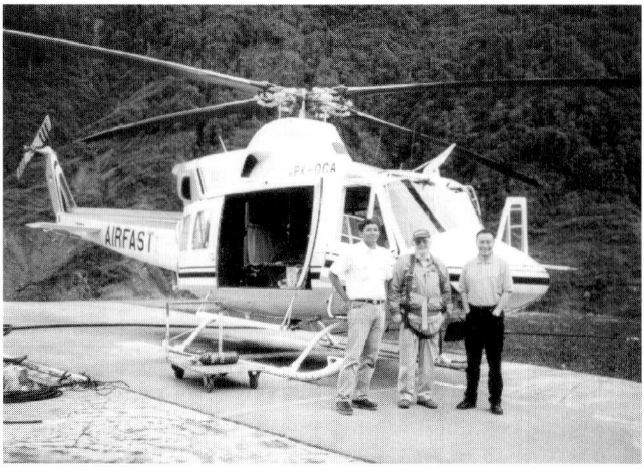

Figure 6.11 *Bell 412 helicopter with authors and (at left) pilot operating in West Papua, New Guinea.*

DCS-460 worked extremely well, with only two stoppages, possibly due to the PCMCIA card being exposed to such a low temperatures for 40 minutes. However, it was possible to restart the camera by removing and then replacing the PCMCIA card.

Air camera mounts

Basically there are four different types of air camera mount:

1. Anti-vibration.
2. Anti-vibration with levelling.
3. Anti-vibration with levelling and drift control.
4. Stabilised.

Although all types of mount need to incorporate vibration isolation, only the stabilised mount can offer a system where the air camera has automatic compensation for aircraft movements such as pitch, roll and yaw (see Chapter 2).

Anti-vibration mounts

Although all air cameras, analogue or digital, suffer image degradation due to vibration, digital cameras that download their images to an integral disk (PCMCIA, flashcard etc.) are particularly vulnerable since the slightest disturbance to the disk will stop the camera! It should be remembered that all disks involve rapidly moving parts and, like most mechanical functions, are subject to variations in temperature, humidity and vibration. Indeed, during a series of experiments with the DCS-460 camera flown with the Thruster aircraft (Fig.6.9) we found that take-off vibrations were sufficient to prevent camera operation. This came as quite a surprise since earlier work with a similar mount had given us no trouble with the DCS-200 camera, and we always flew from a smooth grass strip with the camera mount suspended on a semi-rigid platform behind the fuel tank (Fig.6.12). Obviously the PCMCIA card was the problem, and from a series of empirically controlled experiments Alexander designed a slightly different suspension (still in the same location) but with different types of spring-mounted dampers until the problem was solved. The mounting has now been used sucessfully with the DCS-420 CIR, 460 CIR and 660 camera, all in the same location.

It is also important to note that if a PCMCIA card can suffer from vibrations so can an airborne computer, a problem to be aware of when using a digital camera that downloads images via a 'scuzzi' (SCSI) attachment to a laptop.

Although the simple fixed installation shown in Fig.6.12 does not allow for manual in-flight levelling or drift compensation, this can always be provided by remote control, but was not necessary here. As the Thruster's (trimmed) pitch attitude was known for all our research flying, it was possible to level the mounting for camera verticality while on the ground, and where survey lines were flown we always flew into wind, in order to avoid drift.

Simple fixed installation mounts with vibration damping are usually restricted to military aircraft installations. Tactical reconnaissance aircraft employ cameras with high-speed focal plane shutters, often with shutter speeds of 1/2000 s or more, and since modern Tac-R aircraft are high speed jets, fast shutter speeds are not only essen-

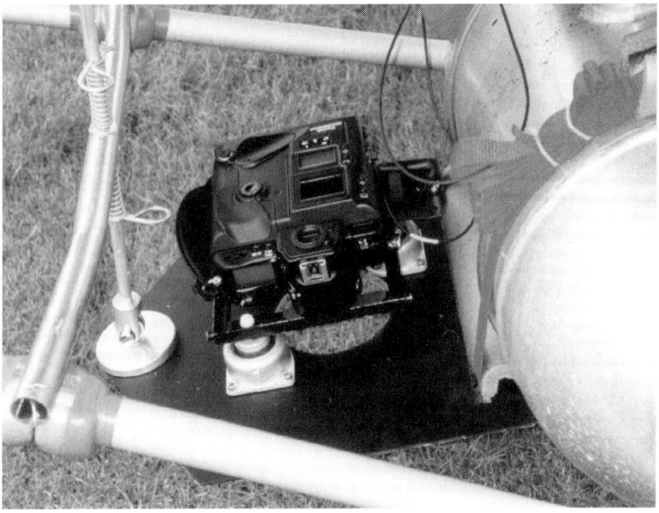

Figure 6.12 *The fixed (non-drift) anti-vibration mount for DCS-460CIR camera on Thruster aircraft externally mounted behind the cockpit.*

tial to curb image blur, but are excellent for reducing the effects of vibration as well (Graham *et al.*, 1996). For most reconnaissance systems the hysteretic damping in rubber is usually sufficient, with camera mounts consisting of different layers of non-rigid materials such as neoprene, foam rubber, hard rubber and silicon-rubber compounds.

For commercial aircraft, either fixed wing or rotary, most camera mountings employ a range of dampers such as hollow-cone mounts filled with natural rubber, spring mounts, air-dampers (rubber-balloons) or special glass-fibre mounts. All are often used in conjunction with metal-spring isolators. The use of oil as a viscous fluid is only suitable in relatively few applications since oil viscosity is greatly affected by temperature. As a consequence oil-filled dashpots cannot be recommended for aviation. Yet another type of dashpot damper is the piston-rod type, available from Radio Spares (RS products,: see App. C). The RS dashpot employs a metal cylinder where the force to be damped is transmitted through a piston rod within the cylinder. The cylinder has a small adjustable orifice to control the rate of air-flow (and damping) as the piston moves in response to the force exerted. However, these semi-pneumatic dashpots would not be suitable for air cameras operating in thin air.

It is of interest to note that in aviation the most popular anti-vibration unit is the spring mount which, in multiples, are used to protect a large range of sensitive instruments such as radios, radar, gyro's, etc. The spring mount is therefore the obvious choice for isolating airborne cameras from both vibration and shock, even though its freedom of movement is generally limited to one direction only. The camera mount shown in Fig.6.12 is a typical example, where three identical spring mounts are employed. Each mount comprises an enclosed aluminium alloy cylinder with internal steel springs and resilient knitted steel wire pads (similar in construction to the well known 'Brillo' pad used for cleaning cooking tins). These anti-vibration and shock mounts are available for a whole range of static loads, ranging from 0.7kg to 33kg and can be ordered from Radio Spares.

The RS unit employed for the mount shown in Fig.6.12 is listed as RS Stock No: 254-7416, for static loads between 2kg and 4.5kg, and was selected for having dynamic characteristics that include a natural frequency between 7 and 10Hz (vertical) and 4.5 to 6Hz (transverse), depending on the load. The maximum displacement input is ±0.8mm. When employed with the DCS-420, 460 and 660 digital cameras we never experienced any trouble, either with the Thruster microlight or when installed on the port step of the Bell-412 helicopter used from sea-level to 18,000 feet in New Guinea – a severe test indeed. This installation, showing the three spring-mounts and aluminium protection plates, is shown in Fig.6.13.

Yet another type of RS anti-vibration mount can be selected from the RS Paulstra range. Designed for small loads, these small silicone-rubber mounts protect low mass components and instruments from vibration and shock, and are highly recommended. Indeed, the authors have successfully flown a number of Kodak DCS digital cameras on a camera-platform supported by four Paulstra type 55500701 mounts, each capable of sustaining static loads of between 0.1 to 1.5 kg in both compression and shear, and 0.1 to 0.4 kg in roll. The mounting designed for the MF-DMC camera is supported by four Paulstra type 55500702 mounts (see Fig. 6.19) capable of sustaining loads within 1.5 to 3.0 kg in compression, 0.5 to 1.0 kg in shear and 0.4 to 0.8 kg in roll. And as all of these mounts can be operated within a temperature range of –40° to +70°C, they are highly suitable for small digital air cameras.

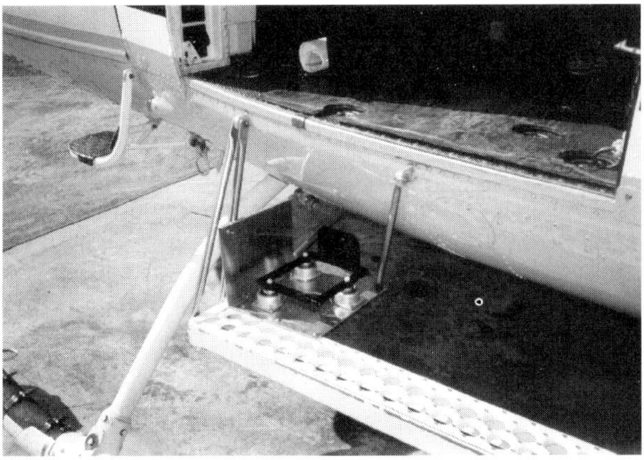

Figure 6.13 *Externally fixed (non-drift) anti-vibration mount connected to port step of Bell 412 helicopter (West Papua. 2000).*

Selection of the appropriate mount can either be based on engineering principles (where static loads, plus disturbing and forced-vibration frequencies all govern the choice of the resilient mounting support), or a suitable support can often be found empirically. In general the latter approach is usually adopted, mainly because there are so many conflicting variables to consider in aviation. Even a simple household device can be employed as an anti-vibration mount, such as three or four Cadnit Kettle Fur Collectors. These fine stainless-steel wire columns have a height and diameter of less than an inch and can easily be fitted with a central spring to afford suitable vibration insulation (see Household Articles Ltd, App. C).

Whereas a simple anti-vibration mount may be sufficient for a fixed position in a military aircraft, it cannot satisfy the requirements essential to aerial survey, where all mapping-camera mounts should be able to satisfy four basic functions which are:

1. Suppress vibration and shock.
2. Allow the camera to be levelled for vertical photography.
3. Provide for at least 15° of drift correction, left and right of the aircraft's heading.
4. Allow for remote-control operation.

Since most small and medium- format cameras have mounts designed for a particular aircraft, the fourth condition may not be necessary if the camera is operated directly from cockpit or cabin. The mount shown in Fig.6.12 for example, has been used with a number of aircraft, all of which allowed for hands-on operation and where drift compensation was either unnecessary (as with the Thruster aircraft) or when the effects of wind-drift are negligible.

Anti-vibration and levelling mounts

Apart from vibration suppression it is important that a mapping camera can be levelled in flight, that is to say the camera mount should be adjustable fore and aft along the aircraft's longitudinal axis so that the camera is as vertical as possible. Aircraft never fly at the same pitch attitude throughout the entire flight envelope of speed and altitude. At slow speeds the aircraft will tend to fly nose-up, whereas at faster speeds the tendancy will be to fly nose-down. Also, with increased altitude the air density decreases and the nose will tend to rise. As a consequence a spirit level should be fixed to the camera mount so that levelling can be confirmed once the aircraft has been trimmed for level survey-flight.

A very simple fore-and-aft level control has been designed by Roger Read (Graham *et al.*, 1996) and consists of a length of transparent plastic pipe bent into a curve and mounted on to the side wall of the aircraft. The transparent pipe is filled with spirit and a bubble to give the level, as shown in Fig.6.14. A lever, with an indicator point at the same radius as the curve of the pipe, is fitted with a cable attachment running back to the camera mount. When the point of the lever is against the bubble, this means that the camera is level fore and aft, providing the two are calibrated before flight.

Anti-vibration, levelling and drift control mounts

Survey flight in wind-free air is rare. As a consequence it is always necessary to allow

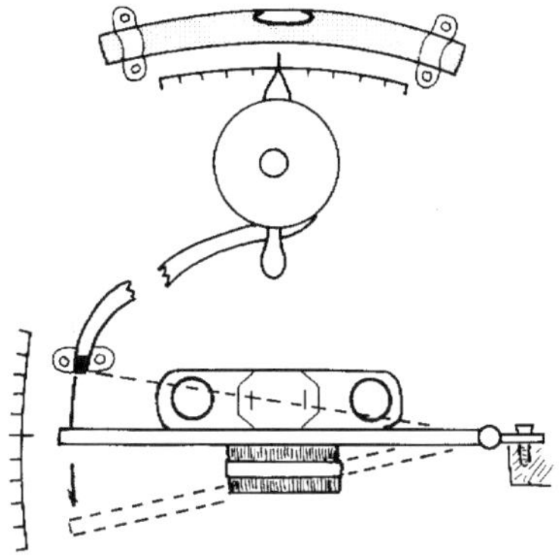

Figure 6.14 *A simple fore-and-aft level control for small-ormat camera mounts. Courtesy Roger Read.*

for wind-drift when the aircraft's heading is different to its track over the ground. This is not only a question of survey navigation however, since we also require some form of drift compensation installed in the camera mount so that the camera format is square to the aircraft's track – rather than its heading.

Wind-drift

Although we shall discuss the effects of wind-drift in Chapter 7, where we consider survey flight tracking, it is important to introduce the difference between an aircraft's heading (hdg) and its track (trk). An aircraft's heading is the direction to which its nose is pointing (indicated by the gyro-compass and direction indicator), and in the absence of wind then the aircraft's heading and track over the ground are the same. This condition is shown in Fig.6.15a, where an aircraft is flying a survey-line with heading and track along the line AB. But if a wind pushes the aircraft to one side or the other, it may still be pointing (hdg) in a given direction, but its track over the ground will be different. Inspection of Fig.6.15b shows the aircraft still heading in the same direction, but the wind-angle (WA) now pushes the machine along the track AC, completely missing the required survey line AB. In order to correct this off-track-error the pilot must now fly the aircraft into the wind-corrected-angle (WCA) as shown in Fig.6.15c.

Survey-crew procedure for correcting effects of wind drift

Pilot's action

(a) Prior to coming to the start of the survey line (point A in Fig.6.15), the pilot must first line up on the line AB according to his flight plan (normally this will be about 5km short of point A). Nowadays the pilot will have entered all the survey lines in his GPS receiver and will fly the aircraft onto the first GPS way-point where the first camera exposure will be made.

(b) During the run onto the first way-point (point A), the pilot will be able to fly on track by reference to his GPS receiver (which shows both trk and hdg) and, at the

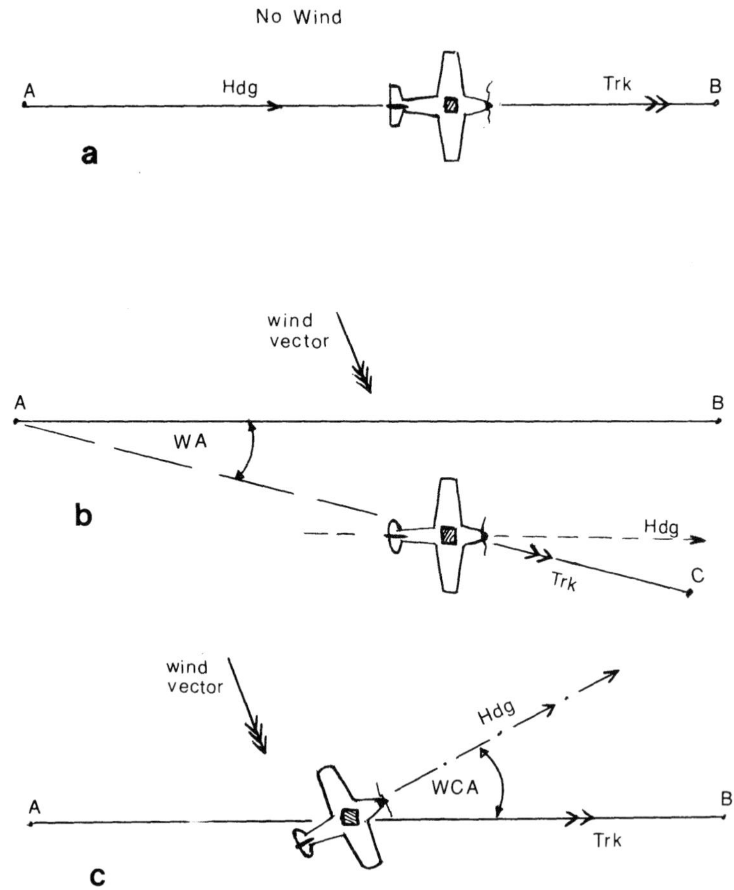

Figure 6.15 *Wind-drift and aircraft heading (hdg).*

same time, check his heading from the aircraft's gyro-compass. Thus, if the desired track is due east, the pilot will fly a compass heading of 90°, but the GPS may show his track as 100°, obviously a northerly wind must be pushing the aircraft southwards, resulting in a wind angle (WA) of 10°.

(c) The pilot must now fly the aircraft into the wind-corrected-angle (WCA), which in this instance would be 80°, allowing the wind to make good the track along the line AB, as verified by the GPS receiver (see Fig.6.15c).

Camera operator's action

(a) Inspection of Fig.6.15a shows the (square) camera format symmetrical to the aircraft's track and its heading. This is the normal situation where a camera is lined up in its mounting for zero-wind conditions (the drift-mount has a zero datum with up to 15° marked to the right and left of the datum) to provide a photo-sequence such as that shown in Fig.6.16a (this sequence is not perfect in order to illustrate a typical survey-line, and to make each frame easier to see). If (by error) we were to take photographs along the track AC (Fig.6.15b), we would gain a photo-sequence like that shown in Fig.6.16b, simply because our camera format is not square to the track AC. Apart from the fact that we had not flown the correct line, our photographs would be totally unacceptable. Obviously the camera must be rotated square to the track AB, as the aircraft is flown into the WCA, as shown in Fig.6.15c.

(b) As soon as the pilot has found the correct WCA and headed into it (Fig.6.15c), he must inform the camera-operator who will then rotate the camera-mount (from datum) into the WA (opposite to the WCA) in order to make the camera format square to the track AB. He must then be prepared to start the exposure intervalometer at least two photographs before the start at point A of the survey line. At the end of the line (point B) the camera is allowed to run for two extra frames before the camera is shut down. The pilot has a difficult task keeping his aircraft 'on-line' and in order to relieve him of unnecessary stress the camera operator should instruct the pilot with "Camera On" when he starts the intervalometer and " Camera Off" at the end of the run.

(c) It is usual, and economic, to begin the second run (adjacent to the first, and with a certain amount of side-lap) by making a 180° turn sometime after the last photograph was taken on the first run. Once the pilot has made this U-turn into

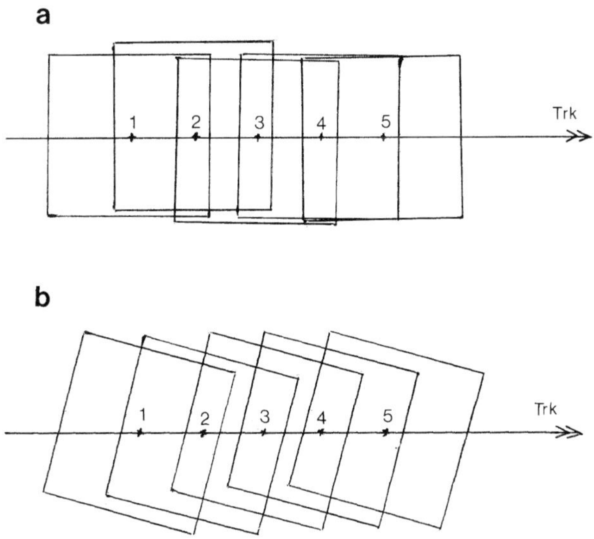

Figure 6.16 *(a) Correct forward overlaps along a flight-line(see Fig. 6.15c). (b) Uncorrected foward overlaps due to lack of drift correction on camera mount.*

the second line he will line up to fresh GPS waypoints, but now the wind will be incident upon the other side of the aircraft creating an opposite WCA. The camera operator must now be prepared for this and, unless the wind has shifted, rotate the camera mount to the same degree of wind-angle, but now on the opposite side of the drift-mount's datum.

The drift-mount

Although a reasonably good drift-mount, complete with drift-scale, can be fashioned from simple materials it may only be suitable for manual operations unless it has the smooth rotation required for remote control. Remotely operated drift-mounts are usually driven by electrical stepping motors and it is essential that the camera platform rotates on a ball-race, as shown in Fig.6.17. Anything less than this can result in the the camera platform sticking, particularly when positioned outside of the airframe.

Normally the drift scale will have a central datum with up to 15° of drift clearly marked left and right of datum (drift corrections greater than 15° are considered to be outside of good survey conditions).

The Geotechnologies digital survey system

Geotechnologies' drift-mount for the Kodak DCS range of digital cameras is shown in Fig.6.18, where a fully 360° rotating camera ring is supported on a similar fixed ring by a smooth ball-race. The lower (fixed) ring is secured to a removable camera base-plate by four small anti-vibration Paulstra mounts (type 55500702). As may be seen from Fig. 6.18, the upper ring of the mount has a vertical post to which the camera is fitted via its tripod-bush, which allows the camera to be levelled (in-flight) fore and aft.

The fittings shown in Figs. 6.18 and 6.19 are within the cabin of a Partenavia 68B, where the camera base-plate is secured over the camera-hole (protected by cabin-operated camera doors). In Fig. 6.19 we see a complete air-survey camera kit consisting of a 16 MPx MF-DMC(2) fitted to a much larger non-drift mount (a drift ring can be fitted on top of the fixed mount as required), the mount being secured to the base-plate by four anti-vibration supports. Left to right is the Quantum battery power source

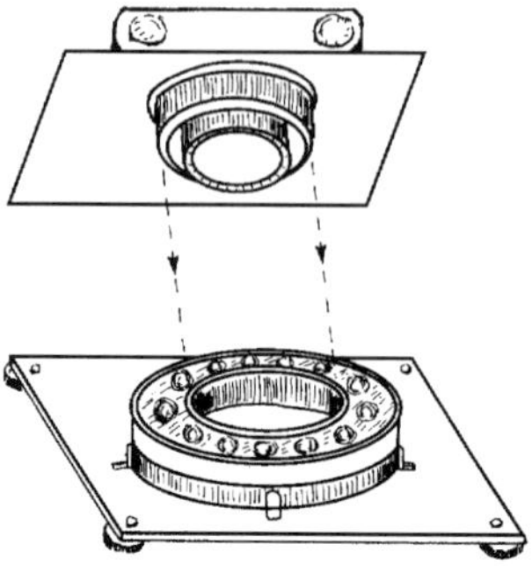

Figure 6.17 *Ball-race configuration for drift-mount assembly.*

and a Garmin hand-held GPS Map 76 unit for the photographer. Both the navigator's GPS Map 295 and the camera operator's GPS Map 76 are connected to roof-mounted antennae (see Chapter 12).

Helicopter mounting for MF-DMC survey system

An excellent nose modification to the Bell-412 helicopter is shown in Fig. 6.20, where a Geotechnologies MF-DMC(2), complete with anti-vibration mount, is shown suspended from the aircraft's radio rack. Modified under an Indonesian STC for the

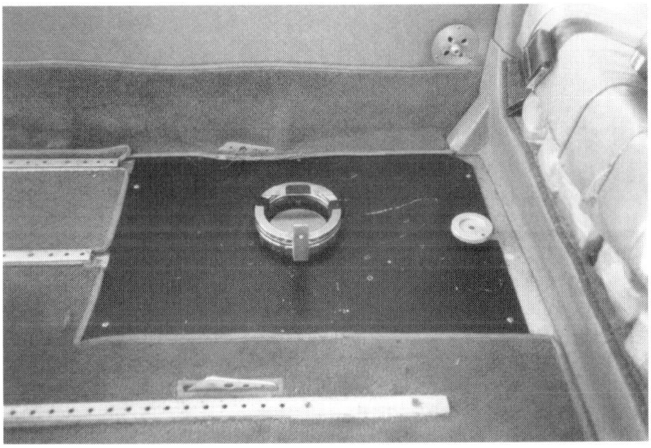

Figure 6.18 *Geotechnologies drift mount for SF and MF digital cameras. Here seen incorporated in a Partenavia 68B aircraft.*

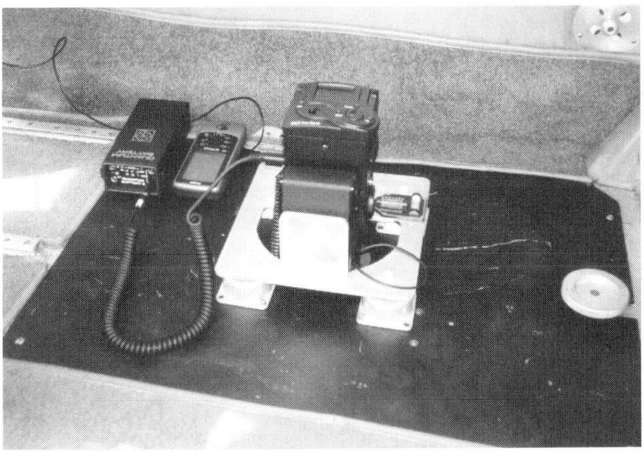

Figure 6.19 *A complete digital air survey system fitted in the cabin of a Partenavia 68B. The 16 MPx, MF-DMC(2) camera is fitted to a non-drift mount secured to the aircraft's base-plate by four anti-vibration supports. The camera mount can be fitted with a rotating drift-ring as required. From the left are the Quantum battery and GPS Map 76 receiver for the camera operator.*

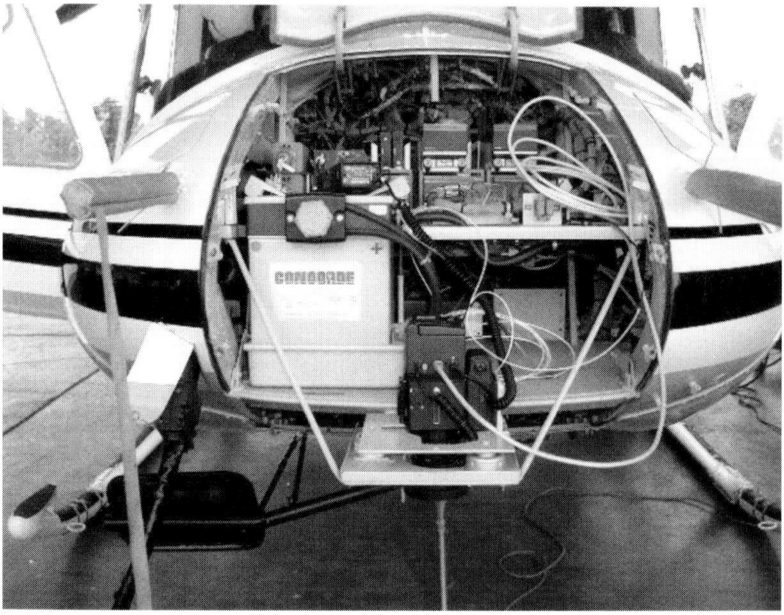

Figure 6.20 *The MF-DMC(2) mounted within a survey modified Bell-412 helicopter. The camera is protected with a modified nose radar-dome (not shown here) and operated from the copilot's seat. The nose-dome has a remotely-controlled sliding cover to protect the lens upon take-off and landing.*

PT Freeport survey helicopter, the camera system is protected under a modified radar dome (not shown here). The MF-DMC(2), mounting and Quantum QB2 power pack were installed at Freeport's aviation centre at Timika, Irian Jaya, and sucessfully tested with a 40 mm lens from sea level to 18,000 ft. Primary considerations for this installation were environmental conditions, where the Bell 412 has to land and take off from dusty (or rain sodden) terrain, and fly surveys under conditions ranging from extreme jungle humidity to high altitude mining camps (see Chapter 12). It was therefore essential to protect the camera lens with a sliding cover in the radar dome, this being remotely operated (as are the exposures) from the copilot's seat.

Stabilised mounts

In an ideal world our survey aircraft would fly straight and level, without pitch, roll or yaw, and the camera would always be truly vertical. Indeed, if this were so we would be able to fly surveys with little or no ground control, making the mapping industry much less expensive and the photogrammetrist's work much easier. But in the real world all aircraft are subject to constant variations in attitude which, for survey platforms, give rise to undesireable image distortions that can only be corrected by reference to accurate ground control. As a measure for minimising these problems many mapping cameras are now installed within stabilised mounts designed to keep the camera vertical – even in turbulence.

Although stabilised mounts have been available for a number of years, these sophisticated systems are designed for large-format film cameras such as the RC-30 and RMK-TOP, and are too large (and expensive) for small and medium-format cameras, either analogue or digital. Nevertheless, a high precision stabilised mount designed for small and medium-format cameras has been made, and is available for remote sensing and digital orthophotos (Heimes *et al.*, 1997).

The Bochum stabilised camera platform

Designed by a team of Geodesists at the Fachhochschule Bochum, University of Applied Sciences, Germany, the Bochum stabilised mount has been fully tested from various aircraft and can be recommended for accurate mapping with small and medium-format digital cameras. Cooperation between Geotechnologies and FH-Bochum promises an interesting future for the MF-DMC, stabilised mount and Pulsar aircraft as a highly accurate medium-format mapping system that allows photogrammetric surveys to be operated without ground control points. Full details can be obtained from Dr. Franjo Heimes, Professor of Photogrammetry at Bochum (see App. C), but a brief resume of this mount is given here.

The mechanical components comprise a stable three-point suspension and three highly dynamic servo-motors to compensate for the aircraft's angular motions. The system stabilises images precisely, even for low flying aircraft under turbulent conditions with precision from differential global positioning systems (d)GPS, and inertial navigation systems (INS). The data to control the platform as well as the data for the survey flight management (SFM) are provided by the (d)GPS augmented FOG INS (fibre optical gyros inertial navigation system) from Litef, Germany.

The original 64Hz inertial measurements (angular rates and accelerations) are acquired via a standard interface by the processor unit and are then combined in a Kalman filter with the measurements of a (d)GPS.

Residual image inclinations and yaw deviations are recorded. Together with data from the (d)GPS augmented inertial platform (INS) the complete exterior orientation data X, Y, Z, κ, φ, ω are delivered.

The two GPS units are Leica 9400, 12 channel single frequency receivers, one used as reference station and the other as rover, providing a position accuracy of c.30 cm. The inertial platform is an LLN-G1, standard strapdown attitude and heading reference system. In the GPS augmented mode the inertial system delivers phi and omega angles with an accuracy of 0.01° and kappa with an accuracy of 0.05°.

Direct georeferencing with the Bochum stabilised mount

The following data result from a test flight made on the 9th August 2000, using the Kodak DCS-460 colour camera with a 28mm lens. A total of 70 images were exposed from a flying height of 700 m providing an image scale of 1:25,000. The forward and side laps were 60% and 25% respectively. The processing procedure for georeferencing these images is shown in Table 6.2.

Table. 6.2 *Direct georeferencing for Bochum stabilised mount imagery.*

1. Reference: Bundle-block adjustment. (c. 500 tie points).
2. Spatial resection using tie-points, X_0 / Y_0 fixed, from (d)GPS (to determine camera orientation values, avoiding the problem of correlations).
3. Determination of misalignment values between camera and INS.
4. Correction of INS angular orientation values.
5. Direct georeferencing (photogrammetric forward intersections using the elements of exterior orientation determined in flight).
6. Comparison of coordinates with those from reference: Bundle-block adjustment.

Standard Deviations: $\sigma_x = 0.30$ m, $\sigma_y = 0.43$ m, $\sigma_z = 1.50$ m.

The strapdown LLN-G1 incorporates two mechanical dry-tuned gyros and three pendulum accelerometers. The original 50Hz inertial measurments (rates and accelerations) are acquired via a smart ARINC 429 board in the processing unit and then combined in a Kalman filter with the (d)GPS measurements. A flight management system is responsible for the camera shutter release, as well as delivering flight-line information to the pilot. Based on a low cost AHRS (attitude and heading reference system) the Bochum camera platform is also available just for fast stabilisation, without georeferencing.

There can be no doubt that the Bochum stabilised mount is the last word in sophistication and, although expensive, will justify its cost in terms of metric accuracy and temporal economy. Designed for light aircraft installation, it can be installed in the Pulsar (Fig.6.7) and most other suitable aircraft to provide an excellent MF digital mapping system which, if necessary, can be flown as a pilot-only operation as well.

Intervalometers

For mapping purposes photographs are taken sequentially along any given flight-line and, in order to provide for stereoscopic coverage, each image should overlap the next by 60% ± 5%. Such cover then allows earth scientists to find terrain heights with the aid of a mirror stereoscope and parallax-bar, and for photogrammetrists and cartographers to create maps, with spot-heights and contours, by use of more sophisticated methods.

A forward overlap of 60% requires calculation, and although we can never expect perfect accuracy (due to wind and small changes in ground speed) this is not too important providing an overlap of at least 55% can be maintained. Although a forward overlap of 60% is usually specified, this is only a nominal figure quoted for average conditions. For mountainous regions, where there are large variations in height above and below the survey datum (average terrain height) a 60% overlap for the datum could well reduce the overlap to only 50% or 40% for the mountain tops. So for these conditions forward-overlap is planned to perhaps 70% or even 90% depending on the terrain. Similarly, where a few small clouds float below the aircraft the overlap is increased to provide a greater number of photographs. In this fashion there is a greater chance that a terrain point covered by a cloud in one image will be revealed in the next.

Gaining the required forward overlap necessitates (a) calculating the flying height above datum, (b) a good knowledge of the aircraft's ground speed, (c) the focal length of the lens and (d) the size of the image format. From these parameters we can calculate the necessary exposure interval (ΔT) required before the next exposure has to be made (in accordance with the formulae listed in Chapter 7).

Obviously ΔT requires some form of timing device (intervalometer) either simple or sophisticated, which could be either (i) a clock, (ii) an audio timing device (iii) an electronically-controlled navigation sight (iv) an electronic timer or (v) a GPS receiver.

Clock timers

A stopwatch can always be used, but a busy survey crew have more to do than just look at a clock. Nevertheless, a stopwatch should always be carried as a reliable back-up, just in case a more sophisticated timer fails during the mission. A large-faced stopwatch, such as the 'Transair Pilots Stopwatch' is recommended (see App. C).

Audio timing devices

A simple tape-recorder with a recorded alarm, set at fixed intervals, is a good system that can be used where necessary. Naturally an audio alarm is not going to be a first choice, but they have proved useful for certain conditions. A large display digital timer, with two individual stopwatch timers and audio alarm is available from Transair Pilot's Shop. This unit allows the timers to count up, or down, for a 24 hour period (see App. C).

Electronically-controlled navigation sights

Traditionally, large-format mapping cameras are controlled by a navigation sight, although nowadays most crews employ survey flight management (SFM) systems with GPS guidance. However, both methods have their respective merits and it is usual to find survey aircraft equipped with both instruments. Even if the navigation sight is not used for survey tracking it is still the best way of deciding whether the atmosphere is clear enough for photography – particularly at high altitudes.

Navigation sights, such as the Leica-Wild PSF3, or Zeiss T-NT, incorporate controls on the sight-head for measuring both drift, and the exposure interval ΔT. For the control of ΔT we are able to set the required overlap, flying height (H), aircraft velocity over the ground (V) and lens focal length. And after setting the appropriate focal length and foward overlap, the two remaining parameters are controlled (subjectively) as the V/H ratio. In the optical head of the navigation sight there is a series of illuminated lines superimposed on the terrain image, and by controlling the speed of these lines to match the apparent image motion, the navigator automatically determines the V/H ratio. This information then goes to a computer which calculates the required exposure interval. As soon as the first exposure is made the camera then recycles, at ΔT, until it is turned off.

Interestingly, the earliest form of navigation sight was created in 1915 for military reconnaissance. Known as a Side-Sight it comprises two horizontal rods placed where the pilot can see them outside the cockpit. The spacing of the two rods is calculated so that when a terrain feature passes from the first rod to the second (at a given height) an exposure is made, and immediately another terrain feature is found at the first rod, and so on. This technique is very simple and is still used today, particularly for light aircraft where ground speed is constantly changing due to gusts of wind (Graham, 1988b). The Side-Sight can still be found useful, but has universally given way to the simple electronic timer.

Electronic timers

An electronic timer is perhaps the best method for providing a sequence of timed exposures in aerial mapping. A few decades ago, most camera-timers were of the electro-mechanical type. Then, in the era of transistorised components, timers suitable for aerial survey were usually made to specific requirements. But in the present electronic era it's possible to purchase an off-the-shelf multifunction digital timer, costing about £100, that can be suitably interfaced with a digital camera to act as an intervalometer. The Geotechnologies Digital Intervalometer is specially made for the job and costs about £900.

This unit has a timer range extending from 0.5 seconds to 9999 minutes and has a resolution of 0.1 s. It is powered by a single 9 V battery and directly interfaces with the MF-DMC(1) and MF-DMC(2).

Multifunction digital timers

A typically suitable timer for aerial survey is the RS Components 'Trumeter' multifunction digital timer. Powered by two lithium batteries (960mAh each), the Trumeter can be programmed to operate in one of eight modes, including single shot, delayed operation and, of course, repeat cycles. It can provide for a large range of timed intervals (beyond those needed for aerial survey) including hours, minutes and seconds.

The MF-DMC (Hasselblad 555 ELD) can use a Trumeter timer for sequencing exposures. This timer inputs a pulse ≥ 20ms to a 30 V output relay whose contacts are connected (via a Hasselblad camera release cord, see Fig.5.26c) to the remote-exposure socket of the camera body. Once an exposure has been signalled the digital-back is reset and the mechanical shutter released. The shutter is then re-cocked and the CCD image downloaded to the on-board computer or internal CF+ microdrives. As soon as the image download is completed the timer can then signal the next sequenced exposure.

The GPS receiver as intervalometer

Since a simple hand-held GPS receiver can provide all necessary survey navigation data, including waypoints and ground-speed, it can also be programmed to indicate every photo-centre as a navigation waypoint. For example, if there are 20 photographs required along a given flight-line, then 20 waypoints can be entered into the GPS unit and the photographer simply has to employ the GPS receiver in its moving map (Route)

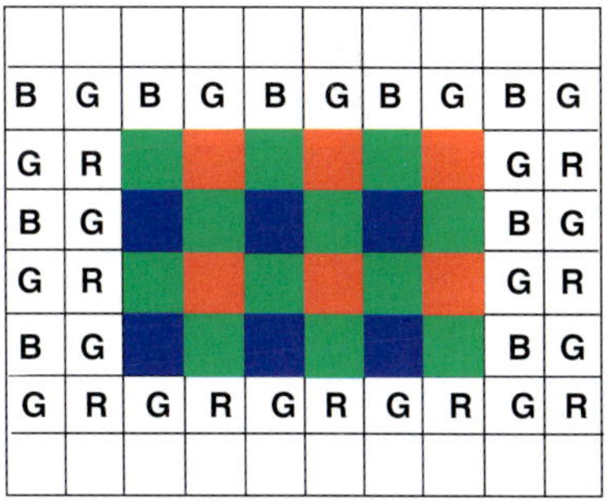

Figure 4.3 *Bayer mosaic. This Kodak blue/green and green/red matrix is one of the many different CFA geometries used with the 'adjacent pixel colour interpolation' algorithms employed for colour CCD imaging.*

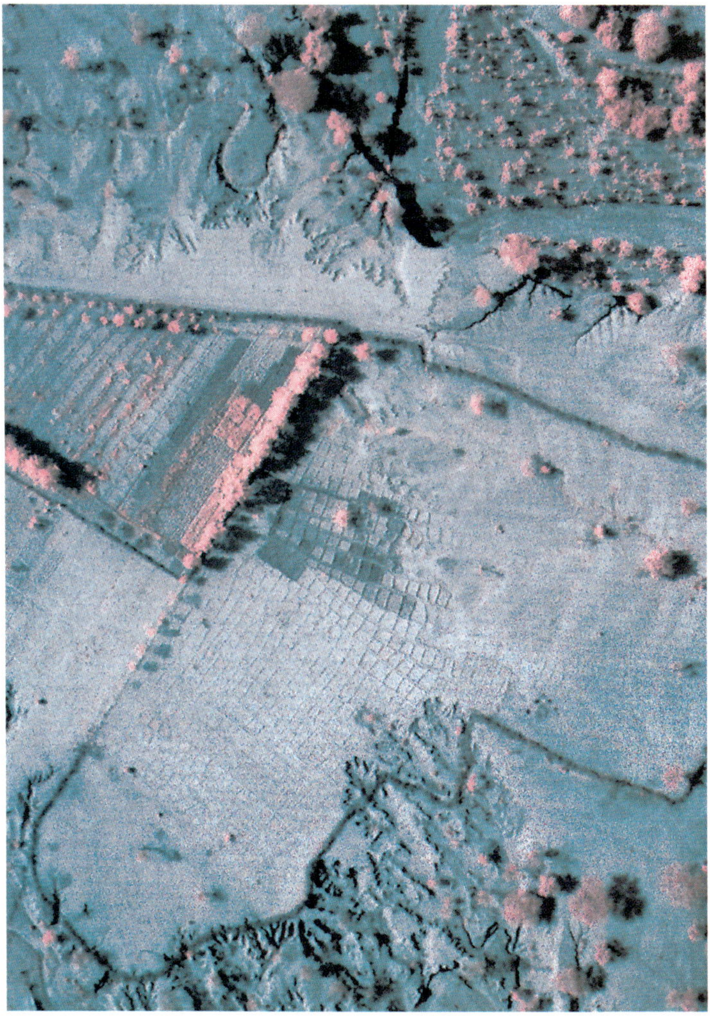

Figure 5.4 *False colour composite (FCC) taken from a DCS-420 camera. Photograph: Alexander Koh.*

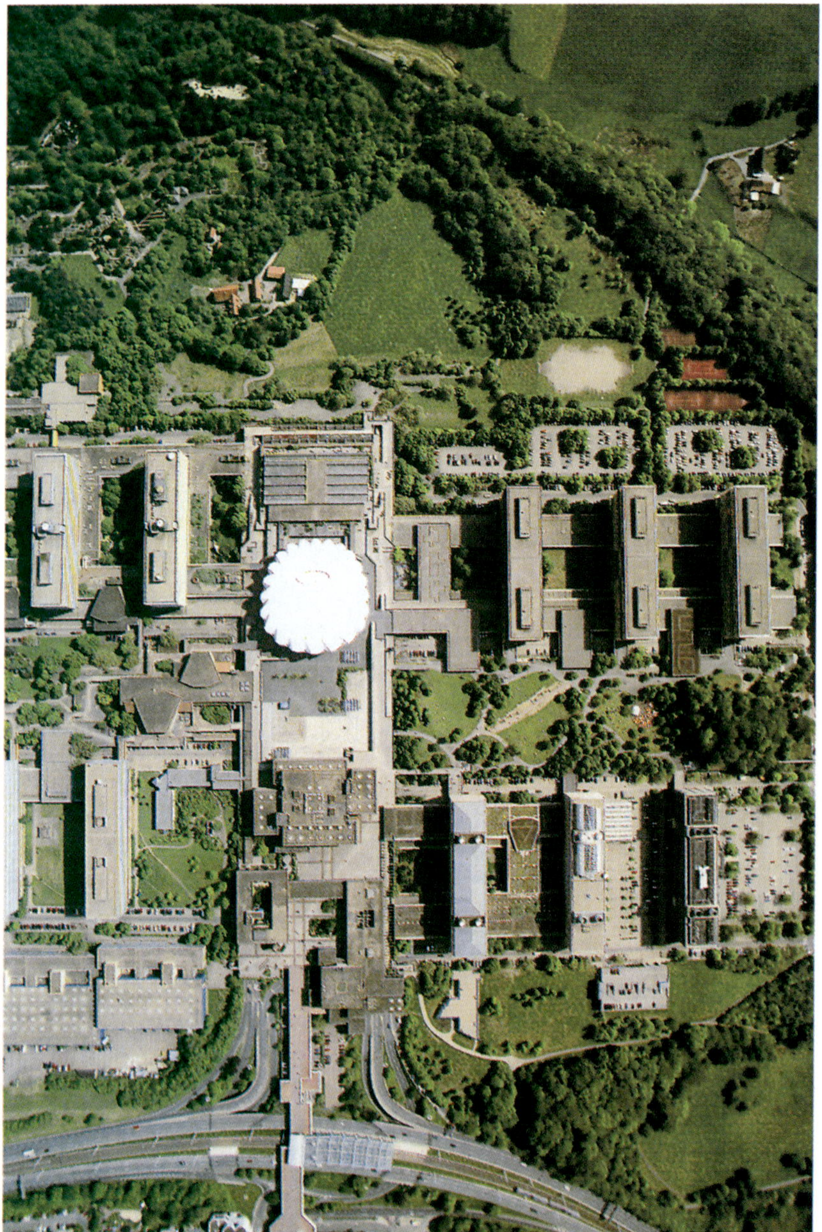

Figure 5.9 *Aerial view of the Fachhochschule Bochum, Germany. Flown by Prof. Dr-Ing, Franjo Heimes. DCS-460c with 28 mm lens and Bochum stabilised mount. Photograph: Franjo Heimes.*

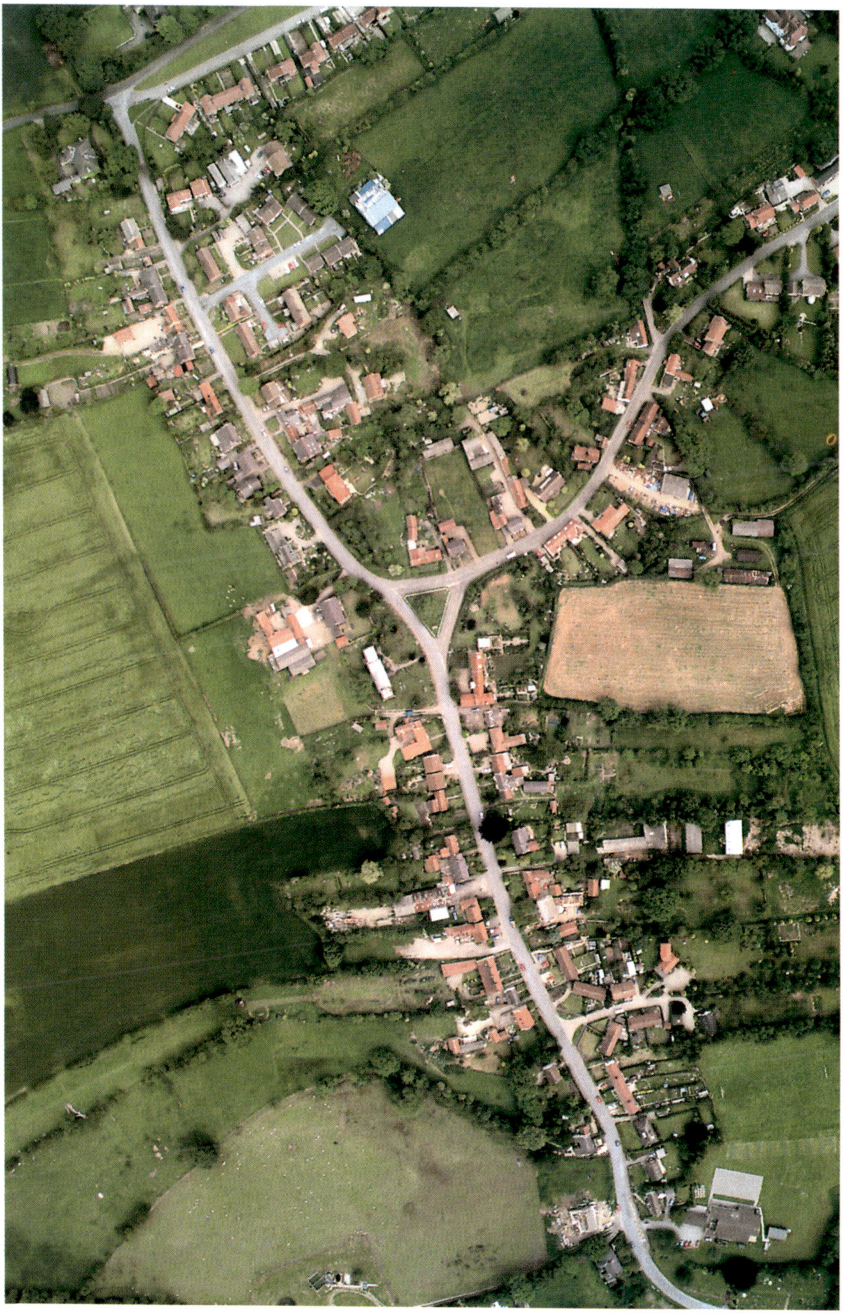

Figure 5.10 *Husthwaite village, North Yorkshire. One of a block of DCS-460 CIR survey images taken in conventional colour mode. Photoscale 1: 25,000, 28mm lens at 2,600 feet. Photograph: Dr. Jon Mills. (Newcastle University).*

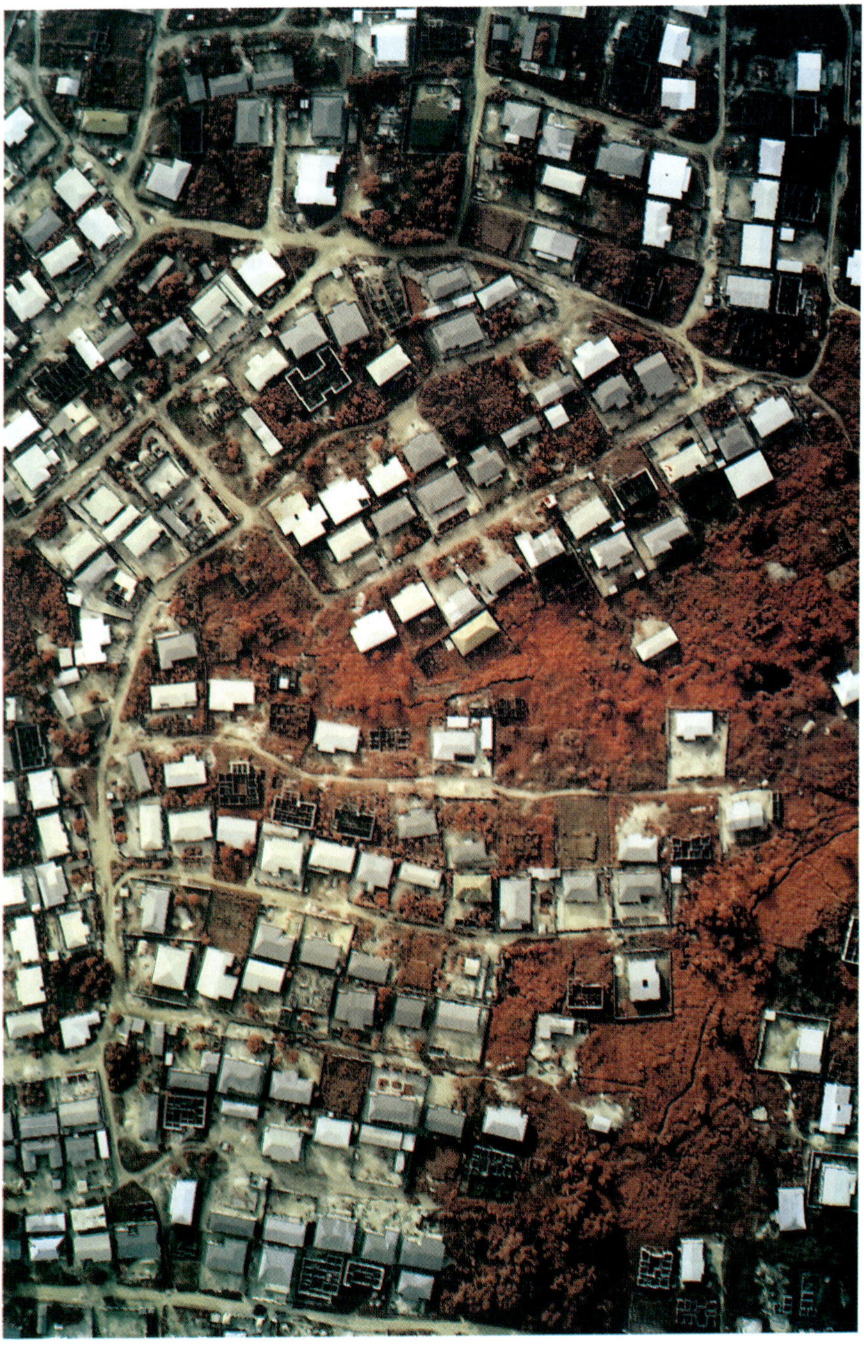

Figure 5.11 *False colour infrared (CIR) image taken at 1200 ft over Kumasi, Ghana, with DCS-460 CIR digital camera. Photograph: Alexander Koh.*

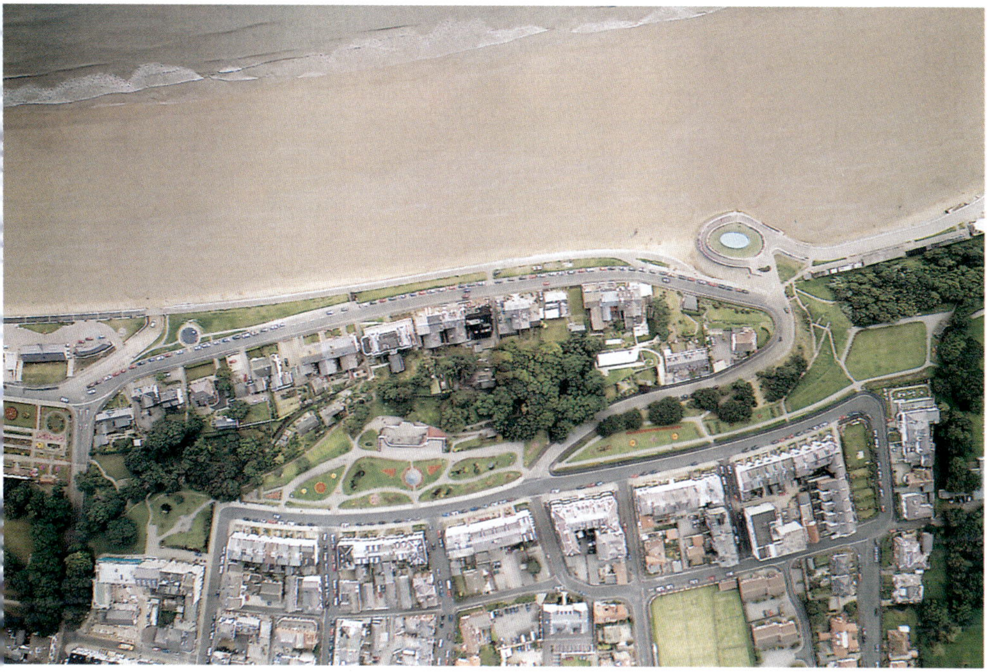

Figure 5.12 *Filey bay, East Yorkshire (coastal errosion survey) taken with a DCS-660 digital camera with 28mm lens at 1800 ft. Photograph: Dr. Jon Mills (Newcastle University).*

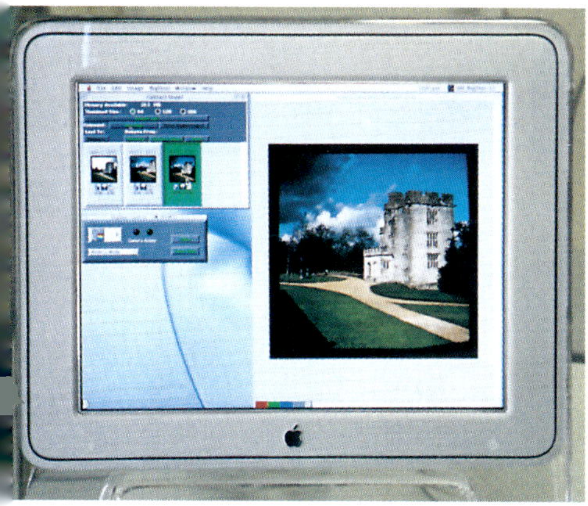

Figure 5.30 *Typical MF-DMC(1) images. Conventional colour (top) and near infrared (right).*

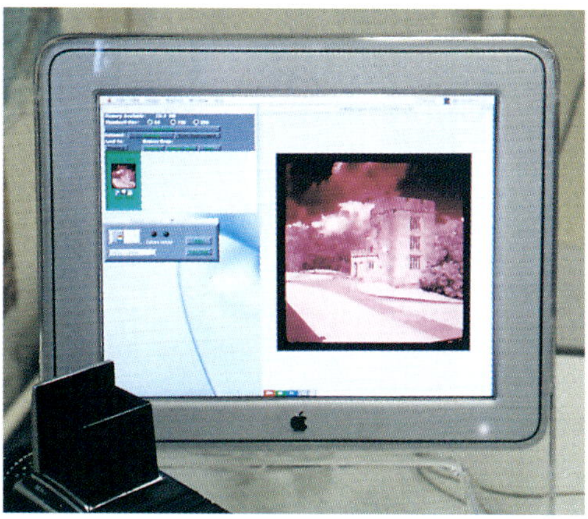

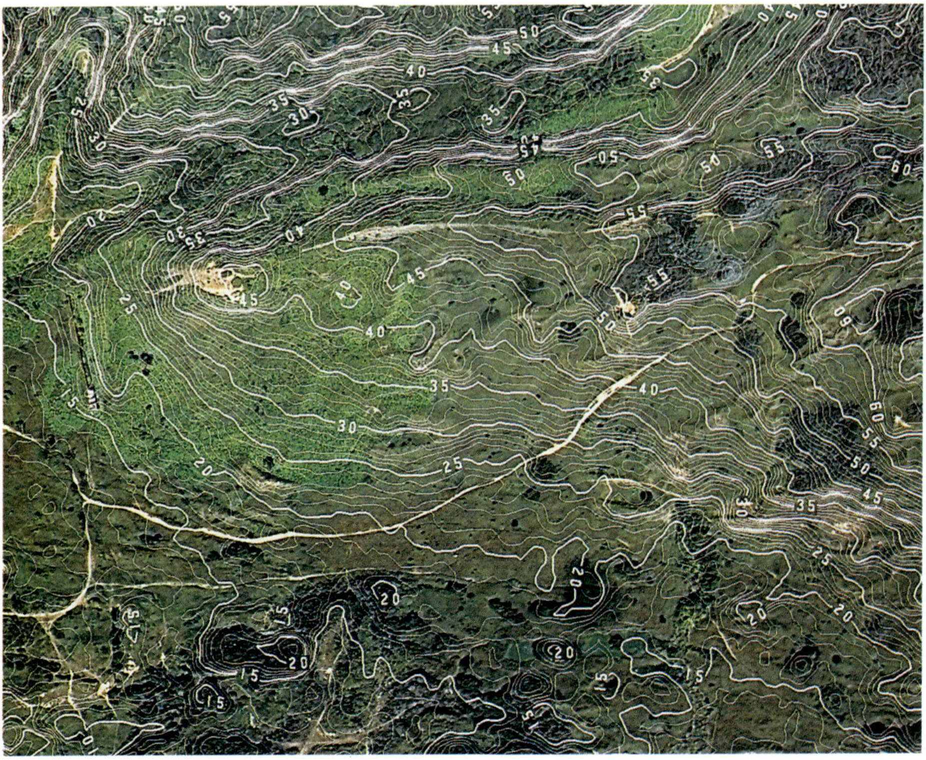

Figure 9.1 *Contoured Orthophoto. DCS-420CIR image taken in Columbia, processed in VirtuoZo software complete with ground control, for DTM and extraction of orthophoto with 5 m contours.*

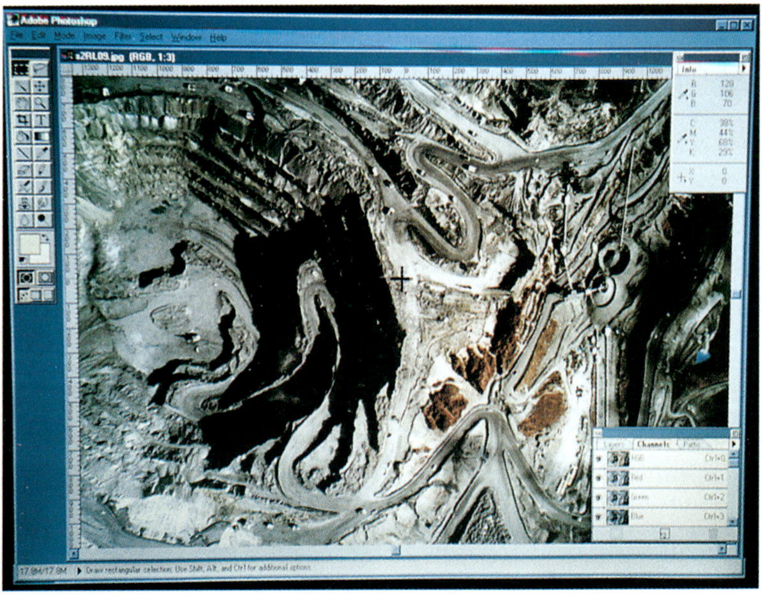

Figure 9.3 *DCS-460CIR image of P.T. Freeport copper mine from 18,000 ft West Papua, New Guinea. Image processed in Adobe Photoshop with drop-down menus for radiometric analysis. (false-colour infrared). Photograph: Ron Graham & Alexander Koh.*

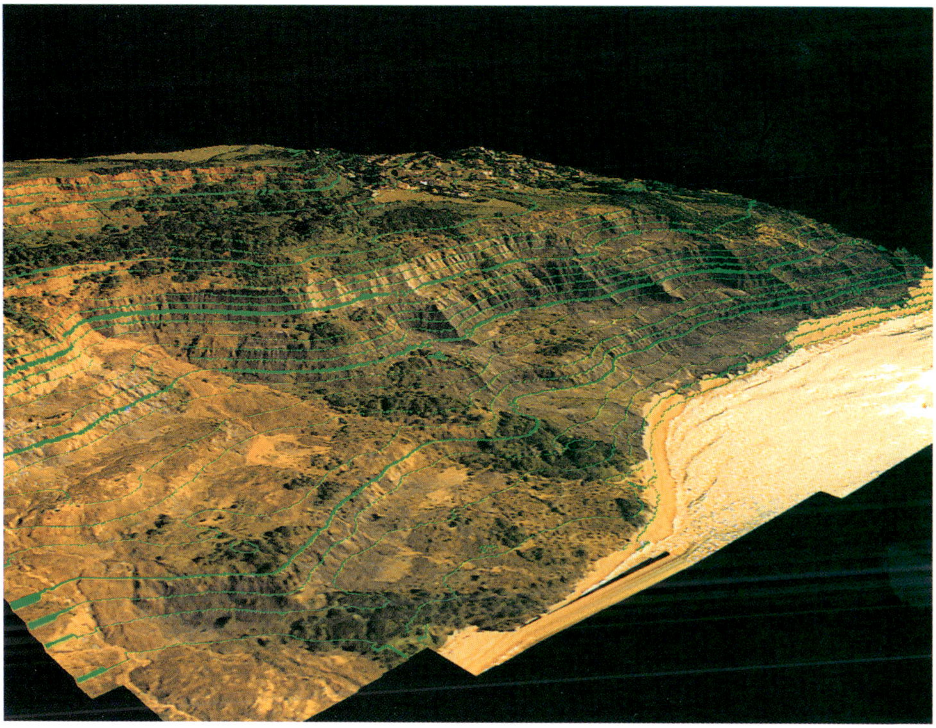

Figure 9.2 *Computer-generated perspective view of Lyme Bay area, Dorset coast. Generated from orthophoto (DCS-460CIR image) in VirtuoZo with 25 m contours. Photograph: Alexander Koh.*

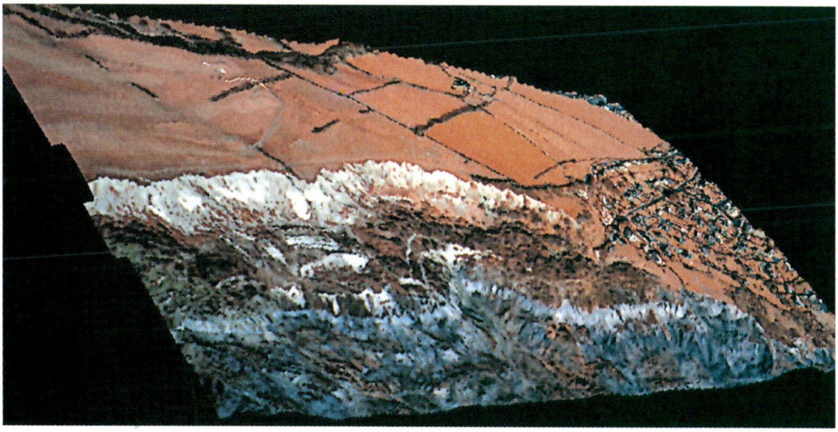

Figure 11.4 *Perspective view of the Black Ven landslide complex. DCS-460CIR imagery,* f = *15mm, GSD = 50cm. Photograph: Alexander Koh.*

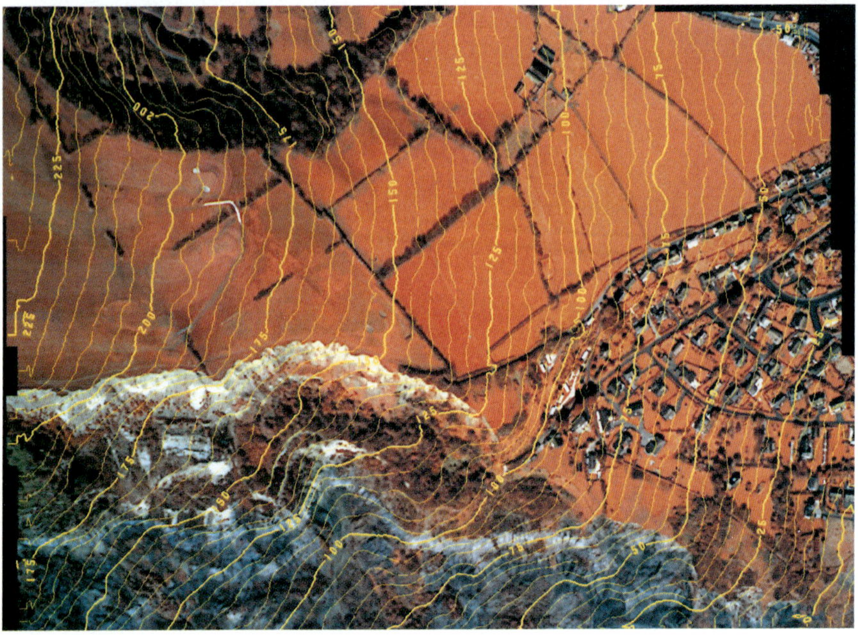

Figure 11.5 *Contoured orthophoto image of the Black Ven landslide complex. DCS-460CIR imagery,* f = *15mm, GSD = 50cm, contours at 5 m. Photograph: Alexander Koh.*

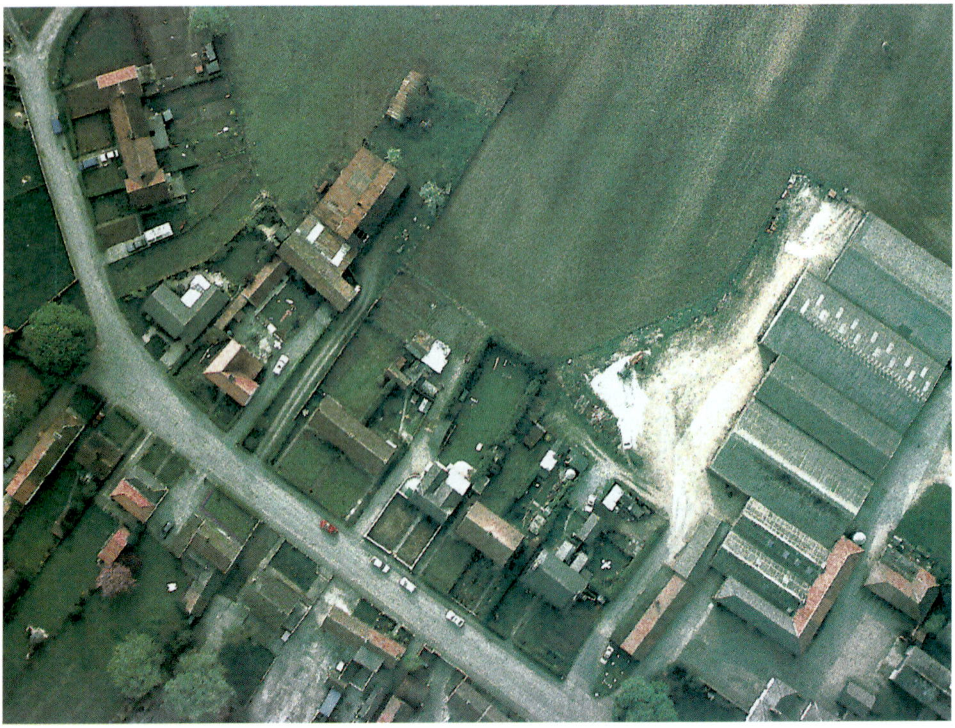

Figure 12.1 *Raskelf village, North Yorkshire. DCS-200 camera, 28 mm lens. Photoscale: 1:17,000. Thruster microlight at 1550 ft. Photograph: Dr Jon Mills.*

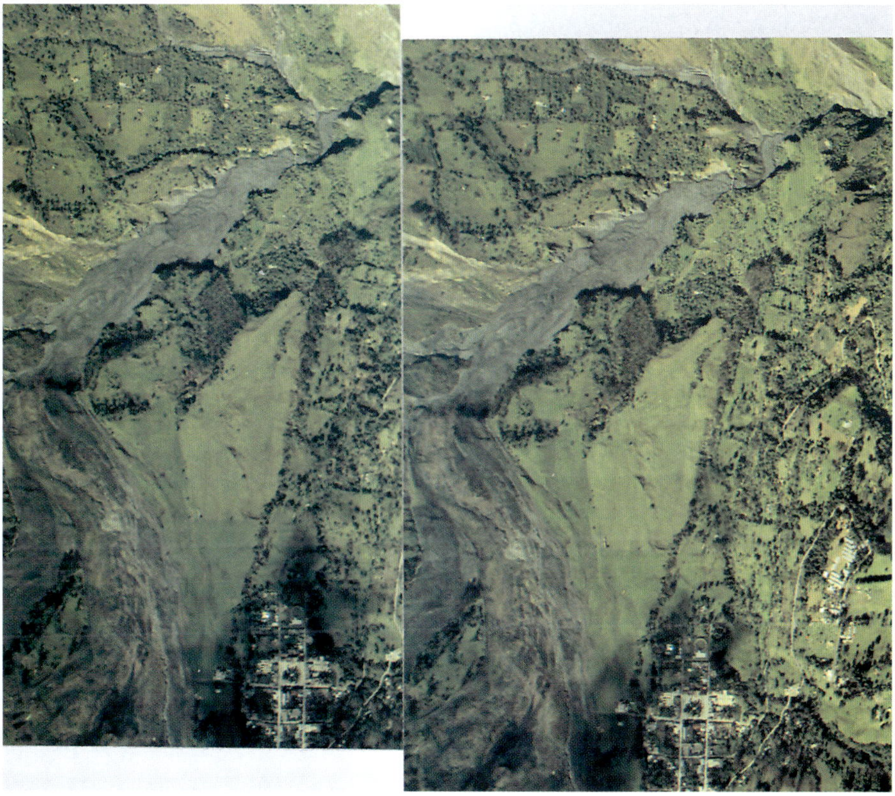

Figure 12.5 *Stereo-pair of the small mountain town of San Cayetano, Columbia (mean height c. 12,000 ft). The DCS-460CIR camera was flown at about 17,000 ft to provide a photo-scale of 1:55,000 and GSD of 50 cm. The massive landslip can be seen at the foot of the mountain just to the left of the town. Photographs: Esther Edwards and Alexander Koh.*

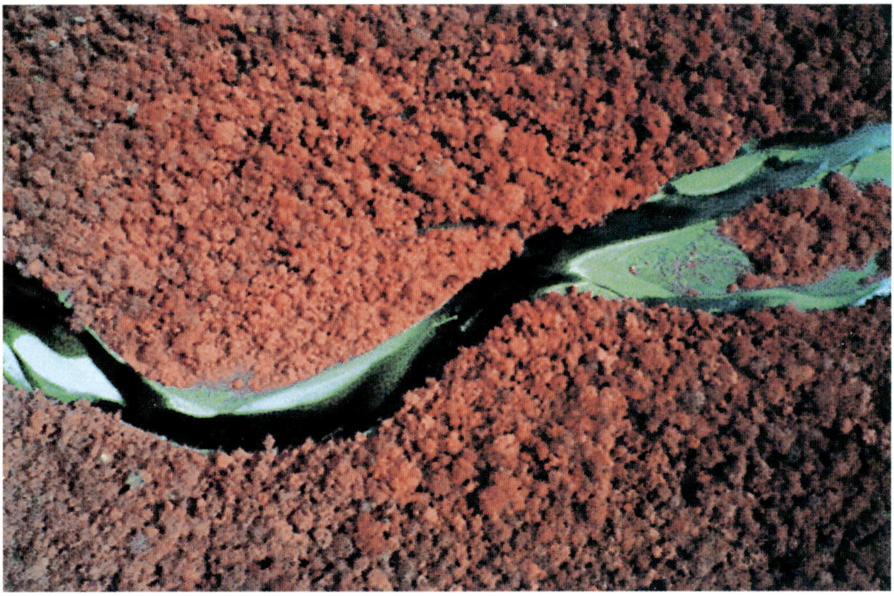

Figure 12.6 *Part of the river Aikwa deposition area, West Papua (New Guinea). Heavy sediment tailings and their effects on adjacent forest areas are made obvious by CIR photography. DCS-460CIR image (28 mm lens) and photo-scale 1:57,000. Photographs: Ron Graham and Alexander Koh*

Figure 12.8 *The West Bay landslip area, Dorset. This DCS-460 colour photograph was taken at an average height of 5600 ft amsl. Photo-scale is 1:60,000 and the GSD is 54 cm. Photograph: Esther Edwards and Alexander Koh*

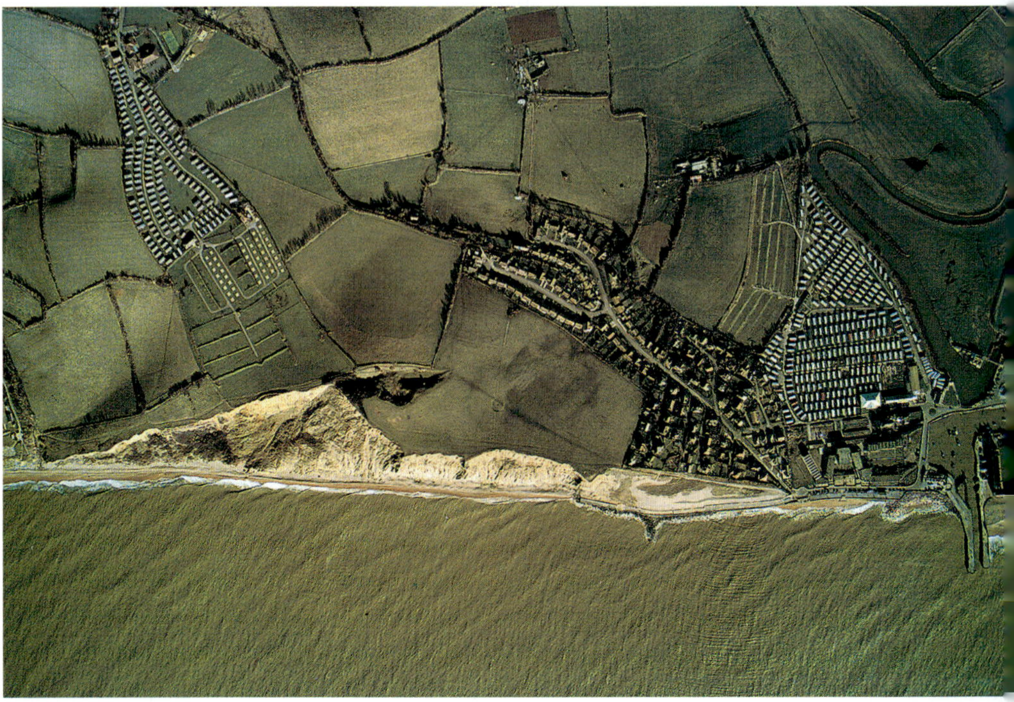

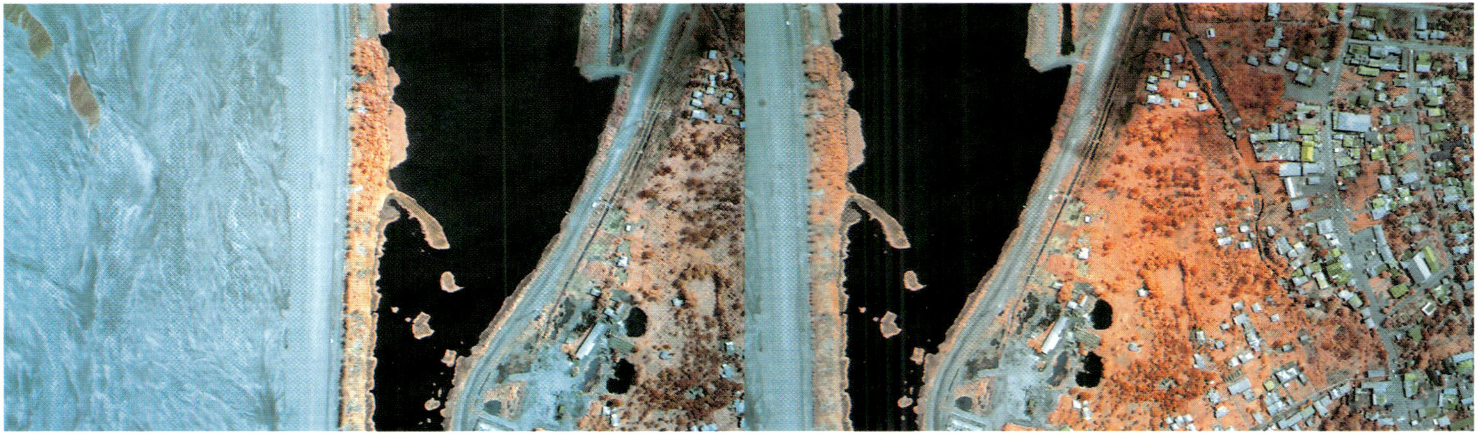

Figure 12.7 *The Aikwa deposition area, West Papua. The town of Timika can be seen on the right of this DCS-460CIR stereo-pair, and the levee system protecting the town from silting overflow is shown on the left of the river Aikwa. Note the strong infrared absorption (black) by the river, indicating an absence of tailing deposits. Photographs: Ron Graham and Alexander Koh.*

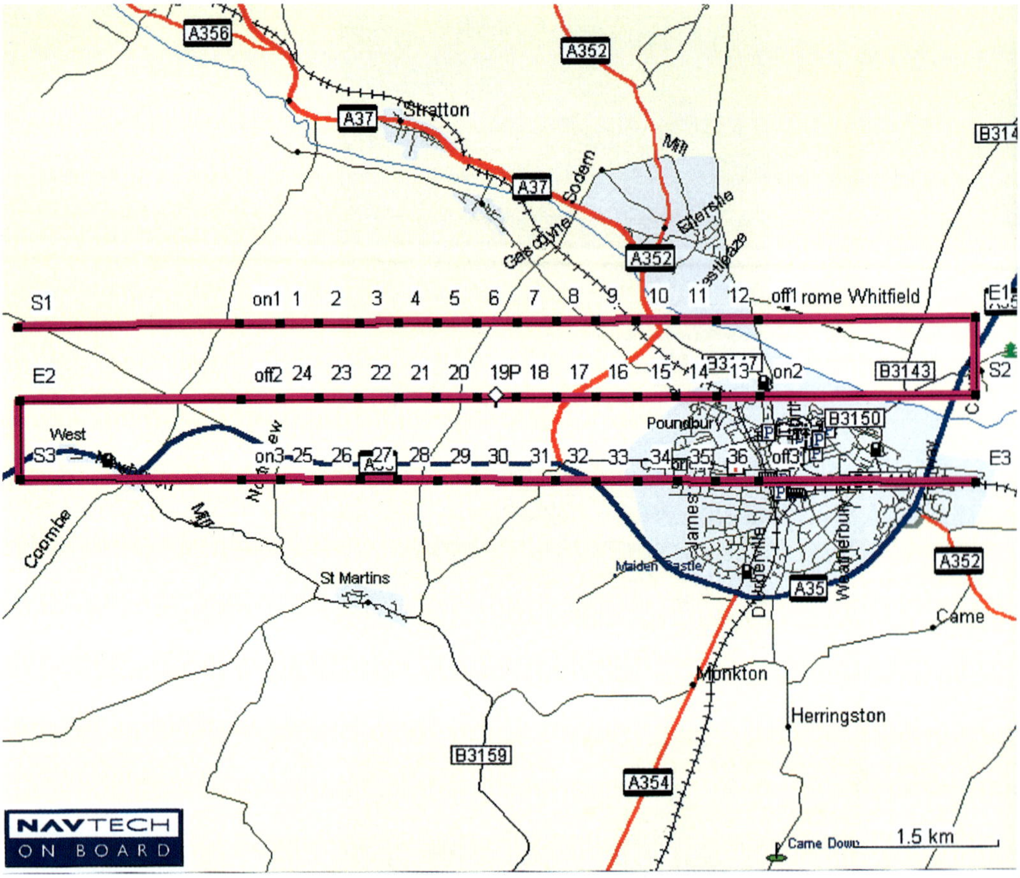

Figure 12.15 *GPS flight planning is conveniently made with the aid of Garmin MapSource software. Here a small three-line survey of Poundbury (Dorchester) is mapped with UTM WGS84 coordinates on West-East, East-West tracks over 10 km flight-lines.*

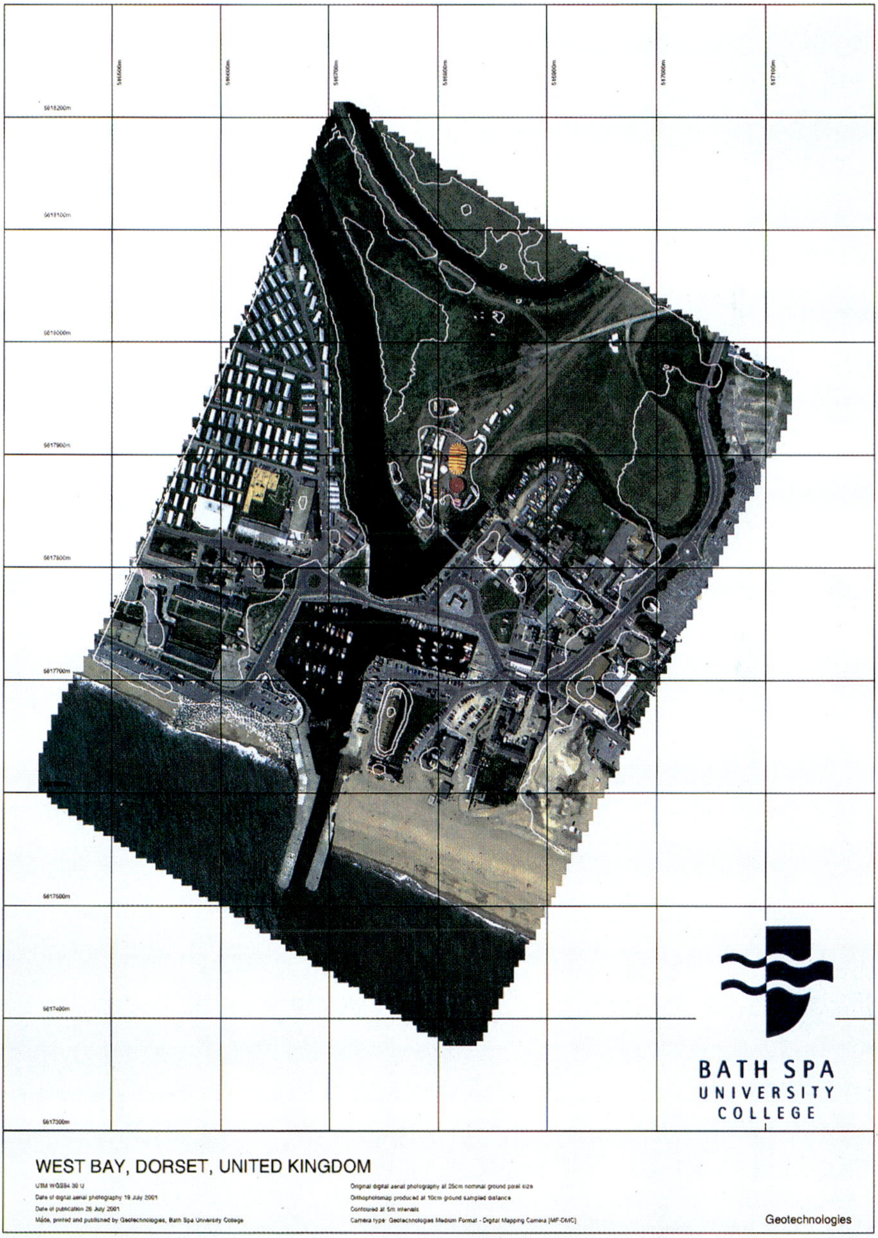

Figure 12.16 *A 5 m contoured orthophotomap (1:1000 original scale) of West Bay, Dorset, overlaid with UTM WGS84 30 U coordinate grid. Taken from MF-DMC(2) imagery with digital photogrammetry by VirtuoZo. Map production from MapInfo software. From a Geotechnologies training program, produced by Jaacub bin Yusoff and Yazir Sardi, July 2001.*

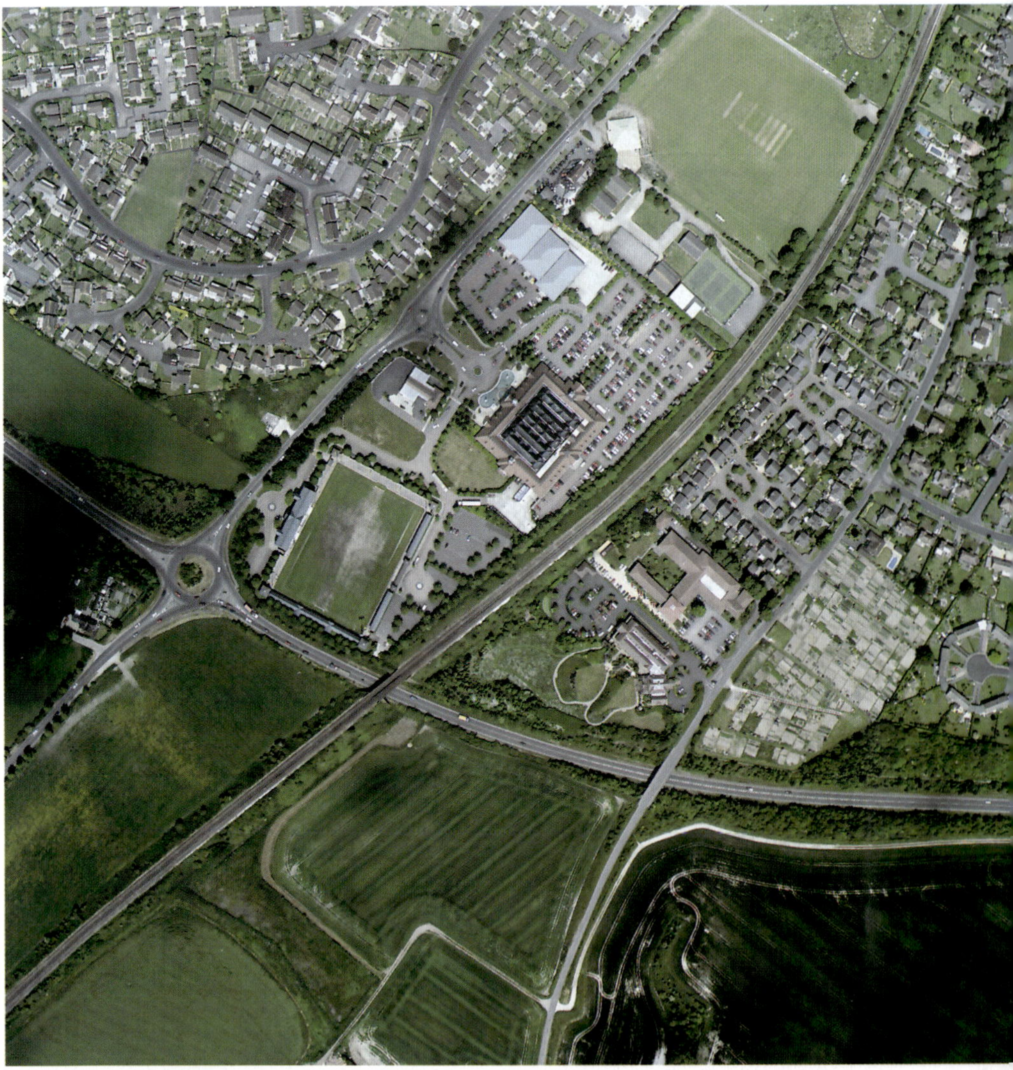

Figure 12.17 *MF-DMC(2) image taken over Dorchester at c. 6000 ft. Zeiss planar 80mm lens, photo-scale 1:22,200. Exposed at 1/250 sec at f/5.6 with a GSD = 20 cm. Photograph: Alexander Koh.*

OPPOSITE: **Figure 12.21** *A composite orthophotomap produced from overlaying a digital orthophotomap (colour insert at centre) on a black and white orthophotomap produced from analogue mapping. The digital insert was made from five MF-DMC(2) images taken at 18,000 ft from a Bell 412 helicopter. The Grasberg copper mine (at 12,5000 ft) can be seen to the left of centre in the digital section.*

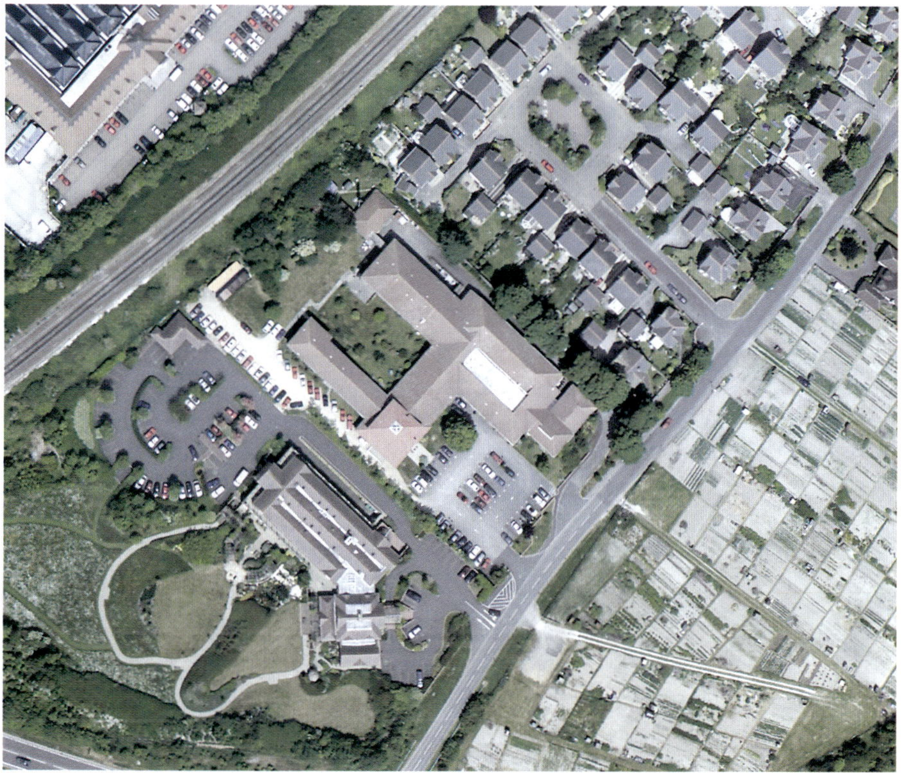

Figure 12.18 *A portion of the 16MPx image shown in Fig.12.18 is here enlarged to gain maximum detail.*

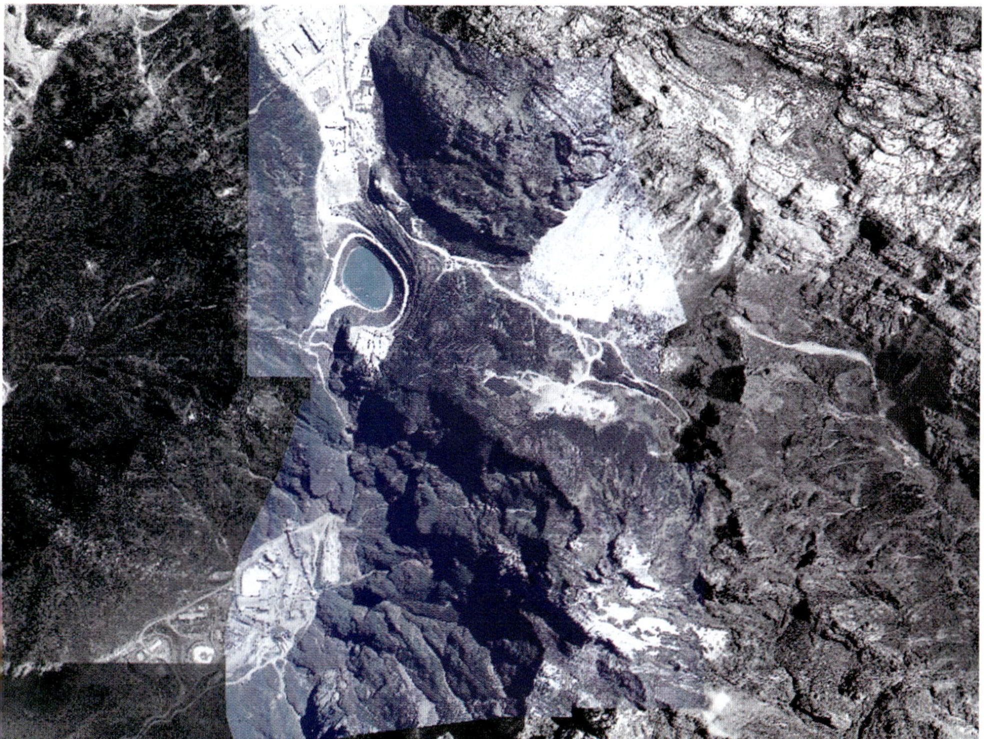

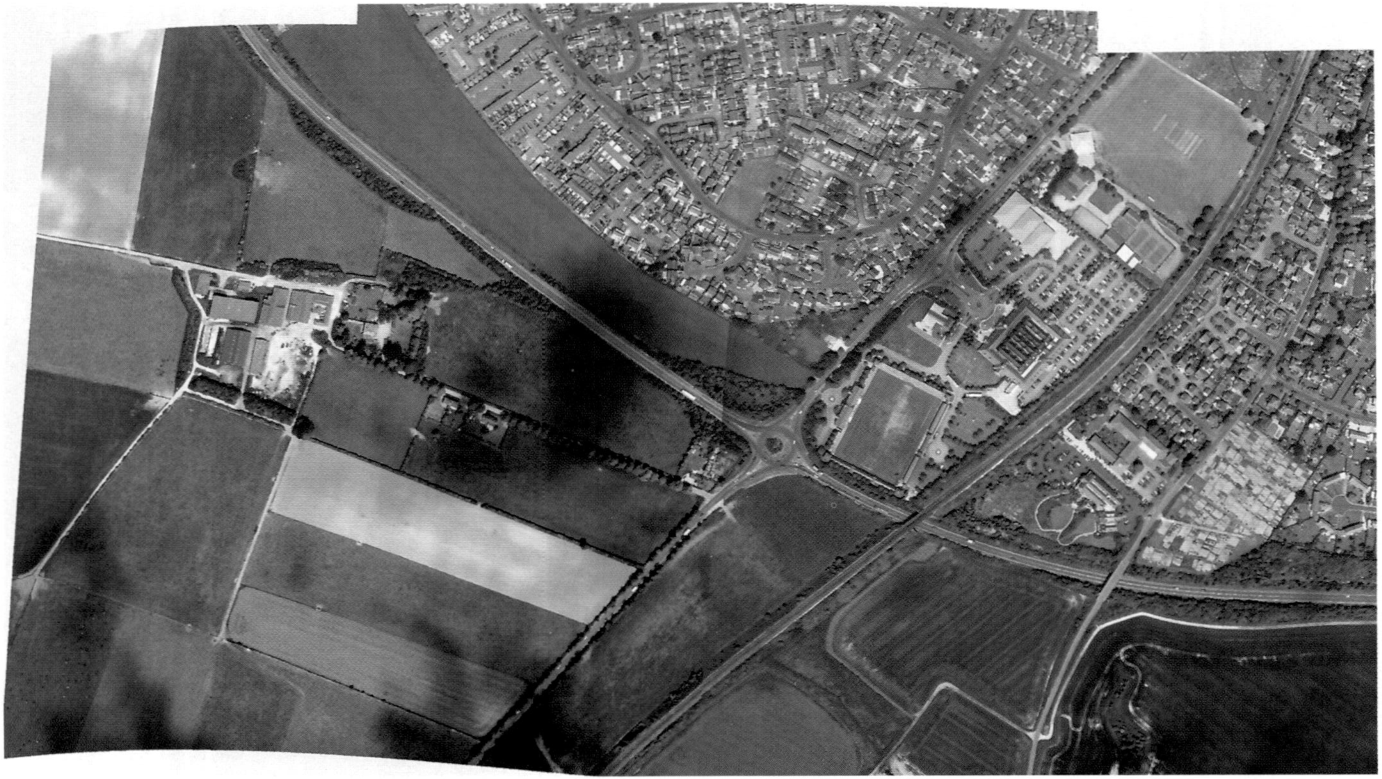

Figure 12.19 *A three photo (uncontrolled) mosaic of the lower Dorchester area. MF-DMC(2) images mosaiced in ER Mapper. Mosaic made by Dr. Rick Curr (Geotechnologies).*

mode to make a camera exposure as soon as the position cursor illuminates each waypoint (WP) along the flight-line track.

Even with an inexpensive receiver, such as the Garmin GPS-12 (costing no more than $180), this method has proved to be very efficient. When a programmed route has been called up to the GPS map display, an appropriate screen scale can be applied and the aircraft's progress monitored along the flight-line so that each leg (from one WP to the next) is followed by the position cursor. As each WP represents progressive photo-centres (at a given forward overlap) the GPS system ensures an accurate flight-line, with accurate overlap, providing the aircraft is flown accurately down the prescribed route.

The advantage of GPS intervalometry is that regardless of wind vectors, the aircraft can be flown to a correct ground speed and its position over the terrain is known to within a few meters. Indeed, even the Garmin GPS-12 (with a good selection of satellites) can provide a 3D navigational accuracy of 5 m EPE (estimated position error).

As we shall see from Chapters 7 and 8, survey flight planning requires very careful attention, and the technique employed by Geotechnologies is to first complete survey flight-planning in the Excel-based ASLP program (Chapter 8). These data are then entered into the Garmin MapSource software (stored in the on-board computer) which draws the flight-lines and waypoints for the survey block at a suitable scale on any of the world-wide range of maps available from MapSource. The stored survey data is then sent to the navigator's GPS receiver (such as the Garmin GPS Map 295). Survey navigation is then simply a question of flying each line in accordance with the GPS moving map display, and making the appropriate exposure when each waypoint (photo-centre) is reached.

7 Survey flight management: tracking, GPS, mission planning

Very few job descriptions manage to survive technological change beyond a few decades, and although some survive through common usage, the majority just fade away. In aviation there will always be the need for navigation, but the specialised role of navigator has now been replaced by anyone who has a global positioning system in their hands. Indeed, even the Royal Air Force has now removed the 'navigator' from its air crew categories.

The title of this chapter could have been 'air survey navigation' but, to be exact, very little true navigation is involved in the average survey operation. In the past, a typical mapping company would employ a three-man crew (ladies included) made up of a pilot, a survey-navigator (tracker) and camera operator. When air camera technology allowed the survey navigator to also operate the camera, the survey air-crew could be reduced to two people.

The real task of navigation has always been in the hands of the pilot, who has the responsibility of taking the aircraft to its survey area, and then flying over a series of survey-lines under the direction of his correctly designated 'survey flight tracker'. This seeming pedantry has always been justified because the term 'tracker' is more appropriate to the task of directing the pilot onto pre-planned survey flight-lines so that the entire survey block (terrain area) is covered with appropriate photography.

Survey-flight tracking

The role of the survey-flight tracker is two-fold; (a) mission planning (on the ground) and (b) in-flight tracking of the required survey lines. The job is the same as previously, but current methods lead to far greater efficiency and flight-line accuracy. Working procedures are much changed too, with the work-load on the ground being much greater than it is in the air – all due to survey flight management system (SFMS) technology.

A survey tracker's basic ground work includes drawing up flight-lines on 1:50,000 or 1:25,000 scale maps, calculating the relevant survey parameters, preparing the entire camera system, checking the weather and, with the pilot, pre-flighting the aircraft and organising all necessary flight approvals. Whereas the navigation element was mainly a question of drawing lines on maps, today it is more a question of entering data into the computer of the SFMS.

In-flight survey work (in cooperation with the pilot) consists mainly of determining wind drift, checking ground speed, and directing the pilot onto various flight-lines. In the past (and even today) the tracker kept the pilot 'on-line' by tracking the desired flight-line through a navigation sight while passing small heading corrections to him as required. During this time the tracker is constantly monitoring drift corrections and checking ground features against the map. Initially the tracker may have needed to determine the wind as a vector quantity, providing both velocity and direction. Such in-flight calculations were drawn via a wind-star diagram – truly a navigator's task of the old school! Indeed, these tasks created a heavy work-load on the tracker/navigator who, in addition, would probably be correcting the camera for drift, checking exposure and changing film magazines (or PCMCIA cards).

In-flight operations with an SFMS are much easier. The tracker will have a GPS display showing at a single glance the aircraft's track, heading and ground speed. Any variation between track and heading is readily interpreted as drift, which is then corrected on the camera mount. The SFMS will also apply the required exposure interval (ΔT), record GPS data (latitude, longitude time of exposure etc.) and most of all provide navigation waypoints for each line. The pilot may also have a repeater GPS monitor which allows him to fly each line without any directions from the tracker.

The role of the tracker now requires even less navigation skill than before, particularly since the basic concepts of 'dead-reckoning' are no longer required. For this reason he is now (correctly) employed as a survey flight manager (SFM), a term universally accepted as the appropriate job description for a survey navigator (tracker).

Today, all competitive survey companies use SFMSs, all of which run off an airborne GPS installation. Almost overnight, the traditional navigation sight was relegated to second place and almost rendered redundant. One of the original units was the SFMS designed by Prof. Dr F. J. Heimes and his team at the Fachhochschule Bochum, Germany. This unit was then taken over by Leica-Wild and is now sold as the Ascot for their RC-20 and RC-30 air cameras.

At about the same time Zeiss produced their own SFMS called 'T-Flight'. Perhaps the most successful SFMS (also from Germany) is the IGI CCNS-4, designed by Prof. Dr. Albrecht Grimm. This unit has sold well throughout the world and is used with many types of air camera. Depending on its level of sophistication a typical SFMS is quite costly because of the the computer, survey-flight software, GPS unit and various interfaces. However, a basic SFMS known as the 'Tracker' has a good reputation with many operators and is relatively cheap at c. $18,000. A full list of SFMS suppliers is given in Appendix C.

The role of the pilot

All commercial pilots are familiar with monitoring the extensive display of instruments on their cockpit dashboard. There are the main flying instruments, such as the magnetic compass, direction indicator, altimeter, air-speed indicator (ASI), rate of climb, artificial horizon and turn and slip indicator. The practised survey pilot will constantly sweep through these instruments while keeping 'on-line' and, in addition, monitor the radio as well keep a sharp look out for other traffic. Other instruments, such as weather-radar, fuel states, engine performance etc., also require constant inspection and are often integrated into an EFIS (electronic flight information system) display.

It could be thought that an additional instrument would only create an unwanted burden on the pilot and, as a consequence, early trials with a GPS-controlled SFMS were conducted by SFMs who directed their pilots (over the intercom) in the usual fashion, i.e, "two-left... steady...one right" etc. But after a while most pilots found that they could handle the extra EFIS without difficulty and actually preferred to "fly the needle" – just as they do with VOR navigation.

The CCNS4 is a highly developed SFMS, incorporating a 5 inch CRT display with a separate panel for information and management functions (Fig.7.1). Known as the 'Command & Display Unit' (CDU), the l/h display offers graphic flight guidance information, leaving the r/h panel for a variety of changeable management functions.

A typical SFMS display with GPS navigation inputs is shown in Fig.7.1. Controlled by pilot flight inputs and corrected by displayed data, the aircraft can easily be steered onto the desired flight-line. The display shown in Fig.7.1 is a typical CCNS4 in-flight example, which is also common to most SFMSs. The SFMS will be under the direct supervision of the SFM, but usually the pilot will have his own (repeater) monitor from which he can fly the aircraft on-line.

Figure 7.1 is an in-flight illustration of a typical survey mission. The aircraft's current heading (Hdg) of 353° is displayed at the top of the screen. The vertical dashed line is static and represents the true ground track (Trk) now being flown (showing 359° at its top). The vertical solid line moves in accordance with the pilot's inputs, and as the pilot flies to the required track it will move onto the dashed line. Pilots generally discuss this type of instrument flying as 'following the needle'.

The right-hand panel of Fig.7.1shows the principal survey-flight parameters which are, from top to bottom: the first flight line starting at + 01 (it ends at –1), the desired

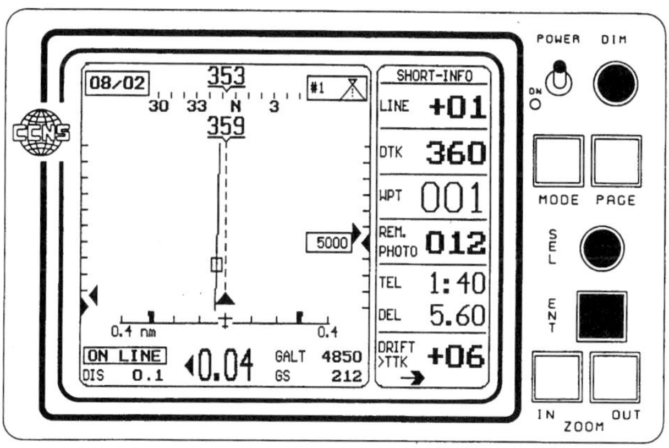

Figure 7.1 *A typical SFMS display from CCNS4 showing current heading (353°). The vertical (dashed) line is static and represents the required ground track (Trk) now being flown at 359°. The solid line (now vertical and close to the required track) moves according to pilot input.*

survey track (DTK) is 360°, the first waypoint (WPT) is 001, the remaining photos are 12, the time to the end of the line (TEL) is 1:40, the distance to the end of the line (DEL) is 5.60nm and the drift is +6° to the right of the aircraft's heading, i.e, true track (TTK) = 359° from the heading of 353°.

For the pilot now 'flying the needle' he sees that the aircraft must be flown towards the desired true track (DTK) shown by the solid line, so he steers left. But as the only movable line in the display is the solid line, this must move to the right – until the solid line is superimposed on the dashed line. He will also have noticed (in the bottom left hand corner of the display) that the magnetic bearing to his first marker point (MKR) shows ON LINE (i.e, 360°), so he is very close. The small square on the solid line slides down the line to indicate the next exposure as it reaches the bottom.

The pilot will also see that the distance to the next waypoint (DIS) is 0.1nm, and his off-track error is only 0.04nm (the off-track distance scale shown here is set to a maximum of 0.4nm). At the bottom right of the display is the true altitude (TALT) at 4850 ft (the required altitude is flagged at 5000 ft, as shown in the right hand column) and his ground speed (GS) which is 212 kts. The pilot can monitor the time to the next exposure by watching the arrow at the left-hand column as it moves down to the base (the full scale is 2nm) . This helps him concentrate and keep the aircraft steady before the critical exposure is made. The rectangle shown at the top left of the display contains information regarding the number of satellites currently received by the GPS receiver (here shown as eight), and the positioning accuracy provided by AEROcontrol (here shown as 2 m).

By such instrumentation the pilot finds survey flying simple, reliable and accurate. The SFMS computer can also print-out the position accuracy for each survey line within the block, as shown by Fig.7.2.

The role of the survey flight manager (SFM)

Regardless of technical innovation, all survey missions have to be carefully prepared and this is the survey flight manager's job. This responsibility also stretches to the survey flight itself, where the SFM is totally in charge of the mission. The pilot is, of course, in charge of the aircraft and the safety of his crew, but the mission has to be controlled by the SFM who still has some data to enter into an SFMS such as the CCNS4.

As the aircraft approaches to within 20 miles of the first survey line a few aircraft instruments must be read, calculations made and fresh flight data entered into the SFMS. Firstly the true altitude (TALT) needs to be calculated which (with the CCNS4 at least) can be done by entering pressure altitude (altimeter set at 1013.2 mb), QNH (altimeter set at regional sea level pressure) and outside air temperature (OAT) into the calculation page on the r/h side of the CDU. Secondly, the SFM must check with the pilot that the aircraft is trimmed for level flight, so that the camera (and navigation sight if used) can be levelled.

The global positioning system (GPS)

Planned by the USA in 1971, the first Block 1, 'Navstar GPS' (standing for NAVigation Satellite Timing And Ranging Global Positioning System) satellite was launched

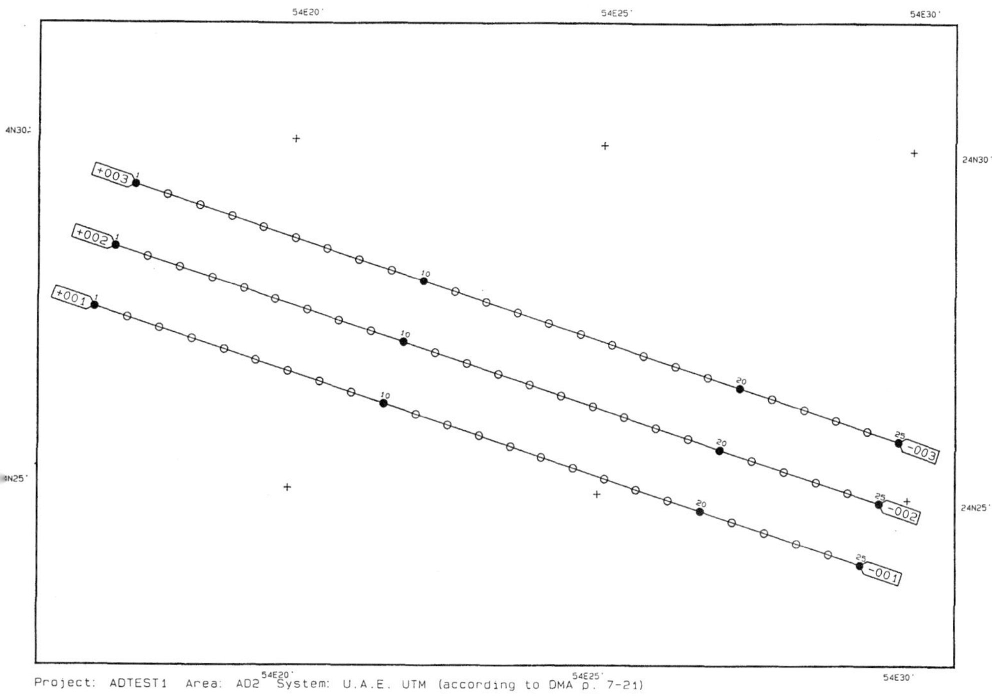

Figure 7.2 *Computer print-out of CCNS4 flight-lines.*

in 1978. By 1985 there were seven satellite vehicles in orbit for calibration, testing and development. By the early 1990s survey aircraft were making use of GPS signals and SFMSs were being tested and developed. The NavStar system consists of three segments:

The space segment

Consisting of 24 orbiting satellites, these space vehicles are arranged in 6 different orbital planes (4 satellites in each) at an orbital altitude of 20,193km (10,898nm). The satellites orbit every 12 hours at an inclination of 55° to the earth's polar axis, with 21 fully active and the remaining three in reserve. At any time, night or day, at least four satellite signals can be received at any place on earth, each transmitting a continuous string of data at precise intervals on two different (L-Band) carrier frequencies, L1 and L2 (L1 = 1575 MHz and L2 = 1228MHz). This allows for three-dimensional positioning in longitude, latitude and altitude (x,y,z), whether on land, sea or air, provided that no less than four satellites are in view.

The control segment

Control of the satellite network is provisioned by five ground stations throughout the world. These are situated at: Ascension Island (Atlantic Ocean), Kwajalein and Hawaii (Pacific Ocean), Diego Garcia (Indian Ocean) and the master ground station at Falcon Air Force Base near Colorado Springs USA. Transmitted data received by a ground station is then passed on to the master control centre where the exact orbit of each satellite is calculated (known as ephemeris). By combining these data with a complex mathematical model of the earth's gravity field, it is possible to predict the position of the satellite for many hours ahead. This predicted orbit data is then transmitted to the satellite to be stored in the on-board computer. These data are then re-transmitted to the user segment of the overall system (see Fig.7.3).

The user segment

The user segment is the GPS receiver. Its purpose is to receive all satellites 'in-view' or above the horizon at any one time, and to measure the delay-time between signal transmission and reception. These data are then converted into an accurate navigational position. The distance from each satellite has to be measured accurately in order for these calculations to be made, and since the location of each satellite is known, its distance from the GPS receiver can be found providing we know exactly how long it took for the signal to reach the receiver. The radio signal travels through space as electromagnetic radiation (EMR travels at 300,000 km/s) and if we know how long it took the signal to travel from satellite to receiver, we can determine the exact distance (speed = distance/time).

The most critical element in the entire process is timing, and the GPS receiver starts the process by measuring the signal's time of arrival, and for this to happen the receiver must know (a) when the signal left the satellite and (b) when it arrived at the receiver. Obviously some form of synchronisation between the satellite and receiver is essential.

Each of the satellites has a distinct encoded signal in the form of a pseudo-random noise (PRN) code (see Fig.7.4) and the process the GPS receiver goes through to measure the transit time of each satellite signal is in five steps:

1. Receive and decode the satellite's repeated signal pattern (PRN).

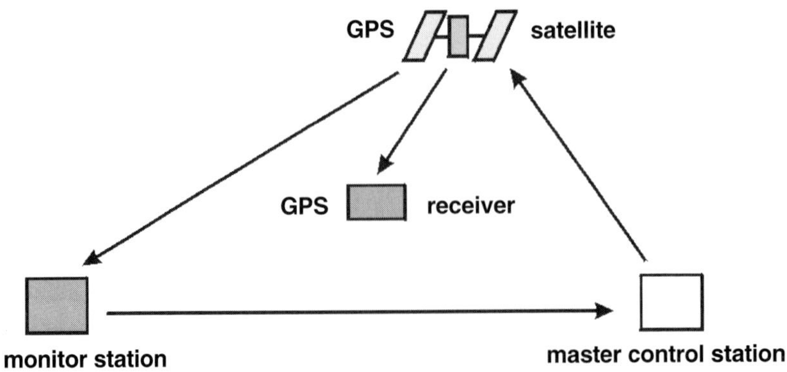

Figure 7.3 *Basis of the global positioning system (GPS).*

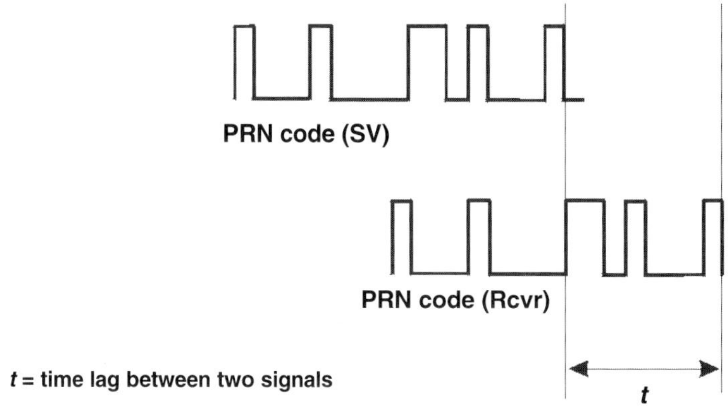

Figure 7.4 *GPS pseudo-random noise (PRN) code.*

2. Generate the same version of the satellite's signal internally.
3. Compare the received signal pattern and the internally generated signal pattern.
4. Quantify the time lag (phase difference) between the two signals.
5. Apply the speed - time- distance equation to determine distance.

Highly accurate clocks have to be employed in GPS since their precision affects the eventual accuracy of the system. Atomic clocks using cesium, rubidium and other elements are constantly being improved and usually four atomic clocks are installed in each satellite (one prime unit and three for back-up). Since the cost of high precision atomic clocks would be too costly for a GPS receiver, they use a slightly less accurate quartz regulated clock.

GPS accuracy

NavStar GPS was originally a military concept, and in order to provide for some measure of protection the US military introduced selective availability (SA) in which errors (of the order of 100 m) were introduced into the timing signals of selected satellites to give small shifts in the calculated position for 95% of the time. For its own purposes the US military had access to the more precise P Code. Fortunately for civilian purposes SA was removed by act of congress in May 1999. However, during the time SA was in force a system known as differential GPS ((d)GPS) was introduced as a partial answer to the dilution of precision (DOP). Two methods were possible: the simplest was to make corrections to the recorded data, or corrections were incorporated at the time of exposure by transmitting differential GPS up-dates in real-time. Both of these (d)GPS systems require a static receiver held at a suitable ground station within 50 km of the survey area.

The object of the second (static) receiver held at a GPS ground station is to establish the exact position of the imagery. The long term aim is to reduce, or even eliminate, the need for costly ground control. Ground control operations are always expensive and sometimes prohibitively so, particularly where large areas of tropical forest, desert or other regions of inhospitable terrain have to be surveyed.

In a typical (d)GPS survey the aircraft records a line of GPS data every second (although now it is possible to record at 20Hz), and the centre point exposure-time of each image is also recorded. After the flight, exposure times are compared to the similar data line recorded at the ground station. The raw data from both stations will contain identical errors at the same instant of exposure, both being subjected to almost identical factors, such as: clock/ephemeris, atmosphere, receiver noise, multipath errors and (when it was applied) SA. But with the ground station being static and operated from an accurately measured WGS84 (World Geodetic System 1984) position, the received positional data from the satellite can be corrected in x, y and z, to establish the actual error at the time of exposure. The ground station correction can then be applied to the x, y and z data recorded in the aircraft to give the corrected position of the aircraft GPS antenna at the time of exposure. A further correction is required to allow for the displacement between camera and GPS antenna.

Naturally GPS technology never stands still and improvements are constantly being made. Among these are systems that employ an inertial measurement unit (IMU) as well as a 12 channel (d)GPS receiver to gain platform positioning accuracies of 0.3–0.5m real-time, and 0.1– 0.2m post aero-triangulation accuracy, depending on the distance between platform and receiver. Such is the IGI-CCNS AERO control system mentioned previously.

Yet another system that shows great promise for future aerial surveys is the Fugro-Omnistar (d)GPS system. This system with global coverage allows the aircraft to receive signals from the Omnistar satellite as well as the GPS satellites. GPS signals are received by the Omnistar ground station and in conjunction with data received at the satellite, retransmits corrected position and ephemeris data to the aircraft. In the aircraft the Omnistar unit integrates the incoming uncorrected signal to give real-time correction to the SFMS (such as the CCNS4). In this fashion (d)GPS is achieved using only the aircraft's receiver, as opposed to the conventional air-station, ground-station and separate navigation system. Further details are discussed in Chapter 9, and in Read and Graham (2002).

Survey mission planning

Obviously all missions start with a client, who wants a mission to be completed according to certain requirements, and within documented specifications. The client will need to discuss these requirements with the SFM. Primary mission details, open to discussion between client and contractor, lead to agreed specifications and are the basis for a formal contract. Typical items for discussion are outlined in Table.7.1.

Survey flight planning: formulae and calculations

Photo-scale and ground coverage

For calculations we use the scale number (m) which is related to the focal length of the camera lens (f) and the flying height above ground (H).

$$m = H/f \qquad (7.1)$$

Table. 7.1 *Survey discussion points: specifications and agreements*

(i)	Defined mission area: boundaries, terrain and available maps.
(ii)	Photo-scale (camera image scale).
(iii)	Type of photography (colour, monochrome, infrared etc.).
(iv)	Survey products (repro-scales, line maps, orthophotos, mosaics, loose prints).
(v)	Survey specifications (forward and side lap, crab, heights, contours and datums).
(vi)	Flying conditions: (mountains, borders, weather, visibility, solar altitude etc).
(vii)	Survey mobilisation and conclusion dates: (limitations and constraints).
(viii)	Airborne GPS, (d)GPS and special survey instrumentation.
(ix)	Survey logistics: Flying hours, airfield and fuel availablity, maintenance etc.
(x)	Camera calibration: certificate and expiry date.
(xi)	Delivery date of survey products (with exceptions for weather etc).
(xii)	Flight reports and indexing.
(xiii)	Image quality: spatial and radiometric resolution, contrast, noise, dynamic range, artifacts etc.
(xiv)	Form of contract: fees, expenses, ownership, copyright, arbitration, demurrage rates (aircraft on ground).
(xv)	Licences and experience of survey crew.

Scale may also be considered in terms of the ratio between the side-dimension of the image (s) and its related side of the ground covered (S).

$$m = S/s \tag{7.2}$$

from which we can put:

$$S = sm = Hs/f \tag{7.3}$$

These relationships are shown in Fig. 7. 5.

Air base (B) and forward overlap (p)

If we adopt the standard forward overlap of 60%, the distance between centre-points of successive photographs will be an air base (B) of 40% of the ground coverage, i.e, $B = 0.4S$. For p expressed as a percentage the base (B) is calculated as:

$$B = S(1 - p/100) \tag{7.4}$$

or, more conveniently, with p expressed as a decimal we can use:

$$B = S(1 - p) \tag{7.5}$$

The air base and associated overlap between two consecutive photographs is shown in Fig.7.6.

Number of exposures (N_p) per flight-line (L_p)

The number of photographs required to cover a given length of flight-line (L_p) can be calculated from:

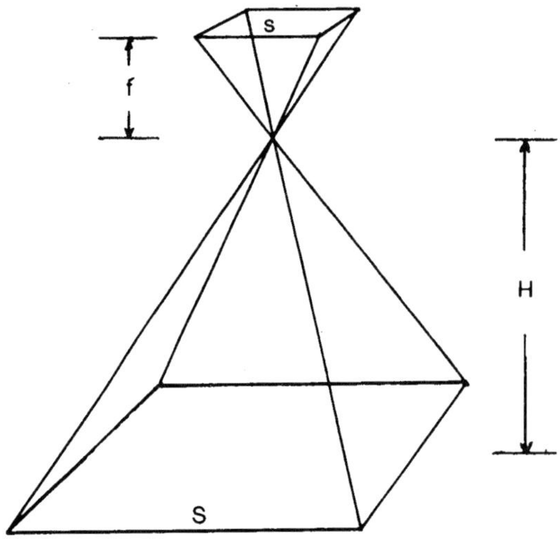

Figure 7.5 *Photo-scale relationships, where:* $m_b = H/f \equiv S/s$.

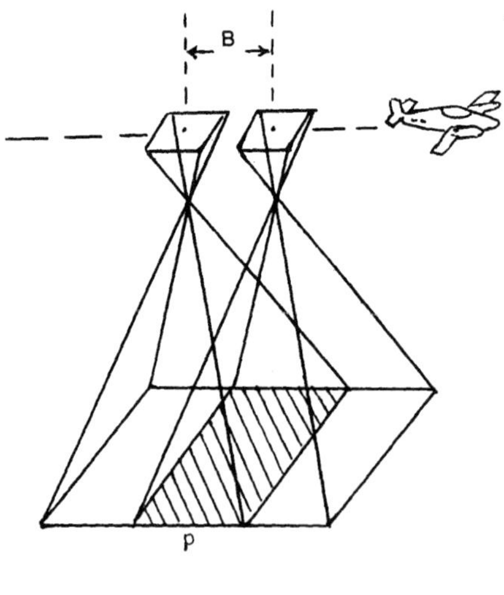

Figure 7.6 *Air-base (B) and forward overlap (p). For stereoscopic cover p is usually 0.6S.*

$$N_p = (L_p/B) + 1 \tag{7.6}$$

Note: At his discretion, the SFM will usually add one or two photographs before and after the number calculated above, depending upon terrain and flying conditions. The camera-on point for example is best planned to include at least two air-base distances outside of the block, to avoid the possibility of a stereo-gap at the start of the run.

Side-overlap (q) and number of flight-lines (N_q)

Very few survey missions consist of only a single flight-line, and normally the survey block will require a number of runs, each separated from its neighbour by a distance (a), and overlapping its neighbour by a specified amount of side-lap (q), as shown for the two flight-lines of Fig. 7.7. On average, a typical side-lap will be anything from 25% to 35%, depending on either client specifications or, more usually, according to the SFM's advice. For relatively flat terrain, side-overlap can be reduced to about 15% and will provide significant economic advantages (perhaps saving an extra line or two) but if the terrain is hilly, or mountainous, a wide tolerance to perhaps 40% side-lap may be essential.

The spacing between neighbouring flight-lines (a) is calculated according to the amount of side-lap required:

$$a = S(1 - q/100) \tag{7.7}$$

Having found a value for a we may now calculate the number of flight-lines (N_q) required from Eq . 7.8.

$$N_q = \{(L_q - S) / a\} + 1 \tag{7.8}$$

where L_q is the width of the survey block.

For economic survey flight, each turn onto the next flight line is like that shown in Fig.7.7, but there are situations where each flight-line must start (+ve) from the same end. In Fig. 7.7 we show a direct turn onto the next flight-line, but this is only one of a few types of survey turn.

Air survey turns

Normally each survey turn is done by visual tracking, where flying over prominant ground features is quite simple. But when flying over deserts, jungle, moorland or swamps, tracking from one line to the next can be almost impossible by visual means. Under these circumstances it is possible for a well-practiced pilot to fly from one flight-line to the next by instruments alone. Keeping the platform straight and level during

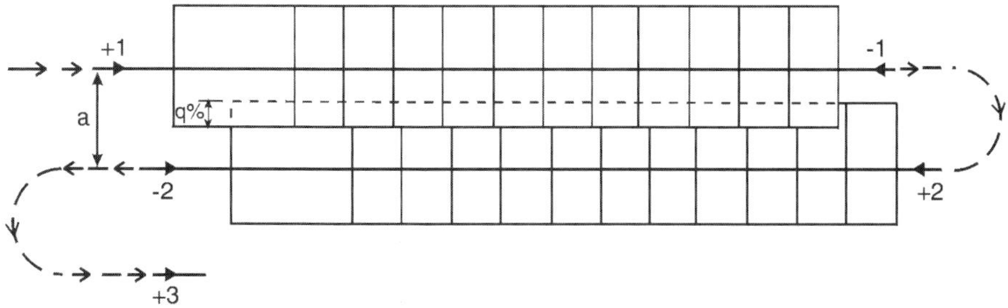

Figure 7.7 *Side-overlap (q) of adjacent flight-lines is usually between 20% and 35% of S. Distance between lines is given by: $a = S(1 - q/100)$ where q is given as a %.*

each run, and with a knowledge of the aircrafts drift and required track, the pilot can keep altitude and turn onto the next line by careful regard to instruments.

Survey turns can can take a number of forms, but the three most well known are: (a) direct turns, (b) U-turns and (c) S-turns, all of which can be flown by instruments with the aid of the Q-Basic computer programs listed in App. D.

Direct survey turns

By far the most efficient and simplest of survey turns is the direct turn onto the reciprocal track, as shown in Fig. 7.7. If the mission plan indicates that a certain distance a has to be kept between flight-lines then, in the absence of navigation aids such as GPS, the pilot can make a direct turn onto the next line from a knowledge of :

1. True air speed (TAS), see App. D.
2. Flight-line separation (a).
3. Drift angle ϕ (GPS recorded difference between heading and track).
4. Wind direction k (i.e, are the turns upwind or downwind?).

The pilot's task is to calculate the 'rate of turn' and 'angle of bank' required in order to turn directly onto the reciprocal track (at distance a from the previous line centre), then fly straight and level on this parallel track, until (at a given ground speed) he has to make the next turn. This must be done without losing height!

A so-called 'rate 1 turn' is 3°/s (180° per min), a 'rate 2' is 180° /30 s and a 'rate 3 turn' is 180° /15 s. The rate of turn depends upon air speed and angle of bank, and if coordinated correctly the ball in the 'turn and slip' indicator should remain central. The normal range of bank angles is between 15° and 50°. The correct angle of bank for a standard (rate 1) turn can either be calculated from the Diturns program in App. D, or for still air conditions by rule-of-thumb, as:

(a) Take 10% of the IAS (knots) and add 7, or

(b) Take 10% of the IAS (miles/hr) and add 5.

So a rate 1 turn at an indicated air speed of 90 kts is 16°. However, still air conditions are rare, so if the wind is significant it is best to use the Diturns program (executed from a lap-top computer while in-flight). A typical example, experienced by one of the authors flying a Cessna 172, and checked by GPS to determine the accuracy of the turn, is as follows:

TAS = 120 kts.

a = 1500 meters.

ϕ = 12°.

For an upwind turn, required rate of turn is 3°/sec (rate 1), and angle of bank = 20°. For a downwind turn, required rate of turn is 6°/sec, and angle of bank = 35°.

Survey U-turns

For large distances between flight-lines it is usually better to employ a U-turn as it is a direct turn with a linear region in the centre of the turn (see Fig.7.8). To apply a U-turn the pilot needs exactly the same data as required for a direct turn, but here the turn will always be at 'rate1'. The answers the pilot wants from the calculations are:

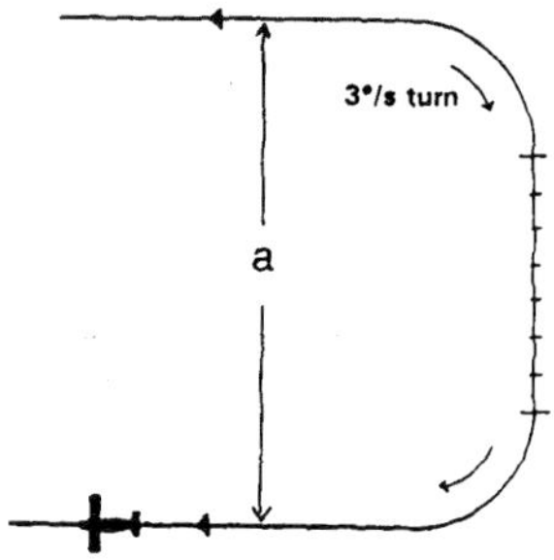

Figure 7.8 *Survey turns: The U-turn (rate of 1 turn of 3° per second).*

(i) The time required to fly the linear component of the turn (which starts as soon as he/she is at 90° to the flight-lines, and ends after time *t* when the pilot returns to the reciprocal track, with appropriate WCA applied to the reciprocal heading.

(ii) The required angle of bank (rate 1 turn).

The Q-Basic listings for a U-turn computer program (UTURNS) can be found in App.D, and the following true example is for a flight-line separation (U) of 3000 m, a TAS of 110 kts and a drift angle $\phi = 5°$.

(a) For an upwind turn: Upwind linear time (t_u) = 22 s.

(b) For a downwind turn: Downwind linear time (t_d) = 9 s.

(c) Required angle of bank (rate1 turn) = 17° (in each case).

In some areas of mission planning it is sometimes useful to calculate the flight-line separation for estimated inputs of TAS, ϕ and the linear component time, in which case we can employ the Q-Basic program (UTURN-A) found in App.D.

Survey S-turns

A more complicated type of turn is required when the distance between flight-lines is too narrow for a direct turn. This is the S-turn and it can be formed in a variety of ways and configurations, but the simplest method is turn-off into an offset angle (δ) as shown in Fig.7.9, then make a direct turn onto the GPS waypoint (WP) of the next line. This type of turn procedure is best left to the pilot who can practice such turns with the aircraft concerned.

Altimetry, height and reference elevation

One of the most important parameters in flying survey is height above ground (*H*). Since this is strongly related to barometric altitude we must pay attention to the subject of altimetry.

Altimetry is the measurement of changes in relative atmospheric pressure at different flight levels. The average mean sea-level barometric pressure is given as 1013.2 mb (14.7 lb/sq inch), and at a mountain top of say, 10,000 ft amsl, we are subjected to a column of air that is 10,000 feet shorter than that at sea level and will be under the influence of less pressure. Basically the altimeter is no more than a highly sensitive aneroid barometer with its dial calibrated in feet instead of pressure units.

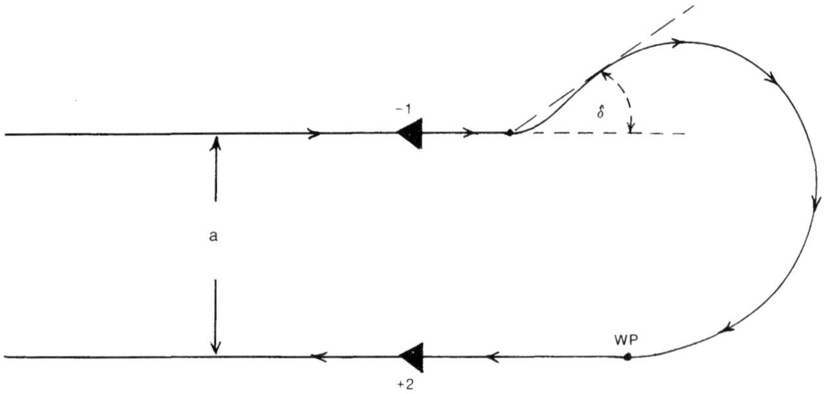

Figure 7.9 *Survey turns: The S-turn.*

The altimeter is calibrated to international standard atmospheric conditions which assume a sea-level pressure of 1013.2 mb, a sea-level temperature of 15°C and a decrease in temperature with height at a lapse-rate of 2°C/1000 ft (up to a height of 36,000 ft, above which temperature is assumed to be constant). Barometric pressure alters from time-to-time and area-to-area, so provision is made for pre-setting the altimeter by means of a small knob at the bottom of the instrument and a sub-scale which reads in millibars (Note: each drop of 1mb represents a gain of 30 ft).

Prior to take-off the pilot is informed of the local barometric pressure by radio, either from an automated terminal information service (ATIS), if available, and always by air traffic contol (ATC). While in flight the pilot uses his radio to up-date information by making requests for the regional barometric pressure. Although the so-called Q-Code is no longer fully used in UK airspace, it is useful to know what they are since they are still to be found in various texts and continue to be used in various areas to specify different 'altitude references'. In the USA altimeter settings are usually discussed in terms of 'altimeter.....'.

QNH

Sea-level barometric pressure is given in terms of QNH, a value that is different throughout various parts of the world. For the UK, and its surrounding seas, there are 14 QNH regions, the altimeter setting for each being provided by the appropriate regional authority. When a QNH is given this will be the lowest forecast value for the region and for this setting the altimeter will read altitude above sea-level. If the airfield QNH is set, this will give the height of the field above sea-level.

QFE

With this setting, the altimeter reads zero when the aircraft is on the ground, and ATC used to provide the pilot with both QNH and QFE prior to take-off and on approach to an airfield. With the altimeter set at QFE the pilot reads height above field, which enables him to know how much he must descend before touch-down.

However, QFE is not usually given today as it is thought to be unnecessary since the vast majority of airfields have a known height amsl.

Pressure altitude

As the pilot climbs away from the airfield he changes the altimeter from QFE to QNH to read altitude above sea level. Then, at a prescribed altitude (usually 3,000 ft amsl within the UK), the aircraft is said to have reached transition altitude when the altimeter should be re-set to the pressure altitude of 1013.2 mb. This means that above transition altitude all aircraft fly on the same altimeter setting regardless of variable barometric pressure, a good safety measure! When the altimeter is set on pressure altitude its readings are referred to as flight levels, e.g, at 5,000 ft the FL is 50, and at 25,000 feet FL is 250.

Height and reference elevation

All of our survey photography is conducted at a certain photo-scale and, as seen from Eq. 7.1, we calculate the scale-number from the platform's height above ground. For flat terrain this is easy of course, but for hilly or mountainous areas we must determine the reference elevation (datum) for the terrain. In most cases the appropriate datum can be calculated from a suitable map, where the SFM can calculate the mean of a selection of spot heights amsl. This datum is then added to the scale height to provide the correct platform altitude (height above datum).

But it is important to remember that the accuracy of the resultant map is inversely proportional to flying height, all other factors being equal. Obviously there will be scale differences between mountain top and valley, and if we fly high enough these differences will be minimised, but so will the overall map accuracy. However, in mountainous terrain our difficulties do not just stop at photo-scale differences!

Line spacing variations

Although we can easily find the required line-spacing (a) from Eq. 7.7, this equation is really only valid for flat terrain, so the SFM usually allows for hills and undulations by increasing the side-lap tolerances. Flying over high ground obviously increases the photo-scale, and will also reduce photo-cover (S^2) at the heights. But if we were to plan a mission over such terrain with regular line-spacing (as in flat terrain planning), we could easily fall below the specified side-lap in areas where high ground falls between runs (see Fig.7.10). To obviate these problems the SFM can make the specifications for side-lap with an associated side-lap tolerance. Thus, for a side-lap of 25% ± 10%, the high ground overlap should be planned to be not less than 15%. This means that every flight-line must be individually planned to arrive at the minimum side-lap on the high ground.

However well we may satisfy the problem of side-lap there is still the question of photo-scale, and if our planned flight-lines are running up the the side of a mountain, as shown in Fig.7.11, we shall need to change altitude for each flight-line in order to keep a reasonably constant height above ground for each run. This condition can be very important where the overall cover is to be used for a block mosaic, and even more important when a specific base/height ratio is required.

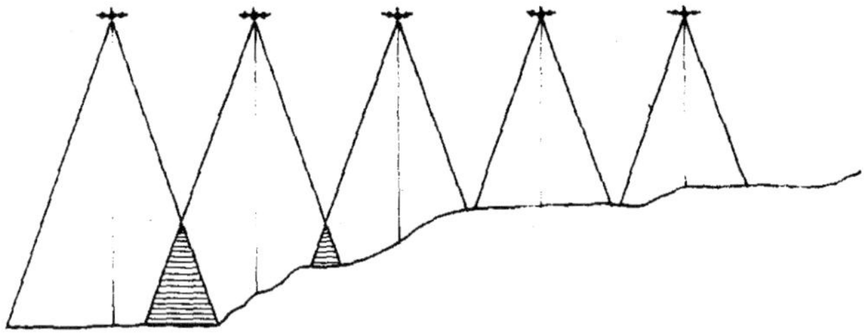

Figure 7.10 *Line spacing and scale variations due to rising ground.*

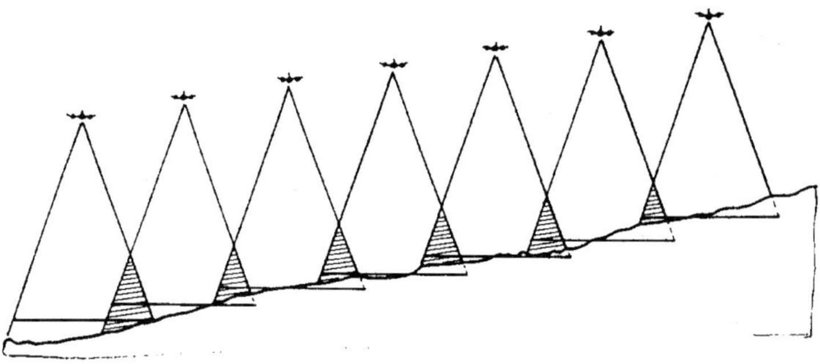

Figure 7.11 *Keeping constant line-separation (and scale) by increasing flying height for each line.*

Base/height ratio

A photogrammetric parameter of some importance is the B/H ratio. Large ratios favour higher plotting accuracy and are usually provided for by employing wide-angle lenses so that greater parallactic angles (a in Fig.2.3) are gained with the increased ratio. This ratio is often dominant in specifications where accurate contours have to be made on a map, particularly in flat regions prone to flooding. In delta regions, such as those near to Dhaka, Bangladesh for example, accurately contoured maps are essential, where contour intervals of less than one meter need to be plotted. For such cover a B/H ratio of 0.6 is a minimum requirement, e.g, with a 38mm lens on the MF-DMC, a height (H) of 1000 ft (305 m) and 60% forward overlap, the air base (B) is 192 m and the B/H is 0.63.

A rule-of-thumb founded by experience with analogue systems suggests that a very rough guide to heighting accuracy is about $10^{-4}.H$. For the MF-DMC example quoted above, we might expect a possible heighting accuracy in the region of 3 cm. A more accurate evaluation is possible using the well known machine parallax equation (Eq. 7.9) which was established for photogrammetric plotters:

$$\Delta H = (\Delta P.m_b.H)/B \tag{7.9}$$

where: ΔH is the calculated heighting accuracy. ΔP is the machine operator parameter which (for digital sensors) is calculated as $\Delta P \approx \sqrt{2}(\sigma_p)$ where σ_p is the pixel measuring error so for 9 μm pixels and a given pixel error of 0.1Px, $\Delta P \approx 4.10^{-5}$ m. H is the platform height above ground (metres), B is the air base and m_b is the scale number.

Using Eq.7.9 in our example for the MF-DMC with a 38 mm lens and using a pixel error of 0.1 Px, we now find a value for the heighting accuracy (ΔH) to be in the region of 50 cm. But (as suggested by the variable measuring error) such answers are inevitably subjective and open to discussion.

Exposure interval ΔT

The exposure interval (ΔT) between camera stations is easily calculated once the air base (B) and ground speed of the aircraft (V_g) are known, where we have:

$$\Delta T = B / V_g \tag{7.10}$$

where B = air base (in meters) and V_g = aircraft velocity over the ground (m/s).

Calculating ground speed (in m/s) is a simple matter these days since values of V_g are accurately shown on our GPS receiver screen. Although these values are usually given in knots, dividing by two will provide a suitable answer since the m/s is 0.515 knots. Thus, for an air base of 250 m and a ground speed of 60 knots, the required ΔT is 250/30 = 8 s (note: we always round down to the closest second).

Apparent image motion (AIM)

Although it is really the camera platform that moves in aerial photography, the resulting apparent image motion causes a degree of image-blur that can seriously lower both contrast and resolution in the photograph. In discussing AIM we must only consider linear image motion, since disturbances due to vibration are not in question here.

The main causes of AIM are:

1. Low height above ground (H).
2. High aircraft ground speed (V_g).
3. Longer camera shutter speeds (t).
4. Longer focal length lenses (f).

All of these variables can be summed up in the equation for AIM, which considers the amount of image-blur (ΔS) resulting from the above parameters, giving us:

$$\Delta S = (V_g . f . t) / H \tag{7.11}$$

Thus, for a typical MF-DMC mission, with an 80mm lens, shutter speed of 1/500 s (0.002 s), ground speed of 90 kts and a height of 1500 ft amgl, the AIM is:

$$\Delta S = (\, 45 \text{ m/sec} \times 0.038\text{m} \times 0.002 \text{ sec}\,) \,/\, 457\text{m} = 7.5 \text{ μm}.$$

Such a degree of image motion is quite acceptable, indeed, it has long been accepted that a permissible amount of AIM is 25 μm. As explained in Chapter 4, when considering contrast and modulation, image blur manifests itself by the loss of sharp edges and a lowering of modulation (Eq. 4.17).

All of the primary calculations for mission planning can be undertaken with the aid of equations 7.1 to 7.11, and their Q-Basic listings are available in App.D under the following headings:

(a) SURPLAN (survey flight planning).
(b) AIM (apparent image motion).
(c) SA1 (solar altitude).
(d) SZ1 (solar azimuth).
(e) DITURNS (direct survey turns).
(f) UTURNS (U-turns for air survey – linear region time).
(g) UTURN-A (U-turns for air survey – line separation).
(h) TAS (true air speed).
(i) TALT (true altitude).
(j) SS (shutter speeds)

Note: These programs are listed in Q-Basic because all DOS programs have Q-Basic installed. However, in Windows 95 and 98 there is only a limited amount of DOS and the user should enter the full DOS program to gain access to Q-Basic. It is also possible to enter survey flight planning programs into computerised calculators, or spreadsheets.

A typical digital survey: In-flight procedures

A typical digital air survey, as practised by Geotechnologies, employs a crew of two or three persons, depending on the work load involved, the normal crew being pilot, survey flight manager (SFM), and tracker.

In situations where there may be considerable wind-drift, and a large number of photographs are required, the SFM may well be fully occupied handling the camera, where drift compensation, camera levelling, changing PCMCIA cards and changing ΔT on the Intervalometer (shifting ground speeds due to wind require different ΔT settings to maintain constant forward overlap) need constant attention.

In the event that the pilot does not have a GPS with moving map display on his instrument panel, he will require instructions from the tracker who, even with a modest hand-held GPS, can keep the pilot on-track via the crew intercom system. The tracker will have each flight-line stored with its respective start and end waypoints and can keep the aircraft on line by monitoring the aircrafts progress on the GPS.

Most of survey aircraft now have a good quality GPS (with moving map display) fitted into the instrument panel, and once the aircraft has been trimmed for level flight it is perfectly possible for the pilot to fly the survey block on his own! However, while this may be possible for small-scale surveys, where the aircraft is at sufficient height to ensure good ground coverage, it is always best to have guidance from the tracker when flying large-scale surveys at only two or three thousand feet.

A typical GPS (Garmin) with moving-map-display is shown in Fig.7.12. Located in the centre of the pilot's instrument panel this display was photographed during a survey line flown with a Partenavia P68B. The survey was flown at 5600 ft with a Kodak DCS-460CIR digital camera fitted with a calibrated 28mm lens to deliver 55 cm GSDs. The pilot could easily fly the aircraft along each flight line, as we can see from Fig.7.12, where the small white aircraft in the display is shown flying down the Chesil beach (Weymouth, Dorset. England). Nevertheless, the tracker also assisted the pilot since there was a considerable cross wind in force at the time.

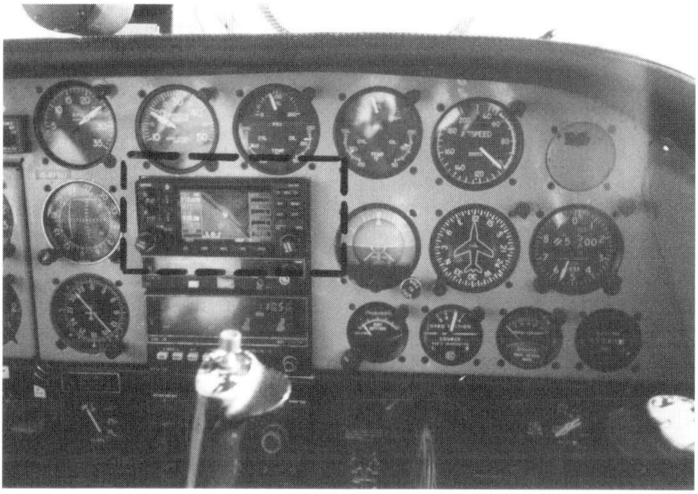

Figure 7.12 *A typical moving map display (inside rectangle) installed in the cockpit of a Partenavia 68B. The small white symbol of an aircraft is shown flying down the track of Chesil beach, Dorset, during a survey flight.*

Although modern avionics, such as GPS, are a great help to a survey pilot, it is not good policy to expect too much from such aids with respect to keeping track. The pilot has enough to do in keeping the wings level, adjusting the aircraft's attitude and throttle (to keep the correct ground speed), and since we need to keep the ground speed as low as possible, taking care not to drop below the critical air speed!

Indexing

Indexing is usually covered within client specifications, where a list of all the items required in such an index is provided. Typically, an index will include items such as:

1. Flight-line numbers.
2. Photo-numbers.
3. Coordinates (map or GPS).
4. Map information (sheet numbers etc).
5. Mean photo-scale.
6. Mean values of forward and side-lap.
7. Dates (as required).
8. Any other information, as required by the client.

The centre point of each photo, in each flight-line, is usually represented by a small circle, connected with a line when consecutive photographs overlap according to specifications (see Fig.7.2). If an overlap exists, but is outside of specifications, the connecting line should be broken at that point, and if there is no overlap then no line is entered.

8 Digital survey planning and logistics

We now take a broader view to embrace every aspect from survey flight operations to the final downstream products required by the client. Comprehensive survey flight management systems (SFMS), such as the IGI-CCNS-4, include much more than basic mission planning calculations since they also allow for many of the items shown in Table 7.1. However, previous SFMSs have been designed for analogue mapping systems and are not entirely appropriate for digital survey planning.

Detailed survey-flight planning formulae are listed in Chapter 7, and their computer Q-Basic listings are provided in App. D for those who would like to apply them in an office desk-top, or airborne laptop. But if we are to conduct an overall mission plan, including full survey-flight logistics, specifications for the type of digital survey required (including product specifications), mapsheet processing and plotting logistics, costings and tender protocols, then we need a computer program that can be used in an iterative fashion.

Working from client specifications, where the final products are the main consideration, it should be possible to apply a host of different values for various parameters, such as base/height ratio, flying height, scale, type of aircraft, ground pixel resolution (GSD), map resolution, etc., in order to evaluate the most cost effective data set. For these purposes it is sensible to employ Microsoft Excel's spreadsheet tools.

The Air Survey Logistic Planner

The Air Survey Logistic Planner (ASLP) discussed here is included in the CD found inside the back cover of this book. When inserted into a computer, the ASLP may be employed for personal digital mission planning.

The ASLP is founded on the equations shown in Chapter 7, with additional material, such as mapping, cartographic, aviation and surveying logistics provided by common industrial standards. However, much of the data comes from empirical observations. Cartographers for example can typically plot lines to a maximum accuracy of 0.1mm, consequently a 1:5000 map will have a resolution of 5000 × 0.1mm, providing a map GSD of 50 cm. Further empirical observations show that mapping accuracy in planimetry (x,y), approximates to twice the camera GSD, and that heighting accuracy (z) is about three times the camera GSD. These empirical observations (based on a maximum map accuracy of 0.1mm) allows us to estimate the required camera GSD from:

$$\text{Camera GSD}_{(x,y)} \approx \text{Map GSD}/2 \tag{8.1}$$

and

$$\text{Camera GSD}_{(z)} \approx \text{Map GSD}/3 \tag{8.2}$$

Thus, for a 1:50,000 survey flown with a MF-DMC camera with 15 μm pixels, the camera GSD = 50,000 × 0.015mm = 75 cm (Eq. 4.25). From Eq. 8.1 and Eq. 8.2, a map GSD of 1.5 m in planimetry should be possible, with a heighting accuracy in the region of 2.25 m.

The ASLP suite is made up of 4 independent spreadsheets, located on the CD. The spreadsheets or modules cover mission planning (filename *Mission Planner.xls*), photocentre waypoint calculator (filename *Photocentre Planner.xls*), camera calibration (filename *Camera Calibration.xls*) and scanning resolution calculator (filename *Scanres Calculator.xls*).

All the spreadsheets have the same format and mode of operation. The user-changeable items are coded red, boxed and highlighted yellow. All costs are in pounds sterling. Items requiring options have the symbol [~] in their dimensional descriptors, which are in square brackets. The user enters one of the options, which are separated by the [~] symbol. A press of the return key confirms an entry and all outputs are immediately updated. Where a result is out of tolerance or fails to meet the performance capability of an instrument, appropriate advisory messages are displayed in red text with accompanying link indicators. It is therefore possible for the user to see the outcome of a certain input and assess the appropriateness of the adjustment with constant reference to the specifications and costs.

Mission Planner

This should be completed with constant reference to requirements specified by the client and fitness for purpose related to applications. The default parameters used within the spreadsheets are based on the experiences gathered over seven years of global commercial operations of Geotechnologies in the delivery of digital aerial imagery (DAI) and contoured orthophoto maps.

Costs for typical daily accommodation and local travel costs are based on the United States Department of Defence Per Diem Rates Committee publication which can be located (at February 2002) at the following internet address;

http://www.dtic.mil/perdiem/ovs02-02.txt

These rates are constantly updated by the United States Department of Defence and provide an excellent starting point for costing aerial survey operations throughout the world. Further information on how the per diem rates are calculated can be found at:

http://www.dtic.mil/perdiem/pdrates.html

The ASLP spreadsheets are designed to follow a logical decision making and support process and are therefore divided into sections. Users should enter their survey parameters in the logical order that information is requested and to verify that the default values for resource costs and number of personnel available are in line with their operations. The spreadsheet determines the flight logistics for the defined area of interest and provides an estimate of aircraft and ground control resources required, lead times to final data delivery and cost of mission. The sections that make up the mission planner module (filename *Mission Planner.xls*) are:

1. Project area location and characteristics
2. Digital camera specifications
3. Aircraft specifications
4. Product specifications
5. Resources and support unit costs/parameters
6. Survey flight logistics
7. Air photo ground point data survey logistics
8. Digital orthophoto mapsheet production logistics
9. Mission costs

Photocentre Planner

This is a utility for calculating the map coordinate eastings and northings, which define the photocentre waypoint for the area of interest. The user should enter the direction of flight lines, the number of flight lines, images per flight line, airbase and flight-line separation. These are derived from the mission planner spreadsheet. The bottom-left-hand-corner coordinate of the area of interest should be determined from the client and entered. Users can then save the block navigation photocentre waypoint file generated in text format for uploading into the GPS units or for use in the production of the photoindex. The maximum number of waypoints that can be generated by this module is 4500.

Routes can then be created within the GPS unit that satisfy any flying restrictions that may be in-force at the time of the planned mission. The sections that make up the Photocentre Planner module (filename *Photocentre Planner.xls*) are:

1. Block parameters
2. Block navigation photocentre waypoint file

Camera Calibration

Camera calibration parameters are frequently presented in mathematical form and it is often useful to expand these mathematical models into a tabular and graphical form to demonstrate the degree of displacement from true an imaged pixel experiences. By inputting the constants and coefficients derived from the calibration routine, a graphical and tabular representation of the camera model is presented by the camera calibration spreadsheet. The sections that make up the camera calibration module (filename *Camera Calibration.xls*) are:

1. Camera calibration parameters
2. Radial distortion plot

Scanres Calculator

It is often common practice to scan existing analogue photography to produce derived digital imagery (DDI) and to process these products in digital photogrammetric workstations. Associated with this scanning process is the need to store the DDI and to ensure that it meets the specifications in terms of ground sampled distance, or to generate image datasets equivalent to captured digital aerial imagery (DAI) for time series or comparative analysis. However, care must be exercised to ensure that the resolution used for scanning does not exceed the resolution of the analogue photography. The scanres calculator enables the user to define the original scale and resolution of the analogue photography and recommends a scan resolution that has been referred to the original scale and analogue photography resolution. The utility may also be used for scanning paper maps for use as backdrops for virtual ground control acquisition. The sections that make up the scanres calculator module (filename *Scanres Calculator.xls*) are:

1. Characteristics of diapositive or print
2. Derived digital image scan requirements
3. Required scan resolution and data storage requirements

9 Photo-interpretation, objective analysis and image quality

Aerial photography provides us with an overall view of the earth which, in a single instant of time, captures an (almost) permanent source of terrestrial information that can be used for many disciplines including remote sensing, GIS, mapping and military reconnaissance.

In terms of remote sensing the full scope of photo-interpretation should also include data from sources such as microwave systems (radar in all its forms), magnetometry, spectroradiometry and thermal scanners. But in a book devoted to digital photography we must concentrate only on the visual and near infrared regions of the recordable electromagnetic spectrum.

The nature of photo-interpretation

Photo-interpretation is a complex business where, on looking at an aerial photograph, some features may be readily identified while others may not, and so the main task for the photo-interpreter (PI) is to relate known facts and recognised features (prior knowledge) to the unknown. Photo-interpretation is both an art and a science requiring subjective judgements on the one hand and objective analysis on the other. The skilled PI will, ideally, have a sound background in his or her chosen field, be it land management, geography, geology, forestry or any other earth science, similarly, military PIs have their own specialisations.

Visual factors in photo-interpretation

Various authors have attempted to classify the major elements involved in the useful information content of imagery, and they generally agree that the prime stages of photo-analysis are resolution, detection and recognition (Rosenberg,1971; Charman, 1977).

Image resolution

Resolution is measured in units defined by physics and is generally assumed to be an objective term, but it also has strong foundations in human perception and visual acuity and so comes within the realm of psychophysics. But regardless of how resolution is measured (see Chapter 4), in its simplest terms it can be said that 'if two points on a photograph cannot be resolved they cannot be seen as two points but only as one'.

Obviously the camera lens and sensor ultimately determine resolution and, as explained in Chapter 4, for digital systems we have to look further than basic optical theory to find all the factors that shape digital image resolution (Eq. 4.21 and 22), and also include sampling theorems such as the Nyquist limit (Eq. 4.26). We also know that without sufficient contrast between our two points they will not be recorded and so we must include MTF (Eq. 4.27) in our considerations.

Having considered the spatial aspects of digital aerial photography, as defined by the ground sampled distance (GSD), we should not ignore the highly important temporal information contained in a time-separated sequence of images of the same scene. By employing repetitive site coverage it is possible to monitor change in crops, land usage, coastal erosion and all manner of changes particularly those that influence maps. Obviously, the smaller the time-interval involved (ΔT) the higher the temporal resolution.

Spectral resolution includes multi-spectral photography (MSP) where the same area is covered by a multiple camera array, each with its own sensor, e.g, filtered-panchromatic, natural-colour and infrared (including false-colour infrared: CIR). Although wide-band filters are usually employed in MSP, special projects often require a higher spectral resolution ($\Delta\lambda$) which demands the use of narrow cut filters with perhaps only 10nm of bandwidth. As we have seen, the DCS-420 and 460 cameras, as well as the MF-DMC(1) are highly suitable for MSP, particularly since it is perfectly possible to isolate the red, green and blue components of a digital colour image with software such as Adobe Photoshop. In addition, digital CIR allows the PI unlimited freedom to exploit every possible combination of false colours in the search for optimum discrimination.

Thus resolution is the ability of an imaging system to distinguish between signals that are close to each other, spatially, temporally or spectrally.

Detection

Before we can make a decision concerning the identity of objects in an image we must first be able to detect their presence, and the first visual reaction is to register variations in tone or colour from their surroundings. Such variations are known as brightness and contrast and, as we have seen above, such contrasts have to be recorded by the camera before they can be seen by a PI.

At this point it is important to look at some of the basic physiological aspects of human vision and their importance with respect to photo-interpretation.

1. The unaided *least distance of distinct vision* is commonly given as 20–25cm, with myopics able to get as close as 15cm to inspect an image. The use of a simple wide-field hand magnifier (about ×3) is an obvious visual aid, and for taking fine measurements on a print, a measuring magnifier (×8) that can focus onto an integrated 0.1mm reference plate is ideal. Enlarging an image to a point where no further information is revealed is known as *empty magnification*, and for the PI serves no useful purpose, particularly where over enlargement of digital imag-

es can introduce pixelation effects. It should be noted that the unaided eye can, at best, resolve 0.1mm under optimum lighting conditions.

2. The human ability to see in *three dimensions* is based upon a number of parameters, including binocular vision, parallax (the average inter-ocular distance being 64mm ± 9mm) and, to varying extents, atmospheric depth (diminishing contrasts with distance), occlusion (objects shift relative to others as the observer moves), subject motion and cultural clues such as shape, size, shadow and patterns, all of which provide guides to depth perception. But for the PI, apart from stereoscopic vision (aided or unaided), only the cultural features have any relevance, which reinforces the need for specialised knowledge.
3. The *spectral sensitivity* of the human eye extends between wavelengths of 380nm to 760nm, but camera sensors can exceed this up to about 1μm in the near infrared. On average the normal human eye is able to see wavelength differences ($\Delta\lambda$) in the region of 3nm, and can distinguish something like 100 colours or more in a single field of view. Nevertheless, as explained in Chapter 4, a typical super VGA card can support a monitor with a maximum simultaneous display of over 16 million colours – not that they can all be perceived of course!
4. An important factor in photo-interpretation is considered in Chapter 4, where the number of grey levels (or colour levels) we can expect to see in a print can be calculated. Known in subjective terms as *just noticeable differences* (JNDs), their objective correlate can be found from Eq. 4.28, from which we can expect to see about 60 JNDs of continuous tones, and more than this if we are looking at colour photographs since small differences of colour are more easily seen than small differences of tone. Naturally these considerations rely upon image quality, where glossy surfaced prints provide the maximum detail in both shadow and highlights.

For interpretating the relative brightness (reflectances) of objects seen in an aerial photograph, an important sensor characteristic is its response curve (relating scene luminance to pixel intensity) and, as we can see from Eq. 3.13, solid state imagers provide a linear response, in contrast to the sigmoid response curve of film. For the PI (who usually assumes a linear radiometric relationship between scene and image anyway) this can only help, particularly in shadow and highlight regions of the photo graph where analogue images are far from linear. This is also important when it comes to objective measurements, using Photoshop to analyse reflectance values of either monochrome or colour images (Graham, 1998).

An interesting feature of detection is that a signal (image) can sometimes be detected even though it is smaller than the resolution of the system. For example, a single (sun lit) elevated telephone wire will easily show up on a small scale aerial photograph. The specular reflectance of the wire shows itself despite its lack of resolution. This should cause no surprise of course since it is a common experience to see stars in the night sky, even though they are well below the resolution of the unaided human eye. In a similar fashion, a narrow road or railway line, the width of which is below the resolution limit, will often appear as a line in a small scale photograph. One of the authors recalls an instance where a military PI detected two small features at the end of an airfield runway. All he saw on the 1:40,000 scale photograph were two identical patterns of radial lines, each emanating from a common centre with each bright line being scaled to about 30cm in length. The separation of the two patterns, plus prior knowledge, gave rise to the PI recognising it as a bicycle, even though the wheel spokes were well below the resolution of the camera lens – a clear case of detection!

Thus we can say that detection is the ability of a system to detect the presence or absence of a signal.

Recognition

Having detected the presence of an object the PI may then proceed to give it some identity, and if certain characteristics agree with the PI's concepts of that object then it can be recognised as such. As we say…'if it looks like a duck, and quacks like a duck, it's most likely going to be… a duck'.

Recognition of elements in a photograph (prior knowledge) allow for further interpretation to take place, e.g, 'a river will naturally follow a valley', just as man-made objects have certain dimensions and features, such as:

1. *SHAPE:* Giving clues to identity. This characteristic alone may serve to identify some objects.
2. *SIZE:* Giving clues to scale. Both relative and absolute sizes are important.
3. *TONE:* Light or dark monochrome areas show differences in terrain.
4. *COLOUR:* A panchromatic sensor will record colour in terms of varying reflectances – as tones. But a true-colour sensor will record terrain colours in their true sense. A false-colour infrared sensor will record natural colours and infrared reflectances in well differentiated (but false) colours.
5. *SHADOW:* Hidden profiles may be revealed in silhouette, e.g, the shape of buildings or the form of field boundaries. Shadow is important in revealing texture. Cast shadows can simplify the recognition of vertical structures. Deep shadows can also hamper identification.
6. *PATTERN:* Repetitive arrangements of both natural and cultural features are quite common. Examples are streets, orchards, buildings, crops, etc. A man-made pattern, such as that produced by contour ploughing might reveal information on the topography, type of soil, or even the nature of the crop.
7. *TEXTURE:* Texture (roughness of surface) is best seen under conditions of low sun angle (solar altitude), such as early morning or late evening – depending on latitude and the time of year. Texture is important when interpreting various types of crop and geological features.
8. *SITE:* The location of objects with respect to terrain features or other objects may be helpful in their identification and classification, e.g, cooling towers (power stations); and solid fuel piles (type of power station).
9. *ASSOCIATION:* By association we refer to the occurrence of certain features in relation to others. A typical example would be in attempting to identify a yacht parked next to a house in the middle of a town, yet this would be easily identified in an area recognised as a marina or on a river.
10. *STEREOSCOPIC APPEARANCE:* The three-dimensional stereo-model gives valuable information not contained in a single photograph.

Semantic information performance

In addition to the three prime stages of photo-interpretation already discussed, we should also include two others which, according to Jerie and Shearer (1972), can be expressed as the semantic information performance of a photograph. These additional features are classification and deduction.

Classification

Classification is an extension of identification (a component of recognition) and may be thought of as more selective identification, e.g., an image identified as a building may, due to certain characteristics (shape and size etc.), be classified as a factory, church or block of flats. Whereas identification sorts objects into very boad classes – roads, buildings, forests – classification refines these classes to track, factory, coniferous trees.

Deduction

Deduction can operate in two distinct ways. Firstly, it can be considered as the link between detection, identification and classification. For example, an image is detected because it has certain characteristics and we deduce (on the basis of prior knowledge) that it has a certain broad identity. In some circumstances we may be able to deduce further that it has a particular identity, i.e, classification. Secondly, deduction can be used to describe the process of deriving information which cannot be directly detected on the photograph. An example might be the deduction of the presence and location of a stream partially concealed by vegetation because of the configuration of the ground. Another example, experienced by one of the authors, was in trying to put a floating mark on black rectangular objects known to be on the slope of a sand dune. The group of black rectangular objects were recognised as Beduin tents – and the Bedu were known to pitch their tents on dune slopes.

Obviously recognition is a complex subject, and in the most simplistic of terms can only be summed up as the ability of a system to recognise, identify and classify a signal.

Aids for photo-interpretation

Traditional aids, such as the simple magnifying glass, ruler and pocket stereoscope, will always be employed in photo-interpretation, regardless of whether the print originates from analogue or digital camera. This is mainly due to their immediate convenience, particularly while travelling, or working in field conditions.

In the office or laboratory we have the mirror stereoscope and parallax-bar, which can be supplemented by more sophisticated equipment such as the Wild Aviopret APT2, or the Zeiss Visopret range of instruments. However, all of these instruments are designed for 23 cm analogue images in the form of prints or diapositives, and although the Visopret 10 DIG and 20 DIG models are supported by various software packages for digital mapping and data acquisition for GIS, they are not appropriate for solid state imagery.

Photo-interpretation of digital imagery

Once a digital aerial photo has been printed it is virtually no different than one printed from film, and can be viewed in the same fashion, either by stereoscope or magnifier. But while the digital image is stored in its host computer, it has the incomparable advantage of being sampled by sophisticated software. In this respect there is no comparison between the two types of photographic information.

Objective analysis: digital image software

Principal among the more well known image software packages is Adobe Photoshop® which, through its many versions, has been welcomed by artists, advertisers, high street photographers, amateur photographers and scientists to name but a few. For those engaged with the products of aerial photography, Photoshop provides an excellent and relatively inexpensive means of enhancing and analysing the primary data.

The image processing features available facilitate histogram balance, colour selection, image ($\cos^4\theta$) correction, metrication, terrain reflectance values, densitometry and the independent analysis of each red, green and blue channel that make up a full colour image. Subject to correct use, we also have an extensive range of tools which allow us to adjust image brightness, colour balance and contrast, and apply filters to help remove noise and pixelation effects. In addition there are low pass (smoothing) filters and a range of high pass filters for sharpening the image, including 'unsharp masking' (Graham, 1998), all of which can be employed for improved interpretation.

Today, there are a number of software programs dedicated to the analysis of aerospace imagery, most of them designed for desk-top image stations. Among these we have the: R-Wel DMS (desktop mapping system) for photogrammetry, Arc-Info and Arc-View (cartography), ERDAS IMAGINE (GIS), PCI EASI / PACE (remote sensing and GIS), ImageStation SSK (photogrammetry) and the very useful VirtuoZo (digital photogrammetric software) for photogrammetry, GIS and remote sensing (see Chapters 11 and 12 for further information).

Software packages for photogrammetry, GIS and remote sensing can provide useful image variants since they are capable of extracting DTMs and DEMs (see Chapter 2), as well as orthophotos and perspective views. Since they process digital images to extract information, they can legitimately be considerd as tools for interpretation.

Contoured orthophotos

The contoured orthophoto shown in Fig.9.1 (see colour section) has contour intervals of 5 m, and was extracted from a stereo pair of DCS-420 CIR images. Processed in VirtuoZo, and complete with ground control, an absolute orientation was followed by a DTM and DEM from which the orthophoto was extracted. Such images are easily made in the computer and, due to their quantitative information can be of great assistance to the PI where terrain heights are important.

Computer generated perspective view

The perspective view shown in Fig. 9.2 (see colour section), was taken from a stereo pair of DCS-460 CIR images recorded during a survey of the Lyme Bay area of the Dorset coast. The nature of the survey was to record coastal erosion including cliff-falls, and as an aid to photo-interpretation some perspective views were generated from various orthophotos (VirtuoZo) with 25 m contours. Perspective views can be of great assistance to the PI, mainly because they provide terrain relationships not obvious from their parent vertical images. Although computer generated perspective views cannot equal the resolution and clarity of directly exposed obliques (even with a low-end digital camera, such as those illustrated in Figs. 2.5 and 2.6) they still provide oblique views otherwise unavailable.

In Fig.9.2, we can see the cliff slopes quite well and the contoured overlay provides additional heighting information. The primary data was flown at a height of 5,600 ft amsl with a 28mm lens, giving a GSD of 50 cm. At the top right of the cliffs the village of Charmouth can be seen.

Image analysis with Adobe Photoshop

Computer assisted interpretation is at the heart of all digital imagery, and regardless of image content all digital images are software processed before printing. Once seen on the monitor they are usually corrected for image size (zoom 'in' and zoom 'out'), brightness, contrast and colour bias. As already mentioned, Photoshop can provide for all the essential image processing operations and in addition offer some useful analytical functions as well.

Naturally we can only mention a few of Photoshop's command menus since they are best explained in the appropriate manuals for each version of Photoshop. Nevertheless, the few functions discussed here will serve to illustrate their usefulness for analytical image interpretation, and with the aid of Fig. 9.3 (colour section) can be found under various menus.

The DCS-460 CIR image shown in Fig.9.3 is a colour infrared record (spectral range 500–800nm) taken from 18,000 ft over the top of the Freeport copper mine in West Papua (New Guinea) with nominal GSD of 25 cm. The first step for pin pointing any feature within the photograph is to set up a system of coordinates using the Rulers menu.

Rulers

The Rulers are strips along the top (x) and side (y) of the image. The Rulers dialogue box is gained by clicking on the Window menu, then Show Rulers. The Rulers can be displayed in various units selected from the Preferences sub-menu found under File. Once in Preferences it is possible to select any of the following units: pixels, inches, centimeters or points, all of which can be employed for image metrication.

Selecting units of pixels the displayed Rulers are first indicated from 0–3060 in x, and 0–2036 in y, and the product (3060 × 2036) confirms the total number of pixels that make up the DCS-460 image structure i.e, 6.14MPx. Then, if preferred, it is possible to position a ruler's 'origin point' by placing the screen cursor on the small square at the top left of the rulers and dragging a cross-hair to the image point of interest. This 'origin-point' is shown as a black cross in the centre of Fig.9.3, and is centred on a small patch of vegetation on the top suface of the mine, the ruler coordinates are now $x = 0$, and $y = 0$ at this point.

Info box

The Info Box can be seen at the top right hand side of Fig.9.3 and is brought onto the screen by clicking on the Window–Palettes–Show Info. Inspection of the Info Box reveals three sub-panels, the arrangement for which can be changed by clicking on one of the pippets. In Fig.9.3 we see the top panel indicating RGB (red, green and blue) color values for the 'origin point' (shown in the bottom panel as $x = 0$, $y = 0$). Once positioned on a given terrain point radiometric data can be gained from the RGB panel. For the vegetation patch at the origin point we have reflectance values R = 128, G = 106 and B = 70, values given in digital numbers (DN). In the above example, if the image was in true colour, these DNs would refer to red, green and blue reflectances. The centre panel shows CMYK (cyan, magenta, yellow and black) in percentage values, but these are of no interest to us here.

Scene radiometric analysis

For radiometric analysis of an image we must appreciate that each RGB screen value is given in terms of its DN number, and since we are dealing with an 8-bit colour system (from 0 to 255) each RGB spectral reflectance (ρ) is given by the fraction: DN/255. Taking the red DN value for example, we have: 128/255 = 50% red reflectance (in true colour). However, the image shown in Fig .9.3 was taken by a DCS-460CIR camera operating in its CIR mode. As a consequence RGB do not represent conventional, red, green and blue channels of true colour, but completely different colour values, as indicated by Figs. 5.7 and 5.8.

Photoshop analysis of a DCS-460 CIR image

The CIR image shown in Fig.9.3, has to be analysed with care since the image and its RGB DNs are not what they may seem. As we know from the text for Fig.5.7 and Fig.5.8, when the camera operates in CIR mode, the blue pixels provide a near infrared image directed to the red gun on the VDU. Similarly, the red pixels provide an image to the green gun (with red reflectances applied to red DNs), and the green pixels are directed to the blue gun (with green reflectances seen as green DNs).

These complex arrangements are best explained in Table. 9.1, where the Info Box shows the CIR DN values (RGB) in the upper panel.

Table. 9.1 *Photoshop analysis of CIR image channels and Info Box DNs.*

Pixel colour	Spectral reflectance	VDU gun	Info Box DN (radiance)
BLUE	INFRARED	RED	R 128 (NIR DNs)
RED	RED	GREEN	G 106 (Red DNs)
GREEN	GREEN	BLUE	B 70 (Green DNs)

To gain the overall reflectance values from the scene we need to average all three RGB DN values. From Fig.9.3 (CIR) we calculate the average of the RGB DNs as: (128 + 106 + 70) / 3 = 101, and so the total reflectance is: 101/255 = 39%, i.e. the total near infrared, red and green reflectances comes to 39%.

A more direct method for gaining the overall reflectance value is to click on a pipette and select Greyscale. By clicking on Greyscale we see the top panel of the Info Box indicating K grey scale units (where 100% is total black and 0% is pure white), and if we now move the cursor to our image point of interest we find that K = 62%, i.e, a reflectance value of 100 – 62 = 38%, which is a close match to that found from the RGB values.

Radiometric calibration

Obviously all RGB image values are relative to each other within the screen display. But if absolute radiometric calibration is required, then an appropriate range of ground targets must be provided in the form of accurate spectral reflectance panels. Such panels need to be painted on a matt reflecting surface, such as cloth (to avoid specular reflectance) and measured with a spectrophotometer. Generally such panels will need to be large enough to be recognised on the computer screen (ideally not less than 2mm in size at 1:1), and from experience we recommend the ground targets to be not less than 3m square. At these dimensions they are suitable for photoscales up to about 1:10,000 maximum. These large panels are best kept in a damp-proof environment and checked for radiometric accuracy prior to display. Usually the panels can be photographed over the airfield (positioned in a clear area, devoid of shadows) taking care to fly at the same scale and solar conditions as for the mission area.

For use with digital cameras such as the MF-DMC series, DCS-460CIR, or 760 types, a single pure white ground target, 2 m square, should be prepared. for general purpose daylight (clear sun and skylight) calibration. The spectrophotometer (or spectroradiometer if target calibration is to include the infrared) should record spectral reflectance bands matching the dominant wavelengths of the sensor's (Bayer) filters. For the DCS-460 CIR, these are: red (660nm), green (530nm), blue (450nm) and near infrared (780nm) each with a bandwith in the region of 30–40nm. For specialised ground truth, a number of different panels can be made, each painted with a specific colour to match foliage, crops or trees, etc. (Graham, 1980). Naturally each panel will have its own dominant hue, but there will be elements of red, green, blue and infrared reflectance in all targets.

After the survey mission has been flown and the digital imagery loaded into Photoshop, the scene containing the ground target(s) should be processed in the normal way for correct contrast, brightness and colour-balance. This image will now be the standard for the actual survey photography and the ground target enlarged (zooming-in to 1:1) for analysis in the Info Box.

By placing the screen-cursor on the image of the white ground target, the Info Box will reveal its RGB reflectance values, as described above. Taking a full colour image as example, the Info Box may read: R = 135, G = 18 and B = 8 DN values, and from our ground truth the actual reflectance values might be, say, r = 76%, g = 11% and b = 5%.

The calibration between ground truth: red, green, blue reflectances and their Info Box RGB values is simply a question of finding the DN correction factor for each RGB. In this example R = 135 DN, which represents the fraction 135/255 or 0.53 of its 8-bit red channel, and the discrepancy between the ground target's red reflection (76%) and the image Info Box is therefore 0.76/0.53, a correction factor (CF) of 1.43. Similarly, for the green, G = 18 DN and 18/255 = 0.07, so 0.11/0.07 provides a CF = 1.57, and for the blue, B = 7 DN and 7/255 = 0.027, which gives 0.04/0.027 and a CF = 1.48.

The radiometric calibration of image to ground truth is best recorded for all ground targets in the form shown by Table.9.2, which shows red, green and blue reflectances recorded from a white target, and their respective DN and CF values. It should be noted that where a digital camera is recording in CIR mode, all blue target reflectances will be cut-off by the camera's yellow filter, and the blue pixels will be recording in the Info-Box as (R) NIR DN values, the red pixels as Info-Box (G) RED DNs, and the green pixels as Info-Box (B) GREEN DNs shown in Table.9.1.

From such a calibration it is possible to gain reasonably accurate values of terrain RGB reflectances from any part of the screened image. Naturally all ground target reflectances will depend on the paint employed and the material of the target.

Screen densitometry

Since we can easily find values of reflectance (ρ) it is a simple matter to determine the reflection density (D_p) of any point within the image (see Box 4.3), where the reflectance density is given by:

$$D_p = \log_{10}(1/\rho) \tag{9.1}$$

Considering the overall reflectance value at the origin point of Fig.9.3, i.e, 38%, the reflectance density (according to Eq. 9.1) is 0.42.

Channels box

The Channels Box is shown at the bottom right of Fig.9.3 and can be accessed by clicking Windows–Palettes–Channels. As may be seen from Fig.9.3, four channels are

Table. 9.2 *Radiometric calibration of screen RGB values.*

	Ground target spectral reflectances			**Info Box RGB DN values**			**Correction factors (for new DN values)**		
	Red %	Green %	Blue % (or NIR)	R	G	B	R	G	B
WHITE	76	11	4	135	18	7	1.43	1.57	1.48
GREY	-	-	-	-	-	-	-	-	-
BLACK	-	-	-	-	-	-	-	-	-
RED	-	-	-	-	-	-	-	-	-
GREEN	-	-	-	-	-	-	-	-	-
etc.									

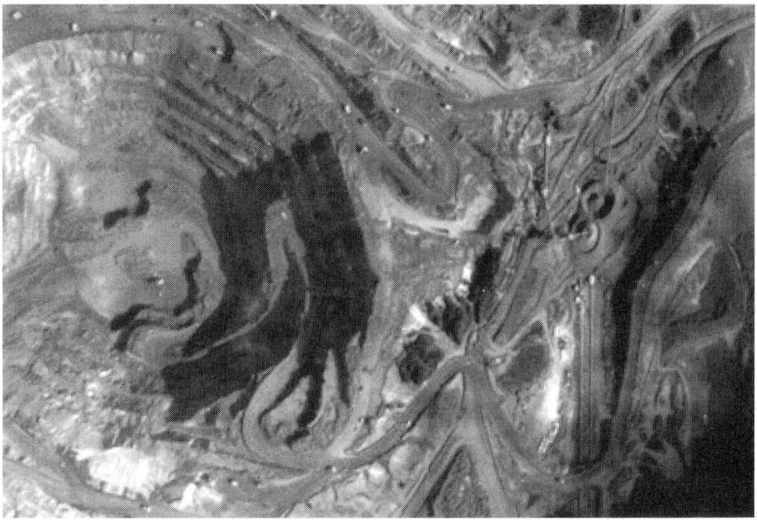

Figure 9.4 *The monochromatic red channel of Fig. 9.3, showing the near infrared (NIR) image component.*

displayed: RGB, red, green and blue (the former being the NIR photosite when the camera is in CIR mode). By clicking on each channel the screen will display either full RGB colour (CIR in this case) or one of the contributing spectral chanels. The Channels Box serves the same purpose as broad-band MSP records and can be useful for analysing the spectral content of crops, forests or any other terrain property.

Figure 9.3 is a CIR photograph of a copper mine, and so the RGB channel icon shows the same CIR image. If the green or blue channel icons are selected we get the red or green spectral images, but if the red channel is selected then we get a near infrared (NIR) image of the scene as shown in Fig.9.4.

Figure 9.4 is the monochromatic red channel of Fig.9.3. Had this CIR image been taken on the jungle floor, 18,000 ft below, we could expect considerable NIR reflectances from the lush vegetation. However, the photograph was taken as part of a survey running up to the mine, the top of which is at 16,000 ft. At 0740 hours the atmosphere was both damp and cold, and so what little vegetation existed was therefore unhealthy and very wet (six small glaciers were nearby) resulting in strong near-infrared absorption and none of the NIR reflectance we usually associate with organic matter.

The Toolbox (on the left side of the image in Fig.9.3) contains a number of icons used mostly to manipulate the image, but none of these are suitable for image analysis.

Sun and shadow influence

As we all know, the sun rises in the east and settles in the west, and at local noon the sun is due south. It is strange therefore to find that all PIs are trained to look at vertical photographs with the shadows falling towards the observer, a practice consistent with the impossible assumption that our midday sun comes from the north rather than the south! But such are the strange subconscious assumptions we make in viewing vertical photographs.

We can conduct a small experiment to prove this lighting illusion. Looking at Fig.9.3, we notice that the solar illumination is coming from the right (the photograph was taken around 0740 hours, about 4° below the equator). If we rotate the image anti-clockwise we have no difficulty in perceiving the crater of the mine, i.e, the shadows fall towards the observer. On the other hand, if we turn the photograph clockwise, then most people will see the crater as a hill. It is this crater/hill illusion that has to be avoided, and is the reason why we should view vertical images with the shadows falling towards us if we are to perceive unambiguous depth impressions.

Artists often produce very convincing illusions of depth by oblique shading, and cartographers have exploited this for many years by shading contoured topographic maps as though they were illuminated from the north west.

These perceptual illusions are well known of course (Gregory, 1998) and should be studied by everyone involved in photo-interpretation. Before leaving the subject it is interesting to mention an even more common phenomenon – the moon illusion. It is a common experience to see the moon, when close to the horizon, as a very large disk which gets progressively smaller as it ascends in the night sky. Yet we know that the moon's disc subtends the same angle to the human eye at all times, proved by photographing it as it rises in the night sky! These effects are not properly understood, although one hypothesis suggests that we assume the sky to be as an upturned bowl, with the observer at its centre. Under these assumptions the horizons are further than the zenith, consequently we perceive both sun and moon to be further away from us when close to the horizon, and perceive them as larger since they afford the same angular subtense as that from zenith.

Image quality

We have dealt with sensors, cameras, flight planning, tracking, interpretation and analysis, all of which are important, but the most significant aspects of aerial survey are those which decide if and when we should fly a particular survey mission. The bottom line is always the local environment in which we must fly, and the choices left open to the survey crew are very few, particularly those which control image quality.

The survey flight manager (SFM) will always have to consider the weather, and make decisions with regard to getting photography while the weather holds – even if it is not ideal. Faced with problems of unsettled weather, waiting for ideal conditions could easily mean months of waiting in some countries (monsoons, snow, wind-blown sand, etc.), but wherever possible atmospheric and solar conditions should always be given the greatest consideration as they have the ultimate bearing on image quality.

Factors contributing to image illumination

Daylight is a mixture of sunlight and skylight in an average proportion of 5:1 at noon, falling to 1:1 in the early morning and late evening. Terrain contrast is obviously affected by solar altitude (θ_s), and solar azimuth (*SZ*), with respect to any terrain feature. For survey missions where mosaics are to be one of the final products it is important to respect the solar variables, particularly in latitudes within 30° of the equator, as changes in solar angles can seriously affect image contrast within the survey block. It is mainly for this reason that long flight-lines are usually flown east-west unless other considerations are more important.

Where expensive areas of arid or open country are being mapped it is important that adjacent flight-lines should be photographed under similar lighting conditions, as no amount of image processing can compensate for strong variations in lighting between adjacent runs. Not least among problems concerned with lighting is the atmosphere, and although we assume a generally cloud free atmosphere for aerial photography this is never the case since there is always some haze.

Haze light

Haze is due to small aerosols in the atmosphere which scatter light in all directions, but not uniformly. Whereas forward-scatter usefully illuminates shadow regions of the scene, back-scatter can enter the camera adding unwanted non-image light to every part of the scene. Back-scattered haze has its own luminance which, even on a clear day, can average about 600 $Cd.m^{-2}$ or more, reducing image contrast considerably.

Haze light is much less in the early morning and late afternoon, making these periods excellent for aerial photography, provided lengthy shadows are not a problem. But for optimum atmospheric conditions we can do no better than to fly in clear skies just after it has rained, when the rain has brought down all of the heavy scattering particles.

What might appear to be a perfect day on the ground may not be so for aerial survey. Looking up we may see a beautiful clear blue sky, but looking down, from say 5000 ft, all we see is a view of the terrain limited by haze. Haze is made up from microscopic particles of gases, sea-salt nuclei, dust, pollen, smoke and other aerosols ranging in size from about 0.1nm to about 1µm.

The purest type of atmospheric scatter is known as Rayleigh Scatter, and is usually only found over large stretches of ocean or primitive landscapes, where the scattering media are mainly gases (oxygen, nitrogen, carbon dioxide and other gases) and sea-salt nucei with molecules and particle sizes ranging from 0.1nm to about 500nm. As a result, we find that Rayleigh Scatter is inversely proportional to the fourth power of the incident wavelengths of light as shown in Eq. 9.2.

$$\text{Rayleigh Scatter} \propto \lambda^{-4} \tag{9.2}$$

If we look at the visible spectrum we see that it extends from 380nm to 760nm where, at the extremes of human vision, red light is twice the wavelength of blue. Since Rayleigh Scatter is inversely proportional to wavelength, we have a factor 2^4 or 16 times more blue scatter than red scatter – which is why we have a blue sky! Pure blue sky is increasingly rare today, mainly due to atmospheric pollution where the aerosols now include industrial smoke and hydrocarbons. As a consequence the usual scattering particles are greater than those for clean air and the process is known as Mie Scatter.

$$\text{Mie Scatter} \propto \lambda^{-s} \quad (9.3)$$

where the scatter index (s) may vary from 0 to the maximum of 4. On average the scatter index is 1.3 ± 0.6.

As we know from experience, even with Mie Scatter prevailing, the sky is generally blue and as such, blue skylight plays a significant part in illuminating the terrain. Indeed, shadows are entirely illuminated with skylight – blue on a clear day and grey under cloud.

Haze can be a serious problem in aerial survey, but is usually only significant above 5000 ft (Graham and Read, 1986). Nevertheless, only experience can help when considering to abort a mission because of haze. The pilot will normally consider haze under the term visibility, where he refers to perhaps 20 or 30 miles of horizontal visibility. But for the survey tracker or photographer looking down at the terrain it remains a difficult decision, particularly when the cost of flying to the survey area is so great. The authors' have often witnessed hazy conditions on one day and found photography to be excellent, whereas similar visual conditions the next day prove the imagery to be unacceptable. One of the reasons for keeping a survey navigation-sight on board, even though survey tracking is done by GPS, is because looking through the sight gives a better view of the terrain and the effects of haze.

A general rule-of-thumb that is useful (but not perfectly accurate) is: " if you can see to navigate, then conditions are good enough for photography."

For monochrome photography we can always cut through some of the haze by using a yellow ('minus-blue') filter over the lens, but for obvious reasons we are denied this ploy with colour photography (except for CIR, where again we must employ a minus-blue filter).

There are significant differences between 'haze' and a 'soft-sun', where the latter is due to high cirrus clouds softening the edges of cast shadows. Ideally we welcome the soft-sun atmosphere for colour photography, mainly because harsh shadows create too much colour contrast, but usually it is necessary to accept the prevailing conditions.

Approximately 26% of the world's land area is dry, and much of this area abounds with mineral deposits. The economic value of having such an area surveyed is beyond doubt, but such ground surveys are not easy, and due to their size they are always expensive projects. As a consequence they are usually photographed with wide-angle lenses, not only to cover large areas at less cost, but also to finish the survey in a reasonable period of time. Unfortunately the use of a wide-angle lens also invites problems associated with the sun.

Solar altitude (θ_s) and hot-spots

Solar altitude (angle) is an important factor in aerial photography, mainly because it controls shadow-length which is important to photo-interpretation. Obviously if long shadows are required then early morning or late evening flight planning is necessary, and for some surveys we must take care that solar altitude is not too high if we are to avoid hot-spots. 'Hot-spots' are a condition due to haze, where back-scattered luminance can be accepted into the camera lens (see Fig.9.5). Depending on the terrain and strength of this back-scattering, the result can be a hot-spot capable of destroying all contrast and detail within one side of the image. This can easily occur in deserts, tundra, forests and snow-fields, but particularly in regions where the solar altitude easily reaches angles higher than 50° above the horizon.

Conditions favourable for hot-spots are illustrated in Fig.9.5 where we can see that they are strongly influenced by the semi-angle of the camera lens ($\phi/2$), its complementary angle (δ) and the solar altitude (θ_s). Although strong hot-spot effects are very obvious (mainly a lack of contrast such that no significant detail can be seen) there is an even greater danger that the hot-spot may not be seen as such and the PI might reasonably assume the effect to be a terrain feature.

Hot-spots (hidden or obvious) are particularly unwelcome in forest surveys, where they can be hidden over extensive canopies, and in many contract specifications there is a clause restricting survey flights to periods where the solar altitude must be less than the complementary lens angle (δ) as shown by Eq. 9.2.

$$\theta_s < \delta \tag{9.2}$$

Solar altitude can be calculated from a knowledge of the geographical location (latitude), the date, month and local time. A suitable hand-held calculator is the Kodak Aerial Exposure Computer R-10. This simple device is designed to calculate the *a priori* correct aerial exposure, and for this purpose includes scales for determining

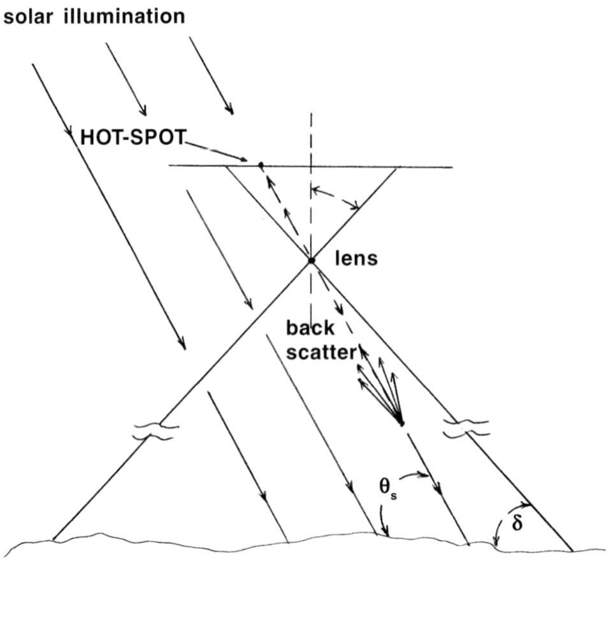

Figure 9.5 *Solar altitude (θ_s) camera semi-angle ($\phi/2$), complementary angle (δ) and their relation to hot-spot generation (due to atmospheric back-scatter, when $\theta_s > \delta$).*

solar altitude. Alternatively, the reader can use the Q-Basic program (SA1) listed in App.D.

In the peak summer months of northern Europe, we can expect noon solar altitudes in the region of 57–64°, and if we are flying with the MF-DMC(3) with its 38mm Biogon lens (FoV = 91°) it has a semi-angle of 45°, and according to Eq. 9.2, our solar altitude must be less than δ (also 45°). Calculating from SA1, we find flying is restricted midday, between 0900 and 1500 hours. On the other hand, if we employ theMF-DMC(2) with an 80mm Planar (FoV = 52°) then the 26° semi-angle and its complementary angle of 64° allows survey flight throughout the entire day, with no restrictions other than normal exposure limits.

Survey flying in the tropics can be even more limiting, particularly in desert regions where at latitudes up to 30° we can expect solar altitudes over 80°, restricting flights to the early morning or late afternoon depending on terrain and camera lens. Nevertheless, there are circumstances where a low solar altitude is useful such as creating long shadows in order to define shallow ridges. One particular instance in the middle east comes to mind where an aerial survey over gravel-plain desert was required. The main interest was wadi areas (dried-up river beds). It was obvious that a low sun was essential, but just as important was the direction of the sun's rays! In other words - the solar azimuth!

Solar azimuth (SZ)

Unlike solar altitude, solar azimuth (SA) has its origins at noon (SZ = 0°), when the sun is due south, i.e, at its 'southing'. As a consequence, all SZ values east of southing are negative, whereas all SZ values westward are positive.

By iterating values of SA and SZ in App. D, we can find the best options for survey flight so that shallow terrain features, such as desert wadis, can be revealed. Unfortunately however, it will mean either early morning or late afternoon flying, and with such low sun conditions a higher than normal exposure rating (ISO equivalent) may be needed.

Wherever a mission is planned for serious photo-interpretation, be it regions of desert, wadi areas, shallow ridges, deep valleys, canyons or mountainous regions, it is essential for the terrain to be suitably illuminated with respect to shadows and their orientation. For this reason it is well worth looking at SA and SZ parameters before completing the survey flight plan.

10 Ground control acquisition

Introduction

Ground control (photogrammetric control) for mapping is a job for surveyors, but not entirely outside the scope of a book such as this. It consists of a network of image-identifiable points on the ground, for which values (referred to a horizontal and vertical datum) have been established. Specifically, 'ground control' is a means for orienting or relating aerial photographs to the ground.

Survey requirements will vary according to the nature and size of each project. A low order of survey will probably be adequate for small, isolated survey projects, computed from an arbitrary origin with assumed starting coordinates and with a conveniently oriented coordinate system. But for larger projects and urban surveys, ground control needs to be of a much higher order – usually tied to the national or state datum.

Photogrammetric control requires both horizontal control and vertical control, the former with respect to a horizontal datum and the latter to a vertical datum. In some cases both horizontal and vertical space positions are known for a given object point, which can then serve as a dual purpose control point. Ideally, each stereoscopic model in the survey should contain at least three horizontal and four vertical control points (Combs *et al.*, 1980).

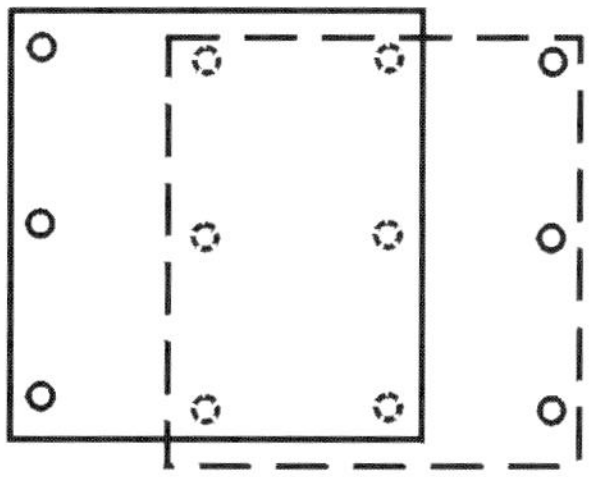

Figure 10.1 *Ideal configuration of ground control points for a stereoscopic model.*

Various control schemes are employed such that a minimal number of control points exist in each model, and a typical configurations for small-area digital surveys, such as those undertaken by Geotechnologies, are for six combined horizontal and vertical points arranged to provide six control points per model, as shown in Fig.10.1.

A high standard of ground control is extremely important for photogrammetric mapping, where we can expect ground control to cost anything from 20 to 50% of the total mapping costs and, as is well known, the accuracy of a completed map can never be better than the ground control upon which it was based.

Generally speaking, images of acceptable photo control points must be sharp and well defined, and lie in favourable locations within the photograph.

Ground control: pre-marking and post-marking

There are many areas, such as deserts, forests and moorlands where natural points for ground control do not exist. As a consequence it is necessary to provide suitable artificial points (targets) to be placed on the ground before photography takes place. The exact positions of these targets are found by field survey in a process known as pre-marking, a procedure both time consuming and expensive, and sometimes impossible if flying has to be done immediately due to problems of approaching bad weather or aircraft servicing.

In the event that pre-marking cannot be completed prior to survey flight, a procedure known as post marking can be adopted where, upon inspection of already flown photography, it is usually possible to identify natural or man-made features that can be visited by ground surveyors to establish their position and serve as ground control targets. Today, it is common practice to employ post-marking techniques, not only for convenience but because the method is more economic and efficient since existing features can be used.

Pre-marking: artificial ground targets

Artificial ground targets should be placed close to the limits of the model, and at a pre-determined interval in the proposed line of flight to serve as wing points for which elevations and coordinates can be later established.

Being made specifically for the purpose of identification, artificial targets have the great advanatage of contrast and visibilty and are unlikely to be confused with natural control points. On the other hand, they incur extra work, are expensive to make and, unless secure against vandalism, animals and weather may suffer destruction.

Types of artificial target for ground control

Although it is possible to purchase permanent ground control markers for surveying, these 50cm or 75cm metal rods are usually made of steel and aluminium and are intended for permanent survey stations. However, survey markers such as the Anchor-Mark variety are not intended for aerial survey marking since their marker-heads are far too small to be recognised in an aerial photograph, such targets therefore need to be supplemented with a much larger target area.

Materials used for targeting vary a great deal, mainly depending on the terrain surface involved. For urban areas (subject to permission) white crosses can be painted on black grounds, be they roads, pavements or any other open area. For soils we must adopt materials, such as wood, plastic or heavy cloth, with each target clearly painted white on black. Another method is to deploy bright umbrellas (the large bright commercial advertising variety are best) that can usually be purchased relatively cheap and are easy to transport and erect. Obviously they are vunerable to winds, but if they can be buried up to the canopy they are usually safe. It is also possible to employ large stones painted white and in the shape of a cross, or use old tyres (painted white) to create cruciform targets.

Perhaps the most difficult and expensive targeting problem is in the desert, particularly where there are large sand-dunes, such as the 100 m high dunes found in the Rub-Al- Khali of Saudi Arabia, or in the Liwa of the UAE. In such areas the main problem is wind-blown sand, and if the carefully surveyed ground control is to be seen, each target must be stable, visible and at some considerable height above the sand. As a consequence it is usual to make concrete monuments, tall enough and large enough to survive, and the aerial photography must take place as quickly as possible – before wind-blown sand covers the targets completely.

The targets are usually cruciform and extend to about 5 or 6 m across, and so their manufacture and positioning is a considerable undertaking. White plastic sheeting (such as 0.15mm opaque polyethylene film) works well on most dark soils and grasses, but is useless on snow or light reflective surfaces. Under these circumstances a dark material such as felt building paper is recommended. Plastic materials do not disintegrate easily and have the advantage of being lightweight and simple to peg down on soil, but if animals are in the survey area there is always the possibility they will be disturbed, or even eaten, particularly by sheep!

Unbleached white muslin or bleached cotton sheets also make ideal targets, and being relatively lightweight (156 grams per square meter) are easily conveyed and cut from rolls to the required panel size. White painted plywood can also be employed, and may be the best option where targets have to be stationed a few feet above ground, but such materials are heavy to handle and much more expensive.

Target size and shape

Ground control targets need to be symmetrical and centered on the station marker. The best shape is a cross (Fig.10.2) so that if one particular leg of the cross is obscured or destroyed the centre can always be found. The physical size of the individual panels making up the cross will always depend on photo-scale, with an image size of about 30–100μm square for the centre panel as a minimum requirement (Wolf, 1974).

Whereas our own field experiments (with digital cameras) tend to agree with those given above, we find that for digital systems panel size is simply related to the GSD and the minimum number of image pixels required to identify a panel. Past survey work and field trials indicate that a minimum of 4 to 5 image pixels is necessary to identify a ground control panel ($5P$ in Fig. 10.2). For a client's request of, say, 50cm GSD, this would mean each panel width will be one GSD (50cm) wide and 5 GSDs (2.5 meters) in length. This can be formalised for the size of ground control panel lengths by putting:

$$\text{Panel length } (5P) = 5(\text{GSD}) \qquad (10.1)$$

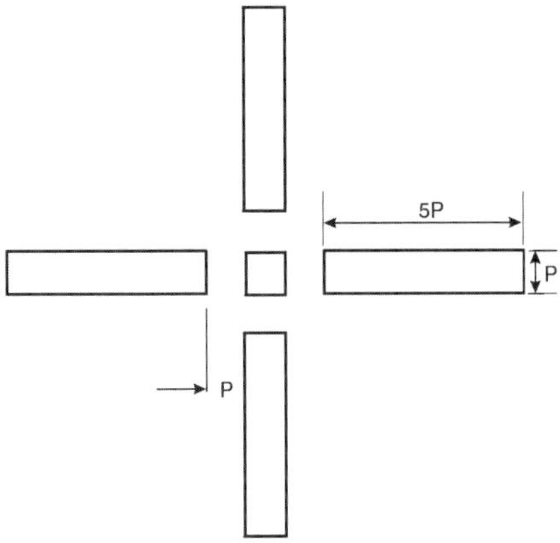

Figure 10.2 *Ground control target showing the ideal shape and size of target elements. For a digital image 5P should occupy at least 4 to 5 pixels.*

In digital air surveys we use the ground sampled distance as a basic specification, where a GSD of 50cm is considered average and one of 25cm a higher ground resolution. Since we incorporate photo-scale within the GSD (Eq. 4.25) all we need to do is apply Eq. 10.1 in order to size the ground control panels. Thus, for a GSD of 50cm, we would need to fly a 28mm lens at 5100 ft, providing a photoscale of 1:55,555. From Eq. 10.1, our requirements are for panels 50cm wide by 2.5 m in length. Alternatively, flying at 2550 ft with the same lens would give us a photoscale of 1:27,700 and a GSD of 25cm. Accordingly, our panel length would need to be 1.25 meters which, divided by 27,700 provides an image of length of 45μm (5 pixels).

It is interesting to note that our 5 pixel image size (45μm) corresponds to the minimum values recommended by Wolf (e.g, 0.03mm to 0.1mm).

Post-marking

As mentioned above, post-marking is mainly employed to day and with the current accuracy of dGPS is in keeping with the economics of digital surveys. Once a survey has been flown it then remains for the images to be examined in order to establish the best locations for ground control points, as indicated in Fig.10.1.

Apart from the economic advantage of not having to manufacture and erect a target, a significant advantage of post-marking is being able to create a notional GC point as an off-set to a large or very identifiable object, particularly where placing a target would not be permitted! A typical example of an off-set GC point is shown in Fig.10.3, where a convenient image reference is the corner of a forest, or building, adjacent to, say, a road or path. The GC point can then be marked (by crayon, aerosol or paint stick) via a Survey Point Stencil and accurately positioned by OmniStar DGPS (see Fig. 5.28).

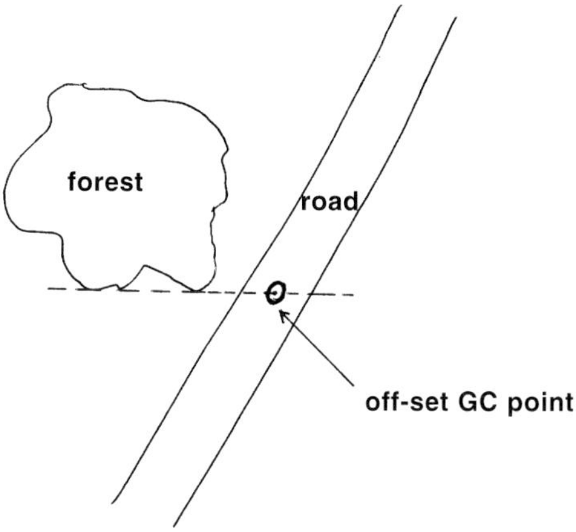

Figure 10.3 *Post marking methods. An off-set ground control point marked by paint-stick or aerosol on a convenient hard surface.*

Off-set technique is further advanced by use of a 'double-prism optical square' device. This hand-held instrument allows the ground surveyor to position a GC point in-line with any feature and is best explained with the example shown in Fig.10.4, where a prominent building (as seen in the image) has one side forming a convenient line of sight to an adjacent road or open space. At the actual location the surveyor can then line-up and mark an accurate GC point with the side of the building, thus creating an accurate image-to-ground reference.

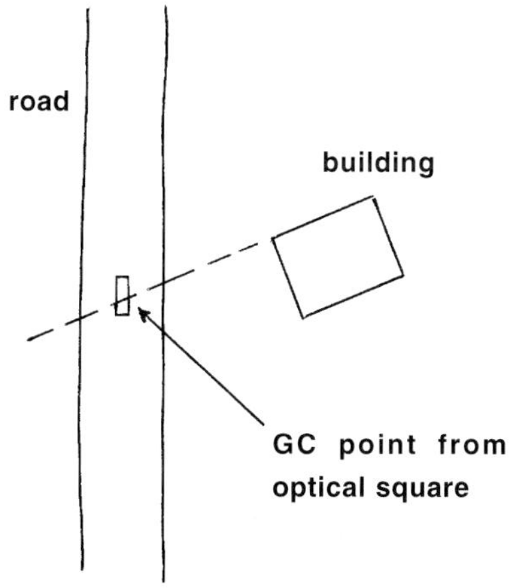

Figure 10.4 *An off-set GC point positioned with the aid of a 'double-prism optical square'*

Ground resolution targets (GRT)

Although most quality cameras have lenses with nominal values of spatial resolution, these values are rarely more than averaged for the lens type, and are usually only quoted in terms of line-pairs per mm, with no indication of the lens MTF (Eq. 4.19). However, metric cameras will usually be provided with a calibration report and this may also include MTF data for its lens.

As already mentioned, with digital-camera surveys we usually quote spatial resolution in terms of ground truth, i.e, GSD, but as we know from Eq. 4.21to 4.24, we are at liberty to evaluate digital images in classical terms of LP/mm if we wish. But regardless of the resolution criteria employed, the survey operator must undertake flight trials to determine realistic values for the camera system in use. It is necessary to emphasise that it is the camera system that is important here, for it is the combination of lens-characteristics, shutter speed, sensor type, image motion and camera mounting that have to be evaluated in airborne imaging.

It is common practice to make suitable ground resolution targets (GRTs) in the form of large 3-bar (or 4-bar) targets as indicated in Figs. 4.5 and 0.5. Since these targets can be painted with bars of various sizes and modulation, when suitably designed and located their images provide realistic evidence concerning the airborne camera system.

A typical GRT example

The two 3-bar GRTs shown in Fig.10.5 were made specifically by one of the authors for testing a Zeiss RMK-TOP 15/23 camera system incorporated within a twin-engined Beech KingAir 350 aircraft. According to contract the camera system had to be tested at two flight levels above the airfield: 2500 ft (1:5000 photo-scale) and at 5000 ft (1:10,000 photo-scale), with the object of providing sure evidence of image quality prior to handing over the aircraft and camera system to the client.

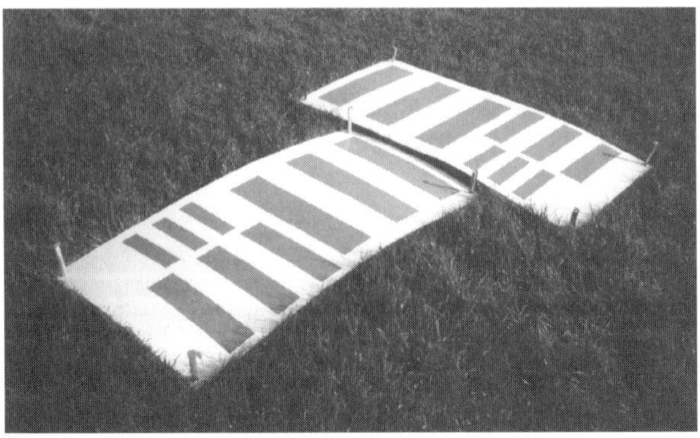

Figure 10.5 *Two identical 3-bar resolution targets, each with a modulation M = 0.5 (see Table 10.1).*

For a thorough resolution test the camera magazine was loaded with colour negative film and was subsequently processed by roller transport machine. The two GRTs were made by painting three 3-bar targets, each at a modulation of 0.5, this being a reasonable value for the type of environment likely to be photographed by the client. The matt paints employed were white and a mid-grey, painted on a 1.2 m by 0.6 m hardboard base. Two identical targets were made and placed at right angles to each other as shown in Fig.10.5, in this fashion they provided both radial and tangential images for evaluation.

Prior tests with various paints established the correct modulation, which was measured with a photometer to give 19 $Cd.m^{-2}$ for the white base, and 6.5 $Cd.m^{-2}$ for the mid-grey bars. Target modulation then followed from

$$M = (L_{white} - L_{grey}) / (L_{white} + L_{grey}) = (19 - 6.5) / (19 + 6.5) = 0.49.$$

Three separate bar sizes were incorporated within the target, each being sized to afford a suitable range of image resolution values as shown in Table.10.1. Analysis of the negative colour image was undertaken by microscope, operating at magnifications up to ×60, and at the nominal scale of 1:5000 the targets measured 0.26mm which, for a target length of 1.2 m gave a true scale of only 1: 4615. All of the 3-bar images could be clearly seen under the microscope at the nominal 1:5000 scale, but were less obvious on the 1:10000 scale images. Indeed, at 1:10000 scale the 3-bar detail was not so clear and only the 62 LP/mm bars could be identified.

Care has to be taken in the analysis of such targets, particularly for analogue systems where the slightest amount of over-exposure gives rise to irradiation (where image resolution is easily destroyed by high density image spread). Other causes of lost resolution include atmospheric effects and camera vibration. Image motion is highly unlikely at heights above 5000 ft.

Athough the above example relates to an analogue system, it serves equally well for digital cameras too. However, a readily available multi-bar target can be found in the streets of most towns throughout the world in the form of an urban pedestrian crossing. Normally such crossings are marked with evenly spaced black and white bars, and all that needs to be done is to measure the bars and widths and take a photometer (or even an exposure-meter) reading to establish target modulation.

Table.10.1 *Ground resolution target ($M = 0.5$).*

Target bars	Target line size line-pair distance	Image line-pair 1: 5000	Image line-pair 1:10000
12 cm x 48 cm	240 mm	21 LP / mm	42 LP / mm
8 cm x 32 cm	160 mm	31 LP / mm	62 LP / mm
5 cm x 20 cm	100 mm	50 LP / mm	100 LP / mm

Although the pedestrian crossing is a convenient GRT, the survey aircraft must then fly at different heights to gain the required image scale and target size before the camera system cut-off resolution can be determined.

Virtual ground point marking

Before leaving the subject of ground point marking, we must also consider a technique that is becoming increasingly common in many parts of the world, where Virtual control points can be recognised from the exposed image.

For various reasons, possibly due to weather, terrain problems, temporal difficulties or simply economic necessity, it may not be possible to either pre-mark or post-mark a mission area. Nevertheless, it may be possible to recognise sufficient image points after the photography has been flown, to provide a system of virtual ground points, with accurate coordinates supplied from existing data.

11 Principles and methods of digital photogrammetry

The rapid developments in digital camera technology and real-time satellite differential global positioning systems, (d)GPS, have yielded new opportunities for 'on-the-fly' mapping when used in conjunction with state-of-the-art digital photogrammetric workstations. This combination efficiently addresses the interior, relative and absolute orientation requirements for the production of contoured orthophoto maps at scales of 1:2500 and coarser. However, despite the progress in digital technologies there is still a considerable lack of awareness on the part of potential users, and it is in response to this that the processing chain described here has been developed.

In this chapter we will explore the major issues that affect quality, mission logistics and cost, and will demonstrate the methodology and application of digital techniques for producing contoured orthophotomaps, with particular reference to employing the Kodak DCS-460CIR camera for coastal environments. This will be achieved through a case study of a dynamic coastal landslide in a residential area located on the Dorset coast in south-west England. In this case study, digital imagery was captured using a CIR aerial digital photographic system (ADPS) at sufficient resolution for the recognition, identification and analysis of features appropriate to the task Ground control was collected using a real-time satellite derived (d)GPS. To obtain planimetric information from the imagery, errors inherent in the photography were resolved using digital photogrammetric techniques. A digital elevation model (DEM) was generated which was subsequently applied to the image base to produce a 5 m interval contoured orthophotomap.

Introduction

The use of stereo analogue vertical aerial photography and photogrammetry for cartographic map production began in the 1900s and partial transition to digital systems, in the form of the analytical stereoplotter of UV Helava, was seen in 1959.

Apart from resistance to digital photogrammetry on the grounds of insufficient accuracy, the inability to process large volumes of digital data with the computers available at that time was a major stumbling block to the further development of the digital approach. Amongst the earliest attempts at providing a digital solution was Intergraph's interfacing of analogue and analytical stereo plotters with a VAX-based

InterMap graphics terminal in the 1980s followed by a stand-alone version in 1990 (Hassini and Carswell, 1992).

The main reason for the push towards digital photogrammetry, cited by Hassini and Carswell, is the promise of massive cost savings in producing typical photogrammetric outputs since digital orthophoto production eliminates the need for slow and expensive analogue orthophoto production equipment. In their 1992 paper, Hassini and Carswell were discussing the use of digitised analogue photographs, but since then, aerial digital photography has become a realistic alternative to analogue systems for many applications (Burger, 1996; Bobbe, 1997; Goodpasture, 1996 and Knapp *et al.*, 1997). We must also consider that in the last few years, parallel advances in desktop computer processing and display technologies, image data compression, lens calibration routines, photogrammetric matching algorithms, output devices and satellite based real-time (d)GPS have made it possible for a totally integrated digital approach to be adopted for contoured orthophotomap production.

The opportunity for decision making regarding the type of imagery to acquire or use presents itself regularly since the shelf life of data can be very short, especially where natural or anthropogenic change is continual and/or rapid, such as in the coastal zone. Although it is now possible to make choices about the type of sensor to use, there are a number of factors, including cost and application, to be considered before any such choice can be exercised. Furthermore, making the change from tried and tested methods to new technology is likely to take some time as it requires forward thinking and courage – described by some as a 'leap in the dark'. Therefore, despite all the advances, traditional aerial photography (using film) is still widely used today in coastal sciences, such as coastal resource management and planning, the study of estuarine sedimentology (MacManus and Soulsby, 1994), monitoring morphological change over time (Jiminez *et al.*, 1997; Leys and Werrity, 1999; Oostwoud Wijdenes *et al.*, 2000) and monitoring coastal wetlands (Ramsey and Laine, 1997). Film, however, is a relatively expensive format which does not lend itself to modern computerised approaches to data handling for resource management and planning. Even though film technology still prevails, other industries including mapping and charting and GIS have now embraced digital technology, and so it is imperative for the imaging side to be able to interface with these industries allowing them to take full advantage of the digital revolution in the production of contoured orthophotomaps.

An orthophotomap gives a true representation of the landscape, whereas the non-rectified photograph does not. The off-the-camera, vertical digital aerial photo has often been used inappropriately for the same purpose as its topographic map counterpart – but without symbology or height information as depicted by contours or spot heights. Use of these unrectified vertical digital photographs as maps is common practice and may be attributed to the obvious spatial relationships between map and photograph, and to the often practised method of fitting and matching consecutive photographs using digital image processing software to form a mosaic (Graham, 1998). Such uncontrolled mosaics may be pleasing to the eye but do not have the metric or geodetic accuracy of the cartographers map, giving a perspective view of the landscape, in contrast to the strictly orthogonal view of a map.

The orthogonal view can be derived from a digital photograph by correcting for the attitude of the camera at the instant of image capture, and by removing displacement errors resulting from the height of objects within the photo-scene. In addition, distortions due to lens aberrations, dimensional instability of the sensor, and translated image motion must be accounted for. The applied science of digital photogrammetry corrects for these errors, accounts for the distortions and derives reliable 3-dimensional measurements from the photograph, supported by quality assurance reports.

The processing chain

Topographic survey operations aim to achieve a maximum degree of accuracy as economically as possible. This remit requires an integrated approach to the process from planning to completion, and the complex problems that face the photogrammetrist can be reduced if pilot, camera operator, navigator (tracker), ground survey team, software and hardware perform effectively and empathetically. The processing chain described here provides a systematic approach that enables this aim to be achieved and at the same time can assuage the fears and reservations of would-be users by presenting a logical and transparent methodology that addresses the data quality issues associated with the use of digital orthophotomaps.

The processing chain may be divided into 4 main areas, which follow logically from one to the next, although it is possible for the user to enter the chain at any one of the 4 main divisions depending on their requirements. The four major elements of the processing chain are shown in Fig.11.1.

Logistics and mission planning

Meticulous planning at the outset is the key to a successful operation and the first element of the processing chain is concerned with establishing a clearly defined purpose for the photography, planning the ground and air survey and drawing up a contractual agreement, all of which ultimately control client satisfaction with the final product. The major parameters that significantly effect quality, mission logistics and

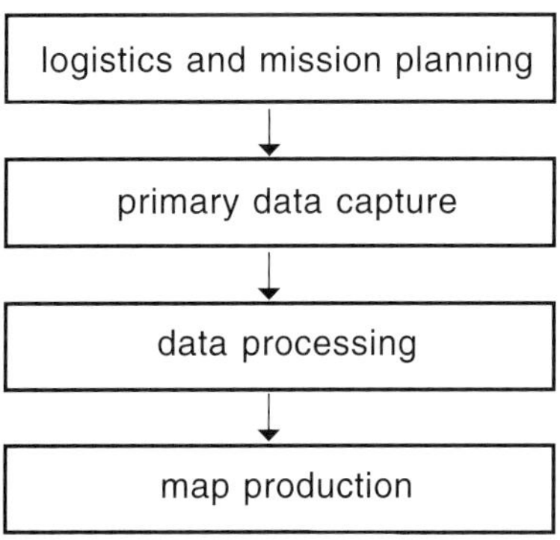

Figure 11.1 *The four major elements of a digital survey processing chain.*

cost when adopting an all-digital contoured orthophotomap production environment are:

1. The camera format.
2. The GSD at point of capture.
3. The block area of the project site.
4. The survey flying height (with respect to a topographic datum).
5. The required scale of the final contoured orthophotomap.
6. The dissemination and compression method used for the image data.

Each of these parameters is addressed during logistics and mission planning and is closely related to the client's requirements. The components of the first major element of the processing chain for logistics and mission planning are shown in Fig.11.2.

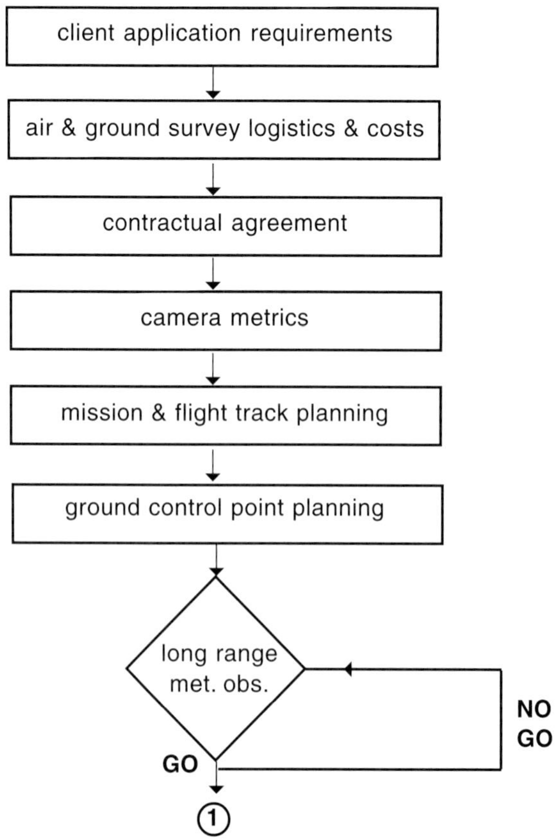

Figure 11.2 *Components of the first major element of the digital processing chain.*

Client application requirements

The first two questions regarding client application requirements are usually 'what does the client want the data for?' and 'when is the data required?' However, defining application requirements is not a trivial task because clients are not usually familiar with specifying application requirements in digital terms. As a consequence, it is the responsibility of the data provider to ensure that the products deliver what has been promised so that the client pays off. For example, an increase in the GSD returns a reduction in the number of overlapping photographs and stereo-models necessary to cover the project site. The number of ground control points required, storage and plotting media, data processing time and aircraft flying hours are all reduced with a corresponding cost benefit. This might at first seem attractive to the client, but will result in a reduction in resolution (GSD) of the digital image, which diminishes the overall accuracy to which ground detail may be coordinated in both plan and height. The GSD dictates the scale of the final map product, and it is of paramount importance that the digital photography is captured at a resolution that can satisfy the client's final mapping requirements.

For some applications, e.g, vegetation mapping, colour infrared (CIR) may be required, but for other applications, e.g, town planning, the client may prefer true colour photography. In addition the client may need to comply with particular data standards or formats and may need to archive and distribute the data in a particular way. From a commercial perspective it is good practice to consider data as assets and to explore opportunities for 'added value' with the client as this may affect the primary data acquisition parameters.

Air and ground survey logistics and costs

Air and ground survey logistics addresses issues such as the relocation of the survey aircraft and crew from their base to the survey site. The type of terrain and ease of access are important considerations for ground control point collection planning, and any photographic requirements which affect operations, such as time of day, season or state of tide must be fully considered. All of these logistical factors influence the cost of the mission, and once the client application requirements have been established it is the cost of an aerial survey that becomes the fundamental issue as far as the client is concerned. Costs are considered below, although comparing the costs of film and digital survey is a complex matter because the two are inherently different in most respects.

Capital costs for film and digital systems

The capital cost of most analogue airborne large-format cameras is roughly $500,000, with relatively high operational costs owing to the need for larger, more expensive, aircraft. In addition, the logistical and navigation support for these large-format systems could add an additional $150,000 to the capital investment, and facilities for scanning must be provided. The complete and totally digital small-format system discussed here is based on the Kodak DCS-460 CIR camera with a dedicated GPS interface. This configuration costs less than $60,000 with modest operational costs of typically $450 per hour for a twin-engined aircraft hire (e.g, Partenavia P68), or considerably less for a single-engined machine, particularly if it is not a survey-dedicated aircraft. Naturally these figures increase slightly when using the medium format MF-DMC system.

Developing, printing and scanning costs (analogue systems)

The costs of chemicals for developing and printing films, and their expensive disposal imposed by environmental regulations are considerable. This is particularly pertinent to colour and CIR (colour infrared) films, since they often require specialist processing available only at a few professional laboratories in the USA, Japan, and Europe. However, no such costs are incurred with digital systems because their images are stored directly to disk at a GSD resolution appropriate for the identified application area. Costs are also dependent on the required product, and if the end product is needed in digital format then film must be scanned and a photogrammetric scanner will be required. Scanning is time consuming (possibly twenty minutes per photograph at 7.5mm scanning aperture (Hohle, 1996) and is a costly operation ($100 per 23cm square image (Light, 1996)). Furthermore, there is often a loss of radiometric detail and geometric integrity in the scanning process (Bakker and Van Kootwijk, 1993; Burger, 1996). In order to minimise this, film is often scanned at a higher resolution than is required, preprocessed if required, and resampled to the GSD specified for the application. Mills *et al.* (1996) have noted that the increased cost of a digital camera compared with its 35mm film counterpart is easily offset by the cost of a high resolution flat-bed scanner.

Block survey and orthophoto production

For block air survey operations the area of photo-coverage for a given GSD dictates the economic feasibility of using one format in preference to another. Up to now the largest commercial off-the-shelf digital cameras have been the Kodak DCS-460 or 760 types with their 18mm × 28mm format and Kodak's 37mm square Pro-Back.

In the case study considered here, we are talking about the DCS-460 CIR which, for the same GSD, has a photo coverage of about 1/90th of a 23cm square mapping camera. For small areas the digital format is less expensive, and it has been reported (Wright, 1998) that the comparative costs of a digital survey and a conventional (23cm) survey of Exmoor National Park, UK, are £8971 for digital, and £18,400 for analogue, with a further £12,800 to £17,232 for scanning the colour prints of the latter.

However, for the production of ortho-rectified photographs a threshold is reached where it becomes uneconomical to use a small-format camera. Typical area threshold limits for ortho-rectified images with 50cm and 100cm GSDs are presented in Table 11.1, where DCS-460 costs are compared with 9 inch × 9 inch (23cm) format photography. These summary costings are derived from a survey of recent charges in Europe. For corridor or feature line surveys, such as pipelines, roads, railway lines and coastlines that can be photographed in a single flight-line, digital is always cheaper. In addition, because the image coverage is smaller, there is minimal wastage in terms of area coverage, considerable savings in the cost of data archiving and considerable efficiency gains when disseminating such data sets using local or wide area networks.

Table 11.1 *Comparative orthophoto production costs of digital surveys (DCS-460CIR) against those for an analogue system (9" x 9" film); both systems yield a 50cm GSD (upper) and 100cm GSD (lower).*

survey block area (km^2)	460 CIR cost, £	9 × 9 film cost, £
	50cm GSD	
1 × 1	2814	22385
10 × 10	28802	44308
25 × 25	151872	85031
	100cm GSD	
1 × 1	2460	15476
10 × 10	10473	25960
25 × 25	43399	47799
50 × 50	155989	85873

The cost of collecting ground control data contributes significantly to the overall cost of the production of ortho-rectified photographs, since at least 6 control points are required for each stereo-pair (model). As the photo coverage is much greater for large format surveys, so the number of control points needed is considerably less for the entire block than is needed for small format digital surveys. This is the main factor where digital surveys can incur higher costs.

Camera metrics

Camera calibration allows the type of camera used for the photography to be determined and enables process distortions due to camera geometry to be fully or partially removed. In this study the digital camera was calibrated by projecting a test pattern onto a near planar wall, and a multi-station convergent network of 16 images of the pattern were captured and imported to EOS Systems Photomodeller Pro camera calibration software. The test targets were identified interactively and the software automatically and iteratively determined the principal distance (correct focal length), principal point offset from image centre (PPx and PPy) and the radial distortion parameters, K_1 and K_2.

Mission and flight-track planning

Mission and flight-track planning is achieved using an interactive mission planner (see ASLP in Chapter 8). Following consideration of the type of photography required (true colour or CIR), the dimensions of the survey block, the minimum and maximum ground elevations within the block, the capability of the aircraft and the desired GSD of the imagery, the mission planner (ASLP) calculates the number of flight-lines, the number of images per line, the duration of the survey, the storage requirements, the location of waypoints, the number of ground control points required and provides a breakdown of the costs involved for the complete processing chain.

It is essential to know the number of images in each flight-line as this controls the required image data storage capacity, as well as the density of GC points needed for rectification. Flight-track planning is the most important component in terms of safety, mission economics, and the planimetric quality of the imagery. It is the responsibility of the SFM (tracker) and the pilot to ascertain whether there are any flying restrictions in and around the survey block and to communicate with the camera operator (if this is not the SFM) any abnormal navigation or local weather conditions. In most cases tracking is by real-time (d)GPS and survey waypoints must be uploaded to the GPS receiver, and critically verified, well in advance of the actual survey. Where

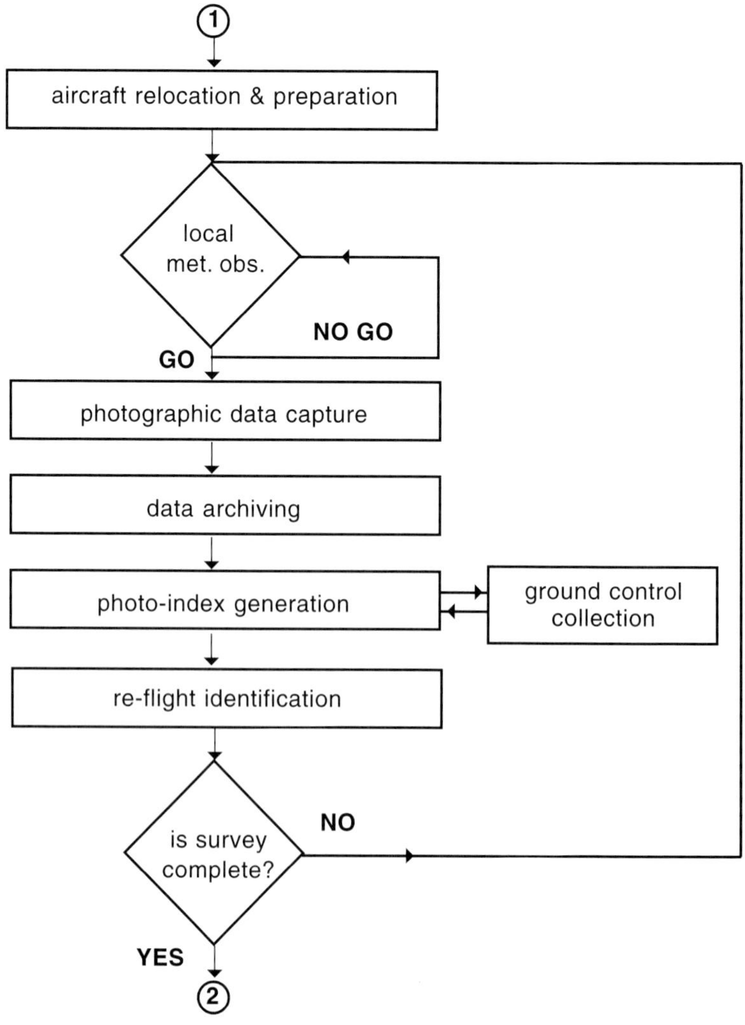

Figure 11.3 *Flow-chart outline for primary data acquisition.*

navigation systems allow, an 'accelerated-time' simulation of the entire survey procedures should be conducted.

The flow-chart shown Fig.11.3 illustrates the overall procedure involved in primary data acquisition. It is to be noted that only after the photo-index has been completed can the mission be considered a success or not, and if not, where re-flights have been identified they must be flown at the first opportunity.

Ground control point planning

Ground control point collection is by real time (d)GPS using the OmniStar service provided by Fugro. This system is capable of sub-meter accuracies in three dimensions and is considered appropriate for GC point acquisition for orthophotomap production up to 1:5000 scale. For higher accuracies RTK (real time kinematic) (d)GPS solutions are necessary. Where accurate detailed maps are available it is often possible to plan the GC point collection before the air survey has taken place. Where existing maps are poor, or in locations where there are no maps, but where there are many natural targets, it may be necessary to plan control point collection after the photography has been collected when potential targets can be identified in the photographs (virtual ground point marking). Where there are no maps and few or no natural targets, such as in the intertidal zone, location of artificial targets is planned and implemented immediately before the survey. In the latter case careful planning and team coordination is essential; for example, in a survey for sediment distribution in the Westerschelde, field workers were required to follow the tide out and plant white 0.5m diameter umbrellas (originally designed for advertising purposes) in the sand at locations fixed using real time (d)GPS immediately before the aerial survey at low tide.

It is recommended that the GC point survey should be subject to the specific requirements for the stereo-analysis and generally include the following:

1. The marking of pre-mark points.
2. The survey of these pre-mark points.
3. The survey of post photography GC points.

The production logistics and methodology of the DEM and orthophotos should prescribe the exact nature and localities of ground control, but in general, this may be guided by the following principles:

1. Points of detail selected as GC points must be identifiable on the photograph and these must be sharply defined and in the same position as when the photograph was taken.
2. When a GC point falls on two adjacent flight-lines, it must be visible on both.
3. Height points in high grass must be avoided.
4. It is more important that a point be positively identifiable rather than the ease with which its position can be determined.
5. The decisive factor of identification is a point's identifiability on the digital photogrammetric workstation.
6. A sketch must be provided for each point fixed.
7. Points shall be fixed in position and height to a general accuracy of ± 0.07% of the flying height above ground, but this shall be finally determined as required by the specifications of the DEM and orthophotos.

Meteorological constraints

Regardless of any operator or client-imposed conditions the ultimate controlling factor over an aerial survey is the weather and in particular, cloud cover. It is essential to consult a long-range (5 day) weather forcast before the decision to mobilise can be taken for routine surveys. This is not always an option for disaster management surveys, but the use of a digital camera considerably increases the opportunity of obtaining photo-coverage in such situations. This is because the difference between large-format film and small-format digital cameras dictates the focal length of lens that is acceptable, and for a similar GSD, large-format cameras require significantly higher survey flight-levels because they generally use 150mm or 210mm lenses. This geometry-induced requirement may limit survey flying to clear-sky conditions and often renders the large format unsuitable for disaster management roles when low-cloud cover accompanies the disaster scene. Under such critical conditions small-format digital systems are often able to operate below cloud cover due to a variety of short focal lengths (15mm, 20mm 24mm or 28mm). Furthermore, digital cameras usually have apertures of either *f*/2.8 or *f*/2, allowing them to gain perfectly good images under lower light levels.

It is interesting to note that when used in their CIR mode, cameras such as the DCS-460CIR exhibit excellent NIR sensitivity, and in one example (Bobbe, 1997) it was demonstrated that the DCS-460 CIR performed better under adverse lighting than a 70mm Hasselblad camera using colour infrared film under the same conditions. This can be put down to the extensive dynamic range of the digital sensor (12 selective bits per channel). Similar results were reorted by Knapp *et al.* (1997) when comparing data from a DCS-420CIR with 35mm and 70mm film cameras. This property can be exploited in regions where cloud cover is frequent, or in areas that are logistically accessible only during the early morning or late afternoon when light levels are less than perfect.

Photogrammetric considerations and data processing

The metric accuracy of a vertical digital photograph is dependent on the reduction of effects of image distortions, height displacement and camera attitude during the instant of image capture. These combine to contribute to positional errors in the spatial mapping of objects within the off-the-camera photograph.

The high quality of optics and materials available today has eliminated the majority of image distortions leaving the nine orientation elements of a near- vertical photograph to be addressed using digital photogrammetric techniques. As described in Chapter 2, the nine orientation elements comprise of six 'outer' and three 'inner' orientations.

The outer-orientation elements include three translations of the camera in cartographic space, represented by the eastings (E), northings (N) and height (ht) of the camera above a datum plane, and three rotations of the camera, represented by pitch (ϕ), roll (ω) and yaw (κ) of the aircraft. Inner orientation elements, which are known to a high degree of accuracy, include the calibrated focal length of the lens and the location of the principle point as represented by the shifts (PPx) and (PPy).

Until recently, photogrammetric techniques for the extraction of elevation data from stereo-pairs of photographs required expensive analytical stereo-plotters (Welch, 1992) but digital (or softcopy) photogrammetry is now becoming increasingly available on low cost PCs running Windows operating system.

Data storage and dissemination is an important consideration when adopting an all-digital approach. The use of lossy image compression reduces the cost of data storage and dissemination, but will create artifacts such as blockiness in the image which may be unacceptable from a cartographic point of view. Experiences in the use of standard JPEG lossy compression techniques up to level 6 results in an accuracy loss that can be tolerated for GSD resolutions up to 50cm. Uncompressed formats such as TIFF do not create artifacts in the image but require much larger data storage facilities with a consequent increase in cost. For example, a 3-band colour digital image sensor of 1.54Px, produces a 4.41Mb image file, whereas the same image compressed to level 6 typically produces a 347Kb JPEG file.

Primary data capture for the case study area

The case study area discussed in this chapter is the Black Ven landslide complex which lies between the two coastal towns of Lyme Regis to the west, and Charmouth to the east, in Dorset on the south coast of England. The Dorset coast has many sites of key geomorphological importance, and Black Ven contains one of the largest systems of landslides in Europe. The area has experienced a long history of instability and the landslide comprises rotational slides, topples, rock falls and slumps of Upper Greensand rock and mudslides, mudflows and sandflows which feed down to the beach. Cliff retreat of around 5m per year is typical during periods of activity. In between major events erosion at the toe of the slope is 15–40m per year (Koh, 1992).

The instability of this part of the Dorset coast presents serious problems for property owners and local authorities as the effects are wide ranging and require expensive engineering solutions. The acquisition of up to date reliable information is a necessary first step in the management of this highly dynamic and inhospitable environment, and colour infrared contoured orthophotographs, which can be delivered within days of the air survey, provide a very valuable resource to engineers and managers alike.

Primary data collection: Black Ven landslide complex

Colour infrared vertical aerial photography was acquired in May 1999, using a DCS-460CIR camera fitted with a 15mm wide-angle lens and 650BP300 filter. The digital camera was mounted (vertically) in a light, twin engined, Partenavia 68b aircraft. The mission was flown at a ground speed of 85 kts and a height of 880 m (2900 ft) amsl, to capture stereoscopic imagery at a GSD of 50cm. A frame rate of 15 s was used to capture the stereo-imagery with a minimum forward overlap of 60%, and a side-lap of 30%. By using a super wide-angle (15mm) lens, the base/height ratio was very high at 0.74, giving rise to increased heighting accuracy.

Six stereo-models were required to create a digital elevation model (DEM) and contoured orthophoto mosaic of the landslide. The ground control data were acquired using real time (d)GPS after the survey was flown, and these points were marked on the unrectified hard copy of the images, which were immediately printed on landing and made available for use in the field to ensure an adequate and appropriate distribution of GC points.

Photogrammetric processing

Following camera calibration each image pair was processed using VirtuoZo photogrammetric software. The production of orthophotos involves a straightforward set of procedures where the computer is provided with the basic data needed to perform the calculations. In the first place the survey block is defined which establishes the number of lines, number of frames per line, imaging scale, the direction of flight, the magnitude of the overlaps and the required output resolution. The GPS derived GC points are recorded in a GCP file to enable relative and absolute orientation of the image pairs.

Interior and exterior orientation

Digital images present a special case for off-the-shelf photogrammetric software since most packages have not been designed with digital photographs in mind. Rather they have been designed for large-format photography where fiducial marks at the four corners of the image are automatically detected using a combination of automatic pattern recognition techniques and known standard format dimensions. From these, the interior orientation is calculated. To address this issue the images were considered to be metric, since there is no appreciable distortion of the CCD sensor under normal operational conditions, and the corners of the image were identified as the fiducials.

This information was recorded as an image mask in the camera parameter file along with the camera calibration details. The interior orientation of both the left and right images in each model was calculated using the camera calibration data and the image mask, and this procedure removes distortions in the image attributable to the lens and camera geometry.

Ground control points were identified on both the left and the right hand images for each model. Following the manual input of six points on both photographs in the model, VirtuoZo is capable of indicating the suggested positions of unused ground control points in the database with a good degree of precision. When all the required GC points have been identified an automatic tie-point generation routine is activated, which typically generates in excess of one hundred common points that relate the overlapping areas of the left and right images, allowing considerable savings in time over other software packages.

The y-parallax residual errors for each related point are then calculated, and the left and right portions of the stereo-model are resampled to remove y-parallax, so simplifying the calculations required to solve for elevation. The images are then matched so that x-parallax can be calculated and hence the elevation. Absolute orientation using the GC points allows the stereo-model to be mapped into a real world co-ordinate system, in this case OSGB36 or UTM WGS84.

DEM extraction

A digital elevation model (DEM) was extracted at 2 m grid intervals. This was considered a sensible interval to reflect the accuracy of the (d)GPS system used to collect GC data and the GSD of 50cm of the digital aerial photography. The DEMs were edited to remove noise and unreliable data derived over dynamic targets such as the sea. The resultant DEM was then used to orthorectify the digital photography and generate a 5 m interval contour image, a perspective image for visual verification and a contoured orthophoto image for map production (Figs. 11.4 and 11.5 respectively – see colour section). The individual contoured orthophoto products were then automatically mosaiced to produce the contoured orthophotomap of the coastline between Lyme Regis and Charmouth at a scale of 1:5000.

The perspective view of the Black Ven landslide complex, shown in the false colour photo of Fig.11.4, is from an azimuth of 150° and an elevation of 45°. The blue tones represent the exposed sequences of the Lower Lias (Belemnite Marls, Black Ven Marls and Shales with Beef), the white tones the exposed sequences of the Lower Cretaceous (Chert, Upper Greensand and Gault). Vegetation types and performance are represented in tones of browns and reds.

Fig.11.5 shows the CIR 5m contoured orthophoto of the Black Ven landslide complex on 16th April 1999, orientated OSGB grid north up, and with a final GSD of 50cm. The original image for Fig.11.5 was taken with a Kodak DCS-460CIR with a 15mm lens providing a GSD of 50cm, and was captured at 1100 hrs local time. The flight was conducted at 2900 ft at a ground speed of 85 kts, and under a cloud base of 3100 ft.

The accuracy of the DEM can be assessed either qualitatively by the user who is familiar with the site or quantitatively by comparing it with checkpoints collected during the field survey. Global measures of DEM accuracy can be obtained by comparing the post-processed GPS elevations at the GC points with the elevation recorded in the DEM at the same location. An independent data source collected to a higher level of accuracy would probably yield the most reliable assessment, but further time consuming surveys may defeat the object of extracting the DEM in the first place.

The monitoring of highly dynamic landscapes such as the Black Ven coastal landslide using digital photography and digital photogrammetry, can provide the engineer and coastal manager with a cost effective supply of timely data enabling them to address urgent management issues such as public safety, loss of property and infrastructure, including dwellings, commercial buildings, roads, sewerage and loss of public amenity facilities. Detailed understanding of the response of the landslide complex to environmental forces is urgently and constantly required. This technique can also provide measurements of a number of important parameters including the volume of material moved, the direction of the movement and the timing and magnitude of landslide events.

12 Digital survey missions: profiles and their applications

As mentioned in Chapter 1, first attempts at small format digital aerial surveys started in the early 1990s (Graham and Mills, 1994; Curr and Koh, 1994) using Kodak DCS digital cameras. But before this (January 1992) units of the US military experimented with a DCS-100 model for reconnaissance work. (Kodak, 1998). Hosted by a Nikon F-3 SLR camera, the DCS-100 embodied a 1280 × 1024 CCD array with 16 mm pixels, the images being stored on a 200Mb hard disk within the associated digital storage unit (DSU). Flown in a Mohawk OV-1 under an 1800 ft ceiling and inclement weather, this early digital reconnaissance imagery was gained with a 180mm lens exposed at 1/500 s at *f*/8 with a rating of 1600 ISO. Apart from the good quality of this recon imagery (even under adverse flying conditions) the main advantage was immediate access via a built-in LCD display or operator viewed video monitor.

The Kodak DCS-200 model then appeared in 1993. In particular the DCS-200 was employed by the US Navy Combat camera teams where the goal was to acquire imagery anywhere in the world and make it available to the Pentagon within one hour of capture. Subject to the actual event, the full or cropped image was compressed and then transmitted either through INMARSAT, data radios or telephone lines, depending on unit location. Average transmission time in the region of 30 s. The digital camera is now a well established reconnaissance sensor for many armed forces throughout the world.

The DCS-200 was the first professional style digital camera and was hosted by the Nikon SLR 8008s carrying the Kodak M-5 chip. In company with all small format digital cameras, the Kodak DCS range are marketed for general use by photographers and not for aerial surveyors. As a consequence the image format follows the aesthetic rectangular form (c. 3:2 ratio) rather than the square format ideal for mapping or reconnaissance. Nevertheless, the M-5 chip with its 1524 × 1012 pixel array (1.54MPx) gives very adequate images which, despite their sub-film quality, are certainly good enough when printed on a dye-sublimation or modern ink-jet printer. With 9 μm square pixels, and 24 bit colour depth, the DCS-200 can operate at equivalent ISO speeds from 50 to 400 in colour and from 100 to 800 in monochrome. The images are stored on a 80Mb hard disk.

Digital aerial surveys with the DCS-200

Initiated by Dr Jon Mills, department of Geomatics, University of Newcastle, the earliest trials were rather hurried owing to aircraft availability. Nevertheless, in July 1994 we fitted a calibrated DCS-200 into the existing camera mount of a Cessna 337 survey aircraft for the urban mission explained in Chapter 5. Typical imagery from this mission, taken at a photoscale of 1:40,000, is shown in Fig.5.1 and the subsequent large scale map of part of St.Neots is shown in Fig.5.2. Calibration values for the 28mm lens on the DCS-200 are shown in Table 5.1. It is of interest to note that this same camera (no longer produced) is still in use many years after its purchase!

It was during these trials that we first came to appreciate a significant problem with all DCS digital cameras when used for aerial survey, and that is the time taken to download each image onto the hard disk or, as with later models, PCMCIA card. Although camera specifications suggested a period of around 3 s for the DCS-200 (which is perfectly adequate for most work) in practice we found it to be closer to 5 s.

Although we wanted to fly the camera with its longer format (14 mm) parallel with the aircraft's axis (so that we could better gain a 60% forward overlap) unfortunately our make-shift mounting adaptation would only allow the camera to be fitted with its short format side (9.2mm) parallel to the aircraft axis. Furthermore, since the camera hole was designed for a larger camera, we had to baffle the opening to prevent exhaust gases from entering the cockpit. This hasty arrangement also precluded the use of the mount's drift facility, forcing us to fly into-wind to avoid drift problems with the line of sequenced imagery.

The essential survey flight calculations were then rapidly made from the usual formula (see Chapter 7) with respect to scale (m), side of ground covered (S), air base (b) and the all important exposure interval (ΔT). Consideration of adjacent lines was not thought appropriate for this first trial. For a scale number of 40,000 our flying height was 3700 ft. With the short side of the format (S') being 9.2 mm, ground coverage (S) on the short side was equal to 368 m, from which a base (b) of 147 m was calculated for 60% forward overlap.

Without GPS or time to estimate our true ground speed, we could only guess our into-wind ground speed from an indicated air speed (IAS) of 100 kts. Consequently we based our exposure interval on a GS of 90 kts (46 m/s) which, with an air base of 147 m, gave the required ΔT as 3 s.

The Cessna 337 is a twin engined (push-pull) aircraft capable of taking the usual large-format mapping camera and can maintain a suitable air speed of 100 kts without falling out of the sky. But, with a full complement of fuel and five people aboard, we didn't wish to fly slower as we considered it possible to download each image within the specified 3 s period.

Upon analysis the images were found to be correctly exposed at ISO 100, and *f*/4, but the average forward overlap was only 41%, indicating that the download period was closer to 5 s than three. Although the lack of 60% overlap excluded the possibility of providing heighting contours, the images were suitable for planimetry and, as shown in Fig.5.2, were plotted on a Leica DVP to provide a large scale map from two overlaping images. Nevertheless, the most significant lesson gained from these trials was to be aware of the camera's true download period, since this single feature has a direct bearing on nearly all other survey planning parameters.

Photogrammetry for the DCS-200

Photogrammetry of the St.Neots trials was conducted by Dr. Jon Mills (Newcastle University) and is described in full by Graham and Mills (1997). However, it should be noted that the method outlined here was devised for use with equipment available at that time i.e, 1994–96.

As briefly explained in Chapter 5, fiducial marks were added to the DCS-200 imagery by using a template image of the same size, which has marked pixels to represent the fiducial marks. The positions of the fiducials being deduced by extrapolation from known coordinates of the calibrated principal point (PP). The template was then overlaid as a transparent layer onto the image being rectified in Adobe Photoshop so that when measured in the photogrammetric software, the lines of intersection yielded the calibrated PP position.

The second stage in applying the calibration data to correct the imagery was to remove any radial and tangential distortions, which was carried out using the 'displace filter' in Adobe Photoshop. A second image is used, termed a 'displacement map', in which the DN of each pixel represents how far the pixel in the image being rectified is to be displaced. A DN of 128 represents no displacement, a value of 0 a maximum negative displacement and 255 a maximum positive displacement. In order to eliminate lens distortion two displacement maps are required, one for x and one for y displacement. These displacement maps are created using an in-house C++ program written specifically for this purpose. The camera calibration data was then entered into the program and each pixel in the image array interrogated, its centre being determined relative to the calibrated PP position, and its displacement (Δx and Δy) being calculated from equations: Eqns. 5.1 and 5.2.

Digital image download period

Obviously the image download period is a major factor in controlling photo-scale and just about every other survey parameter when using off-the-shelf high end digital cameras. Ideally we would be happy with a period of two seconds or so, but to date only a few high-end cameras satisfy this critereon using Firewire interface. We have little doubt that many future high-end digital cameras (both small and medium format) will have two second download times, and these will most likely be CMOS types. As discussed (Chapter 5), the Foveon II employs three CMOS chips and with a Firewire interface downloads in two seconds! We can expect many digital innovations including CCD developments such as the Fuji Super CCD with its honeycomb CFA and high ISO sensitivity. And although the Fuji FinePix S1 Pro takes far too long (15 s) to be useful for aerial survey, the medium-end FinePix 4700 employs a 2.4MPx Super CCD chip that can download to a Smart Media card in one second, and has a top (electronic) shutter speed of 1/2000 s – all of which indicates future possibilities.

Currently there are several suitable high-end small-format Kodak DCS cameras that are being used for survey purposes, including the DCS-200, 410, 420 and 460 models, all of which download within 5–12 s. Later DCS models, such as the 560 and 660 (both with ITO 6MPx chips) and the DCS- 620x (2MPx) camera are fitted with an IEEE-1394 (Firewire) high-speed serial interface, and consequently have much faster download periods, the 620x being capable of two-second downloading. Yet another high-end camera suitable for survey work is the Nikon D1 (2.74MPx, CCD array) which also connects to the computer by Firewire and has an ISO speed range from 200 to 1600 with an electronic shutter capable of 1/16,000 second.

So, although the latest Firewire-compatible cameras are generally capable of two-second download periods, and the MF-DMC cameras are similarly fast, the remaining problem is with the older cameras and how to deal with 5–12 s downloads.

As we know from the survey flight planning formulae shown in Chapter 7, the planned photo-scale of any mission must be considered with respect to: flying-height, lens focal length, air-base, sterescopic cover, ground coverage, aircraft ground-speed and exposure interval. If the camera cannot function rapidly enough then a smaller photo-scale may have to be considered.

For the DCS-200 and 420 cameras with their M-5 chip the main restriction is the safe ground speed of the aircraft and the nominal 100 knot safe air speed that dictated our photo-scale should be 1: 40,000 for the 28mm lens employed. A similar restriction is where the desired photoscale is as large as, say, 1:15,000, and a 60% forward overlap is essential in order to gain stereoscopic coverage. Under these circumstances we have a choice of three possible solutions (Graham and Mills, 1997):

1. Employ an aircraft that can fly suitably slow – say at 50 knots (see Chapter 6).
2. Employ two similar cameras and stagger their exposure intervals to cover the required photo-sequence.
3. Re-fly each flight-line with GPS-controlled exposures to fill-in any missing overlaps with point-to-point precision.

To our knowledge all three options have been adopted by various operators, but the authors usually select the first option for research flights and, where necessary, the last for large photo-scale operations.

Mapping trials with the DCS-200 and Thruster Microlight

The Thruster microlight aircraft (Fig. 6.9) has proved to be a valuable research platform, not only due to its economic operation, but mainly because it can safely fly within an envelope of 30–60 kts and can easily be fitted with various types of experimental drift mount (Graham, 1988). Indeed, much of our research into suitable anti-vibration mounts has been conducted with this aircraft where, in taking off from grass fields, vibration can be considerable. The usual mounting configuration for the Thruster is a suspension type just behind the cockpit (Fig. 6.9).

Our second series of DCS-200 trials were conducted over the North Yorkshire village of Raskelf using the calibrated 28mm lens. Operated from a simple aluminium mount behind the open cockpit, the camera was exposed according to pre-calculated intervals of 8 s to provide a nominal forward overlap of around 56% at a height of 1550 ft providing a photo-scale of 1:17,000 (Graham and Mills, 1997).

Using the SURPLAN (air survey mission planning) Q-Basic program (see App. D), the entire mission planning for the Raskelf village survey was formulated with the camera's 14mm image axis parallel to line-of-flight. Photographed in early May 1995 at 1700 hours and under slightly hazy conditions, the resultant photography was excellent with soft shadows and good detail (Fig.12.1 – see colour section). Due to the late hour for this flight, camera exposure was set in the 'shutter priority' mode at 1/250 s, which was perfectly adequate since the aircraft was flying into-wind at a ground speed close to 35 kts. It is interesting to note that the ground resolution of this early digital camera was extremely good, and due to measured ground truth (an open barn roof with 15cm wide rafters) it was possible to confirm the ground sampled distance (GSD). According to Eq. 4.25 GSD = m_b.Px, which is 17,000 × 9 mm or 15.3 cm.

Photogrammetric processing of the Raskelf imagery (which was rectified for the effects of lens distortion) took place within the softcopy Photo mapper module of the R-Wel Desktop Mapping System (DMS), a powerful software package suitable for photogrammetry, remote sensing and GIS applications with off-the-shelf PCs (Welch,1989). Ground control and check points were measured in a ground control survey using a Leica TC 400 total station. In total 60 points were coordinated. Sixteen

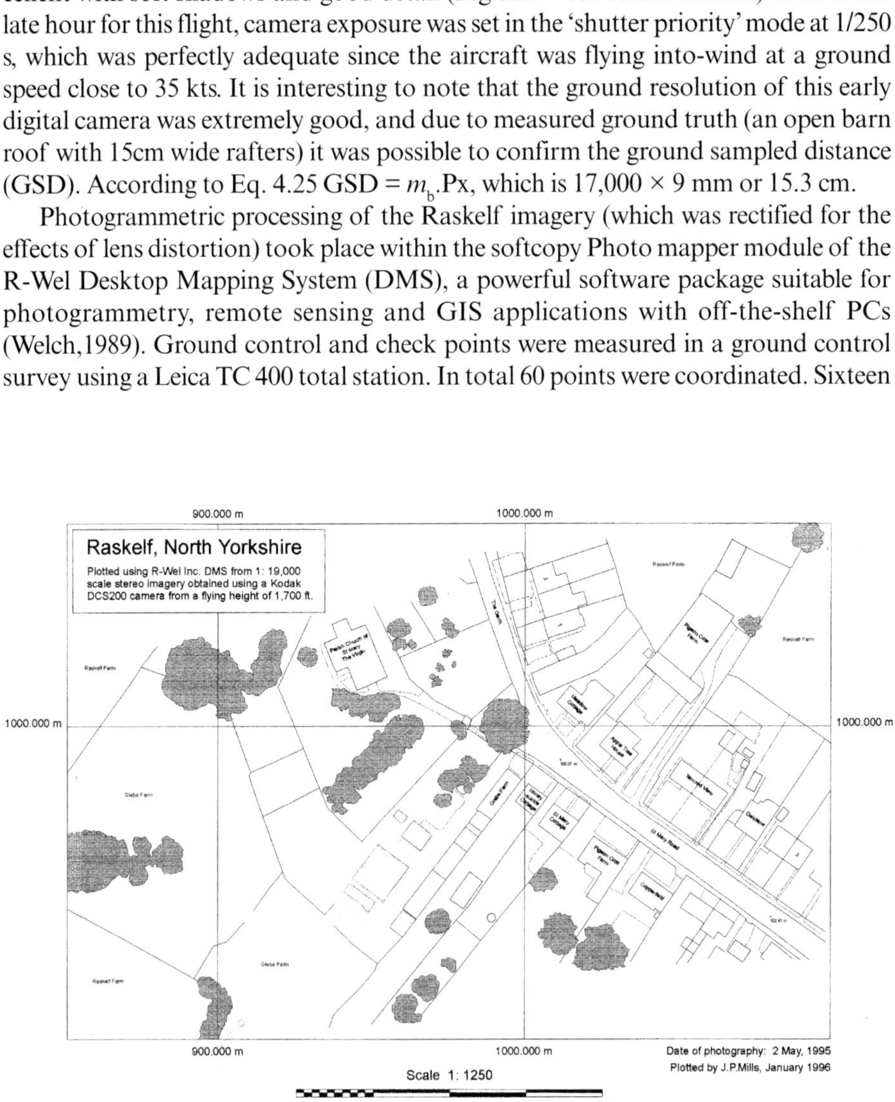

Figure 12.2 *Vector map of Raskelf. DCS-200 with 28mm lens. Map plotted from R-Wel: DMS, from 1:19,000 scale stereo imagery. Flying height 1700 ft. Courtesy Dr. Jon Mills.*

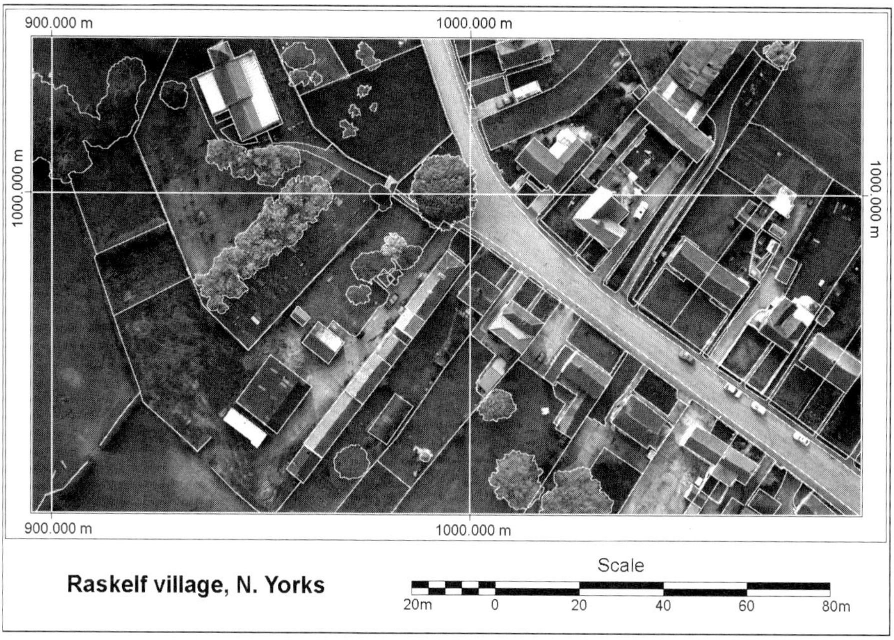

Figure 12.3 *Orthophotomap (complete with vector overlay) of Raskelf village. DCS-200 camera. Courtesy Dr. Jon Mills.*

of these points were used to control the three photographs that were used in the processing (eight in each image). The RMS error for each resulting space resection was well within the ground resolution of the pixel.

Stereo tests with the DMS's anaglyph stereoplotting facility were performed showing a planimetric RMS error of 100 mm (0.6 pixels) and in height of 250 mm (1.6 pixels). The imagery was then processed to produce a DEM and orthophoto. Monoscopic observations (with heights from the DEM) to the same points measured in the stereo tests showed a similarly good planimetric error of 200 mm (1.3 pixels) but a rather poor heighting accuracy of 1300 mm (8.1 pixels).

The orthophoto was then used for mapping, resulting in the vector map of Raskelf, produced by monoplotting with heights from the underlying DEM (Fig.12.2). An orthophotomap of the area, complete with vector overlay can be seen in Fig. 12.3. Examination of Figs. 12.2 and 12.3 illustrates how much more information an orthophoto can contain for GIS purposes when compared to a vector map. Extensive details of this trial can be found in Mills *et al.*, (1996).

Mapping trials

Following the 1995 DCS-200 trials, Jon Mills anticipated further mapping experiments (June1997) in cooperation with the RSGIS unit of Bath Spa University College. The plan was to use the RSGIS unit's DCS-420CIR camera in the Thruster microlight aircraft, but as the newly arrived DCS-460CIR camera was available from Kodak, we were pleased to continue our joint trials with this instrument instead.

The DSC-460CIR has an identical resolution (9 μm square pixels) to both the DCS-200 and the DCS-420 series, but the 460, with its M-6 chip, has an array of 2036 × 3060 pixels within a 18.4 × 27.6 mm format, making the associated 'footprint' four times that of either the DCS-200 or 420 cameras. Although the nominal pixel resolution is the same for all three cameras, the 460 image quality is far superior to the other two due to the improved CFA interpolation algorithm of the latter.

DCS-460CIR trials: Husthwaite Village, North Yorkshire

The original mapping plan for the village of Husthwaite entailed a three-line block with each line consisting of 13 full-colour images with 70% forward overlap. The flying height was to be 2600 ft and, as before, each flight-line would be flown into wind using the same type of non-drift mount as used for the Raskelf mission.

An initial test flight was flown with an installed GPS unit from which the prevailing wind vector was established, and a heading of 100° gave the correct into-wind track. The GPS also provided an accurate ground speed of 40 mph. Further checks were made to establish ground features that would allow the pilot to fly along predetermined tracks with way-points indicated on the GPS unit. These way-points were set for 30% side-lap at the planned photo-scale of 1: 25,000.

Unfortunately it was discovered on landing that no images had been taken. The problem was soon found to lie with the PCMCIA card which failed due to vibration, despite the soft spongy suspension mount. Obviously a suitable anti-vibration mount with drift facility was now imperative, and after many experiments a highly suitable mount was manufactured by Alexander Koh (see Chapter 6). In the meantime we continued to fly the DCS-460CIR in the hand-held vertical mode, with Jon Mills hanging over the open cockpit of the Thruster and a two-way spirit level mounted on top of the camera. In this fashion a suitable small block of the village was covered somewhat uncomfortably, but with remarkable accuracy. An example of this imagery is shown in Fig.5.10.

DCS-460CIR camera calibration

The DCS-460 was calibrated from imagery taken of a test pattern projected onto a laboratory wall at the Department of Geomatics, University of Newcastle. A multistation convergent network of 16 images was recorded and up-loaded into the EOS Systems Photomodeler Pro camera calibrator software for automatic calibration. The significant determined parameters are shown in Table 12.1. Unfortunately, the software gives little indication of the accuracy of the calibration, other than an error factor, in this case 1.21 (after three iterations), on completing the bundle adjustment.

Table. 12.1 *DCS-460CIR calibration parameters for a 28mm lens at infinity.*

	f (mm)	p_x (mm)	p_y (mm)	k_1(μm)
Value	28.846	0.593	– 0.355	–146.6565

Photogrammetric processing of the Husthwaite imagery with VirtuoZo

After camera calibration the imagery was subjected to further analysis using the VirtuoZo softcopy photogrammetric workstation. In this instance the software was running on a Silicon Graphics O2 R5000 workstation equipped with 96Mb of RAM and 30 Gb of hard disk space. VirtuoZo was developed in 1979 at the Wuhan Technical University, China and will accept non-metric as well as metric aerial imagery and will also process satellite imagery. The primary output from the software is ortho-imagery, DEMs and contour maps. Further details on the system can be found in Zhang *et al.* (1994) and are also provided here in Chapter 11.

Imagery from the Husthwaite mission was processed up to the relative orientation stage in VirtuoZo using the corner of the images as fiducial marks at the inner orientation stage. Then the stereopair could be checked by viewing on the screen using Crystal Eye's shuttered glasses system (Fig. 12.4).

The imagery used in the processing was not corrected in any way for lens distortion since VirtuoZo claims to remove all y-parallax during epipolar resampling. This may be the case for large-format precision scanned imagery, however it is clearly not the

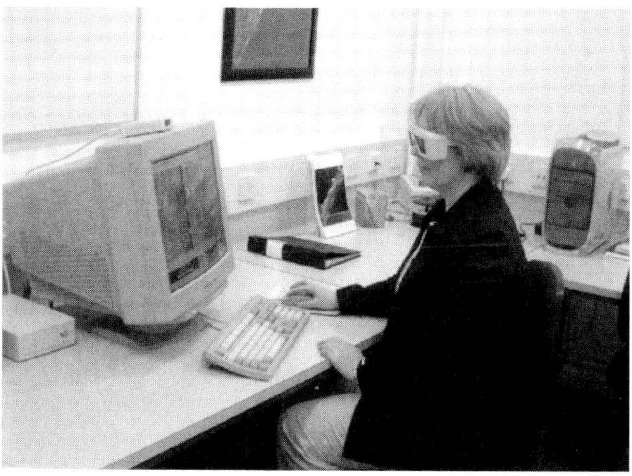

Figure 12.4 *Operating the VirtuoZo photogrammetric workstation. Note the use of Crystal Eye shuttered glasses for stereoscopic viewing.*

case for such unconventional imagery. Indeed, when performing relative orientation, the automatic procedure appears to reject any points with an RMS error greater than the pixel size (9 μm). As a result, the points are clustered in the middle of the model away from areas of large quantities of lens distortion. Relative orientation therefore involved adding points at the periphery of the image until *y*-parallax was removed as well as possible. Between 112 and 233 points per model were automatically and semi-automatically measured by the software at the relative orientation stage with an RMS error on any stereopair no larger than 7 μm (0.8 pixel).

To progress beyond the relative orientation stage, ground control was required but, due to certain restrictions, only a limited GPS ground survey could be conducted at the Husthwaite site using two Ashtech Z-12 geodetic receivers with real-time kinematic (RTK) radio link. Such equipment provides instantaneous coordinates to the centimeter level. Sufficient points were gained to control a small block of 6 × 2 images (2 × 2 stereopairs) of the centre of the village but provided no coordinates with which to carry out any meaningful accuracy check. Each stereopair in the block was controlled using 6 points with RMS errors of 210–780 mm for planimetry and 100–640 mm in height.

VirtuoZo's area, feature and bridge mode-based global-image matching procedures were used to measure a DEM at a 5 m interval, with success of the autocorrelation varying from between 73.6% and 95.4% for individual models. The DEM was edited manually using the stereo viewing facility for any major errors (usually showing up as large spikes in the DEM).

For the Husthwaite survey the individual DEMs and orthophoto's were mosaiced together to form a single image using VirtuoZo's automatic mosaicing feature (which feathers the overlapping models to form a smooth continuous image).

Although no accuracy assessment was possible from the Husthwaite survey, examination of the ground pixel size gives an indication of the suitability of such imagery for mapping. The largest Ordnance Survey mapping of such an area would be at a scale no larger than 1: 2500. With a GSD of 25 cm, the effective print resolution of the orthophoto at 1:2500 would be 254 dpi (dots per inch), and as most printers operate at 300 dpi, the image scale is only 15% from the optimum resolution. Such trials certainly justify our faith in the digital camera concept, and confirm the view that digital small-format surveys for small area mapping, GIS and remote sensing is a viable solution for many operators.

San Cayetano, Columbia

Typical of many small-format digital surveys carried out by Geotechnologies in Africa, Europe, New Guinea and South America is the June 1999 survey of the San Cayetano region of Columbia using a DCS-460CIR camera. But untypically this was an extremely large task involving two people (Alexander Koh and Esther Edwards) flying 40 survey hours over a period of 19 days.

The mission profile required a full colour survey of the small mountain town of San Cayetano (north east of Bogota) which had narrowly survived a massive landslip catastrophe from adjacent hills. The photo-scale was 1:55,000 and the mission was flown at an average height of 5000 ft above mean ground level (c.12,000 ft). The agreed

GSD was 50 cm, and overall stereo cover was essential in order to evaluate landslide damage, and also determine possible sites for township relocation.

The survey aircraft was a Cessna 182 which flew at an average ground speed of 70 kts (35 m/s). A massive total of 118 flight-lines were flown under GPS control, with 28 exposures per flight-line. The camera intervalometer setting was 17 s, and each flight-line was photographed in about 13 min. Flight-line separation was 510 m, and the airbase (60% forward overlap) was 610 m.

In addition to the usual problems associated with survey flight over tropical mountainous terrain, the survey tracker had to navigate without any useful maps and depended entirely on GPS data. Notwithstanding, the results were excellent and when processed with 5 m contours provided the clients with all the necessary information. The stereo-pair (Fig.12.5 in colour section), shows the town of San Cayetano at the bottom-edge, with the offending landslip immediately above and to the left of the town.

Digital surveys for PT Freeport Papua (New Guinea)

Reference has already been made (Chapter 9) to the Geotechnologies Freeport Copper Mine mission in early 2000, when the authors flew a digital survey to record the mine (see Figs. 9.3 and 9.4) and the Cartensz Glaciers. But during our stay we were requested to fly numerous other missions, from sea level over the jungle floor to various river confluences in the Iryan Jaya highlands, as well as malarial sites, new towns, environmental regions, levees and native relocation areas. Operating from the Timika base-camp airstrip in the coastal swamp area, our usual flying started at 0600 hours local time in order to fly up to the intermediate camp at Tembagapura (6000 ft) from where we could assess the weather and attempt to cover the mine area at 18,000 ft. On most days intermittent cloud cover prevented us from flying over the mine area after 1000 hours.

The Kodak DCS-460CIR camera was mounted between the cabin door and the step of the Bell 412 helicopter (Fig.6.13) and operated from within the cabin, where the PCMCIA cards could be changed after every 80 exposures.

Among the missions flown we operated the DCS-460 in both conventional colour and in CIR. These included a 10 × 5 km block over the new jungle township of Kuala Kencana, just north of Timika. This was completed as a CIR orthophotomap (GSD of 50 cm) from which a mosaic was completed within eight hours of landing.

During numerous flights over lowland forest areas it was obvious that some of the rivers leading from the upland mine area were polluted with mill tailings. These sediments were particularly evident in the wide corded Aikwa river which runs ash grey in parts, due to the unique nature of its sediment load, a large part of which consists of the rock flour or silt that is the waste product of Freeport's mill and concentration plant. These tailings, and their effects, are made obvious by CIR photography (Fig.12.6; see colour section) where diverse forest growth and decay are shown in various false-colours and the river (naturally a deep brown colour) is shown black where sufficient water is available to absorb the near infrared (NIR). The heavy sediment tailings in the Aikwa show clearly in Fig.12.6, as does their influence on adjacent vegetation which becomes starved of oxygen supply to their roots, causing stress and killing the trees.

The Aikwa Deposition Area (ADA) mission

The issue of tailings was not so much one of toxicity but of sheer volume, and the problem became drastic when the silty Aikwa overtopped its bed and began to 'sheet flow' eastward to the Kopi river. Freeport engineers then built a levee system on the western edge of the Aikwa's old channel to protect the population of Timika, shown in the right-hand stereo-pair of Fig.12.7 (colour section). One of the primary concerns was to avoid harming the Lorentz nature reserve, a 1.5 million-hectare land area that begins two river systems east of the Freeport projects area. The Lorentz reserve covers a broad swath of Iryan Jaya (now called Papua) from the mountains to the sea, and is one of the most biologically diverse and important reserves in the world (Mealey, 1996). Protection of this valuable area was through a system of levees which were designed to create a controlled flood plain, called the Aikwa Deposition Area (ADA).

Our helicopter mission over the ADA was to establish a surveillance system suitable for regular monitoring of the levee system, and the deposits. The following survey flight logistics were prepared (as per Chapter 8) for the Bell 412 and DCS-460CIR camera fitted with a 28 mm lens, flown at a photoscale of 1:57,000 with a GSD of 50 cm. These logistics are shown in Table. 12.2.

The West Bay landslide survey

Following the Black Ven survey discussed in Chapter 9, yet another landslide occured in the same coastal region when the worst landslip in 50 years hit the Dorset coast at Stonebarrow, just east of Charmouth. As a consequence, Geotechnologies surveyed the Dorset coast-line from Portland to Lyme Regis in January 2001, covering the

Table. 12.2 *ADA Timika: survey flight logistics*

Survey area:	ADA Timika, West Papua
Lens focal length:	28 mm
Altitude (amgl):	1600 m (5250 ft)
Ground speed of aircraft:	60 kts (Bell 412 helicopter)
Permitted across-track error:	100 m
Flight-line separation (a):	820 m
Air base (b):	610 m
Flight-line *'Lead-in & Out'* :	3 km and 1.6 km
Camera 'ON' at distance-to-go (DTG):	14 km (DTG)
Camera 'OFF' at distance-to-go (DTG):	2 km (DTG)
Camera framing rate (ΔT):	20 s intervals
Number of images per flight-line:	20
Number of survey lines per block:	2
Raw image data storage requirements:	0.71 Gb
Duration of survey per line:	12 min
Total relocation flying hours:	0.5 h
Total survey flying for mission:	0.4 h
Total aircraft hours for mission:	0.9 h

entire Lyme Bay coast including the West Bay landslip area. The purpose was to provide stereoscopic images of the threatened coast for future evaluation.

A series of single flight-lines were flown with a Partenavia 68B at an average height of 5600 ft amsl, using a calibrated DCS-460 CIR camera in a drift mount. East-west lines were flown at an average ground speed of 117 kts, and west-east lines (into wind) at an average of 80 kts. Drift compensation was made for each separate run. All of the flight-lines were flown with the aid of GPS waypoints and wind-drift corrections made by reference to GPS track and compass headings.

Bearing in mind the importance of keeping the beaches and cliffs directly beneath the camera, each coastal line was flown so that an off-shore distance of at least 100 m was included in each image. The survey was carried out in conventional colour with a 28 mm lens. The calibration parameters can be found on the enclosed CD under Table 12.3. Comparison of the calibration data shown in Tables.12.1 and 12.3 show that two different 460 cameras have a very similar principal distance. However, the calibration shown in Table.12.3 is more complete and includes radial distortion data (first quarter cartesian coordinates).

A typical colour photograph taken from this mission is shown in Fig. 12.8 (colour section), where the local features of West Bay, such as the caravan sites, village, cliffs and beaches are clearly seen. The photoscale is 1:60,000 providing a GSD of 54 cm and helped by clear winter sunlight at noon, the detail is excellent.

Digital aerial surveys with the MF-DMC(2)

As far as we know, Geotechnologies were the first team to employ the Kodak DCS Pro Back in aerial survey. As a consequence we were delighted to find it a great success when we flew a series of small blocks and lines for cartographic and training missions over southern England in June and July 2001. The areas for these missions were Dorchester, a small country town in Dorset, and various coastal areas along the Dorset coast.

As discussed in Chapter 5, the MF-DMC(2) is a Hasselblad 555ELD camera fitted with the Kodak Pro-Back 16MPx sensor. For these operations we employed either a calibrated 80 mm Zeiss Planar (CFE 2.8/80 mm) or a 40 mm Zeiss Distagon (CF 4/40) lens, both with databus connections (to retain calibration the Pro Back is fitted to the MF-DMC(2) with alignment lugs). On each mission the camera was flown without a computer since the two (1Gb) CF+ cards held in the Pro Back provided sufficient capacity for an anticipated maximum of 120 images. The Macintosh G4 computer, Garmin GPSMAP 295 receiver and MF-DMC(2) are shown in Fig.12. 9, where the lens Sync Cable connection to the Pro Back can be seen leading from the lens to the Sync Cable jack. The Sync Cable jack, IEEE 1394 port and Quantum battery jack can be seen in Fig.12.10, and the highly portable camera/battery configuration we employed is shown in Fig.12.11. For a more extensive survey the alternative camera configuration (where images can be downloaded via Firewire to a computer) is shown in Fig.12.12.

Access to the two CF+ cards is shown in Fig.12.13, where a 'card busy' LED indicates the active card. Any number of cards may be ejected and replaced simply by

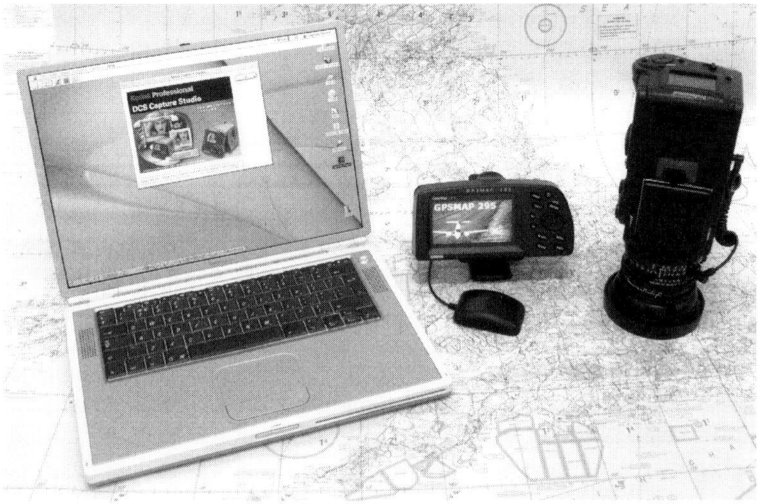

Figure 12.9 *The MF-DMC(2) system. Macintosh G4 laptop, GPS 295 and Hasselblad 555ELD with Kodak DCS Pro Back (16MPx).*

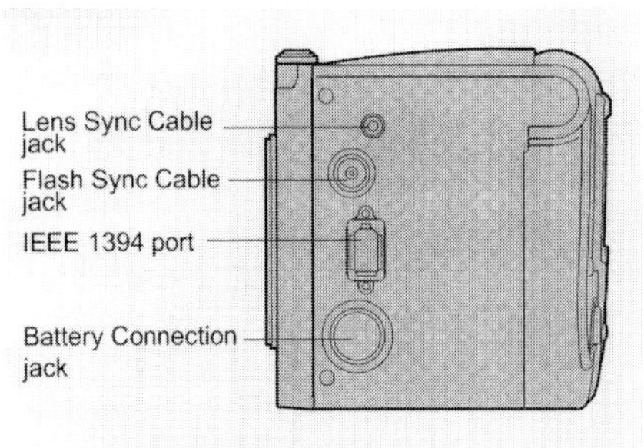

Figure 12.10 *Kodak DCS Pro Back showing (top to bottom) the Sync Cable jack, IEEE 1394 port, and the Quantum battery (QB2) jack. Diagram courtesy of Eastman Kodak Limited.*

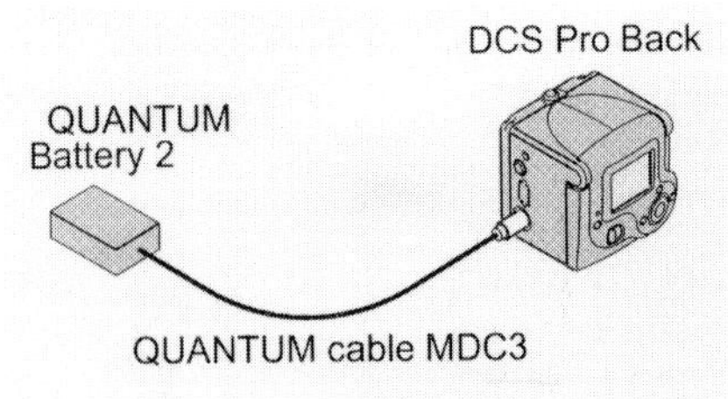

Figure 12.11 *Kodak DCS Pro Back with QB2 power source, a simple in-flight configuration for the MF-DMC(2) system. Diagram courtesy of Eastman Kodak Limited.*

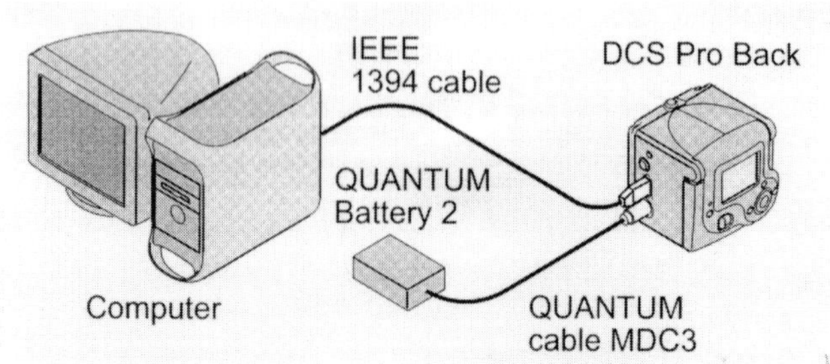

Figure 12.12 *The DCS Pro Back can be connected via IEEE 1394 to either a Macintosh desk-top or G4 laptop (in-flight preference) with QB2 power source and MDC3 cable. Diagram courtesy of Eastman Kodak Limited.*

using the appropriate 'card eject button'.

During in-flight operation the image LCD (Fig.12.14) is extremely useful since image quality (with respect to exposure and dynamic range of the scene) can be monitored and controlled via the histogram menu. The intervalometer menu can also be called up for operating sequenced exposures, which is particularly useful for short flight-lines. For more extensive survey lines and blocks, each required photo-centre can be entered into the GPS as a waypoint coordinate (ideally in UTM WGS84) and where exposures are made as each photo-WP appears on the moving map display. In this way, flight-line navigation and exposure intervals are conveniently integrated.

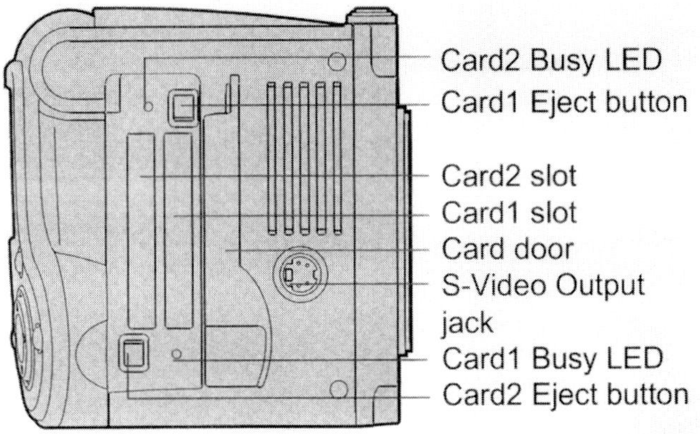

Figure 12.13 *The MF-DCS(2) supports the Kodak Pro Back which provides for two 1Gb CF+ cards, each of which can be replaced by using the appropriate 'eject button'. Diagram courtesy of Eastman Kodak Limited.*

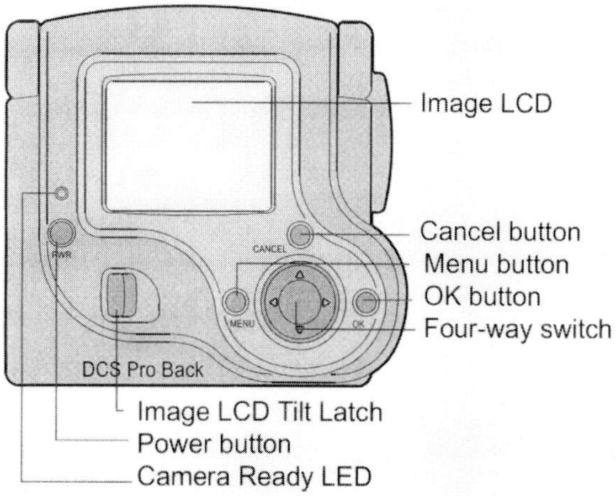

Figure 12.14 *The DCS ProBack has a useful LED image display that can also call up various menus, such as histogram and intervalometer. Diagram courtesy of Eastman Kodak Limited.*

Poundbury (Dorchester): a typical MF-DMC(2) survey mission

As discussed in Chapter 8, digital survey planning may be conveniently plotted in the Excel Air Survey Logistic Planner (ASLP), and for the Poundbury (training) mission the details of this short flight plan can be seen on the CD under Tables 12.4 and 12.5.

From CD Table 12.4, we can see that a calibrated 40 mm lens was employed with camera exposures made at 1/250 s at *f*/5.6, and since this was mid-morning in July at nearly 4100 ft, with less than 1octa of fair-weather cumulus below at about 3500 ft, conditions were good for aerial survey. The base/height ratio can be seen as 0.37, good enough for photogrammetric accuracy, although not a major issue for this particular training mission. The aircraft (a Partenavia P68b) was fitted with the Geotechnologies drift-mount and as part of our trials program we flew at an estimated ground speed of 80 kts (with 1/3 flap) to check the camera mount's ability to tilt against the slightly pitched-up attitude of the aircraft – which was completely successful.

The ground coverage for the Pro Back's 36.65 mm square image area is shown as 1.02 km for a photo-scale of 27,778. Forward overlap is 60% and side-lap 25%. The estimated ground sampled distance (ground resolution) is given by the product of photo-scale and pixel size, or GSD = 27,778 × 9 μm = 25 cm.

CD Table 12.5 shows the survey height above ground level as 1231 m (4039 ft) and the permitted across-track error is shown as 110 m (a wide margin for GPS navigation). The airbase is 410 m and distance between flight-lines 613 m. We may also note that the flight-line 'lead-in' and 'lead-out' distance is 3k, that is to say, the distance allowed to fly onto the first waypoint (first required photograph on line) is 3km, which gives the pilot and navigator/camera operator sufficient time to fly an accurate line and stabilise both the aircraft and the camera mounting. Similarly, the 'lead-out' distance of 3km allows the pilot to prepare for the next line.

The camera on signal is calculated as 8 km from the DTG (distance to go), where the DTG is the end of the flight line, and the camera off is given as 2km from DTG. These values are quite excessive for a short number of photographs per flight-line (here shown as only 14 photographs for each of the three flight-lines), but since the extra photography could be used for other purposes this was acceptable. At an estimated ground speed of 90 kts (45m/s) the camera framing rate was timed at 8 s intervals.

Mapping the Poundbury flight plan

Since our navigation is done with the aid of a Garmin GPS (with moving map display) it is sensible to use the Garmin MapSource software for setting up the flight planning data made with the Excel ASLP. MapSource is extremely useful since all the flight-line WPs can be entered into the program against a wide range of available map scales. As each of the three Poundbury flight-lines was about 10 km, a MapSource scale of 1.5 km was selected for a general view of the area (Fig.12.15; see colour section). As we can see, flight-line S1 to E1 is West-East, the second line S2 to E2 is East-West and the third line S3 to E3 is West-East. All three lines were planned to cover the Poundbury new-town area west of Dorchester starting from UTM cordinates at S1 (30 U 531547 5619309) and ending at E3 (30 U 541534 5617746), a total of 49 waypoints (including the central point of interest at P in the second line).

Once the flight plan has been checked as correct the data can be downloaded into a GPS receiver, such as the Garmin 76 or 295 models. The flight-plan data is loaded into the GPS as a route which can then be called up during the mission for survey navigation and camera operation purposes.

Flying the mission

For short flight-lines such as those indicated for Poundbury, it is normally only necessary to fly from stored waypoints S1 to the camera on and camera off WPs and then turn at the E1 WP onto WP S2 etc. The individual photocentres are then exposed by intervalometer or stop watch. But as this was a training mission all 49 WPs were uploaded into a Garmin GPS Map76 (for the photographer) and to a Garmin Map 295 for the survey navigator (seated next to the pilot). With the GPS Map-Page zoomed to a map-scale of 2 km or larger it is a simple matter to guide the pilot along each flight line and for the photographer to expose each photo-centre as the waypoints pass the diamond icon along the track.

West Bay training mission

As part of a training course in digital aerial survey (Geotechnologies, Bath Spa University College) two students completed a digital survey of West Bay Dorset with the MF-DMC(2) system.

Planned as a short single line with 60% forward overlap, the project was flown with a calibrated 16MPx MF-DMC(2) camera fitted with the Distagon 40 mm lens. The first task for the two students was to calibrate the camera (the calibration report is shown in CD Table 12.6), then provide a simple flight plan in Garmin MapSource which was then downloaded into the GPS Map 76 and Map295 receivers. Acting as navigator and photographer in turns, the students then flew over West Bay to provide sufficient photography for two models with a GSD of 25 cm.

After downloading the digital imagery to computer a number of rough prints were made from stereo pairs and a suitable model area delineated. With OmniStar equipment and GPS receivers the team then collected suitable ground control points at West Bay for photogrammetry, these points were then located within the model area of the prints.

Photogrammetry was undertaken with VirtuoZo under a Silicon Graphics Unix system, from which interior, relative and absolute orientations were resolved for a single model area using six GCPs. Under supervision, the students then progressed to map production using MapInfo software. From the epipolar imagery and, after suitable image matching and editing, a DEM was gained from which an ortho image with 5 m contours and UTM grid coordinates was generated.

The contoured orthophotomap shown in Fig.12.16 (colour section) is produced with 10 cm GSD and contour intervals of 5 m, at an output scale of 1:1000.

Infrared photography

As mentioned in Chapter 5, the Pro Back normally has an infrared blocking filter placed directly in front of the ITO sensor, which can easily be removed during flight.

This IR blocking filter is provided to afford improved colour rendition by removing unwanted IR radiation from each of the Bayer CFA cells within the chip, but if it is removed and a yellow (Wratten 12 or 15) filter placed in front of the lens, then all blue elements of the Bayer CFA will only record in the NIR. Subsequent to selecting the blue channel from RGB colour during image processing the displayed image would then be in monochromatic NIR. A number of such images were made over rural areas (without exposure compensation) using a Wratten 12 filter.

MF-DMC(2) image quality (Photoshop processing)

On inspection of many MF-DMC(2) screened images it is evident that the 16MPx Pro Back is a great success since the imagery shows excellent resolution easily confirming estimated GSDs from 15–25 cm. Contrast and colour rendition are also of high quality even in cast shadow areas. Converted to tiff images in Photoshop, a number of prints have been made without further processing. Figure12.17 is a photograph taken from one of the Dorchester flight-lines. Giving proof to the 20 cm GSD is the enlarged portion of Fig.12.17 (Fig.12.18), where the two hospitals and adjacent allotments are shown in fine detail.

Taking three photographs adjacent to that shown in Fig.12.17 an uncontrolled mosaic was swiftly made by Dr Rick Curr (Geotechnologies) using ER Mapper with 20 reference points applied to adjacent images. The (almost) seemless result is shown in Fig.12.19.

Perhaps our most pleasing surprise was the success of the NIR imagery which, although slightly overexposed, gave typical NIR monochrome results, making the MF-DMC(2) useful for multispectral photography (MSP) as shown by Fig.12.20.

Helicopter operations with the MF-DMC(2) in New Guinea

As mentioned in Chapter 6, the Freeport (copper and gold) Mining Company in Timika, Irian Jaya, purchased a MF-DMC(2) for mapping and remote sensing surveillance over their Grasberg mine which lies 12,500 ft above the jungle floor. As we had previously shown the value of such work with the DCS-460CIR camera (through Freeport's mapping consultants: McElhanney, Jakarta), the inclusion of the DCS(2) into an expensive helicopter modification was a logical step. Geotechnologies installed the system into one of Freeport's Bell 412 helicopters and tested the camera at various altitudes. A particularly interesting application was to photograph the Grasberg mine with the MF-DMC(2) from 18,000 ft with a 40 mm lens, and process five of these images into a coloured digital orthophotomap. This was then overlaid on an existing (analogue) monochrome orthophotomap, in order to compare changes due to mining operations. The coloured digital overlay is seen on its monochrome base in Fig. 12.21, where it can be seen that the match is very good. The Grasberg mine can be seen at the upper left of centre in the coloured area.

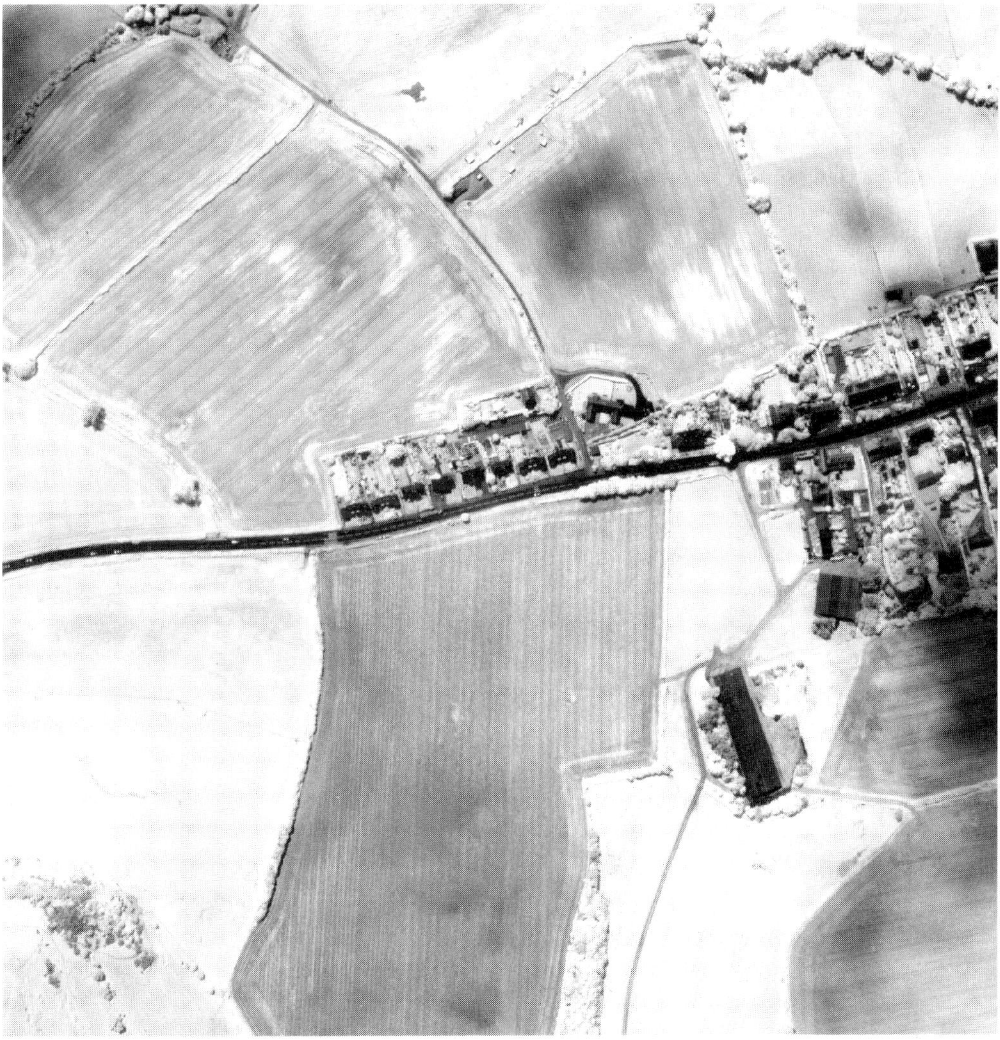

Figure 12.20 MF-DMC(2) NIR image taken with the IR blocking filter removed from the ProBack and a Wratten yellow 12 filter placed over the lens. Monochrome NIR component taken from the blue channel of the RGB image. Photograph courtesy Alexander Koh.

MF-DMC conclusions

From what we have seen with the MF-DMC(2) survey flight imagery, it is obvious that digital aerial surveys with medium format cameras now represent a serious alternative to analogue systems, particularly for small to medium sized surveys. They not only compare favourably with film in terms of resolution and image quality, but also offer faster and cheaper imagery that can be processed directly with available software. Options for monochrome, full colour, infrared and CIR are all available from a single system where soft copy photogrammetry can provide DTMs, contoured orthophotos and controlled mosaics within a few hours.

Economic factors

At the time of writing we can be sure that until CCD sensors larger than that in the MF-DMC cameras become available, we can safely compare the economic costs of digital against large format (23 cm) analogue operations for contoured orthophoto map production. Table 12.7 provides information in this respect.

Table 12.7a *Comparison between digital aerial imagery (MF-DMC(2)) and analogue (23 cm × 23 cm) derived digital imagery at GSD = 25 cm for contoured orthophoto map production.*

Linear feature distance (km)	*cost of data acquisition (US$) MF-DMC(2) (digital aerial imagery)*	*cost of data acquisition (US$) analogue (23 cm × 23 cm) (derived digital imagery)*
10	33,000	48,000
20	38,000	50,000
40	48,000	55,000
80	89,000	64,000
160	111,000	86,000
320	194,000	132,000

Table 12.7b *Comparison between digital aerial imagery (MF-DMC(2)) and analogue (23 cm × 23 cm) derived digital imagery at GSD = 25 cm for contoured orthophoto map production.*

Area of interest (km^2)	*cost of data acquisition (US$) MF-DMC(2) (digital aerial imagery)*	*cost of data acquisition (US$) analogue (23 cm × 23 cm) (derived digital imagery)*
2.5 × 2.5	33,000	48,000
5 × 5	45,000	52,000
10 × 10	83,000	72,000
20 × 20	226,000	128,000
40 × 40	764,000	348,000

It is clear that analogue data acquisition and map production soon becomes more economic as distances and area coverage increase. Table 12.7a indicates that for linear feature cover of distances above 70 km, digital surveys are less economic than conventional film. Simlarly, digital area coverage becomes less economic for areas over 80 km^2 (Table 12.7b).

Such economic factors look only at operational costs however, and do not represent the entire picture. Temporal and logistic issues have also to be considered and ultimately dictate towards the faster data acquisition offered by digital systems.

Appendix A
Unit conversions

To convert from A to B, mutiply by factor C.

A	B	C
Length		
metres	centimetres (cm)	100
metres	millimetres (mm)	1000
metres	micrometres (μm)	1,000,000
metres	nanometres (nm)	1,000,000,000
inches	millimetres (mm)	25.4
feet	metres (m)	0.3048
metres	feet (ft)	3.2808
metres	yards	1.0936
miles (statute)	kilometres (km)	1.6093
miles (statute)	nautical miles (Nm)	0.8688
nautical miles	statute miles	1.1509
nautical miles	kilometres (km)	1.8523
Area		
square metre	square feet	10.764
square kilometre	square metres	1,000,000
hectare	square metres	10,000
hectare	acre	2.471
square metre	square yards	1.196
acre	aquare yards	4840
Mass		
ounces	grams (g)	28.3495
kilograms	pounds (lbs – avdp)	2.2045
pound	kilograms (kg)	0.4536
metric tons	kilograms	1000

Volume

gallons (UK)	litres (l)	4.546
gallons (US)	litres (l)	3.785
gallons (UK)	gallons (US)	0.8326
gallons (UK)	cubic metres (m^3)	0.004546
pints	litres (l)	0.568
pints (UK)	pints (US)	1.2009

Velocity

miles per hour	kilometres per hour	1.6093
kilometres per hour	miles per hour	0.6214
knots (kts – Nm/h)	miles per hour	1.151
knots (kts – Nm/h)	metres per second (m/s)	0.515
knots (kts – Nm/h)	kilometres per hour (km/h)	1.852
feet per second	miles per hour	0.6828

Pressure

torr (mm Hg)	pounds per square inch	0.0193
standard atmosphere	torr (mm Hg)	760
standard atmosphere	bar	1.0132
standard atmosphere	millibar	1013.2
standard atmosphere	inches of mercury (0°C)	29.921
standard atmosphere	Pascal (Pa)	101325.03
Pascal (Pa)	Newton per square metre	1.0

Temperature

Centigrade (°C)	Fahrenheit (°F)	(°C × 9/5) + 32
Fahrenheit (°F)	Centigrade (°C)	(°F – 32) × 9/5
Temperature conversion by addition		
Kelvin (K)	Centigrade (°C)	add 273.15 to °C
Outside air temperature		
°C (at sea level)	OAT at altitude (°C)	add 2°C per 1000 ft

Appendix B
Binary and ASCII codes

Binary code

Like decimal notation, the binary system of numbering is a positional notation, where the value of a binary number depends not only on the bits it contains, but also teir position in the number. The positional value increases from right to left by powers of 2, as the following list makes clear.

Decimal No.	Powers of 2	Binary No.
0	(0×2^0)	0000
1	(1×2^0)	0001
2	(1×2^1)	0010
3	$(1 \times 2^1) + (1 \times 2^0)$	0011
4	(1×2^2)	0100
5	$(1 \times 2^2) + (0 \times 2^1) + (1 \times 2^0)$	0101
6	$(1 \times 2^2) + (1 \times 2^1) + (0 \times 2^0)$	0110
7	$(1 \times 2^2) + (1 \times 2^1) + (1 \times 2^0)$	0111
8	(1×2^3)	1000
9	$(1 \times 2^3) + (0 \times 2^2) + (0 \times 2^1) + (1 \times 2^0)$	1001
10	$(1 \times 2^3) + (0 \times 2^2) + (1 \times 2^1) + (0 \times 2^0)$	1010
11	$(1 \times 2^3) + (0 \times 2^2) + (1 \times 2^1) + (1 \times 2^0)$	1011
12	$(1 \times 2^3) + (1 \times 2^2) + (0 \times 2^1) + (0 \times 2^0)$	1100
15	$(1 \times 2^3) + (1 \times 2^2) + (1 \times 2^1) + (1 \times 2^0)$	1111
16	(1×2^4)	10000
20	$(1 \times 2^4) + (0 \times 2^3) + (1 \times 2^2) + (0 \times 2^1) + (0 \times 2^0)$	10100
32	(1×2^5)	100000
100	$(1 \times 2^6) + (1 \times 2^5) + (0 \times 2^4) + (0 \times 2^3) + (1 \times 2^2) + (0 \times 2^1) + (0 \times 2^0)$	1100100

In order to convert from binary to decimal we multiply each bit in the binary number by the power of 2 with the least significant bit (on extreme right) having the positional value of 2^0, then add them all together. In the above examples (see under power of 2) we can see that the coefficient of each term is either a one or a zero and it is the coefficents that make up the binary number. Thus, for decimal 20, we add (from the right) as: $0 + 0 + (1 \times 2^2) + 0 + (1 \times 2^4)$ which sums to $4 + 16 = 20$.

ASCII Code

Binary digits (bits) can also be used to represent letters of the alphabet, numbers and punctuation marks. One such 7 bit code is the ASCII (American Standard Code for Information Interchange) which is used extensively in small computer systems to translate from the keyboard chracters to computer language. Since this code represents letters as well as numbers it is known as an *alphanumeric code*.

Character	ASCII	Character	ASCII
0	0110000	A	1000001
1	0110001	B	1000010
2	0110010	C	1000011
3	0110011	D	1000100
4	0110100	E	1000101
5	0110101	F	1000110
6	0110110	G	1000111
7	0110111	H	1001000
8	0111000	I	1001001
9	0111001	J	1001010
		K	1001011
		L	1001100
		M	1001101
		N	1001110
		O	1001111
		P	1010000
		Q	1010001
		R	1010010
		S	1010011
		T	1010100
		U	1010101
		V	1010110
		W	1010111
		X	1011000
		Y	1011001
		Z	1011010

Appendix C Suppliers, manufacturers and institutes

Adam Technology (photogrammetry) Enterprise House, Boathouse Meadow Business Park, Cherry Orchard Lane, Salisbury. SP2 7LD, UK. Tel: +44 (0)1722 414221.

Advanced Imaging (digital imaging journal) 445 Broad Hollow Road, Melville, N.Y, 11747. USA. Phone: (631) 845-2700. Fax (631) 845-2736.

Aerofilms Gate Studios, Station Road, Boreham Wood, Herts. WD6 1EJ. UK. Tel: +44 (0)208 207 0666. Fx: +44 181 207 5433.

Aerial Imaging Systems Ltd. (air surveys and consultants) Roger Read, Oostveenweg 126, 7533 VX Enschede, The Netherlands. Tel: +31 53 4323518. Fax +31 53 4307359. E-mail: rojread@wxs.nl and at:

Aerial Survey Inc. Tongue River Rt, Miles City, MT 59301. USA. Tel :+1 (406) 232-2058.

Agritec Rua Augusto Severo, 1.030, Centro Civico, Curitiba, Parana, Brazil. Tel: 55 41 254-5122. Fax: 55 41 254-2775.

Airborne Data Systems Inc. Route 2, Box 38, Wabasso, MN 56293. USA. Tel: (507) 984-5419. fax: (507) 984-3150. E-mail: airdat@rconnect.com

Alan Mann Group of Companies (aircraft modifications and maintenance) Fairoaks Airport, Chobham, Woking, Surrey. GU24 8HX. Tel: +44 (0)1276 857887. Fax: +44 (0)1276 857677.

American Society for Photogrammetry & Remote Sensing 5410 Grosvenor Lane, Suite 210, Bethesda, Maryland 20814-2160, USA. Tel: 301-493-0290. Fax: 301-493-0208. E-mail: asprs@asprs.org

Aquarious International (aerial surveys) Hangar 9, Toronto Buttonville Airport, 2833 16th Avenue, Box 175, Markham, Ontario, Canada. LR3 0P8. Tel: (905) 475-2885. Fax: (905) 475-8750 and at:

World Trade Centre, Jakarta, Wisma Metropolitan 11 16th Floor, JL. Jend. Sudirman 31, Jakarta 12920, Indonesia. Tel: (62-21) 2510644, Fax: (62-21)2510643.

PT Asconusa (survey mapping and engineering) Wisma Benhil. 7th Floor, JL.Jend. Sudirman Kav.36. Jakarta Pusat. Indonesia. Tel: 8463521 - 8467262. E-mail: asconusa1@rad.net.id

Ball Aerospace & Technologies Corp. 1600 Commerce Street, Boulder, CO 80301, USA. Tel: 303-939-6100. Fax: 303-939-6104.

Canada Map Office. 615 Booth Street, Ottowa, Ontario, Canada.

Canadian Forest Service, Great Lakes Forestry Centre, PO Box 490, Sault Ste, Marie, Ontario P6A 5M7, Canada.

Carleton University Dept. of Geography, 1125 Colonel By Drive, Ottowa, Ontario, K1S 1B6, Canada.

Carto Instruments Inc. P.O Box 2379, Corvallis, Oregon 97339, USA. Tel/Fax: (541) 753-9160. E-mail: carto@cartonet.com

DAP Technologies 955 Place Dufour, Ville de Vanier (Quebec), Canada G1M 3B2. Tel: (418) 681-9394. Fax: (418) 681-0799.

Eastman Kodak Company, Aerial Systems Rochester, New York 14653-7128, USA. Tel: 716 253-1817. Fax: 716 253-0705.

Eastman Kodak, Image Sensor Solutions 1669 Lake Avenue, Rochester, NY. 14650-2010, USA. Tel: 716-722-4385. Fax 716-477-4947.

Eastman Kodak, Scientific Imaging Systems 343 State Street, Rochester NY, 14652, USA. Tel: 203-786-5600. Fax: 203-786-5656. 1 Tudor House, Lysander Close, Clifton Moor, York, YO30 4XB. Tel: +44 (0)1904 691469. Fax: +44 (0)1904 691569.

Eurosense, Nervierslaan 54, B-1780 Wemmel, Belgium. Tel: +32 (0)2 460 70 00.

Fachhochschule Bochum (Prof. Dr. F.J. Heimes) Department of Photogrammetry and Aerial Photography, Lennershofstrasse 140, Bochum, Germany. Tel: +49 (0)234 3210 517.

Federal University of Parana Department of Forest Management & Silviculture, Curitiba, Parana, Brazil.

Fly Buy Ultralights Ltd. (Ikarus C42 small light aeroplane) Ambleside, Bourne End Road, Cranfield, Beds MK43 0BD. Tel: +44 (0)1234 751110. Fax: +44 (0)1234 751784. E-mail: sales@flybuyultralights.com

Foveon Inc. 3565 Monroe St, Santa Clara, CA 95051, USA. Tel: (408) 350-5100. www.foveon.net

Geotechnologies (Alexander Koh) Bath Spa University College, Newton St. Loe, Bath, BA2 9BN. Tel: +44 (0)1225 875580. Fax: +44 (0)1225 875776. Internet: www.bathspa.ac.uk E-mail: a.koh@bathspa.ac.uk

Ron Graham 3 St. Michaels Close, Over Compton, Sherborne, Dorset. DT9 4QR, UK. (air survey training and consultancy) Tel: +44 1935 421303. Fax: +44 1935 421304.

Hamamatsu Corporation 360 Foothill Road, Bridgewater, NJ 08807-0910, USA. Tel: 908-231-0960. Fax: 908-231-1518.

Hansa Luftbild GmbH Elbestrasse 5, PO Box 3609, D-48145 Munster, Germany. Tel: +49 (251) 2330-0, fax: +49 (251) 2330-112. E-mail: hansaluftbild@hansaluftbild.de

Victor Hasselblad AB Box 220, SE-401 23, Goteborg, Sweden. Tel: +46 31 10 24 00. Fax: +46 31 13 50 74.

Hong Kong Lands Department 24/F, North Point Government Offices, 333 Java Road, North Point, Hong Kong. Tel: (852) 2231 3304. Fax: (852) 2752 8119.

Household Articles Ltd. (Cadnit kettle fur collector) Sanderstead Station Approach, South Croydon, Surrey, CR2 0YY, UK.

IGI mbH (CCNS-4), Langenauer Strasse 46 57223 Kreuztal, Germany. Tel: +49 2732 55 25 0. Fax: +49 2732 55 25 25.

ImageSense (Norman Goba) 66 Tilson Road, Toronto, Ontario M4S 1P5, Canada. Tel: (416) 487-2818. Fax: (416) 487-8879. E-mail: ngoba@the-wire.com

ITC International Institute for Aerospace Surveys & Earth Sciences, PO Box 6, 7500A, Boulevard 1945, Enschede, The Netherlands.

JUPEM Department of Survey & Mapping Malaysia. Bangunan Ukur, Jalan Semarak, 50578 Kuala Lumpur, Malaysia. Tel: 603-2924034. Fax: 603-2970140.

Kodak Ltd. Government Markets & Aerial Systems, Kodak UK, PO Box 66, Station Road, Hemel Hempstead, Herts, HP1 1JU. UK. Tel: +44 (0)1442 844992. Fax: +44 (0)1442 844283.

Local Earth Observation (Peter Poole) 225 Carlton Street, Toronto, Ontario, M5A 2L2, Canada. Tel: 416-929-6484. Fax: 416-929-6575.

LH Systems Ltd. Building D1, Fairoaks Airport, Chobham, Surrey, GU24 8HU, UK. Tel: +44 (0)1276 855756. Fax: +44 (0)1276 855365.

LH Systems GmbH Heinrich-Wild Strasse, CH-9435 Heerbrugg, Switzerland. Tel: +41 71 727 3411. Fax: +41 71 727 4691.

PT McElhanney Jl. Haji Saidi No. 38B Cipete, Jakarta 12150, Indonesia. Tel: (6221) 9211473. Fax: (6221) 7255380. E-mail: fgoncalves@mcelhanney.com

Midwest Aerial Photography 6530 Singletree Dr., Columbus, Ohio 43229, USA. Tel: 614-431-3686. Fax: 614-844-6414. E-mail: info@midwestaerialphoto.com

Infoterra Delta House, Southwood, Farnborough, Hampshire. GU14 0NL, UK. Tel: +44 (0)125 236 2033. Fax: +44 (0)125 5016.

Omega Optical (CCD Filters) PO Box 573, 3 Grove Street, Brattleboro, Vermont 05302, USA. Tel: (802) 254-26980. Fax: (802) 254-3937.

Ordnance Survey Romsey Road, Southampton, SO16 4GU, UK. Tel: +44 (0)1703 792349. Fax: +44 (0)1703 792472.

Philips Semiconductors Image Sensors (PSIS) Prof. Holslaan 4, Postbox WAG05, 5656AA Eindhoven, The Netherlands. Tel: +31 40 2744 400. Fax: +31 40 2744 090.

Radio Spares RS Components, PO Box 99, Corby, Northants, NN17 9RS, UK. Tel: +44 (0)1536 201234.

Remote Sensing & Photogrammetric Society, c/o School of Geography, University of Nottingham, University Park, Notts., NG7 2RD, UK. Tel: +44 (0)115 9515435. Fax: +44 (0) 115 9515249. E-mail: rspsoc@nottingham.ac.uk

Rotax Engine Specialists ConAir Sports Ltd, Burnside, Deppers Bridge Southam, Leamington Spa, Warwickshire, CV47 2SU, UK. Tel/Fax: +44 (0)1926 614422. E-mail: Ibeale@avnet.co.uk

Shadow Aircraft (Group 'A' and SLA) CFM Aircraft Ltd, Unit 2D, Eastlands Industrial Estate, Leiston, Suffolk IP16 4LL. Tel: +44 (0)1728 832353. Fax: +44 (0)1728 832944. E-mail: cfmaircraft@compuserve.com

ST Aviation Ltd (Jabiru: Group 'A' & SLA) Technology House, High Street, Downham Market, Norfolk PE38 9HH, UK. Tel: +44 (0)1366 385558. Fax: +44 (0) 1366 385559.

Thruster Air Services Ltd. Malthouse Ginge, Nr Wantage, Oxen. OX12 8QS, UK. Tel: +44 (0) 1235 833305. Fax: +44 (0) 1235 833390. www.thruster.co.uk. E-mail: info@thruster.globalnet.co.uk

USDA NRCS, 2820, Walton Commons West, #123 Madison, Wisconsin 53718, USA. tel: (608) 224-3014. E-mail: bhuberty@mw.nrcs.usda.gov

University of Newcastle Department of Geomatics. Newcastle Upon Tyne, NE1 7RU, UK. Tel: +44 (0)191 222 5393. Fax: +44 (0)191 222 8691. E-mail j.p.mills@ncl.ac.uk

University College London Department of Geomatics. Gower Street, London, WC1E 6BT, UK. Tel: +44 (0)207 504 2726. Fax: +44 (0)207 380 0453.

USDA ARS Remote Sensing Research. 2413E, Hwy 83, Weslaco, Texas 78596, USA. Tel: (210) 969-4824. Fax: (210) 969-4893. E-mail: j-everitt@.tamu.edu

USDA Forest Service Remote Sensing Applications Centre, 2222 W 2300 S, Salt Lake City, Utah 84109, USA.

USDA Forest Service. Pacific North West Research Station, Seattle, Washington, USA.

Vinten Ltd. Vicon House, Western way, Bury St. Edmunds, Suffolk, IP33 3SP, UK. Tel: +44 (0)1284 750599. Fax: +44 (0)1284 750598.

York Survey Supplies Centre. Prospect House, George Cayley Drive, Clifton Moor, York, YO30 4XE, UK. Tel: +44 (0)1904 692723. Fax: +44 (0)1904 690385. E-mail: sales@yorksurvey.co.uk Web: http://www.yorksurvey.co.uk

Z/I Imaging UK Delta 100, Delta Business Park, Great Western Way, Swindon, Wiltshire, SN5 7XP, UK. Tel: +44 (0)1793 618506. fax: +44 (0)1793 618508. E-mail: ewickens@ziimaging.com

Z/I Imaging GmbH Postfach 1106, 73442 Oberkochen, Germany. Tel: +49 (7364) 20-28 86. Fax: +49 (7364) 20-37 24.

Appendix D
Air survey computer programs

The nine programs in this appendix are written in Quick Basic. This programming language is available with versions 5 and upwards of the MS-DOS operating system doe IBM compatible PCs. Once installed in desktop, laptop or notebook PC, these programs allow for rapid, iterative calculations of missions.

(a) SURPLAN (survey flight planning)
(b) AIM (apparent image motion)
(c) SA1 (solar altitude)
(d) SZ1 (solar azimuth)
(e) DITURNS (air survey line turns: direct turns)
(f) UTURNS (air survey line turns: U turn –linear region time)
(g) UTURN-A (air survey line turns: U turn –line separation)
(h) TAS (true air speed)
(i) TALT (true altitude)
(j) SS (shutter speed calculation for given *f*/no., EAFS, FF, date and time)

(a) SURPLAN

```
1   PRINT "
5   CLS
10  PRINT "                    SURPLAN. BAS."
15  PRINT "                   Press F5 to RUN."
20  PRINT
25  PRINT "                          AIR SURVEY MISSION PLANNING."
30  PRINT
35  INPUT "         ENTER MISSION NUMBER:         ", MT
40  PRINT
45  PRINT "         Scale = M  = 1/m                 (where m = Scale Number).";
50  PRINT "         H = Height above ground.         F  = Focal length of lens.";
55  PRINT "         S = Ground distance covered.    Ne = Negative side.";
60  PRINT "         Scale No (m) = H/F = S/Ne "; ""
65  PRINT
70  INPUT "         Enter Scale No (m) required:            ", m
75  INPUT "         Enter Focal length of Lens (F) in mm: ", F
80  PRINT "                                                          ANSWER.";
85  H = m * (F / 304.8)
90  PRINT
95  PRINT "         Required Height above Ground(feet)         =  ";
100 PRINT INT(H + .5); "Feet.";
105 PRINT
106 INPUT "         Enter average elevation or datum (feet)    =     ", EL
107 TALT = (H + EL)
108 PRINT "         Required True Altitude (TALT) in feet:     =  ";
109 PRINT INT(TALT + .5); "Feet."; ""
110 INPUT "         Enter Negative Side (Ne) in mm:            =     ", Ne
115 PRINT
120 S = (Ne * m) / 1000
125 PRINT "         Ground Covered (S) (Single Frame)          =  ";
130 PRINT INT(S + .5); "Meters.";
135 PRINT
140 REM      Area Covered by a single frame: FA = S^2.
145 FA = (S / 1000) ^ 2
150 PRINT "         Single Frame Area (FA)                     =  "; FA; "Sq.KM"
155 PRINT
160 INPUT "         Enter Forward Overlap p(%):                =  ", P
165 REM      Base (b) = S(1 - p/100)
170 b = S * (1 - (P / 100))
175 PRINT "         Length of base (b)                         =  ";
180 PRINT INT(b + .5); "Meters.";
181 R = (b / (H / 3.28))
182 PRINT "         Base over height Ratio:                    =  "; R;
184 PRINT
185 INPUT "         Enter Side Lap      q(%):                  =  ", q
190 REM      a = Distance between Flight-Lines, with q Side-Lap.
195 a = S * (1 - (q / 100))
200 PRINT "         Distance between Flight-Lines (a)          =  ";
205 PRINT INT(a + .5); "Meters.";
210 PRINT "         Ga = Area of Block (Length (Lp) * Width (Lq)) "
215 PRINT
220 INPUT "         Enter Length of Flight-Line Lp (km)        =  ", Lp
225 INPUT "         Enter Width of Block Lq (km)               =  ", Lq
230 PRINT
232 Ga = Lp * Lq
235 PRINT "         Area of Block                              =  "; Ga; "Sq.km";
240 REM  Np = Number of Photographs/Line (plus 2 prior & 2 post frames).
245 Np = ((Lp * 1000) / b) + 5
250 PRINT "         Number of Photos/Flight-Line (plus 4):     =  ";
255 PRINT INT(Np + .7); "(inclusive)."
```

(a) SURPLAN *continued*

```
260 REM      Nq = Number of Flight-Lines.
265 Nq = (((Lq * 1000) - S) / a) + 1
270 PRINT "          Number of Flight-Lines:                  =  ";
275 PRINT INT(Nq + .7); ""
280 PRINT
285 REM   Fm =  Model Area (Stereo-cover) = ((S-b)*S)
290 Fm = ((S - b) * S) / 10000
295 PRINT "          Fm = Model Area (Stereo Cover)           =  "; Fm; "Ha";
300 PRINT
305 REM   Sa = New Stereo Area = a.b
310 Sa = (a * b) / 10000
315 PRINT "          Sa = New Stereo Area                     =  "; Sa; "Ha";
320 PRINT
325 Nt = Ga / (Sa / 100)
330 PRINT "          Required Number of Photos/Block (Nt)     =  ";
335 PRINT INT(Nt + .5); "Photos";
340 PRINT
345 PRINT "                SELECT CODE FOR AIRCRAFT GROUND SPEED (Vg):"; ""
350 PRINT "          Code: 1 = m/sec. "; ""
355 PRINT "          Code: 2 = Knots. "; ""
360 PRINT "          Code: 3 = MPH.   "; ""
365 PRINT "          Code: 4 = Km/Hr. "; ""
370 INPUT "          Enter Aircraft Ground Speed Code:        =  ", C
375 PRINT
380 IF C > 4 THEN PRINT "               ERROR! Codes are between 1 to 4!"; ""
385 IF C > 4 GOTO 370
390 INPUT "          Enter Aircraft Ground Speed (Vg):        =  ", Vg
395 PRINT
400 IF C = 1 THEN Vg = Vg
405 IF C = 2 THEN Vg = Vg / 1.9417
410 IF C = 3 THEN Vg = .447 * Vg
415 IF C = 4 THEN Vg = .276 * Vg
420 REM  Exposure Interval T = b/Vg (seconds).
425 T = b / Vg
430 PRINT "          T = Exposure Interval                    =  ";
435 PRINT INT(T - .5); "(seconds)"; ""
440 REM  Apparent Image Motion (AIM) = 1000.(SS.Vg.F)/(H/3.28083) microns.
442 PRINT
445 PRINT "                    APPARENT IMAGE MOTION (AIM)."; ""
450 PRINT
455 INPUT "          Enter Shutter Speed (decimals):          =  ", SS
460 PRINT
465 AIM = 1000 * (SS * Vg * F) / (H / 3.28083)
470 PRINT "          AIM (Apparent Image Motion)              =  ";
475 PRINT INT(AIM + .5); "Microns"; ""
480 PRINT
485 PRINT "                END OF MISSION PLANNING CALCULATIONS.";
490 PRINT
493 PRINT "                 For HARDCOPIES connect the PRINTER."
495 PRINT
500 GOSUB HARDCOPY
502 END
505 HARDCOPY:
510 INPUT "          FOR HARDCOPY OPTION: KEY (1), RETURN TO PGM KEY (2).", HC
515 PRINT
520 IF HC = 1 THEN
530 PRINT
535 PRINT "    If the PRINTER is NOT CONNECTED wait ONE MINUTE for an automatic"
540 PRINT "    return to the Pgm then, press ENTER and EXIT Pgm."
545 PRINT
```

(a) SURPLAN *continued*

```
550 PRINT "                         CONNECT PRINTER AND RE-OPEN."
570 LPRINT "                                  SURPLAN."
575 LPRINT
580 LPRINT "                        AIR SURVEY MISSION PLANNING."
585 LPRINT
590 LPRINT "                              MISSION NUMBER:       "; MT
595 LPRINT
600 LPRINT "      Scale Number (m)                           =  "; m
605 LPRINT "      Focal Length (mm)                          =  "; F
610 LPRINT "      Required Height above Ground (feet)        =  ";
615 LPRINT INT(H); "Feet.";
616 LPRINT "      Average Terrain Elevation (or Datum): =     "; EL; "Feet"
617 LPRINT "      Required True Altitude (TALT)              =  ";
618 LPRINT INT(TALT); "Feet.";
619 LPRINT "      Negative Side:                             =   "; Ne; "mm"
620 LPRINT "      Ground Covered (S)                         =  ";
625 LPRINT INT(S); "Meters.";
630 LPRINT "      Forward Overlap (p):                       =  "; P
635 LPRINT "      Side-Lap        (q):                       =  "; q
640 LPRINT "      Single Frame Area (FA)                     =  "; FA; "Sq.Km"
645 LPRINT "      Length of Base (b)                         =  "; b; "Meters."
646 LPRINT "      Base over Height Ratio (R)                 =  "; R;
650 LPRINT "      Distance between Flight-Lines (a)          =  "; a; "Meters."
655 LPRINT "      Length of Flight-Line (Lp)                 =  "; Lp; "Km."
660 LPRINT "      Width of Block (Lq)                        =  "; Lq; "Km."
665 LPRINT "      Ga = Area of Block.                        =  "; Ga; "Sq.Km"
670 LPRINT "      Number of Photos/Flight-Line (Np)          =  ";
675 LPRINT INT(Np + .7); "(includes 4 extra)";
680 LPRINT "      Number of Flight-Lines (Nq)                =  ";
685 LPRINT INT(Nq + .7);
690 LPRINT
695 LPRINT
700 LPRINT "      Fm = Model Area (Stereo-Cover)             =  "; Fm; "Ha."
705 LPRINT "      Sa = New Stereo Area                       =  "; Sa; "Ha."
710 LPRINT "      Required Number of Photos/Block (Nt)       =  ";
720 LPRINT INT(Nt + .7); "Photos";
722 LPRINT
724 LPRINT
725 LPRINT "      Aircraft Ground Speed Code                 =  "; C;
730 LPRINT "      Aircraft Ground Speed (m/sec): Vg          =  ";
735 LPRINT INT(Vg + .5);
740 LPRINT "      T = Exposure Interval = b/Vg               =  ";
745 LPRINT INT(T - .5); "Seconds."
746 LPRINT "      Applied Shutter Speed (SS)                 =  "; SS
750 LPRINT "      AIM (Apparent Image Motion)                =  ";
755 LPRINT INT(AIM + .5); "Microns.";
760 ELSEIF HC = 2 THEN
765 PRINT
770 ELSE
775 GOTO 530
780 END IF
800 END
```

RWG

(b) AIM

```
1     PRINT "
5     CLS
6     PRINT "                              AIM.BAS."
8     PRINT "                         Press F5 to RUN."
10    PRINT
15    PRINT "                    APPARENT IMAGE MOTION: AIM "; ""
20    PRINT
25    PRINT "             A Program to evaluate Exposed Image Motion"; ""
30    PRINT "             in Vertical Air Survey Photography."; ""
35    PRINT
40    INPUT "          Enter Shutter-Speed (decimals of a second): ", SS
45    CLS
50    REM Different units of Estimated Ground Speed can be expected!
55    PRINT
60    PRINT "          SELECT CODE FOR AIRCRAFT GROUND SPEED:"; ""
65    PRINT
70    PRINT "          Code: 1  =  m/sec."; ""
75    PRINT "          Code: 2  =  Knots."; ""
80    PRINT "          Code: 3  =  MPH.  "; ""
85    PRINT "          Code: 4  =  Km/h. "; ""
90    PRINT
95    INPUT "          Enter Aircraft Ground Speed CODE: ", N
100   PRINT
105   IF N > 4 THEN PRINT "              ERROR! Codes are between 1 and 4!"
110   PRINT
115   IF N > 4 GOTO 95
120   INPUT "          Enter Aircraft Ground Speed: ", Vg
125   CLS
130   PRINT
135   INPUT "          Enter Lens Focal Length, in mm: ", F
140   CLS
145   PRINT
150   INPUT "          Enter Height above Ground, in feet: ", H
155   CLS
160   IF N = 1 THEN Vg = Vg
165   IF N = 2 THEN Vg = Vg / 1.9417
170   IF N = 3 THEN Vg = .447 * Vg
175   IF N = 4 THEN Vg = .276 * Vg
180   AIM = 1000 * (SS * Vg * F) / (H / 3.28083)
185   PRINT
190   PRINT
195   PRINT "            AIM =  ";
200   PRINT INT(AIM + .5); "microns"; ""
205   PRINT
210   PRINT "            END OF CALCULATION.";
215   END
```

RWG

(c) SA1

```
1  PRINT "
5  CLS
6  PRINT "                                SA1. BAS."
7  PRINT
8  PRINT "                            Press F5 to RUN. "
10 REM      Duplicate $A Pgm for further modifications, as may be required.
15 PRINT
20 PRINT "                          SOLAR ALTITUDE "; CHR$(91); "SA"; CHR$(93)
25 PRINT
30 PRINT "              Sin SA = ((SinLA.SinSD) + (CosLA.CosSD.CosHA))"; ""
35 PRINT
40 INPUT "                             Enter Latitude:   ", LA
45 CLS
50 PRINT
55 INPUT "                      Enter Number of Month: ", M
60 CLS
65 IF M = 1 THEN M = 0
70 IF M = 2 THEN M = 31
75 IF M = 3 THEN M = 59
80 IF M = 4 THEN M = 90
85 IF M = 5 THEN M = 120
90 IF M = 6 THEN M = 151
95 IF M = 7 THEN M = 181
100 IF M = 8 THEN M = 212
105 IF M = 9 THEN M = 243
110 IF M = 10 THEN M = 273
115 IF M = 11 THEN M = 304
120 IF M = 12 THEN M = 334
125 PRINT
130 INPUT "                                DAY NUMBER: ", D
135 Z = M + D
140 PRINT
145 INPUT "    Enter Longitude (Degrees WEST are -ve): ", LO
150 CLS
155 PRINT
160 INPUT "          Enter Local Time (0 to 24 hours): ", LT
165 CLS
170 Pi = 3.1416
175 Angle1 = LA:                                REM in Degrees.
180 Arads1 = Angle1 * (Pi / 180):               REM in Radians.
185 A = SIN(Arads1)
190 PRINT
195 Angle2 = ((360 / 365.25) * (Z - 83)):       REM in Degrees.
200 Arads2 = Angle2 * (Pi / 180):               REM in Radians.
205 SD = 23.45 * SIN(Arads2) + .6
210 Angle3 = SD:                                REM in Degrees.
215 Arads3 = Angle3 * (Pi / 180):               REM in Radians.
220 B = SIN(Arads3)
225 F1 = A * B
230 C = COS(Arads1)
235 D = COS(Arads3)
240 HA = (LO + ((LT - (LO / 15)) - 12) * 15)
245 Angle4 = HA:                                REM HA = Hour Angle, Degrees.
250 Arads4 = Angle4 * (Pi / 180):               REM in Radians.
255 E = COS(Arads4)
260 F2 = C * D * E
265 F3 = F1 + F2
270 REM  F3 = Sin SA and must be converted to Tan SA for further calculation.
275 REM  F4 = Tan SA = (Sin SA)/(SQR(1 -(Sin SA)^2)).
280 F4 = (F3) / (SQR(1 - (F3) ^ 2))
285 Arads5 = ATN(F4)
290 Angle5 = Arads5 * (180 / Pi)
295 PRINT
300 PRINT "                        SOLAR ALTITUDE = ";
305 PRINT INT(Angle5 + .5); "Degrees";
310 END
```

RWG

(d) SZ1

```
1  PRINT "
5  CLS
6  PRINT "                                          SZ1. BAS."
7  PRINT
8  PRINT "                                       Press F5 to RUN."; ""
10 PRINT
15 PRINT "                             Q BASIC: SOLAR AZIMUTH PGM: SZ1"; ""
20 PRINT
25 PRINT "                              SZ = (Sin HA.Cos SD)/Cos SA."; ""
30 REM THE formula for SA (Solar Altitude) includes all parameters for SZ.
35 PRINT
40 INPUT "                                 Enter Latitude: ", LA
45 CLS
50 PRINT
55 INPUT "  Enter Longitude (Degrees WEST are -ve): ", LO
60 CLS
65 PRINT
70 INPUT "                          Enter Number of Month: ", M
75 CLS
80 PRINT
85 INPUT "                               Enter Day Number: ", D
90 CLS
95 PRINT
100 INPUT "                Local Time (0 to 24 hours): ", LT
105 CLS
110 IF M = 1 THEN M = 0
115 IF M = 2 THEN M = 31
120 IF M = 3 THEN M = 59
125 IF M = 4 THEN M = 90
130 IF M = 5 THEN M = 120
135 IF M = 6 THEN M = 151
140 IF M = 7 THEN M = 181
145 IF M = 8 THEN M = 212
150 IF M = 9 THEN M = 243
155 IF M = 10 THEN M = 273
160 IF M = 11 THEN M = 304
165 IF M = 12 THEN M = 334
170 Z = M + D
175 Pi = 3.1416
180 Angle1 = LA:                                  REM in Degrees.
185 Arads1 = Angle1 * (Pi / 180):                 REM in Radians.
190 A = SIN(Arads1)
195 Angle2 = ((360 / 365.25) * (Z - 83)):         REM in Degrees.
200 Arads2 = Angle2 * (Pi / 180):                 REM in Radians.
205 SD = 23.45 * SIN(Arads2) + .6
210 Angle3 = SD:                                  REM in Degrees.
215 Arads3 = Angle3 * (Pi / 180):                 REM in Radians.
220 B = SIN(Arads3)
225 F1 = A * B
230 C = COS(Arads1)
235 D = COS(Arads3)
240 HA = (LO + ((LT - (LO / 15)) - 12) * 15)
245 Angle4 = HA:                                  REM in Degrees.
250 Arads4 = Angle4 * (Pi / 180):                 REM in Radians.
255 E = COS(Arads4)
260 F2 = C * D * E
265 F3 = F1 + F2
270 REM                                    F3 = Sin SA.
275 REM                                    F4 = Cos SA = (SQR(1-(F3)^2))
280 F4 = (SQR(1 - (F3) ^ 2))
285 REM                                    B  = Sin SD.
290 REM                                    F5 = Cos SD = (SQR(1-(B)^2))
```

(d) SZ1 *continued*

```
295 F5 = (SQR(1 - (B) ^ 2))
300 REM                                       E  = Cos HA.
305 REM                                       F6 = Sin HA = (SQR(1-(E)^2))
310 F6 = (SQR(1 - (E) ^ 2))
315 S = (F6 * F5) / F4
320 REM  S = Sin SZ (Sin Solar Azimuth) and must be converted to Tan S.
325 REM  F7 = Tan S = (Sin SZ)/(SQR(1-(Sin S)^2))
330 F7 = S / (SQR(1 - (S) ^ 2))
335 Arads5 = ATN(F7)
340 Angle5 = Arads5 * (180 / Pi)
345 IF LT < 12 THEN Angle5 = -Angle5
350 IF LT > 12 THEN Angle5 = Angle5
355 PRINT
360 PRINT "                        SOLAR AZIMUTH = ";
365 PRINT INT(Angle5 + .5); "Degrees."; "   "; CHR$(1); ""
370 PRINT
375 PRINT
380 PRINT "     "; CHR$(1); ""
385 END
```

RWG

(e) DITURNS

```
1   PRINT "
5   CLS
6   PRINT "                                        DITURNS.BAS."
8   PRINT "                                      Press F5 to RUN."
10  PRINT
15  PRINT "                                   AIR SURVEY LINE-TURNS."; ""
20  PRINT
25  PRINT "                                       DIRECT TURNS."; ""
30  PRINT
35  PRINT "      FROM:      True Air Speed (TAS), Line Separation (a),"
40  PRINT "                 Drift Angle (D), and Wind Direction (k):"; ""
45  PRINT
50  PRINT "            COMPUTE REQUIRED RATE OF TURN (R) & ANGLE OF BANK (B):"
55  PRINT
60  REM                 R = (2.TAS/a).(((180/Pi)CosD)+k((90+kD)SinD))
65  PRINT "            Select CODE (C) for Aircraft True Air Speed (TAS): ";
70  PRINT
75  PRINT "            CODE 1 = m/sec.     "; ""
80  PRINT "            CODE 2 = Knots.     "; ""
85  PRINT "            CODE 3 = MPH.       "; ""
90  PRINT "            CODE 4 = Km/h.      "; ""
95  PRINT
100 INPUT "            ENTER TAS CODE:                    ", C
105 PRINT
110 IF C > 4 THEN GOTO 70
115 PRINT
120 INPUT "            ENTER TAS:                         ", TAS
130 PRINT
135 INPUT "            ENTER LINE SEPARATION (meters):    ", a
140 PRINT
150 INPUT "            ENTER ANGLE OF DRIFT:              ", D
160 PRINT
165 REM   Turns are either UPWIND (k=-1) or DOWNWIND (k=1) with respect to
170 REM   direction of turn and crosswind component.
175 Pi = 3.1416
180 Angle1 = D
185 Arads1 = Angle1 * (Pi / 180)
190 X = COS(Arads1)
195 Y = SIN(Arads1)
200 IF C = 1 THEN TAS = TAS:                    REM e.g,     77.25 m/s.
205 IF C = 2 THEN TAS = TAS / 1.9417:           REM e.g,     150   Knots.
210 IF C = 3 THEN TAS = .447 * TAS:             REM e.g,     173   MPH.
215 IF C = 4 THEN TAS = .276 * TAS:             REM e.g,     280   Km/h.
220 REM  UPWIND RATE OF TURN = RU,     DOWNWIND RATE OF TURN = RD.
225 PRINT
230 RU = (2 * TAS / a) * (((180 / Pi) * X) - ((90 - D) * Y))
235 RD = (2 * TAS / a) * (((180 / Pi) * X) + ((90 + D) * Y))
240 REM  UPWIND ANGLE OF BANK = BU,    DOWNWIND ANGLE OF BANK = BD.
245 REM  B = Atan((TAS.Pi.R)/(g.180): where g (gravy y const) = 9.81 m/sec^.
250 REM  B = Atan(F1) = Atan(0.00178.TAS.R)
255 F1 = .00178 * TAS * RU
260 F2 = .00178 * TAS * RD
265 Arads2 = ATN(F1)
270 Angle2 = Arads2 * (180 / Pi)
275 Arads3 = ATN(F2)
280 Angle3 = Arads3 * (180 / Pi)
285 PRINT "                                      UPWIND."; ""
290 PRINT
295 PRINT "        REQUIRED RATE OF UPWIND TURN    (RU)    =  ";
300 PRINT INT(RU + .5); "Degrees/Second.";
```

(e) DITURNS *continued*

```
305 PRINT "          REQUIRED UPWIND ANGLE OF BANK   (BU)    =  ";
310 PRINT INT(Angle2 + .5); "Degrees."; ""
315 PRINT
320 PRINT "                                   DOWNWIND."; ""
325 PRINT
330 PRINT "          REQUIRED RATE OF DOWNWIND TURN  (RD)    =  ";
335 PRINT INT(RD + .5); "Degrees/Second.";
340 PRINT "          REQUIRED DOWNWIND ANGLE OF BANK (BD)    =  ";
345 PRINT INT(Angle3 + .5); "Degrees."; ""
350 PRINT
355 PRINT "                             END OF CALCULATIONS."; ""
360 PRINT
370 PRINT "  NOTE:  Normal range for Bank-Angle is from 15 to 40 degrees."; ""
380 PRINT
500 PRINT "                  For HARDCOPIES connect the PRINTER."
505 PRINT
510 GOSUB HARDCOPY
520 HARDCOPY:
524 INPUT "           FOR HARDCOPY OPTION: KEY (1), RETURN TO PGM KEY (2).", HC
526 PRINT
528 IF HC = 1 THEN
530 PRINT "   If the PRINTER is NOT CONNECTED wait ONE MINUTE for an automatic"
532 PRINT "   return to the Pgm then, press ENTER and EXIT Pgm."
534 PRINT
536 PRINT "                      CONNECT PRINTER AND RE-OPEN."
538 LPRINT "                              DITURNS."
540 LPRINT "      TAS CODE                                 =  "; C
541 LPRINT "      TAS (Always printed in meters/sec)       =  "; TAS
542 LPRINT "      LINE SEPARATION (meters):                =  "; a
543 LPRINT "      DRIFT ANGLE:                             =  "; D
545 LPRINT "                              UPWIND."
550 LPRINT
555 LPRINT "                    REQUIRED RATE OF UPWIND TURN   (RU)   =  ";
560 LPRINT INT(RU + .5); "Degrees/Second.";
565 LPRINT "                    REQUIRED UPWIND ANGLE OF BANK  (BU)   =  ";
570 LPRINT INT(Angle2 + .5); "Degrees. ";
575 LPRINT
578 LPRINT
580 LPRINT "                           DOWNWIND. "
585 LPRINT
590 LPRINT "                  REQUIRED RATE OF DOWNWIND TURN  (RD)  =  ";
695 LPRINT INT(RD + .5); "Degrees/Second.";
600 LPRINT "                  REQUIRED DOWNWIND ANGLE OF BANK (BD)  =  ";
605 LPRINT INT(Angle3 + .5); "Degrees.   ";
610 ELSEIF HC = 2 THEN
615 PRINT
620 ELSE
625 GOTO 530
630 END IF
650 END
```

RWG

(f) UTURNS

```
1   PRINT "
5   CLS
6   PRINT "                                         UTURNS. BAS."
8   PRINT "                                       Press F5 to RUN."
10  PRINT
15  PRINT "                                AIR SURVEY LINE-TURNS."; ""
20  PRINT
25  PRINT "                                         `U' TURNS."
30  PRINT
35  PRINT "     THIS PROGRAM WILL FIND THE REQUIRED TIME (t) for FLYING THE"
40  PRINT "     LINEAR PART OF A `U' TURN WITH A RATE 1 TURN (3 Deg/Sec)."; ""
45  PRINT
50  PRINT " Parameters:"; ""
55  PRINT "       True Air Speed (TAS), Line-Separation (a), Drift (D),"
60  PRINT "       Direction of turn with respect to crosswind component (k)."
65  PRINT "       Fixed Rate of Turn (R = 3 deg/Sec)."; ""
70  PRINT
75  REM  t = (a - ((2TAS/R).(((180/Pi)CosD)+k((90+kD)SinD))))/(TAS(1+kSinD)).
80  PRINT "       Select CODE (C) for Aircraft True Air Speed (TAS): ";
85  PRINT
90  PRINT "       CODE 1 = m/sec.    "; ""
95  PRINT "       CODE 2 = Knots.    "; ""
100 PRINT "       CODE 3 = MPH.      "; ""
105 PRINT "       CODE 4 = Km/h.     "; ""
110 PRINT
115 INPUT "       ENTER TAS CODE:                               ", C
120 PRINT
130 IF C > 4 THEN GOTO 85
135 INPUT "       ENTER TAS:                                    ", TAS
140 PRINT
150 IF C = 1 THEN TAS = TAS:              REM e.g,    77.25  m/sec.
155 IF C = 2 THEN TAS = TAS / 1.9417:     REM e.g,   150     Knots.
160 IF C = 3 THEN TAS = .447 * TAS:       REM e.g,   173     MPH.
165 IF C = 4 THEN TAS = .276 * TAS:       REM e.g,   280     Km/h.
170 INPUT "       ENTER FLIGHT-LINE SEPARATION (meters):        ", a
175 PRINT
185 INPUT "       ENTER ANGLE OF DRIFT:                         ", D
190 PRINT
200 Pi = 3.1416
205 Angle1 = D
210 Arads1 = Angle1 * (Pi / 180)
215 X = COS(Arads1)
220 Y = SIN(Arads1)
225 REM  Turns are either UPWIND (K=-1) or DOWNWIND (k=1) with respect to"
230 REM  direction of turn and crosswind component.
235 REM  tu = UPWIND time,     td = DOWNWIND time.
240 REM  tu = (a - ((2TAS/3).(((57.29)X)-((90-D)Y))))/(TAS(1-Y))
245 REM  td = (a - ((2TAS/3).(((57.29)X)+((90+D)Y))))/(TAS(1+Y))
250 F1 = (2 * TAS / 3)
255 F2 = ((57.29) * X) - ((90 - D) * Y)
260 F3 = (TAS * (1 - Y))
265 tu = (a - (F1 * F2)) / F3
270 IF tu >= 4 THEN
275 PRINT "              UPWIND LINEAR TIME   (tu)    =  ";
280 PRINT INT(tu + .5); "Seconds.";
285 ELSEIF tu <= 3 THEN
290 PRINT "              UPWIND TIME IS TOO SHORT - TRY DIRECT TURN PROGRAM!"
295 ELSE
300 GOTO 275
305 END IF
310 F4 = ((57.29) * X) + ((90 + D) * Y)
315 F5 = (TAS * (1 + Y))
```

(f) UTURNS *continued*

```
320 td = (a - (F1 * F4)) / F5
325 IF td >= 5 THEN
330 PRINT "                    DOWNWIND LINEAR TIME (td)      =  ";
335 PRINT INT(td + .5); "Seconds.";
340 ELSEIF td <= 4 THEN
345 PRINT
350 PRINT
355 PRINT "                    DOWNWIND TIME TOO SHORT!"
360 ELSE
365 GOTO 330
370 END IF
375 REM   Angle of Bank (B) = Atan((TAS.Pi.R)/g.180). g(gravity) = 9.81m/s^.
380 REM   Since R = Const = 3 deg/sec, then: B = Atan(0.00534.TAS).
385 REM   For R = Const, Upwind and Downwind Bank(s) are equal.
390 F6 = .00534 * TAS
395 Arads2 = ATN(F6)
400 Angle2 = Arads2 * (180 / Pi)
405 PRINT
410 PRINT "                    ANGLE OF BANK (RATE 1 TURN)  =  ";
415 PRINT INT(Angle2 + .5); "Degrees."; ""
420 PRINT
425 PRINT "                              END OF CALCULATIONS.  ";
430 PRINT
435 PRINT " NOTE:"
440 PRINT "     If distance between lines (a) is required (for a given time)";
445 PRINT "     either tu, or td, use the Program: UTURN-a."; ""
450 PRINT
460 PRINT "                        For HARDCOPIES connect the PRINTER."
465 PRINT
470 GOSUB HARDCOPY
475 HARDCOPY:
500 INPUT "                FOR HARDCOPY OPTION: KEY (1), RETURN TO PGM KEY (2).", HC
505 PRINT
510 IF HC = 1 THEN
512 PRINT
514 PRINT "    If the PRINTER is NOT CONNECTED wait ONE MINUTE for an automatic"
516 PRINT "    return to the Pgm then, press ENTER and EXIT Pgm."
518 PRINT
520 PRINT "                            CONNECT PRINTER AND RE-OPEN."
525 LPRINT "                                   `U' TURNS."
526 LPRINT "    TAS CODE                                 =    "; C
527 LPRINT "    TAS (Always printed in meters/sec)       =    "; TAS
528 LPRINT "    FLIGHT-LINE SEPARATION (meters)          =    "; a
529 LPRINT "    DRIFT ANGLE:                             =    "; D
530 LPRINT
532 LPRINT "    UPWIND LINEAR TIME (tu)                  =    ";
535 LPRINT INT(tu + .5); "Seconds.";
537 LPRINT
538 LPRINT
540 LPRINT "    DOWNWIND LINEAR TIME (td)                =    ";
545 LPRINT INT(td + .5); "Seconds.";
547 LPRINT
548 LPRINT
550 LPRINT "    Angle of Bank (Rate 1 turn)              =    ";
555 LPRINT INT(Angle2 + .5); "Degrees.";
560 ELSEIF HC = 2 THEN
565 PRINT
570 ELSE
575 GOTO 525
580 END IF
600 END
```

RWG

(g) UTURN-A

```
1   PRINT "
5   CLS
6   PRINT "                                   UTURN-A     "
8   PRINT "                               Press F5 to RUN."
10  PRINT
15  PRINT "                            AIR SURVEY LINE-TURNS."; ""
20  PRINT
25  PRINT "                           `U' TURNS (Line Separation). "; ""
30  PRINT
35  PRINT "      THIS PROGRAM WILL FIND THE REQUIRED LINE SEPARATION (a) FOR";
40  PRINT "      A `U` TURN MADE AT THE STANDARD RATE OF 3 deg/sec, AND AN ";
45  PRINT "      INTERTIME (LINEAR REGION) OF (t) SECONDS."; ""
50  PRINT
55  PRINT " PARAMETERS:"; ""
60  PRINT "     True Air Speed (TAS), Drift (D), Fixed Rate of Turn (R), ";
65  PRINT "     Direction of Turn with respect to Cross-Wind Component (k),";
70  PRINT "     Time of Linear component (t)."; ""
75  PRINT
80  REM   a = ((2TAS/R).(((180/Pi).CosD)+k((90+kD)SinD))) + TAS(1+kSinD)t.
85  PRINT "     Select CODE (C) for Aircraft True Air Speed (TAS):  "; ""
90  PRINT
95  PRINT "     CODE 1 = m/sec.     "; ""
100 PRINT "     CODE 2 = Knots.     "; ""
105 PRINT "     CODE 3 = MPH.       "; ""
110 PRINT "     CODE 4 = Km/h.      "; ""
115 PRINT
120 INPUT "     ENTER TAS CODE:                                         ", C
130 PRINT
135 IF C > 4 THEN GOTO 85
140 INPUT "     ENTER TAS:                                              ", TAS
150 PRINT
155 IF C = 1 THEN TAS = TAS:              REM e.g,    77.25  m/sec.
160 IF C = 2 THEN TAS = TAS / 1.9417:     REM e.g,   150     Knots.
165 IF C = 3 THEN TAS = .447 * TAS:       REM e.g,   173     MPH.
170 IF C = 4 THEN TAS = .276 * TAS:       REM e.g,   280     Km/h.
175 INPUT "     ENTER ANGLE OF DRIFT:                                   ", D
185 PRINT
190 INPUT "     ENTER LINEAR COMPONENT TIME (Seconds):                  ", t
200 PRINT
220 Pi = 3.1416
225 Angle1 = D
230 Arads1 = Angle1 * (Pi / 180)
235 X = COS(Arads1)
240 Y = SIN(Arads1)
245 REM  Turns are either UPWIND (k=-1) or DOWNWIND (k=1) with respect to
250 REM  direction of turn and crosswind component.
255 REM  au  =  UPWIND distance between lines, ad = DOWNWIND distance.
260 REM  au = ((2TAS/3).(((57.29)X)-((90-D)Y))) + TAS(1-Y)t.
265 REM  ad = ((2TAS/3).(((57.29)X)+((90+D)Y))) + TAS(1+Y)t.
270 F1 = (2 * TAS / 3)
275 F2 = ((57.29) * X) - ((90 - D) * Y)
280 F3 = (TAS * (1 - Y) * t)
285 F4 = (TAS * (1 - Y) * t)
290 F5 = ((57.29) * X) + ((90 + D) * Y)
295 F6 = (TAS * (1 + Y) * t)
300 au = (F1 * (F2)) + F3
305 ad = (F1 * (F5)) + F6
310 PRINT "              UPWIND DISTANCE BETWEEN LINES   (au) =  ";
315 PRINT INT(au + .5); "Meters.";
320 PRINT "              DOWNWIND DISTANCE BETWEEN LINES (ad) =  ";
```

(g) UTURN-A *continued*

```
325 PRINT INT(ad + .5); "Meters."; ""
330 PRINT
340 PRINT "                           END OF CALCULATIONS."; ""
345 PRINT
350 PRINT "                      For HARDCOPIES connect the PRINTER."
355 PRINT
360 GOSUB HARDCOPY
365 HARDCOPY:
370 INPUT "         FOR HARDCOPY OPTION: KEY (1), RETURN TO PGM KEY (2).", HC
375 PRINT
380 IF HC = 1 THEN
382 PRINT
384 PRINT "    If the PRINTER is NOT CONNECTED wait ONE MINUTE for automatic"
386 PRINT "    return to Pgm then, press ENTER and EXIT Pgm."
388 PRINT
390 PRINT "                 CONNECT PRINTER AND RE-OPEN."
392 LPRINT "                          `UTURN-A'."
395 LPRINT "    TAS CODE                                 =  "; C
396 LPRINT "    TAS (Always printed in meters/sec)       =  "; TAS
397 LPRINT "    DRIFT ANGLE:                             =  "; D
398 LPRINT "    LINEAR COMPONENT TIME (Seconds):         =  "; t
399 LPRINT
400 LPRINT "       UPWIND DISTANCE BETWEEN LINES (au)    =  ";
405 LPRINT INT(au + .5); "Meters.";
410 LPRINT "       DOWNWIND DISTANCE BETWEEN LINES (ad)  =  ";
415 LPRINT INT(ad + .5); "Meters.";
420 ELSEIF HC = 2 THEN
425 PRINT
430 ELSE
435 GOTO 382
440 END IF
450 END
```

RWG

(h) TAS

```
1   PRINT "
5   CLS
6   PRINT "                              TAS. BAS."
8   PRINT "                           Press F5 to RUN."
10  PRINT
15  PRINT "                         TRUE AIR SPEED (TAS). "; ""
20  PRINT
25  PRINT "           To determine TAS from IAS (Indicated Air Speed)."; ""
30  PRINT
35  PRINT "    PARAMETERS:"
40  PRINT "       Pressure Altitude, i.e, Altimeter set at standard 1013.2 mb"
45  PRINT "       atmospheric pressure (A); Outside Air Temperature (OAT), in"
50  PRINT "       degrees Celsius (C); Indicated Air Speed (IAS)."
55  PRINT
60  REM   TAS = IAS(SQR((273.16 + C)/(288/10^D)))
65  REM     D = A/(63691.776 - (0.2190731712.A)
70  REM   TAS increases (roughly) as 2% per 1000ft amsl.
75  INPUT "              Enter INDICATED AIR SPEED (IAS):           ", IAS
80  CLS
85  PRINT
90  INPUT "              Enter ALTIMETER PRESSURE ALTITUDE (ft):    ", A
95  CLS
100 PRINT
105 INPUT "              Enter OUTSIDE AIR TEMPERATURE (C):         ", C
110 CLS
115 PRINT
120  D = A / (63691.776# - (.2190731712# * A))
125  TAS = IAS * (SQR((273.16 + C) / (288 / 10 ^ D)))
130 PRINT
135 PRINT "                          TAS =    ";
140 PRINT INT(TAS + .5);
145 END
```

RWG

(i) TALT

```
1  PRINT "
5  CLS
6  PRINT "                                 TALT. BAS."
10 PRINT "                                Press F5 to RUN."
15 PRINT
20 PRINT "            FINDING THE NECESSARY PRESSURE ALTITUDE (PALT) TO FLY";
25 PRINT "            THE TRUE ALTITUDE (TALT) REQUIRED FOR AN AIR SURVEY. "
30 PRINT
35 REM  TALT will be different to PALT due to differences between the QNH
40 REM  (Altitude) setting for atmosphere, and the Pressure Altitude, which
45 REM  employs the International Standard Atmosphere (ISA)of 1013.25mb; and
50 REM  also the difference in Outside Air Temperature (OAT) and the ICAO
55 REM  temperature of 15 degrees Centigrade.
60 REM  Note:  1 mm Hg = 1.33322 mb.
65 PRINT
70 INPUT "            Enter REQUIRED TRUE ALTITUDE (TALT),(ft):       ", TALT
75 CLS
80 PRINT
85 INPUT "            Enter OUTSIDE AIR TEMPERATURE (OAT), (C):       ", OAT
90 CLS
100 PRINT
105 INPUT "           Enter QNH value (mb):                           ", QNH
110 CLS
115 PRINT
120 REM  PALT = Pressure Altitude to be flown with altimeter set at 1013.25mb.
125 REM  PALT = TALT(1 + ((dT/288.15) - (187.8/1000000).dP) + 27.3*dP.(feet)
130 dT = OAT - 15
135 dP = QNH - 1013.25
140 PRINT
145 PALT = TALT * (1 + ((dT / 288.15) - (187.8 / 1000000) * dP)) + dP * (27.3)
150 PRINT
155 PRINT "                      REQUIRED PALT  =     ";
160 PRINT INT(PALT + .5); "feet"; ""
165 END
```

RWG

(j) SS

```
1    PRINT "
5    CLS
6    PRINT "                         SS. BAS."
8    PRINT "                      Press F5 to RUN."
10   REM   Shutter Speed (SS) Calculations for Aerial Photography.
15   PRINT
20   PRINT "                              SHUTTER SPEED"; CHR$(91); "SS"; CHR$(93)
25   PRINT
30   PRINT "           SS = ((286*(EAFS)*(FS)*(FH))/(FF)*(Aperture)^2))"
35   PRINT
40   PRINT "       (FS) =  Function of Solar Altitude."
45   PRINT "       (FH) =  Function of Height above Ground."
50   PRINT "       (FF) =  Filter Factor."
55   PRINT
60   PRINT "       Variables: Lat, Month, Day, Long, Local time, EAFS,"
65   PRINT "       Height, Filter factor, Aperture."
70   PRINT
75   INPUT "              Enter Latitude:                              ", LA
80   PRINT
90   INPUT "              Enter Number of Month:                       ", M
100 IF M = 1 THEN M = 0
105 IF M = 2 THEN M = 31
110 IF M = 3 THEN M = 59
115 IF M = 4 THEN M = 90
120 IF M = 5 THEN M = 120
125 IF M = 6 THEN M = 151
130 IF M = 7 THEN M = 181
135 IF M = 8 THEN M = 212
140 IF M = 9 THEN M = 243
145 IF M = 10 THEN M = 273
150 IF M = 11 THEN M = 304
155 IF M = 12 THEN M = 334
160 PRINT
165 INPUT "              Enter Day Number:                            ", DAY
170 PRINT
175 Z = M + DAY
185 INPUT "              Enter Longitude (Degrees West are -ve):      ", LO
190 PRINT
195 INPUT "              Enter Local-Time (0 to 24 hours):            ", LT
205 pi = 3.1416
210 Angle1 = LA:                                  REM in degrees.
215 Arads1 = Angle1 * (pi / 180):                 REM in radians.
220 A = SIN(Arads1)
230 Angle2 = ((360 / 365.25) * (Z - 83)):         REM in degrees.
235 Arads2 = Angle2 * (pi / 180):                 REM in radians.
240 SD = 23.45 * SIN(Arads2) + .6
245 Angle3 = SD:                                  REM in degrees.
250 Arads3 = Angle3 * (pi / 180):                 REM in radians.
255 B = SIN(Arads3)
260 F1 = A * B
265 C = COS(Arads1)
270 D = COS(Arads3)
275 HA = (LO + ((LT - (LO / 15)) - 12) * 15)
280 Angle4 = HA:                                  REM in degrees.
285 Arads4 = Angle4 * (pi / 180):                 REM in radians.
290 E = COS(Arads4)
295 F2 = C * D * E
300 FS = F1 + F2
305 REM   FS = Sin(SA) must be converted to Tan(SA) for further calculations.
310 REM   F3 = TAN(SA) = (SIN.SA)/(SQR(1-(SIN.SA)^2)).
```

(j) SS *continued*

```
315 F3 = (FS) / (SQR(1 - (FS) ^ 2))
320 Arads5 = ATN(F3)
325 Angle5 = Arads5 * (180 / pi)
330 PRINT
335 PRINT "                    Solar Altitude =                        ";
340 PRINT INT(Angle5 + .5); "Degrees"; ""
345 PRINT
350 INPUT "                    Enter EAFS:                             ", EAFS
355 PRINT
360 INPUT "                    Enter Flying Height (feet):             ", H
365 PRINT
370 FH = ((.4343 * LOG(H)) - 2.14):          REM Function of height in feet.
375 INPUT "                    Enter Filter Factor (none = 1):         ", FF
380 PRINT
385 INPUT "                    Enter Camera Aperture:                  ", N
390 PRINT
395 SS = ((286 * (EAFS) * (FS) * (FH)) / ((FF) * (N) ^ 2))
400 PRINT "                            SHUTTER SPEED =                 ";
405 PRINT "1/"; INT(SS); "Seconds."; ""
410 PRINT
415 PRINT "                                  END OF CALCULATIONS."
420 PRINT
500 PRINT "                        For HARDCOPIES connect the PRINTER."
505 PRINT
510 GOSUB HARDCOPY
515 END
520 HARDCOPY:
525 INPUT "                FOR HARDCOPY OPTION: KEY (1), RETURN TO PGM KEY (2).", HC
530 PRINT
560 IF HC = 1 THEN
570 LPRINT "                        SHUTTER SPEED CALCULATION (SS). "
575 LPRINT
580 LPRINT "       Latitude (LA)                             =  "; LA
585 LPRINT "       Total days (from 1st Jan) to Month M:     =  "; M
590 LPRINT "       Day Number (DAY)                          =  "; DAY
595 LPRINT "       Longitude (LO)                            =  "; LO
596 LPRINT "       Local-Time (LT)                           =  "; LT
600 LPRINT "       Solar Altitude (SA)                       =  ";
605 LPRINT INT(Angle5 + .5); "Degrees.";
610 LPRINT "       EAFS                                      =  "; EAFS
615 LPRINT "       Flying Height (H) above Ground (ft)       =  "; H
620 LPRINT "       Filter Factor (FF)                        =  "; FF
625 LPRINT "       Lens Aperture (N)                         =  "; N
630 LPRINT
635 LPRINT "       SHUTTER-SPEED (SS)                        =  ";
640 LPRINT "1/"; INT(SS); "Seconds.";
645 ELSEIF HC = 2 THEN
650 PRINT
655 ELSE
660 GOTO 570
665 END IF
700 END
```

RWG

Glossary

Absolute temperature thermodynamic temperature expressed in units of Kelvin. Zero degree on this scale (absolute zero) represents the lowest temperature theoretically possible, and is the temperature – 273.15°C.

A/D converter a device that converts continuously varying analogue signals into discrete digital signals or numbers.

Adobe Photoshop well known and popular imaging software for Mac and PC computers.

Automatic exposure control (AEC) in air cameras, a light sensor monitors the terrain luminance and controls the lens aperture to keep the exposure correct, this is called *Shutter-Priority* since the shutter is pre-set to maintain a certain shutter-speed and so lets the aperture (*f*/no) float. If *Aperture Priority* is selected, then the camera aperture is pre-set and the shutter-speed floats to the correct exposure.

Air-base (*B*) the length of a line joining two air camera stations; also, the distance (at the scale of the stereoscopic model) between adjacent perspective centres as reconstructed in the plotting instrument.

Algorithm a rule for solving a mathematical problem in a finite number of steps.

Aliasing an effect in computer graphics and bit-mapped images, where diagonal lines, curves or circles produce a stair-stepped appearance when resolution is too course.

Alphanumeric consisting of letters, numbers, spaces and other characters (see ASCII).

Altitude the height of an aircraft above a specific datum point or *reference elevation* (usually mean sea level).

Analytical photogrammetry photogrammetry in which solutions are obtained by mathematical methods.

Analogue any device that represents changing values by a continuously variable physical property, such as voltage in a circuit. An analogue device can manage an infinite set of values within its range, whereas a digital device can only manage a fixed number of values.

Analogue display a video display (such as VGA) is capable of a continuous range of grey levels or colours. By comparision, a digital display can only resolve a finite range of greys or colours (such as the old EGA system).

Apparent horizon in an aerial photograph, the line where land and sky meet. It is slightly below the true horizon.

ASCII acronym for American Standard Code for Information Interchange. This standard code assigns numeric values to letters, numbers, punctuation marks and control characters, to provide compatibility between computers and peripherals.

Attitude the angular orientation of the camera, or of the photograph taken with the camera, with respect to some external reference system. Three angles are required to satisfy attitude 1. ω (*x*-tilt), 2. ϕ (*y*-tip) and 3. κ (*z*-rotation); otherwise called 1.Tilt, 2. Swing, and 3. Azimuth; or 1. Roll, 2. Pitch and 3. Yaw.

Bandwidth in communications and optics, bandwidth refers to the range between highest and lowest frequency (or wavelength) available for transmission.

Base, photo the distance between *Principal Points* of two adjacent prints of a series of aerial photographs. It is usually measured on one print after transfer of the principal point of the other print.

Base/height (*B*/*H*) ratio base over height ratio, where *B* (the air base) is the displacement of the camera between two exposures at *H*, the height above the object being photographed.

Bayer mosaic filter a very popular colour filter array **(CFA)** system, consisting of an array of red, green and blue, or cyan, magenta and yellow filter lines.

Binary a term reserved for any system that uses two different states, components, conditions or conclusions. In mathematics the binary system uses combinations of the digits 0 and 1 to represent all values.

Binary numbers numbers stored in binary form (see Appendix B).

Bit contraction of *binary digit*. A bit is the basic unit of information in a binary system of numbering, where 0 equals *off* and 1 equals *on*. Bits can be grouped to make larger units, such as the byte, where 8 bits equals one byte.

Bit-mapped graphics an image created by a series of dots (pixels), rather than a set of lines (vectors). Bit-mapped graphics consume large amounts of disk and memory space.

Brightness a subjective term that describes the sensation of light entering the eye. Roughly related to the objective term luminance, which is a physical unit.

Buffer an area of memory used for temporary storage of data.

Byte a contraction of the term *binary digit eight*. A byte is a group of eight bits that usually holds a single character. Bytes are further grouped into kilobytes (1024 bytes), megabytes (1,048,576 bytes), or gigabytes (1,073,741,824 bytes).

CAD computer aided design.

CFA (colour filter array) In a typical digital camera, full colour is formed from a series of monochrome sensors (CCDs) where, through the process of colour interpolation and an individual red, green or blue filter over each pixel, a full colour image is created.

Calibrated focal length an adjusted value of the equivalent focal length computed to distruibute the effects of lens distortion over the whole angle of field of an air camera. It is equal to the principal distance.

Camera, metric a camera whose *Interior Orientation* is known, stable and reproducible.

CCD charge coupled device. A solid state imaging sensor that uses an array of *metal oxide semiconductors* (**MOS**) to produce an electrical output proportional to the amount of light (electromagnetic radiation, EMR) incident upon each picture element (pixel). Each signal charge is 'clocked-out' to the *Output Register* by coupling all adjacent cells. Analogue signals the undergo A/D conversion to create a digital image.

CD-ROM acronym for 'compact disk – read only memory'. A high capacity (650Mb) optical storage device used to store large image files, dictionaries, images etc.

CFA interpolation colour filter array interpolation. Algorithm for improving a CCD colour image by using 'cross-talk' between an array of coloured filters.

Charge packets an optically induced signal charge stored in the potential well of each CCD storage element (pixel).

CMOS complementary metal oxide semiconductor (an alternative solid state imaging sensor to the CCD).

CMYK cyan, magenta, yellow and black. The four colours used in printing, where CMY are the complementary colours to RGB (red, green and blue).

Cos^4 law this states that for an ordinary lens (ignoring aberrations) the illuminance at the plane of focus is directly proportional to the fourth power of the cosine of the semi-angle of field.

Coverage the ground area represented on aerial photographs, photo-mosaics, or maps.

Coordinates linear or angular quantities which designate the position that a point occupies in a given reference system. Also used as a general term to designate the particular kind of reference system, e.g, cartesian coordinates, expressed as x, y, z.

Crab a condition in aerial photography where the camera format is not aligned with the track of the aircraft.

D/A converter a device that will convert a digital signal into an analogue one.

Dark current thermally generated electrical noise in a CCD imaging system.

Datum a reference element, such as a line or plane in relation to which the position of other elements are determined. Also called reference plane or datum plane. In aerial (survey) photography it is usual to take the mean of map spot heights to establish a suitable reference datum for the aircraft's height *above mean ground level* (amgl).

Density (*D*) an opto-imaging term mainly used in analogue photography where density refers to the common logarithm of opacity (the reciprocal of the transmission or reflection of an image). Density is given as $D = \log.(1/T)$ for diapositives, or as $D = \log.(1/R)$ for reflection prints.

DFinity A 4MPx CMOS camera with colour separation prism and Firewire interface.

(d)GPS. differential global positioning system. A more precise system of GPS accuracy which uses an airborne GPS receiver and a ground-based reference receiver. See GPS.

Diapositive a transparent positive print intended for viewing by transmission.

Digital a term that describes any system that represents values in the form of binary digits (binary codes consisting of 0s and 1s) see App. B.

Digital number (DN) the number of binary digits (bits) that make up a particular signal. e.g, for an 8 bit (one byte) system we have $2^8 = 256$ discrete levels of information, numbering from 0 to 255 DNs.

DOS acronym for disk operating system.

Electronvolt a unit of energy (symbol eV) equal to the work done on an electron when it moves through a potential difference of one volt.

Error (statistics) The difference between any measured quantity and the true value for that quantity. Like true value, errors are indeterminate and hence they are strictly theoretical quantities (see root mean square).

Absolute absolute deviation from corresponding *true value.*

Blunder the result of carelessness or a mistake, may be detected through repetition.

Random deviation caused by chance only; the relation between magnitude and frequency of the individual errors is regulated by laws of normal frequency, and therefore tend to be compensating.

Systematic an error which follows some definite mathematical or physical law, for which a correction may be determined and applied.

Exposure the total quantity of light received per unit area on a solid state sensor (CCD or CMOS) or film.

Fiducial mark usually four in number, located at the edge or corners of the image plane and recorded on the image to define axes, the intersection of which fixes the *principal point (PP)* or *fiducial centre* of the aerial photograph and fulfils the requirement for *interior orientation.*

File formats There are a number of file formats used in the current generation of digital cameras. They include **TIFF** (tagged image file format), **BMP** (Windows compatible bit-mapped graphic image), **PICT** (Mac supported), **EPS** (encapsulated PostScript), **JPEG** (joint photographic experts group) and **Photoshop** (Photoshop file format).

Firewire The IEEE-1394 high-speed serial input/output interface conceived in 1986 by 'Apple Computers' with the trademark *FIREWIRE.* See Interface.

Flight index a transparent map overlay indicating the principal point of each photograph exposed in an aerial survey.

Focal length the distance measured along the optical axis from the rear nodal point on the lens to the plane of critical focus of a very distant object.

Focal plane the plane (perpendicular to the axis of the lens) in which images of points on the object field of the lens are focused.

Forward motion compensation (FMC) movement of the image sensor during exposure, to compensate for the steady forward motion of the camera image in aerial photography.

Forward overlap the percentage of the image which is recorded twice in successive frames in a forward direction. Usually not less than 60% forward overlap is required in order to provide a stereoscopic model of the terrain.

FoV field of view (of a lens).

Foveon II A 16MPx, CMOS camera with Firewire interface and 2 second download.

Full frame transfer a CCD imager that employs its full array of pixels for imaging, in contrast to the *Frame Transfer* types, which employ half the total CCD elements for imaging and half for temporary storage.

GPS. global positioning system. GPS is a navigation system which employs a constellation of satellites to determine positions of aircraft or anything else that moves on or near the surface of the earth.

Grey scale a term used in computer graphics (*grey levels*) to describe a series of shades from white through any number of grey levels to black. The number of grey levels available depends on the number of bits dedicated to each pixel. Thus, a pixel with 8 bits (one byte) has $2^8 = 256$ grey levels.

Ground control point a point on the ground (usually marked artificially) which is readily identifiable from an aerial photograph. Ground control points are used for checking scale and camera tilt.

Ground sampled distance (GSD) the resolved ground distance, theoretically solved as the pixel size × scale number, i.e, GSD = $Px.m_b$.

Ground state the state of a system (an atom for example) in its lowest energy level, in contrast to its exited state.

Halftone when an original photograph is printed through a (halftone) screen, the image is broken up into a pattern of dots. Dark areas form dense dot patterns that can merge together, whereas highlight areas have few dots.

High pass filter an image processing operation which employs a mathematical 'filter' to provide image sharpening or edge enhancement when applied to the digital image array. A particular example is the Laplacian filter.

HSB acronym for *Hue, Saturation* and *Brightness,* which are the three main attributes of any colour (HSB is also a colour model used in computer graphics). Hue is the name of the colour; saturation is how pure the colour may be (freedom from other colours); and brightness refers to its visual luminance.

Illuminance a photometric unit (symbol E). The light shining from a source onto a scene or subject.

Image motion the smearing or blurring of imagery on an aerial photograph due to the relative motion of the camera with respect to the ground at the moment of exposure.

Image processing the computer processing of a graphical image, made possible by the use of various software packages dedicated to image enhancement and overall control of the image.

Inertial navigation system (INS) a dead reckoning system in which three mutually perpendicular accelerometers feed readings to an integrating device which computes the aircraft's position from acceleration and time.

Infrared (IR) that part of the electromagnetic spectrum lying between 760nm and about 1mm. The near or optical infrared extends from the visible limit (760nm) to about 2μm, and can be focused by optical elements and recorded to about 1μm on both film and silicon CCD pixels. The far infrared, with atmospheric windows allowing transmissions in the 3–6μm and 8–14μm bands, can only be recorded by thermographic scanning cameras (thermal imagers).

Infrared false colour a particularly useful attribute of silicon imaging CCDs is their natural sensitivity to the optical infrared band (760–1000nm). This band can easily be recorded by those CCD cameras that retain this infrared response, and are employed in remote sensing applications of natural vegetation, diseased crops and forest inventories.

Interface A common boundary between two devices. Typical examples of standard computer interfaces are (i) Electronic Industries Association (EIA) **RS232C** interface (common output port for printers etc), (ii) **SCSI** a common interface for digital cameras, (iii) Universal Serial Buses (**USB** port) where, for example, two USBs enable a *daisy-chain* connection of a number of USB equipped devices to one USB, and of particular importance to digital cameras (iv) the **IEEE-1394** ***(Firewire)*** high-speed serial input/output (I/O) connection. An IEEE-1394 interface allows digital image data to be transferred from camera to a Pentium computer much faster and with higher quality than other connections, such as *serial, parallel, SCSI,* or even *USB.* USB based digital cameras will continue to be available, but IEEE-1394 based cameras will surely offer a better product in the future.

ISO International Standards Organisation, establishes world-wide standards in numerous fields. In photographic areas the main standard is that of film speeds or, in the case of digital cameras, the sensitivity of a CCD camera. All digital cameras have their CCD chip rated in terms of 'film speed', in exactly the same way a film is rated.

JPEG Joint Photographic Experts Group. A well known image compression standard and file format. JPEG employs lossy compression methods, achieves compression ratios as high as 20:1 and stores 24 bit colour images.

Kell factor A factor relating 3 pixels to equal one line-pair/mm.

Knot a unit of speed. It is equal to one nautical mile per hour (Nm/hr) or 0.514 m/sec. It is the universal unit for measuring air speed.

Lapse rate generally we may consider that air temperature changes with height at a rate of –2°C per 1000 ft. This is known as the lapse rate.

LCD liquid crystal display. Usually found in portable computers (lap-top and note-book) where display screen technology employs an electric current to align crystals in a special liquid.

Least squares a method of adjusting observations in which the sum of the squares of all residuals derived from fitting the observations to a mathematical model is made a minimum. It assumes the frequency distribution of the errors is normal, i.e, symmetrical and characteristic of the typical bell-shaped curve.

LED Light emitting diode. A semiconductor device which emits light when a voltage is applied across it.

Line-pair (LP) In assessments of optical resolving power using bar targets, the results are quantified in line pairs per millimetre (Lp/mm). A line-pair consists of a dark bar and a light bar. In practice the distance between the centres of two dark bars is used.

Low-pass filter commonly known as a smoothing filter, a low-pass filter is generally used in image processing software to remove image noise and speckle from a digital image.

Luminance the objective correlate of brightness (symbol *L*), luminance is a measure of how much light is coming from a surface. The unit of luminance is the candle/square metre (Cd / m^2).

Magnetic course direction based on magnetic north rather than true north.

Millibar a unit of atmospheric pressure, still current in aircraft altimeters. Originally one bar was one standard atmosphere (now 1013.25 millibars). The SI unit is the Pascal (Pa); 1 millibar = 100 Pa. 1 Pa = 1 Newton per square metre (N/m^2).

Multi-spectral photography (MSP) a battery of airborne cameras each responsible for recording a single specific bandwidth.

Nadir the point on the ground immediately below the aircraft, also known as the plumb point.

Nautical mile a measure of distance. Originally designed to be one minute of longitude at the equator, it is equal to 6080 ft or 1.8523 km.

Nyquist limit for a CCD sensor with pixel spatial frequency k_s, unambiguous resolution of image detail with a spatial frequency k_i, is not possible if $k_i > 0.5k_s$.

Optical square An optical device useful for *Off-Set* measurements and gound control.

Orientation (absolute) Scaling, levelling and orientation to ground control of a relatively-orientated model.

Orientation (outer) The photogrammetric or analytical determination of the position of the camera station and the attitude of the camera at the instant of exposure. When determined by stereoscopic instruments it is separated into two parts *Relative* and *absolute.*

Orientation (relative) The determination of the position and attitude of one photograph with respect to another in a relative pair of aerial photographs.

Orthophotograph a photograph having the properties of *Orthographic Projection;* derived from a conventional aerial photograph so that the effects of both camera tilt and terrain relief are removed. Now a simple procedure when reproduced from a digital image via computer software.

Parallax the change in appearance of an object or scene as the viewpoint is shifted. *X-parallax* is the difference in the absolute stereoscopic parallaxes of two points imaged on a pair of photographs. Customarily used in the determination of the difference in elevation of objects. Also called parallax difference. *Y-parallax* is the difference between the perpendicular distances of the two images of a point from the vertical plane containing the air base.The existence of Y-parallax is an indication of tilt in either or both photographs and/or a difference in flight height.

Parallax bar a device used to obtain relief data from stereoscopic pairs of aerial photographs. Also known as a *Stereometer.*

Photogrammetry the process of making accurate measurements from photographs, and the analysis of such measurements.

PCMCIA PC Memory Card International Association. A standard for *plug-in* adaptors for portable computers and digital cameras.

Photo-electron an electron emitted from a substance due to irradiation by EMR.

Pixel contraction of picture element. The smallest element (resolution) of an image.

Q-Basic a version of Microsoft Basic bundled with MS-DOS 5. Note for Windows 98 there is only a partial DOS 5 incorporated and it will be necessary to load the *complete* DOS (disk operated system) software into the computer to operate Q-Basic programs.

Q-Code This code is used in aviation radio telephony to communicate required altimeter settings, where the altimeter sub-scale is set to a certain barometric pressure in either millibars or inches. It is also used for communicating navigation information among other items.

QDM Magnetic heading to be steered by the aircraft (assuming no wind) to reach the VDF (VHF direction finding) station.

QDR Magnetic bearing of the aircraft from the VDF station.

QFE With this setting (provided by Air Traffic Control) the altimeter will read zero when the aircraft is on the ground, regardless of the height of the airfield above mean sea level (amsl). The setting enables the pilot to know how far he must descend before landing. On QFE the vertical distance above ground is reported as height.

QNE now known as pressure altitude. At a prescribed altitude (3000 ft to 6000 ft in the UK, and 18,000 ft in USA airspace) an aircraft is said to have reached transition altitude when the standard altimeter setting of 1013.2mb (29.92 inches) will be used. This means that above transition altitude, all aircraft fly on the same altimeter setting, regardless of daily barometric pressure. When the altimeter is adjusted to 1013.2mb the vertical distance from that datum is given in flight levels e.g, at 4000 ft we refer to flight level 40, and at flight level 80 the altimeter will read 8,000 ft. It should be noted however, that only when the barometric pressure happens to be at 1013.2 will FL 80 be 8000 ft above mean sea level (amsl).

QNH is the lowest forecast value for the region where the altimeter will read altitude amsl. When flying from one altimeter setting region to another the pilot must obtain the relevant QNH.

QSY "changing transmission frequency to......".

QTE True bearing of the aircraft from the VDF station.

RAM acronym for random access memory – The principle memory system in a computer used for the operating system, application programs and data.

Rate 1 turn a change of direction in an aircraft is accompanied by banking the wings. A rate 1 turn is that angle of bank necessary to enable the aircraft to turn at a rate of 3° per second (180° per minute).

Rectification The process of correcting a (near) vertical aerial photograph for tilt.

Reseau camera a survey camera fitted with a register glass engraved with a reseau of calibrated marks, usually crosses on an orthogonal grid 10 mm apart in each direction.

Resolution the ability of an optical system to record fine detail. In aerial photography it is often given in terms of ground sampled distance GSD, or as line-pairs per millimeter (Lp/mm). The diffraction limited resolution of a perfect lens is given by the Rayleigh criterion, which states that images of two points will be just resolved when the distance (r) between them is given by $r = 1.22\,\lambda N$, where λ is the dominant wavelength of the incident light and N is the relative aperture of the lens (*f*/no).

RGB red, green, blue. The three additive primary colours.

Roll rotation of an aircraft about its longitudinal axis so as to cause a wing-up or wing-down attitude. Known in photogrammetry as tilt the rotation of a camera or photo-coordinate system about the x-axis. Expressed as omega (ω).

ROM acronym for read only memory.

Root mean square (RMS) a technique for obtaining statistical information using a large number of samples. The RMS value is obtained by taking the square-root of the sum of the squares of the differences of the samples from the mean value divided by one less than the total number of samples. The figure obtained is called the standard deviation (σ) and is a measure of precision of a single observation. Its square is called variance.

RS-232-C a standard interface between computer and a peripheral. RS-232 uses either a 9 pin or 25 pin connector, the C denotes a third revision of the recommended standard.

Scale the ratio of distance on a map or aerial photograph to ground distance, e.g, 1:20,000 means that 1mm on the map represents 20 metres of actual distance, the first figure is always 1; the second figure is known as the scale number.

SCSI acronym for small computer system interface (pronounced 'scuzzy'). SCSI is often used to connect hard-disks, tape drives, scanners, printers, CD-Rom drives and digital cameras, in fact any peripheral that involves mass storage of data.

Semantic information information taken from an aerial photograph which comes from recognised terrain features, man-made objects etc.

Semiconductor a material that is in between a conductor and an insulator, and whose electrical properties can be precisely controlled by the addition of dopants (impurities). The most common semiconductors are Silicon and Germanium.

Semi-controlled mosaic A mosaic made with Ground Control but with unrectified photographs; conversely, a mosaic made with rectified photographs but without ground control.

Side overlap The percentage overlap between successive runs (lines) in a photographic survey block.

Slant range In oblique photography, the actual distance between the aircraft and the target.

SLR single lens reflex (camera). Screen viewing through the camera lens.

Solar altitude (θ_s) the angle made between the ground and the sun at any time from sunrise to sun set. This is a function of latitude, day, month and time of day.

Solar hot-spot bright area of low contrast surrounding the geometrical shadow of the aircraft. Usually accompanied by poor indications of relief in the photograph. Mainly caused by exposing aerial photograps when the solar altitude (θ_s) is greater than the complementary angle (δ) of the camera semi-angle ($\theta_c /2$), i.e, $q_s < \delta$ is the required condition to avoid solar hot-spots.

Spot height a point on a map whose height above a specified reference datum is noted, usually by a dot or small cross and elevation value. Also called spot elevation.

SVGA super video graphics display (an enhancement to the standard VGA) which can display at least 800 pixels horizontally and 600 pixels vertically.

Terabyte a terabyte is equal to 1000 gigabytes (2^{40}), or 1,099, 511, 627, 776 bytes.

Thumbnail a very low-resolution digital image, used for library file purposes.

Translation movement in a straight line without rotation.

TWAIN a somewhat humorous term for explaining an interface that is a *Technology Without An Interesting Name.*

Ultraviolet the invisible portion of electromagnetic radiation which is below 380nm in wavelength and extends down to the X-ray spectrum of EMR. Ordinary glass will effectively cut out UV radiation at about 340nm.

Uncontrolled mosaic a mosaic made without use of ground control or rectification.

USB universal serial bus (see Interface).

Valency band the outermost electrons of an atom (those responsible for chemical bonding) occupy the valency band of a solid. If the valency band is filled and there is a wide forbidden band between it and the next highest empty band, then the material is an insulator. However, if the valency band is not completely filled, or if it overlaps with a higher empty energy band, then there are vacant levels that electrons can enter and the material will be a good conductor. Most metals have this property.

Vignetting Usually applied to image illumination 'fall-off' due to the $\cos^4$ law. Strictly, it means cut-off due to obstruction from camera doors etc.

VHF very high frequency (radio).

Wavelet compression Wavelet image compression transforms signals into a sum of small overlapping waves for analysing, storing and transmitting information. This method is mainly used for scientific applications.

Waypoints (GPS) A specific location stored in the GPS receiver's memory. Each waypoint is specified in terms of latitude and longitude, and can be given a bearing and distance from a reference waypoint. En-route navigation can be provided by selecting a GOTO destination to provide graphic steering guidance.

Bibliography

Bakker. H.C. and Van Kootwijk. E.J. (1993). Vegetation Mapping in a Dutch Todal Area using a Combination of Visual & Digital Analysis. In *Remote Sensing for Monitoring the Changing Environment of Europe*, Winkler (Ed), Balkema, Rotterdam.

Bartleson. C. J. and Witzel. R. F. (1967). *Photographic Science & Engineering*, **11**(4), p. 263. July/August.

Bobbe. T. (1997). Applications of a Color Infrared Digital Camera System as a Remote sensing Tool for Natural Resource Management. In *Proceedings of the First North American Symposium on Small Format Aerial Photography*. ASPRS, pp. 80–90.

Burger. B. (1996). The Airborne Advantage. Earth Observation Magazine, **5**(9), pp.46–49.

Carnes. J. E. and Kosonocky, W. F. (1981). *Charge Coupled Devices and Applications*. RCA Publication. April.

Charman, W. N. (1977). *Photographic Science & Engineering*, (**21**) 4, July/August.

Combs. J. E. *et al.* (1980). *Manual of Photogrammetry*, 4th Edition. Chapter VII. ASPRS.

Curr. R. and Koh. A. (1994). *Repeat Multi-band Aerial Video Survey of Baringo, Kenya, for University of London*. Kings College, London.

Eckardt. A., Braunecker. B. and Sandau. R. (2000). Performance of the Imaging System in the LH Systems ADS-40 Airborne Digital Sensor. *Wkg Group 1/3, IAPRS*, **XXXIII**, Amsterdam.

Electronic Imaging. (1999). *Fuji Revolutionises CCD Design*. p.7.

Fryer, J.G. (1992). Recent Developments in Camera Calibration for Close Range Application. *International Archives of Photogrammetry & Remote Sensing*, **29**(B5), pp.594–599.

Goodpasture, A.V. (1996). Digital Imaging and GPS Technology for Resource Management. *Earth Observation Magazine*, **5**(10), pp.45–47.

Gong, Jiana, Zhilin Li, Qing Zhu, Haigang Sui and Yi Zhou. (2000). Effects of Various Factors on the Accuracy of DEMs: An Intensive Experimental Investigation. *Photogrammetric Engineering & Remote Sensing*, **66**(9), pp.1113–1117.

Graham, R.W. (1975). *The Optimum Photographic Representation of Brightnesses in Interior Scenes*. Ph.D thesis CNAA.

Graham, R.W. (1980). The ITC MultiSpectral Camera System with respect to Crop Prognosis in Winter Wheat'. *ITC Journal*, **2**, pp.235–254.

Graham, R.W. (1988a). CFM Shadow. *Pilots International*, Feb., pp.32–33.

Graham, R. W. (1988b). Small Format Aerial Surveys from Light and Microlight Aircraft. *Photogrammetric Record*, **12**(71), pp. 561–573.

Graham. R.W. (1995). Kodak Digital Cameras for Small Format Aerial Photography. *Photogrammetric Record*, **XV**(86), pp. 325–327.

Graham, Ron. (1998). *Digital Imaging*. Whittles Publishing, Caithness, 224 pp.

Graham, R.W. and Mills, J. (1994). *Experiences with Airborne Digital Photography for Photogrammetry & GIS*. Internal Document, Dep't of Geomatics, University of Newcastle, U.K, 1994.

Graham, R.W. and Mills, J. (1997). Experiences with Airborne Digital Photography for Photogrammetry and GIS. In *Proceedings of the First North American Symposium on Small Format Aerial Photography*. ASPRS, pp.17–36.

Graham, R.W. and Mills, J. (2000). Small Format Digital Cameras for Aerial Survey: Where are we now? Report on the One Day Symposium on Digital Cameras for Aerial Survey. *Photogrammetric Record*, **16**(96), pp. 905–909.

Graham, R.W. and Read, R.E. (1986). *Manual of Aerial Photography*. Butterworth.

Graham, R.W, Read. R.E and Warner. W.S. (1996). Small Format Aerial Photography. Whittles Publishing, Caithness. 354 pp.

Gregory, R. L. (1998). *Eye and Brain*, 5th Edition. Oxford University Press.

Hassini, M. and Carswell. J. (1992). Transition from Analogue to Digital Photogrammetry, EARSel. *Advances in Remote Sensing*, **1**(3), pp. 66–70.

Heimes, F.J., Brechtken, R., Richter, T. and Baumker, M. (1997). Practical Experiences with a High Precision Stabilised Camera Platform Based on INS/(D) GPS. *Proceedings of the First North American Symposium on Small Format Aerial Photography*. ASPRS, pp. 45–54.

Hinz, A., Dorstel, C. and Heir, H. (2000). Digital Modular Camera: System Concept and Data Processing Workflow. *Wkg Group II/7. IAPRS*, **XXXIII**, Amsterdam.

Hohle, J. (1996). Experiences with the Production of Digital Orthophotos. *PE & RS*, **64**(10), pp.1189–1194.

Holst. G.C. (1996). CCD Arrays, Cameras & Displays. *SPIE*, p.131.

Hynes. S. (2000). Fuji FinePix S1 Pro Digital Camera. *Professional Photographer*, Sept., pp.64–68.

Intergraph Corp. ITC. (1993). Accuracy of a Digital Photogrammetric Workstation. Presentation at the International Symposium: *Operationalisation of Remote Sensing*. pp.19–23, ITC, The Netherlands.

Janesick, J.R. *et al.* (1990). New Advancements in CCD Technology – Sub-Electron Noise and 4096 × 4096 Pixel CCDs. Charge Coupled Division and Solid State Optical Sensors, *SPIE*, **1242**, pp.223–227.

Jerie, H. G. and Shearer, J.W. (1972). Research Concerning the Semantic Information Performance of Aerial Photography. *12th Congress of the International Society for Photogrammetry*, Ottawa.

Jerie, H.G. and Visser, J. (1969). *Planning of Photogrammetry Projects. Pt.1.* ITC Publication, Enschede, The Netherlands.

Jimenez, J.A. *et al.* (1997). *Journal of Coastal Research*, **13**(4), pp 1256–1266.

Katz, D. (1935). *The World of Colour*. Kegan Paul, London.

King, D.J., Haddow,K. and Pitt,D.G. (1997). Evaluation of CIR Digital Camera Imagery in Regeneration Assessment: Research Design & Initial Results. *Proceedings of the First Noth American Symposium on Small Format Aerial Photography*. ASPRS, pp.186–194.

King, J.E. (2000). Keynote Address by General J.E. King to ASPRS 2000 Annual Conference. *Photogrammetric Engineering & Remote Sensing*, **66**(9), pp.1043–1053.

Knapp, K.A., Disperati, A. and Hoppus, M. (1997). Evaluation of a Colour Infrared Digital Camera Sy stem for Forest Health Protection Applications in the Western United States &

Southern Brazil'. *Proceedings of the First North American Symposium on Small Format Aerial Photography*. ASPRS, pp. 80–90.

Kodak (1998) *Digital Image Capture, Exemplar Imagery*. Kodak Publication.

Koh, A. (1992). *The Coastal Landforms of West Dorset*. Ed. R. J. Allison. Geologists Association Guide No. 47, 67–79.

Koh, A. (1996). *Multispectral Aerial Digital Photographic System, Survey of Baringo, Kenya for the Natural Resources Institute*. Geotechnologies, Bath Spa University College.

Koh, A. (2000). Aerial Surveys with the Kodak DCS-460CIR Digital Camera and OmniStar dGPS'. One Day Symposium on Digital Cameras for Aerial Survey. *Photogrammetric Newsletter*. No.33, January.

Konecny, G., Schuhe, W. and Wu, J. (1982). Investigations on the Interpretability of Images by Different Sensors and Platforms for Small Scale Mapping. *Proceedings ISPRS, Comm.1*, Symposium, Canberra, Australia, pp. 11–22.

Larish, J. (2000). Still Waters, Break Through Design: Fuji Delivers a Super CCD for Digital Photography. *Advanced Imaging*, pp.18–-21.

Leys, K.F. and Werritty, A. (1999). River Channel Planform Change: Software for Historical Analysis. *Geomorphology*, **29**, pp.107–120.

Makarovic, B. and Tempfli, K. (1979). Digitising Images and Automatic Processing in Photogrammetry. *ITC Journal*, **1**, pp.107–126.

Light, D.L. (1996). Film Cameras or Digital Sensors? The Challenge Ahead for Aerial Imaging. *Photogrammetric Engineering & Remote Sensing*, **62**(3), pp. 285–291.

McColl, W.D. *et al.* (1983). Multidetector Electro-Optical Imaging Scanner MEIS II. *Proceedings of the 8th Canadian Symposium on Remote Sensing*, pp.71–79.

McManus, J. and Soulsby, J.A. (1994). Macro and Micro Sediment Forms and Sequences using Multi-Platform Remotely Sensed Imagery in the Eden Estuary, SE Scotland. In *Remote Sensing-From Research to Applications in the new Europe*, R. Vaughan (Ed), Proceedings of the 13th EARSel Symposium, Dundee, pp. 353–356.

Mealey, G. A. (1996). *Grasberg*. Freeport-McMoRan Copper & Gold Inc.

Mills, J.P. (1996). *The Implementation of a Digital Photogrammetric System and its Applications in Civil Engineering*. Ph.D thesis, University of Newcastle-Upon-Tyne..

Mills, J.P., Newton, I. and Graham, R.W. (1996). Aerial Photography for Survey Purposes with a High Resolution Small Format Digital Camera. *Photogrammetric Record*, **15**(88), pp. 575–587.

Mullen, K.T. (1985). The Contrast Sensitivity of Human Colour Vision to Red-Green and Blue-Yellow Chromatic Gratings. *J. Physiol*, **359**, pp.381–400.

Muller, R.S. and Kamins, T.I. (1986). *Device Electronics for Integrated Circuits*, 2nd Edition. John Wiley & Sons. pp.411.

Oostwoud Wijdenes. D.J. et al. (2000). Spatial Distribution of Gulley Head Activity and Sediment Supply along an Ephemeral Channel in a Mediterranean Environment. *Catena*, **39**, pp. 147–167.

Pearson, D.E. (1975). *Transmission and Display of Pictorial Information*. Pentech Press, London, pp.115.

Ramsey, E.J. and Laine, S.C. (1997). Comparison of Landsat Thematic Mapper and High Resolution Photography to Identify Change in Complex Coastal Wetlands. *Journal of Coastal Research*, **13**(2), pp. 281–292.

Read, R.E. and Graham, R.W. (2002). *Manual of Air Survey: Primary Data Acquisition*. Whittles Publishing, Caithness.

Rosenberg, P. (1971). Resolution, Detectability and Recognizability. *Photogrammetric Engineering*.

Sandau, R. *et al.* (2000). Design Principles of the LH Systems ADS-40 Airborne Digital Sensor. *Wkg Group 1/3. IAPRS*, **XXXIII**, Amsterdam.

Schuster, R, and Braunecker, B. (2000). Calibration of the LH Systems ADS-40 Airborne Digital Sensor. *Wkg Group IC-4, IAPRS*, **XXXIII**, Amsterdam.

Shannon, C.E. (1948). *Bell Systems Tech. J.*, **27**, p. 623.

Shortis, M.R. and Beyer, H.A. (1996). Sensor Technology for Digital Photogrammetry and Machine Vision. In *Close Range Photogrammetry and Machine Vision*, Ed. K.B.Atkinson. Whittles Publishing, Caithness, pp.120–121.

Van den Heuvel, F.A. (1993). Automated 3D Measurement with the DCS-200 Digital Camera. *Optical 3D Measurement Techniques* IT. (Eds: Gruen, A. and Kahmen, H.). Wichmann, Karlsruhe, pp. 63–71.

Van Ness, F.L. (1967). Spatial Modulation Transfer in the Human Eye. *J. Opt. Soc, Am.*, **57**, pp.401–406. 1967.

Welch, R.A. (1992). Desktop Mapping with Personal Computers. *Photogrammetric Engineering & Remote Sensing*, **55**(11), 1651–1662.

Wolf, P.R. (1974). *Elements of Photogrammetry*. McGraw-Hill Inc., New York. 562 pp.

Wright, D. (1998). Unpublished MSc thesis, University of Greenwich, Chatham Maritime, Kent.

Yang, E.S. (1988). *Microelectronic Devices*. McGraw Hill, International Edition.

Zhang, J., Zhang, Z., Wu, X., Wang, Z., Qiu, T. and Chao.H. (1994). A Photogrammetric Workstation from WTUSM. *International Archives of Photogrammetry and Remote Sensing*, **30**(3/2), pp. 939–944.

Index